Lecture Notes in Computer

Edited by G. Goos and J. Hartmanis

Advisory Board: W. Brauer   D. Gries   J. Stoer

J. B. Banâtre   D. Le Métayer (Eds.)

Research Directions in High-Level Parallel Programming Languages

Mont Saint-Michel, France, June 17-19, 1991
Proceedings

Springer-Verlag
Berlin Heidelberg New York
London Paris Tokyo
Hong Kong Barcelona
Budapest

Series Editors

Gerhard Goos
Universität Karlsruhe
Postfach 69 80
Vincenz-Priessnitz-Straße 1
W-7500 Karlsruhe, FRG

Juris Hartmanis
Department of Computer Science
Cornell University
5148 Upson Hall
Ithaca, NY 14853, USA

Volume Editors

Jean Pierre Banâtre
Daniel Le Métayer
IRISA, Campus de Beaulieu
F-35042 Rennes Cedex, France

CR Subject Classification (1991): D.3.2-3, D.1.3, D.2.2

ISBN 3-540-55160-3 Springer-Verlag Berlin Heidelberg New York
ISBN 0-387-55160-3 Springer-Verlag New York Berlin Heidelberg

© Springer-Verlag Berlin Heidelberg 1992
Printed in Germany

Typesetting: Camera ready by author
Printing and binding: Druckhaus Beltz, Hemsbach/Bergstr.
45/3140-543210 - Printed on acid-free paper

Preface

The workshop on "Research Directions in High-Level Parallel Programming Languages" was held at Mont Saint-Michel (France) in June 1991. The motivation for organizing this workshop came from the emergence of a new class of formalisms for describing parallel computations in the last few years. Linda, Unity, Gamma, and the Cham are the most significant representatives of this new class. Formalisms of this family promote simple but powerful language features for describing data (set, multiset, tuple space) and programs (multiple assignment, chemical reaction, tuple manipulation). However, these proposals appeared in different contexts and were applied in different domains (distributed algorithms, communications, algorithmics, semantics of parallelism,...). Hence, there has been no real community of researchers in this area. The goal of the Mont Saint-Michel workshop was to review the status of this new field and to compare experiences.

The programme committee consisted of Jean-Pierre Banâtre (Irisa, Rennes, France), Gérard Berry (Ecole des Mines, Sophia Antipolis, France), David Gelernter (Yale University, New Haven, USA), Daniel Le Métayer (Irisa, Rennes, France), and Jayadev Misra (University of Texas at Austin, USA). Each member of this committee was in charge of inviting a number of other researchers interested in this area.

This volume contains most of the papers presented at the workshop. Its outline mirrors the organization of the workshop into four main sessions : Unity, Linda, Gamma and Parallel Program Design. These parts are introduced respectively by Jayadev Misra, David Gelernter, Daniel Le Métayer and Jean-Pierre Banâtre.

A number of people contributed to the success of the workshop. We offer our sincere thanks to all of them. We are particularly grateful to Elisabeth Lebret for her efforts.

The workshop was organized by Inria Rennes (Irisa). We would also like to thank C^3 (the French programme for parallelism) for their financial support.

Rennes, France
December 1991

J.P. Banâtre
D. Le Métayer

Contents

Part 1: Unity

A Perspective on Parallel Program Design*

Jayadev Misra

The University of Texas at Austin, Austin, TX 78712, USA

The papers in this section on UNITY range from "esoteric" theory to "mundane" practice. Yet, they fit into a rather coherent view of programming. To appreciate this continuity, I highlight a few questions about parallel program design: why theory and practice remain so far apart, what UNITY aspired to achieve, where it failed and where it succeeded, and finally, how the following papers fit into a whole.

Common-Sense Reasoning

A fine example of common-sense reasoning is found in proving the following identity over binomial coefficients:

$$\binom{n}{k} = \binom{n-1}{k} + \binom{n-1}{k-1}$$

The left side represents the number of different ways of choosing k distinct items out of n distinct items. Now, a specific item is either left out in a choice—then, we have to choose k items out of the remining $(n-1)$ items, and this can be done in

$$\binom{n-1}{k}$$

ways—or, the specific item is included in the choice—then, the remaining $(k-1)$ items could be chosen out of the remaining $(n-1)$ items in

$$\binom{n-1}{k-1}$$

ways. Since the two possibilities are mutually exclusive, the total number of possible choices is simply the sum of the two terms shown in the right side of the identity.

The simplicity of this common-sense-based proof is far outweighted by its disadvantages. Insufficient attention has been paid to the boundary conditions—is k allowed to be zero or, even negative? Can k exceed n, or can n be a real number? The proof does not allow these possibilities, but even more disturbing is that the prover does not seem to be aware that such restrictions should be stated explicitly. Not only do we not have the generality that is available in the given identity but we are unsure about the conditions under which the identity can be used safely.

Much of programming, and temporal reasoning based on common-sense, has this flavor. A mathematical problem is reduced to an every day problem on which common-sense reasoning can then be applied, , *viz.* if a process receives a reply before sending a

* This material is based in part upon work supported by the Texas Advanced Research Program under Grant No. 003658–065 and by the Office of Naval Research Contract N00014-90-J-1640.

message, then the reply could not have been the response to this message; therefore ... The most "likely cases" are considered, and argued about. The boundary conditions—the number of iterations of a loop being zero, the item being searched lying outside the bounds of the stored items, the buffer being full, etc.—are usually neglected. It is not surprising that most errors arise from such "unforeseen circumstances" (a wonderful tautology).

Sequential programming could cope, to some extent, with these difficulties by identifying a large number of possible boundary conditions as outlined above, testing with pathological inputs, code walk-throughs, and, most often, by simplifying and structuring the design. All these principles are important when we approach parallel program design. However, reasoning based on temporal behavior of a program is now grossly inadequate; we simply can't imagine that one processor can execute a million steps while another has not yet completed even a single step! We are more likely to leave out such pathological cases in our reasoning. The moral is that common sense reasoning is useful for sequential programming, though not a complete solution; it is entirely inadequate for parallel programming.

But proofs are expensive! It is difficult to learn how to prove and very difficult to prove "real" programs. Alas, like democracy as a political system, proofs are terrible and there is nothing better. One aspect of the above complaint is sociological—yes, it takes many years of education to become proficient in any novel activity—and the other is scientific—yes, terrible methods take longer to learn and apply. The scientific community can address only the second question; our methods have to become much better. UNITY has addressed the scientific question in two different ways: restricting the class of properties that we can prove and simplifying the programs whose properties are to be proven.

Restrictions

One would like to derive a number of properties of a program besides the fact that it implements a given specification describing the values of its variables over time. We may wish to know the program's performance on a given machine (or whether it meets some real-time constraints), the amount of buffer spaces it consumes or the network traffic it generates. It seems best to develop different methods to address these different questions. While correctness can be studied entirely within mathematical logic, at least in principle, questions of performance are best treated through a combination of analytical and empirical methods. Similarly, different methods may be employed to prove different kinds of correctness properties. Sequential programs may be proved by employing pre- and post-conditions; parallel programs seem to require more general techniques in order to describe the states that may arise *during* a computation. Correctness of a deterministic program requires a proof about its lone execution sequence, whereas for nondeterministic programs, one may need to state properties of possible execution sequences.

We can simplify the proof methods and make them cheaper to apply if we restrict the class of properties we are willing to consider. This led us to adopt a minimal fragment of linear temporal logic for stating properties in UNITY; the choice of operators was influenced by our desire to employ induction as the basis of our proofs. Hence, we rejected the primary temporal-logic operators $\Box$ (always) and $\Diamond$ (eventually), in favor of *unless*, *ensures* and $\mapsto$ (*leads-to*). An *unless* property is proven by induction on the number of program steps, *ensures* provides a mechanism to capture (a weak form of) fairness and *leads-to* is proven by induction on the number of "*ensures*-steps."

Restricting the logic to such a small fragment has the disadvantage that many interesting properties can no longer be stated. For instance, "for every natural number there is an execution sequence that outputs that number" cannot be stated and "event f occurs between an occurrence of event e and a subsequent occurrence of event g" can only be stated with some difficulty. In spite of these disadvantages, we continue to believe that these restrictions are useful. The proofs are considerably shorter than in the other methodologies and the inference rules provide useful guidelines for program design.

Simplifications

A program that is executed is never proven; what is proven is only an abstraction of that program that is subsequently compiled and linked. We have sufficient confidence in the compilers and linkers that we continue to believe in an executing program even though we have proved only an abstraction of it. Stated in another way, we find it cost-effective to argue about two different correctness problems (using different methods, presumably): The correctness of a high-level program and the correctness of the compiler. UNITY supports this scheme by providing a yet-higher level of abstraction which admits of simpler reasoning. This higher level includes only synchrony and asynchrony as the basic constructs, and assignment as the only statement. Everything else—process, message, communication protocol, deadlock, etc.—has been excluded. How effective is this method? How expressive is the notation in solving "real-world" problems and how does one refine a program and prove the correctness of refinements? Most of these questions can only be answered through empirical methods.

Our experience suggests that UNITY is, surprisingly, extremely effective in expressing solutions to parallel programming problems: Synchronous assignment can be used to indicate a solution in which the tasks are to be executed in lock-step and asynchrony can be used for expressing solutions to problems that will eventually be executed on a MIMD machine. The combination of synchrony and asynchrony makes it possible to develop solutions for geographically distributed synchronous multiprocessors, for instance. The structuring of programs, through union, seems to capture the essence of process-network style of composition. The notion of superposition allows for program construction in layers.

Refinement has posed more serious problems. Refinement of a UNITY program to another involves no conceptual difficulty; correctness is shown by deducing the properties of the former from the properties of the latter using the inference rules of UNITY. In fact, it is preferable to refine only the properties, i.e., by adding more properties or strengthening the existing ones, until a program can be constructed to implement those properties. Refinement of a UNITY program (or its properties) to a program in an existing language has proved to be more difficult, since the latter kind of programs could be considerably more detailed and not as amenable to formal proofs.

Research Directions

UNITY is not a programming language. The data structures in it are ad-hoc in nature. The structuring methods, though powerful, should be enhanced considerably. For instance, sequential compositions of programs is not yet available because we don't yet have the appropriate inference rules. A programming language that reflects the UNITY philosophy will make it possible to introduce a complete methodology of program construction, from specification to code through a sequence of program/data/specification refinement. In this regard, the paper by Rajive Bagrodia represents an important step in the right direction. His results show that one need not sacrifice efficiency in the pursuit of machine independence; in fact, I have every hope that his programs will turn out to be *more* efficient on sizeable problems because it is easier to optimize starting with higher-lever code.

The work of Gruia-Catalin Roman is, again, an attempt to introduce structure in a programming language by limiting the UNITY-style actions to operate on a Linda-style tuple space. Linda's success in the user community attests to the effectiveness of tuple-space as a programming construct. Its interaction with UNITY has been thought out carefully in Roman's paper. This empirical study will eventually address some of the questions regarding refinement.

The paper by Antonio Pizzarello details a "real-world" problem of enormous size that has been successfully tackled by application of UNITY methodology. This work, carried out by the employees of BULL HN in Phoenix and Mark Staskauskas of The University of Texas is impressive in both size and complexity. That the project could be completed successfully, within the budget and schedule constraints, gives us hope that well trained professionals will triumph in the end! Written from the perspective of a manager, this paper is significant for those wishing to avoid some of the pitfalls in applying formal methods in the industry.

The papers by Ambuj Singh and Beverly Sanders are more theoretical in nature. They explore some of the foundational issues of UNITY. Many of the "practical" questions in UNITY—which structuring operators are appropriate, should we denote termination explicitly in a program, etc.—were first answered theoretically; if a concept proves theoretically-troublesome it usually proves practically-troublesome in the end. Sanders examines the original design decisions of UNITY, particularly its logic, in the light of the experience gained in its use in the recent years. She suggests several generalizations that can enhance the power without introducing additional complexity. Singh explores a constrained form of UNITY programs where the asynchrony relation is specified explicitly. He designs a logic for this style of programs in a manner similar to original UNITY.

It is too early to predict that these ideas will "succeed." All we can attempt is that our questions be important, not only for UNITY but for parallel programming, in general. Then the papers succeed magnificently.

This article was processed using the LaTeX macro package with LMAMULT style

UNITY to UC: A Case Study in the Derivation of Parallel Programs

Indranil Chakravarty[1], Michael Kleyn[1], Thomas Y.C. Woo[1]*, Rajive Bagrodia[2]**, Vernon Austel[2]

[1] Schlumberger Laboratory for Computer Science, Austin, TX 78720
[2] Department of Computer Science, University of California at Los Angeles, Los Angeles, CA 90024

Abstract

This paper describes the use of the UNITY [6] notation and the UC compiler [2] in the design of parallel programs for execution on the Connection Machine CM2 (CM). We illustrate our ideas in the context of a computer simulation of particle diffusion and aggregation in a porous media.

We begin with a UNITY specification, progressively refine the specification to derive a UNITY program, translate the program to UC abstractions, which may be further refined to improve efficiency, and finally implement the program on the CM. Performance results on the efficiency of the program constructed using this approach are also included.

1 Introduction

Much of the current work in parallel processing is aimed at finding good abstractions for expressing parallelism in programs. [7, 4, 1, 10, 9]. The goal is to provide a language which allows the user to express an algorithm in a concise and abstract way, independent of any parallel model of computation, and then to transform this specification into an efficient implementation. Efficiency in this context refers to maximizing the use of the computation and communication resources of a target architecture in order to reduce the execution time.

One approach, exemplified by UNITY, is to use a logic and a notation in which the abstract specification of the computation and successive refinements of the specification are expressed. The parallel constructs proposed in UNITY make it possible to express parallelism inherent in the problem, independent of a target architecture. The notation allows a programmer to reason about computation and communication concisely and provides a rigorous approach for ensuring the correctness of the algorithm as it is successively refined to express details of the computation. Mapping such an abstract specification to a target architecture, and ensuring correctness and efficiency, is difficult and requires considerable knowledge about processor interconnectivity, cost of communication channels, and the behavior of the synchronization primitives available. This type of knowledge, however,

---

* M.Kleyn and T.Y.C. Woo are currently at the Department of Computer Sciences, The University of Texas at Austin, Austin TX 78712

** The work of this author was partially supported by NSF under grant CCR 9157610 and by ONR under grant N00014-91-J-1605

can be used to refine both the UNITY and UC abstractions so that the derived programs are more amenable for implementation on a particular kind of target architecture.

The absence of UNITY implementations on specific architectures implies that at some point the UNITY program must be mapped to a lower-level language for implementation. It is important that this mapping be simple, so that it is easy to show that the transformed program is equivalent to the UNITY specification. A language called UC [2] was developed recently and implemented on the CM. As illustrated subsequently, a UNITY program can easily be translated into a UC program and executed on the CM. Our objective in this paper is to demonstrate the use and efficacy of the UNITY and UC notations for designing parallel programs. The eventual objective of this research is to develop a method to derive UC programs from their UNITY specifications. Our goal in this paper is modest and is simply aimed at demonstrating the feasibility of our objectives. For this purpose, we have selected a "real world" problem: computer simulation of the diffusion and aggregation of particles in a cement like porous media[11]. We develop a UNITY specification for this problem and present a UNITY program that meets the specification. In the interest of brevity, we omit the formal proof that the program satisfies its specifications. The initial UNITY program is refined to exploit the inherent parallelism in the application. Architecture-dependent refinements are not introduced at this level. The refined program is then transformed into a UC program. Although a proof methodology to prove the correctness of this transformation has not yet been developed, we informally argue the correctness preserving nature of the transformation. We demonstrate how the UC program can itself be refined further to exploit the data parallelism offered by an SIMD architecture like that of the Connection Machine. The eventual UC program was executed on the Connection Machine and its performance was compared with the performance of an equivalent program written in CM FORTRAN.

The next section gives a brief description of the UNITY notation and programming logic. Section 3 summarizes the main features of the UC language. Section 4 informally describes the diffusion aggregation problem. In section 5, a UNITY specification is developed for the problem and UNITY programs are presented in section 6. Section 7 translates the main portion of the program into UC and discusses further refinements. The paper concludes with performance results and comparisons with the same algorithms programmed in CM FORTRAN[8].

2 UNITY

UNITY stands for "Unbounded Nondeterministic Iterative Transformations". UNITY has two parts, a notation for expressing computations and a logic for reasoning about computations. The notation provides constructs that avoid specifying sequential dependencies which are not inherent in the problem. UNITY programs describe both the operational behavior of the program (using logical assertions) and assignment statements that describe the computation. Unlike sequential languages their order of execution of the assignment statements has no relation to the order in which they are written. UNITY programs terminate by reaching a *fixed point*. A program reaches a fixed-point in its execution when the execution of any statement does not change the state of the program.

2.1 The UNITY Programming Notation
UNITY statements take the following form:

$$\langle \otimes x : r.x :: t.x \rangle$$

where x is a quantified variable whose range is specified by $r.x$ and $t.x$ is the term of the expression. A term can be a simple assignment or an assignment to another quantified statement. $\otimes$ can any of the following operators:

|| - This separates *assignment components* indicating that the set of assignments of the quantified term are *all* executed simultaneously.

| - This separates *assignment statements*, indicating that *only one* assignment of the set of assignments of the quantified term is executed. With | the selection is non-deterministic but *fair*; in an infinite execution of the program every assignment is executed infinitely often.

an associative operator - $\otimes$ can be any associative symmetric operator such as $+$ (addition), $*$ (multiplication), min (minimum), max (maximum), $\vee$ (disjunction), or $\wedge$ (conjunction). The application of such a symmetric operator on N operands can be performed in $O(logN)$ time with $O(N)$ processors on a synchronous machine (e.g. CM).

Enumerated statements are also allowed. For example, $x := 3 \,\|\, y := 0 \,\|\, z := 2$ explicitly enumerates three statements that execute simultaneously.

2.2 The UNITY Programming Logic

The UNITY program structure is described by three *logical relations*, **unless, ensures,** and **leads-to**. These relations can be used to make assertions about the properties of a program, and inference rules associated with these relations together with UNITY's model of program execution allow the programmer to check whether certain desired properties of a program hold. The relations have formal definitions in terms of the pre- and post-conditions of a statement. We provide informal meanings of the relations here:

unless: p *unless* q, means that if p is true at some point in the computation and q is not, after the execution of a (any) statement p remains true or q becomes true.

ensures: p *ensures* q, means that if p is true at some point in the computation, p remains true as long as q is false and eventually q becomes true.

leads-to: Given p *leads-to* q in a program, once p becomes true q is or will be true. However, we cannot assert that p will remain true as long as q is not. This is a major difference between ensures and leads-to.

These three relations can be used to reason about the safety and progress properties in a program. For a detailed description the reader is referred to [6].

Example The following example illustrate how this notation can be used to specify matrix computations. Multiplication of a pair of matrices, $C^{L \times N} = A^{L \times M} B^{M \times N}$, can be specified as:

$$\langle \| \, i,k : 0 \leq i < L, 0 \leq k < N :: C[i,k] := \langle + j : 0 \leq j < M :: A[i,j] \times B[j,k] \rangle \rangle$$

In this example i, j, and k are the quantified variables, $0 \leq i < L, 0 \leq k < N$ specifies the range of i and k and the symbol $\|$ indicates that all the summations (of which there are $L \times N$, one for each pair of i and j), can occur simultaneously. Each summation could be performed in $O(logM)$ time by M processors. Thus matrix multiplication can be performed in $O(logM)$ time with $L \times N \times M$ processors. Using fewer processors, for example $L \times M$, the same operation can be performed in $O(N)$ time.

Note that the notation does not define the mapping of the operations on a target architecture. A more detailed description of the notation can be found in the Chapter 2 of [6].

3 The UC Programming Language

UC provides a synchronous programming notation by extending C with a few primitives. This section describes only those UC constructs that have been used in deriving the program described in this paper. A detailed description of the language can be found in [2, 3].

Consider the UC program shown below. It shows a mapping of the UNITY specification of matrix multiplication described in the previous section. The program computes matrix $c^{L \times N}$ as the product of two matrices $a^{L \times M}$ and $b^{M \times N}$ as specified in the UNITY description in the previous section. For brevity, input-output issues are ignored. The program declarations include the standard C declarations for matrices a, b and c (line 1). In addition, three index-sets I, J and K are declared (line 2). Each index-set consists of L, M, or N integers ranging from 0 to $L - 1$, 0 to $M - 1$, and 0 to $N - 1$, respectively. The declaration of an index-set uses two identifiers, the first one (example I) refers to the index-set itself and the second (example i) to an arbitrary element of the set.

```
1          int a[L][M], b[M][N], c[L][N];
2          index-set I:i = {0..L-1}, J:j = {0..M-1}, K:k ={0..N-1};

3          par (I,K)
4              c[i][k] = $+(J; a[i][j]*b[j][k]);
```

The program consists of a single UC parallel assignment. The UC keyword **par** (line 3) specifies parallel execution of the assignment statement in line 4. This is similar to the || operator in UNITY. The index-set(s) contained in the **par** statement determine the number of instances of the assignment statement that are executed in parallel. In this case, $L \times N$ instances of the assignment will be executed, one for each of the $L \times N$ elements in the product set I × K. Now consider the assignment statement itself. For a given (i, k), the value of c[i][k] is computed as the dot product of two vectors: the ith row of a and the kth column of b. The dot product is programmed in UC as a reduction (line 4). The reduction specifies the addition of M expressions, one for each value of index-element j, where the jth expression is a[i][j]*b[j][k]. Besides addition, other associative, symmetric operators may also be used in a reduction. These include $&& (logical and), $> (maximum), $< (minimum), $* (multiplication), $^ (logical exclusive or), and $, value of an arbitrary operand.

The next example computes the trace of array a(the sum of elements on its main diagonal). The declarations are similar to the previous example and have been omitted. The body is a single reduction which computes the sum of the diagonal elements. This example illustrates how a boolean expression may be used to select a subset of the elements from an index-set. The predicate $(i==j)$ selects only those elements from the index-sets that correspond to the subscripts of the diagonal elements of array a. The keyword **st** in the reduction separates the index-sets from the boolean expression. (Note that this reduction may be expressed more concisely as: $\$+(I; a[i][i])$). A boolean expression may also be used in a **par** statement to restrict the assignment operation to a subset of the array elements.

```
trace = $+(I,J st(i==j) a[i][j]);
```

The last example illustrates repeated execution of a **par** statement (iterative **par**). The asterisk preceding the keyword **par** indicates that the statement is executed repeatedly until every instance of the predicate associated with the statement evaluates to false. In this example, the assignment statement for the ith row is executed repeatedly until the first element of the row is negative.

```
*par (I)
    st (a[i][0] >= 0)
        a[i][0] -= $+(J st (j != 0) a[i][j]);
```

If the keyword **par** of a UC statement is replaced by **seq**, the corresponding statement (or statement block) is executed sequentially for each element in the index-set. The elements are selected in the order of their occurrence in the original specification for the corresponding index-set. The **seq** statement may be thought of as an abbreviated specification of a counting loop.

A UC program need not specify how an array is to be mapped on the CM memory. A default mapping is generated by the compiler using simple heuristics. For instance, if an array is used within a **par** statement, each element of the array will be stored on a unique virtual processor. Arrays that have the same dimensionality are mapped such that corresponding elements of different arrays lie on the same processor and successive elements of an array are mapped to neighboring processors. Thus if a program uses two arrays $a_{n,n}$ and $b_{n,n}$, the $(i,j)^{th}$ elements of each array are automatically mapped on the same data processor. However, even for a relatively simple program like matrix multiplication, a modified data mapping can improve the execution efficiency of a program. UC currently defines four types of mappings: **permute, fold, copy** and **reduce**. These mappings provide a systematic way to rearrange data in the CM memory for execution efficiency. A complete description of UC mappings together with a study of their impact on program efficiency may be found in [3].

4 The Diffusion Aggregation Problem

The purpose of this simulation is to develop computer models that account for changes in porosity and microstructure resulting from fluid flow in a porous material. The simulation begins with a model in which there is a collection of unhydrated material clusters scattered over a plane. These clusters represent the original unreacted rock grains and are separated by pore space. The proportion of the plane occupied by unhydrated material is referred to as the *packing fraction*. The proportion of the plane that is pore space is the *porosity*. The packing fraction and the initial geometric configuration of the unhydrated materials are strong determinants of the simulation result. The starting configuration

Pore Space   Unhydrated
                              Materials

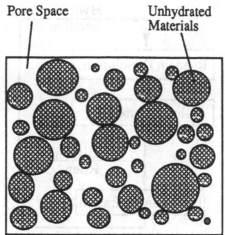

Fig. 1. Initial Configuration

for the simulation is typically an approximation to cement-based materials and use a random placement of circles (e.g., Figure 1).

Dissolution takes place at the surface layer of the unhydrated materials, i.e., those unhydrated materials that are in contact with the pore space. The selection of the surface layer material that dissolves is random. The dissolved unhydrated material become diffusing particles. The particles perform a random walk in pore space until they encounter a solid (unhydrated material or previously hydrated product) whereupon they become an immobile hydrate product. When all diffusing particles have settled, the process repeats again starting from the dissolution step. Taken to the extreme the dissolution/diffusion cycle would be repeated until there were no more surface level unhydrated material. This is not necessarily the way the simulation would be used in practice.

An entire simulation can be viewed as an iteration consisting of three distinct steps (Figure 2). A random dissolution step selects surface unhydrated material to dissolve. Volume correction is then applied to augment the diffusing particle count. The diffusion phase moves the particles in random walks until they all have hydrated. The number of diffusion rounds is determined by the length of the random walk followed by the last diffusing particle to hydrate. All particles are assumed to move at the same speed. The model is assumed to admit a periodic boundary condition for the simulation grid. In the next section we derive a specification of the simulation program using UNITY.

5 Diffusion Aggregation Unity Specification

In this section we derive a formal specification of the UNITY program in terms of a set of invariant, unless, and leads-to properties.

Variables

Phase is represented using a global variable named *phase* which can assume values from the set {*dissolution, correction, diffusion*}. This variable is used to denote a phase

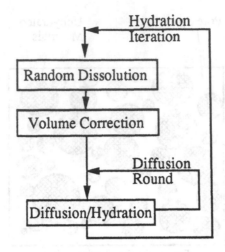

Fig. 2. Random Dissolution/Hydration Model

change during the simulation.

The simulation space (particles space and pore space) is represented using a two-dimensional array $[0..N-1, 0..M-1].s$. Each array cell records the current state, that is, position and material type in it. The material type in each cell can assume values from the following set { U for unhydrated material, H for hydrated material, P for pore space, and D for diffusing particle }. The particle movement is represented implicitly. Thus a movement of a particle from one position to another is represented as a state change (in the type of material) among the positions in the two-dimensional array.

During the dissolution phase, each unhydrated material that has at least one pore neighbor will attempt to dissolve by performing a random move. To record the direction of this move, we use an array $[0..N-1, 0..M-1].m$. An arbitrary mapping, e.g. 0 for N, 1 for NE, 2 for E and so on can be used to denote the direction. Similarly this variable is also used in the diffusion step for recording the direction for the random walk. We assume the existence of a function *dest* which takes a position $[i, j]$ and a move direction m and returns the destination position of the move. For example, if we use 3 to denote SE, then $dest([i, j], 3)$ returns the position $[i+1, j-1]$.

In the following discussion the ranges of i and j are omitted to avoid clutter and are assumed to be $0 \leq i < N$ and $0 \leq j < M$. Each array cell corresponds to a position in the simulation space. We denote the position as $[i, j]$.

Invariant Properties

1. The variable *phase* can only assume values from the set {*dissolution, correction, diffusi*

$$phase = dissolution \lor phase = correction \lor phase = diffusion \qquad (I_1)$$

2. Similarly, for all position $[i, j]$ ($0 \leq i < N, 0 \leq j < M$) the state $s[i, j]$ can only assume values from $\{U, H, P, D\}$.

$$[i,j].s = U \ \lor \ [i,j].s = H \ \lor \ [i,j].s = P \ \lor \ [i,j].s = D \qquad (I_2)$$

If the current state of position $[i,j]$ is t (i.e. $s[i,j] = t$), we will call $[i,j]$ a t-position.

Stable Properties

1. Once a position is occupied by a hydrated material, it will always remain as a hydrated material. In other words, hydrated material as the final state of the simulation.

$$[i,j].s = H \qquad (S_1)$$

2. This is an exact dual of S_1. If a position is not occupied by unhydrated material, it will never be occupied by unhydrated material. In other words, the simulation process will not produce new unhydrated material. Hence, we can view unhydrated material as the initial state of the simulation. The simulation process itself can be viewed as a non-deterministic transformation of unhydrated material into hydrated material driven by the rules of the diffusion and aggregation.

$$[i,j].s \neq U \qquad (S_2)$$

Unless Properties

In order to simplify the following derivation, we introduce three functions $neighbor$, $\#N$ and $\#T$. $neighbor$ is a boolean function, whereas the other two are numeric functions. Their definitions are detailed below:

- $neighbor([s,t],[u,v])$

$$neighbor([s,t],[u,v]) = \begin{cases} true, \text{ if } & (s \neq u \ \lor \ t \neq v) \\ & \land \ (s = u + 1 \bmod N \ \lor \ u = s + 1 \bmod N) \\ & \land \ (t = v + 1 \bmod N \ \lor \ v = t + 1 \bmod N) \\ false, \text{ otherwise} \end{cases}$$

Therefore, $neighbor([s,t],[u,v])$ is true if position $[s,t]$ and position $[u,v]$ are adjacent.

- $\#N([i,j],t)$

$$\#N([i,j],t) \equiv \langle +[u,v] : neighbor([u,v],[i,j]) \\ \land [u,v].s = t :: \\ 1 \\ \rangle$$

The expression $\#N([i,j],t)$ returns the number of neighbors of position $[i,j]$ whose state is equal to t. For example, $\#N([i,j],P)$ returns the number of pore neighbors of $[i,j]$.

- $\#T(t)$

$$\#T(t) \equiv \langle +[u,v] : [u,v].s = t :: 1 \rangle$$

$\#T(t)$ returns the total number of position whose state is currently equal to t. For example, $\#T(P)$ returns the total number of pore spaces.

With these definitions we can proceed to define the unless properties:

1. We need to specify the permissible state transitions for each position $[i, j]$. These are:

   (a) An unhydrated material can only change into a pore by dissolving, and it can do so only in the dissolution phase, and only if its random walk destination is a pore.

$$[i, j].s = U$$
$$\text{unless}$$
$$phase = dissolution \land [i, j].s = P \land dest([i, j], [i, j].m).s = D \qquad (U_1)$$

   (b) A P-position can only change into a D-position. In other words, a pore cannot spontaneously become unhydrated or hydrated material.

$$[i, j].s = P \text{ unless } [i, j].s = D \qquad (U_2)$$

   (c) A diffusing particle may move only in the diffusing phase and if its random walk destination is a pore. Whether the random walk succeeds depends on whether there are other particles trying to move into the same pore space.

$$[i, j].s = D$$
$$\text{unless}$$
$$phase = diffusion \land [i, j].s = P \land dest([i, j], [i, j].m).s = D \qquad (U_3)$$

2. During the dissolution phase, pore spaces and the total number of unhydrated material and diffusing particles must remain constant. This is required to ensure that the dissolving process produces the same number of diffusing particles as it consumes unhydrated materials. Thus, no new material is generated.

$$\#T(U) + \#T(D) = k$$
$$\text{unless}$$
$$phase \neq dissolution \qquad (U_4)$$

3. The total number of pores should remain constant except in the volume correction phase.

$$\#T(P) = k$$
$$\text{unless}$$
$$phase = correction \qquad (U_5)$$

4. Due to the random walk nature of diffusion, we cannot require a program to always have a terminating diffusing step. Therefore we can only specify the weaker unless properties. (See leads-to properties for other phase change below.)

$$phase = diffusion \text{ unless } phase = dissolution \qquad (U_6)$$

Leads-to Properties

1. In the dissolution phase, a pore space must allow exactly one unhydrated neighbor to dissolve into it. This implies that the pore must be the destination of at least one of its unhydrated neighbor.

$$phase = dissolution \ \wedge \ [i,j].s = P$$
$$\wedge \ \langle \vee \ [u,v] :: neighbor([u,v],[i,j]) \ \wedge \ dest([u,v],[u,v].m) = [i,j] \rangle$$
$$\longmapsto$$
$$[i,j].s = D \tag{L_1}$$

2. The dissolution phase ends and the correction phase begins if all unhydrated materials that can dissolve have dissolved.

$$phase = dissolution \ \wedge$$
$$\langle \wedge \ [s,t],[u,v] :: neighbor([s,t],[u,v]) \ \wedge \ dest([s,t],[s,t].m) = [u,v] \Rightarrow [u,v].s \neq P \rangle$$
$$\longmapsto$$
$$phase = correction \tag{L_2}$$

3. The correction phase should be terminating.

$$phase = correction \longmapsto phase = diffusion \tag{L_3}$$

4. In the diffusion phase, a diffusing particle will undergo hydration if its random walk destination is a solid (i.e. unhydrated or hydrated).

$$phase = diffusion \ \wedge \ [i,j].s = D \ \wedge \ (dest([i,j],[i,j].m).s = H \ \vee \ dest([i,j],[i,j].m).s = U)$$
$$\longmapsto$$
$$[i,j].s = P \tag{L_4}$$

5. In the diffusion phase, a pore space must allow exactly one diffusing particle neighbors to move into it, if it is the random walk destination of at least one of its diffusing particle neighbors.

$$phase = diffusion \ \wedge \ [i,j].s = P$$
$$\wedge \ \langle \vee \ [u,v] :: neighbor([u,v],[i,j] \ \wedge \ dest([u,v],[u,v].m) = [i,j] \rangle$$
$$\longmapsto$$
$$[i,j].s = D \tag{L_5}$$

6. The diffusion should terminate once all the diffusing particles have undergone hydration.

$$phase = diffusion \ \wedge \ \#T(D) = 0 \longmapsto phase = dissolution \tag{L_6}$$

Derived Properties

Here we list some properties that can be derived from the specification:

1. An unhydrated material can only dissolve into an adjacent pore position. Thus when an unhydrated material dissolves, it must cause a previous pore neighbor to become non-pore neighbor.

$$phase = dissolution \ \wedge \ [i,j].s = U \ \wedge \ \#N([i,j],P) = k$$
$$unless \tag{D_1}$$
$$\#N([i,j],P) < k$$

2. Similar to above but for diffusing particles in the diffusion phase.

$$phase = diffusion \ \wedge \ [i,j].s = D \ \wedge \ \#N([i,j],P) = k$$
$$unless \tag{D_2}$$
$$\#N([i,j],P) < k$$

3. phase change is cyclic.

6 UNITY Program

The following UNITY program may be derived from the specification constructed in the previous section. Although it is possible to formally derive the program from its specification in the preceding section, the proof is omitted in the interest of brevity.

Program *Rock*1
initially $\quad \langle \wedge \, [i,j] :: [i,j].s = P \ \vee \ [i,j].s = U \rangle$
$\qquad\qquad \wedge \, phase = dissolution$

assign

1: $\quad \langle \| i,j ::$
$\qquad\qquad \langle \| u,v :: [i,j].s,[u,v].s := D, P \text{ if } [i,j].s = P \wedge [u,v].s = U$
$\qquad\qquad\qquad\qquad\qquad \wedge \, dest([u,v],[u,v].m) = [i,j]$
$\qquad\qquad\qquad\qquad\qquad \wedge \, phase = dissolution$
$\qquad\qquad \rangle$
$\qquad \rangle$

2: $\quad \| \quad phase := correction \text{ if } \langle \wedge \, [s,t],[u,v] :: neighbor([s,t],[u,v])$
$\qquad\qquad\qquad\qquad\qquad\qquad\qquad \wedge \, dest([s,t],[s,t].m) = [u,v]$
$\qquad\qquad\qquad\qquad\qquad\qquad\qquad \wedge \, [s,t].s = U$
$\qquad\qquad\qquad\qquad\qquad\qquad\qquad \Rightarrow [u,v].s \neq P \rangle$
$\qquad\qquad\qquad\qquad \wedge \, phase = dissolution$

3: $\quad \| \quad \langle \| i,j :: [i,j].s := D \text{ if } [i,j].s = P$
$\qquad\qquad\qquad\qquad \wedge \, phase = correction$

4: $\quad \| \quad phase := diffusion \text{ if } phase = correction$

5: $\quad \| \quad \langle \| i,j :: [i,j].s := H \text{ if } [i,j].s = D$
$\qquad\qquad\qquad\qquad \wedge \, (dest([i,j],[i,j].m).s = H \ \vee \ dest([i,j],[i,j].m).s = U)$
$\qquad\qquad\qquad\qquad \wedge \, phase = diffusion$
$\qquad\qquad \rangle$

6: $\quad \| \quad \langle \| i,j ::$
$\qquad\qquad\qquad \langle \| u,v :: [i,j].s,[u,v].s := D, P \text{ if } [i,j].s = P \wedge [u,v].s = D$
$\qquad\qquad\qquad\qquad\qquad\qquad \wedge \, dest([u,v],[u,v].m) = [i,j]$
$\qquad\qquad\qquad\qquad\qquad\qquad \wedge \, phase = diffusion$
$\qquad\qquad\qquad \rangle$
$\qquad\qquad \rangle$

7: $\quad \| \quad phase := dissolution \text{ if } \langle +[u,v] : [u,v].s = D :: 1 \rangle = 0$

$$\wedge \, phase = diffusion$$

End *Rock*1

Note, that *Rock*1 does not support any parallel execution of statements since only the ∥ operators are used. In order to exploit the inherent parallelism in the simulation, we need to replace as many of the ∥ by the ‖ operator. Such a refinement can only be performed if correctness is preserved. We demonstrate a few of these refinements and justify their soundness.

6.1 Refinement

Let us first concentrate only on statement (5). Statement (5) expresses the fact that if a diffusing particle is attempting to perform a walk into a solid (unhydrated or hydrated), then it will undergo hydration and become a hydrated product. Since each substatement in (5) modifies different variables, they can be executed independently on each processor. We can show that by replacing the ∥ in (5) with ‖, the correctness is preserved, i.e., the new program also satisfies the specification.

Now let us turn our attention to statement (6). There are 2 levels of nesting in statement (6). We will look at the parallelization of each level in sequence. Since UNITY does not allow a ∥ operator to be nested within a ‖ operator, we first investigate the parallelization of the inner level nesting. Since each substatement can modify two distinct variables, the parallelization requires careful consideration. If we simply replace the ∥ with ‖, the program would be incorrect. We can view this as a contention problem (Figure 3) where two particles A and B are trying to diffuse into the same pore space. If they both succeed then this would result in the loss of one diffusing particle leading to an incorrect result. This illustrates that a straightforward replacement of ∥ by ‖ for the inner level does not work for statement (6).

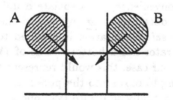

Fig.3. Multiple Particle Contention for a Pore Space

Cast as a resource contention problem, a straightforward solution would be to employ a centralized resource coordinator. In our case, this translates to allowing the destination pore space to select only one of possibly many neighboring diffusing particles to move in. This can be formally expressed as:

6′: $\langle \| i, j :: [i, j].s, [select([i, j], D)].s := D, P \text{ if } [i, j].s = P$
$$\wedge \, \langle \vee [u, v] : neighbor([u, v], [i, j]) ::$$
$$dest([u, v], [u, v].m) = [i, j]$$
$$\wedge [u, v].s = D$$

$$)$$
$$\land phase = diffusion$$

$$)$$

where $select([i,j],t)$ returns a neighboring position whose state is t and whose move destination is $[i,j]$. Formally,

$$select([u,v],t) = [i,j] \Rightarrow \begin{array}{l} neighbor([u,v],[i,j]) \\ \land [i,j].s = t \\ \land dest([i,j],[i,j].m) = [u,v] \end{array} \qquad (C)$$

6.2 Mapping to UC

In this section, we demonstrate how the UNITY program derived in the previous section can be translated into UC. The translation is straightforward since the UC constructs used are close to UNITY. We use statement (6′) as an example. A complete listing of the UC code may be found in [5].

Each position in the simulation space is represented by an array element $d[i][j]$. The corresponding state and move is recorded respectively in $d[i][j].s$ and $d[i][j].m$. The abstract *select* operation in the UNITY program can be mapped into UC as follows. Each pore space particle, say [i,j], surveys its eight neighbors to identify the diffusing particles that have selected [i,j] as their destination. If more than one such particle exists, a random selection is performed by the pore to pick one diffusing particle. We define variables $d[i][j].in$, which is used to store the id of a randomly chosen neighbor that has selected [i,j] as a potential destination and $d[i][j].id$, which is a unique identifier for each element. For instance, $d[i][j].id$ may be set to $(N+1)*i+j$, where N is the number of rows or columns in the array.

In the following mapping, the *dest* function (6′) is replaced by two separate functions xdest and ydest which return the x and y component of the destination position, respectively. In addition, for convenience, we associate a unique id $d[i][j].id$ for each position, the id can be easily obtained using any one-to-one function that maps the set of positions to integers. The *select* operation is mapped to the $, reduction operator in UC. Note that the $, operator has a bottom value of INF, i.e., it returns INF if the boolean condition is false. In our case, this would represent the fact that no neighboring diffusing particle is attempting to move into the pore space.

The original statement is actually split into two: one to select a neighboring particle (if any) to move in, and the other to perform the actual move. The par(I,J) construct maps directly to the $\langle \| i,j : \ldots \rangle$ in UNITY. The st(d[i][j].s==P) takes care of the first conjunct in the boolean condition for (6′). The second conjunct is represented by st(d[i][j].s==P && d[i][j].in != INF) in the second statement, while the third conjunct is implicitly represented by the sequential structure of the UC program.

```
index-set K:k ={-1 ..1};

/* obtain the unique id for each position */
par (I,J)
  st (1) {
    d[i][j].id = f(i,j);
}
```

```
/* randomly select a diffusing particle to move in by using
   the $, reduction operator over the neighboring diffusing
   particles */
par (I,J)
  st (d[i][j].s==P) {
    d[i][j].in = $,(K st (
                          (d[i+k][j+k].s==D) &&
                          (xdest(i+k,j+k,d[i+k][j+k].m)==i) &&
                          (ydest(i+k,j+k,d[i+k][j+k].m)==j)
                          )
                          d[i+k][j+k].id
                     );
  }


/* map the selected id back to the actual position, and change
   state, finverse is the inverse function for f */
par (I,J)
  st ((d[i][j].s==P) && (d[i][j].in != INF)) {
    int ii,jj;
    ii = finverse (d[i][j].in, 'x');
    jj = finverse (d[i][j].in, 'y');
    d[ii][jj].s = P;
    d[i][j].s   = D;
  }
```

Since the CM Fortran does not support an equivalent reduction operator as $,, the UC program was further refined by expanding the $, into a sequence of if-then-else statements so that a fair comparison with the CM Fortran program could be made. The execution times for the UC and CM Fortran versions were equivalent: for a 128 x 128 grid size with a porosity of 30 percent, each iteration took about 30 seconds to complete on an 8K CM2.

7 Conclusions and Further Work

The approach outlined in this paper and the experimental results have given us some insights into the role of formal techniques for parallel program construction. First, we used the UNITY logic and notation to define a program abstraction that satisfied the constraints implied in the specification. We felt that the derivation of the computation was enhanced by UNITY since it provided a systematic way of determining what could be parallelized. Second, we found that the refinement process has to consider a model of parallelism that is reflected by the target architecture and the structure of the data. This choice of using an array to represent the simulation space was guided by our knowledge of a synchronous parallel model, and refinement of the reduction operators was guided by communication costs and constraints in the CM architecture. Third, we found the mapping from UNITY to UC, for this class of problems, was rather easy and the iterative refinement at the UC level for performance efficiency was very useful.

The objective of this paper was to demonstrate that parallel programs can be designed in a high-level notation, refined into a form that highlights the inherent parallelism, and can be easily mapped into a language that exploits the resources of the target architecture. We found that the UC implementations were generally much more concise than those in CM Fortran. We attribute this conciseness to the versatility of the index sets, the parallel constructs, and the generality of the condition expressions. The conciseness is not at the expense of performance. On the contrary, the UNITY/UC form provides all the information needed by the compiler to generate an efficient program.

The contribution of this paper is twofold. First, we have shown the viability of using a high-level notion like UNITY to express the parallelism inherent in a mathematical algorithms, independent of the target architecture. Second, we have been able to successively refine the algorithm from a high-level specification into a form that is directly translatable into UC, preserving the parallelism implied in the abstract specification.

8 Acknowledgments

The authors would like to thank Prof. J. Misra, University of Texas, for his encouragement and to Dr. Peter Highnam for his help in implementing the CM Fortran version of the diffusion aggregation problem. The authors thank Dr. David Barstow for his technical review and suggestions, and Dr. Reid Smith, Director, Laboratory for Computer Science for his support and encouragement of this project.

References

1. J. R. Allen and K. Kennedy, A Parallel Programming Environment", IEEE Software, 2:4, 22-29,July,(1985)
2. R. Bagrodia, K.M. Chandy and E. Kwan, UC: A Language for the Connection Machine, Supercomputing '90, New York, NY, November, (1990), 525-534
3. R. Bagrodia and S. Mathur, Efficient Implementation of High-Level Parallel Programs, ASPLOS-IV, April (1991)
4. J.C. Browne, M. Azam and S. Sobek, The Computationally Oriented Display Environment (CODE) - A Unified Approach to Parallel Programming", IEEE Software, July, 1989)
5. I. Chakravarty, M. Kleyn, T. Woo, R. Bagrodia and V. Austel, UNITY to UC: Case Studies in Parallel Program Construction, Schlumberger Laboratory for Computer Science, TR-90-21, November, (1990)
6. K. M. Chandy and J. Misra, Parallel Program Design - A Foundation, Addison Wesley, Reading, MA, (1989)
7. Marina C. Chen, Very-high-level Parallel Programming in Crystal, Yale University,Dec, 1986, YALEU/DCS/RR-506
8. Connection Machine Fortran, Thinking Machines Corporation, Cambridge, MA (1989)
9. Robin Milner, Communication and Concurrency, Prentice Hall, Englewood Cliffs, New Jersey, (1989)
10. Edgar Knapp, An Excercise in the Formal Derivation of Parallel Programs: Maximum Flows in Graphs, ACM Transactions on Programming Languages and Systems, 12: 2, April, (1990) 203-223
11. T.A. Witten and L.M.. Sander, Diffusion Limited Aggregation, Physical Review, 27:9, (1983)5686-5697

This article was processed using the LaTeX macro package with LMAMULT style

Reasoning about Synchronic Groups*

Gruia-Catalin Roman[1] *and H. Conrad Cunningham*[2]

[1] Department of Computer Science, Washington University, Campus Box 1045, One Brookings Drive, St. Louis, MO 63130 U.S.A.
[2] Department of Computer & Information Science, University of Mississippi, 302 Weir Hall, University, MS 38677 U.S.A.

Abstract

Swarm is a computational model which extends the UNITY model in three important ways: (1) UNITY's fixed set of variables is replaced by an unbounded set of tuples which are addressed by content rather than by name; (2) UNITY's static set of statements is replaced by a dynamic set of transactions; and (3) UNITY's static ||-composition is augmented by dynamic coupling of transactions into *synchronic groups*. This last feature, unique to Swarm, facilitates formal specification of the mode of execution (synchronous or asynchronous) associated with portions of a concurrent program and enables computations to restructure themselves so as to accommodate the nature of the data being processed and to respond to changes in processing objectives. This paper overviews the Swarm model, introduces the synchronic group concept, and illustrates its use in the expression of dynamically structured programs. A UNITY-style programming logic is given for Swarm, the first axiomatic proof system for a *shared dataspace language*.

1 Introduction

Attempts to meet the challenges of concurrent programming have led to the emergence of a variety of models and languages. Chandy and Misra, however, argue that the fragmentation of programming approaches along the lines of architectural structure, application area, and programming language features obscures the basic unity of the programming task [4]. With the UNITY model, their goal is to unify seemingly disparate areas of programming with a simple theory consisting of a model of computation and an associated proof system.

Chandy and Misra build the UNITY computational model upon a traditional imperative foundation, a state-transition system with named variables to express the state and conditional multiple-assignment statements to express the state transitions. Above this foundation, however, UNITY follows a more radical design: all flow-of-control and communication constructs have been eliminated from the notation. A UNITY program begins

---

* Several of the concepts presented here appeared earlier in Roman and Cunningham's paper "The Synchronic Group: A Concurrent Programming Concept and Its Proof Logic," *Proceedings of the 10th International Conference on Distributed Computing Systems*, IEEE, May 1990.

execution in a valid initial state and continues infinitely; at each step an assignment is selected nondeterministically, but fairly, and executed atomically.

To accompany this simple but innovative model, Chandy and Misra have formulated an assertional programming logic which frees the program proof from the necessity of reasoning about execution sequences. Unlike most assertional proof systems, which rely on the annotation of the program text with predicates, the UNITY logic seeks to extricate the proof from the text by relying upon proofs of program-wide properties such as invariants and progress conditions.

Swarm [15] is a model which extends UNITY by permitting content-based access to data, a dynamic set of statements, and the ability to prescribe and alter the execution mode (i.e., synchronous or asynchronous) for arbitrary collections of program statements. The Swarm model is the primary vehicle for study of the *shared dataspace paradigm*, a class of languages and models in which the primary means for communication among the concurrent components of a program is a common, content-addressable data structure called a *shared dataspace*. Elements of the dataspace may be examined, inserted, or deleted by programs. Linda [3], Associons [14], GAMMA [1], and production rule languages such as OPS5 [2] all follow the shared dataspace approach.

The Swarm design merges the philosophy of UNITY with the methods of Linda. Swarm has a UNITY-like program structure and computational model and Linda-like communication mechanisms. The model partitions the dataspace into three subsets: a tuple space (a finite set of data tuples), a transaction space (a finite set of transactions), and a synchrony relation (a symmetric relation on the set of all possible transactions). Swarm replaces UNITY's fixed set of variables with a set of tuples and UNITY's fixed set of assignment statements with a set of transactions.

A Swarm transaction denotes an atomic transformation of the dataspace. It is a set of concurrently executed query-action pairs. A query consists of a predicate over the dataspace; an action consists of a group of deletions and insertions of dataspace elements. Instances of transactions may be created dynamically by an executing program.

A Swarm program begins execution from a specified initial dataspace. On each execution step, a transaction is chosen nondeterministically from the transaction space and executed atomically. This selection is fair in the sense that every transaction in the transaction space at any point in the computation will eventually be chosen. An executing transaction examines the dataspace and then, depending upon the results of the examination, can delete tuples (but not transactions) from the dataspace and insert new tuples and transactions into the dataspace. Unless a transaction explicitly reinserts itself into the dataspace, it is deleted as a by-product of its execution. Program execution continues until there are no transactions remaining in the dataspace.

The synchrony relation feature adds even more dynamism and expressive power to Swarm programs. It is a relation over the set of possible transaction instances. This relation may be examined and modified by programs in the same way as the tuple and transaction spaces are. The synchrony relation affects program execution as follows: whenever a transaction is chosen for execution, all transactions in the transaction space which are related to the chosen transaction by (the closure of) the synchrony relation are also chosen; all of the transactions that make up this set, called a synchronic group, are executed as if they comprised a single transaction.

By enabling asynchronous program fragments to be coalesced dynamically into synchronous subcomputations, the synchrony relation provides an elegant mechanism for structuring concurrent computations. This unique feature facilitates a programming style in which the granularity of the computation can be changed dynamically to accommodate structural variations in the input. This feature also suggests mechanisms for the programming of a mixed-modality parallel computer, i.e., a computer which can simultaneously execute asynchronous and synchronous computations. Perhaps architectures of this type could enable both higher performance and greater flexibility in algorithm design.

This paper shows how to add this powerful capability to Swarm without compromising the ability to formally verify the resulting programs. The presentation is organized as follows. Section 2 reviews the basic Swarm notation. Section 3 introduces the notation for the synchrony relation and discusses the concept of a synchronic group. Section 4 reviews a UNITY-style assertional programming logic for Swarm without the synchrony relation and then generalizes the logic to accommodate synchronic groups. Section 5 illustrates the use of synchronic groups by means of a proof of an array summation program. Section 6 discusses some of the rationale for the design decisions.

2 Swarm Notation

The name *Swarm* evokes the image of a large, rapidly moving aggregation of small, independent agents cooperating to perform a task. This section introduces a notation for programming such computations. Beginning with an algorithm expressed in a familiar imperative notation, a parallel dialect of Dijkstra's Guarded Commands [6] language, we construct a Swarm program with similar semantics.

The program fragment given in Figure 1 (similar to the one given in [10]) sums an array of N integers. For simplicity of presentation, we assume that N is a power of 2. We also assume that elements 1 through N of the constant array A contain the values to be summed. The program introduces variables x, an N-element array of partial sums, and j, a control variable for the summing loop. The preamble of the loop initializes x to equal A and j to equal 1. Thus, the precondition Q of the program's loop is the assertion

$$pow2(N) \wedge j = 1 \wedge \langle \forall i : 1 \le i \le N :: x(i) = A(i) \rangle$$

where

$$pow2(k) \equiv \langle \exists p : p \ge 0 :: k = 2^p \rangle.$$

At termination, $x(N)$ is required to contain the sum of the N elements of A. Thus the postcondition R of the program is the assertion

$$x(N) = sum_A(0, N)$$

where

$$sum_A(l, u) = \langle \Sigma k : l < k \le u :: A(k) \rangle.$$

The loop computes the sum in a tree-like fashion as shown in the diagram: adjacent elements of the array are added in parallel, then the same is done for the resulting values, and so forth until a single value remains. The construct

$$\langle \| \ k : predicate :: assignment \rangle$$

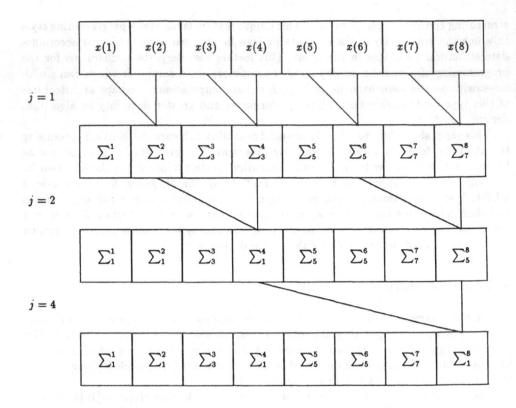

```
j : integer;
x(i : 1 ≤ i ≤ N) : array of integer;

j := 1;
⟨ k : 1 ≤ k ≤ N :: x(k) := A(k)⟩;
{ Q }
do j < N ⟶ { P }
        ⟨‖ k : 1 ≤ k ≤ N ∧ k mod (j * 2) = 0 :: x(k) := x(k − j) + x(k)⟩;
        j := j * 2
od
{ R }
```

Fig. 1. A Parallel Array-Summation Algorithm using Guarded Commands

is a parallel assignment command. The *assignment* is executed in parallel for each value of k which satisfies the *predicate*; the entire construct is performed as one atomic action. An invariant P for the program's loop is the assertion

$$pow2(N) \land pow2(j) \land 1 \leq j \leq N \land \langle \forall i : node(i,j) :: x(i) = sum_A(i-j,i) \rangle$$

where

$$node(k,l) \equiv (1 \leq k \leq N \land k \bmod l = 0).$$

(Clearly $Q \Rightarrow P$ and $P \land j \geq N \Rightarrow R$.) The integer function $\frac{N}{j} - 1$ (call it vf) is an appropriate variant function to show the termination of the loop.

Swarm is a shared dataspace programming model. Instead of expressing a computation in terms of a group of named variables, Swarm uses a set of *tuples* stored in a *dataspace*. Each tuple is a pairing of a type name with a finite sequence of values; a program accesses a tuple by its content—type name and values—rather than by a specific name or address. Swarm programs execute by deleting existing tuples from and inserting new tuples into the dataspace. The *transactions* which specify these atomic dataspace transformations consist of a set of *query-action* pairs executed in parallel. Each query-action pair is similar to a production rule in a language like OPS5 [2].

How can we express the array-summation algorithm in Swarm? To represent the array x, we introduce tuples of type x in which the first component is an integer in the range 1 through N, the second a partial sum. We can express an instance of the array assignment in the do loop as a Swarm transaction in the following way:

$$v1, v2 : x(k-j, v1), x(k, v2) \longrightarrow x(k, v2)\dagger, x(k, v1 + v2)$$

The part to the left of the $\longrightarrow$ is the query; the part to the right is the action. The identifiers $v1$ and $v2$ designate variables that are local to the query-action pair. (For now, assume that j and k are constants.)

The execution of a Swarm query is similar to the evaluation of a rule in Prolog [16]. The above query causes a search of the dataspace for two tuples of type x whose component values have the specified relationship—the comma separating the two tuple predicates is interpreted as a conjunction. If one or more solutions are found, then one of the solutions is chosen nondeterministically and the matched values are bound to the local variables $v1$ and $v2$ and the action is performed with this binding. If no solution is found, then the transaction is said to fail and none of the specified actions are taken.

The action of the above transaction consists of the deletion of one tuple and the insertion of another. The $\dagger$ operator indicates that the tuple $x(k, v2)$, where $v2$ has the value bound by the query, is to be deleted from the dataspace. The unmarked tuple form $x(k, v1 + v2)$ indicates that the corresponding tuple is to be inserted. Although the execution of a transaction is atomic, the effect of an action is as if all deletions are performed first, then all insertions.

The parallel assignment command of the algorithm can be expressed similarly in Swarm:

$$[\| \ k : 1 \leq k \leq N \land k \bmod (j * 2) = 0 ::$$
$$v1, v2 : x(k-j, v1), x(k, v2) \longrightarrow x(k, v2)\dagger, x(k, v1 + v2)]$$

Each individual query-action pair is called a *subtransaction* and the overall parallel construct a *transaction*. As with the parallel assignment, the entire transaction is executed atomically. The cumulative effect of executing a transaction is as if the subtransactions are executed synchronously: all queries are evaluated first, then the indicated tuples are deleted, and finally the indicated tuples are inserted.

In Swarm there is no concept of a process and there are no sequential programming constructs or recursive function calls. Only transactions are available. Like data tuples, transactions are represented as tuple-like entities in the dataspace. A transaction has a type name and a finite sequence of values called parameters. Transaction instances can be queried and inserted in the same way that data tuples are, but cannot be explicitly deleted. A Swarm dataspace thus has two components, the tuple space and the transaction space.

We model the execution of a Swarm program in the following way. The program begins execution with the specified initial dataspace. On each execution step, a transaction is chosen nondeterministically from the transaction space and executed atomically. This selection is fair in the sense that every transaction present in the transaction space at any point in time must eventually be executed (i.e., weak fairness [8]). Unless the transaction explicitly reinserts itself into the transaction space, it is deleted as a by-product of its own execution—regardless of the success or failure of its component queries. Program execution continues until there are no transactions remaining in the transaction space.

We still have two aspects of the array-summation program's do command to express in Swarm—the doubling of j and the conditional repetition of the loop body. Both of these actions can be incorporated into the transaction shown above. We define transactions of type Sum having one parameter as follows:

$$
\begin{aligned}
Sum(j) \equiv \\
[\| \ k : 1 \leq k \leq N \wedge k \bmod (j*2) = 0 :: \\
v1, v2 : x(k-j, v1), x(k, v2) \longrightarrow x(k, v2)\dagger, x(k, v1+v2)] \\
\| \qquad j*2 < N \longrightarrow Sum(j*2)
\end{aligned}
$$

Note that the transaction above uses parameter j as a constant throughout its body. A transaction instance $Sum(j)$—representing the jth iteration of the loop—updates the set of x tuples to reflect the newly computed partial sum and inserts an appropriate transaction to continue the computation.

For a correct computation of array A's sum, the Swarm program must initialize the tuple space to contain the N elements of the array represented as x tuples, i.e., to be the set

$$\{ \ x(1, A(1)), \ x(2, A(2)), \ \cdots, \ x(N, A(N)) \ \}.$$

Similarly, the transaction space must consist of the single transaction $Sum(1)$.

Figure 2 shows a complete array-summation program. Since each x tuple is only referenced once during a computation, we modify the definition of the Sum subtransactions to delete both x tuples that are referenced. If a tuple form in a query is marked by the *dagger* operator, then, if the overall query succeeds, the marked tuple is deleted as a part of the action.

The first sentence in this section describes a Swarm computation with the following metaphor: "a large, rapidly moving aggregation of small, independent agents cooperating

```
program ArraySum(N, A : [∃p : p ≥ 0 :: N = 2^p], A(i : 1 ≤ i ≤ N))
    tuple types
        [i, s : 1 ≤ i ≤ N :: x(i, s)]
    transaction types
        [j : 1 ≤ j < N ::
            Sum(j) ≡
                [|| k : 1 ≤ k ≤ N ∧ k mod (j * 2) = 0 ::
                    v1, v2 : x(k − j, v1)†, x(k, v2)†  ⟶  x(k, v1 + v2) ]
            ||          j < N              ⟶  Sum(j * 2)
        ]
    initialization
        Sum(1); [i : 1 ≤ i ≤ N :: x(i, A(i))]
    end
```

Fig. 2. A Parallel Array-Summation Program in Swarm

to perform a task." So far we have taken a microscopic view of Swarm computations—focusing on the small, rapidly moving, independent agents (i.e., transactions and tuples). We should not, however, ignore the macroscopic view—losing sight of the large *aggregation* of agents *cooperating* to perform a *task*. Although the *ArraySum* program does not define a process in the sense of the CSP [11] model, the evolving "swarm" of transactions does embody a distinct, purposeful activity: computing the sum of an array. Using the assertional programming logics given in Section 4, we can specify and verify such "macroscopic" properties of Swarm computations. As we see in the next section, the synchrony relation enables us to organize simple transactions into complex groups which work on portions of the overall task.

3 Synchronic Groups

The discussion in the previous section ignored the third component of a Swarm program's dataspace—the *synchrony relation*. The interaction of the synchrony relation with the execution mechanism provides a dynamic form of the || operator. The synchrony relation is a symmetric, irreflexive relation on the set of valid transaction instances. The reflexive transitive closure of the synchrony relation is thus an equivalence relation. (The synchrony relation can be pictured as an undirected graph in which the transaction instances are represented as vertices and the synchrony relationships between transaction instances as edges between the corresponding vertices. The equivalence classes of the closure relation are the connected components of this graph.) When one of the transactions in an equivalence class is chosen for execution, then all members of the class which exist in the transaction space at that point in the computation are also chosen. This group of related transactions is called a *synchronic group*. The subtransactions making up the transactions of a synchronic group are executed as if they were part of the same transaction.

The synchrony relation can be examined and modified in much the same way as the tuple and transaction spaces can. The predicate

$$Sum(i) \sim Sum(j)$$

in the query of a subtransaction examines the synchrony relation for a transaction instance $Sum(i)$ that is directly related to an instance $Sum(j)$. Neither transaction instance is required to exist in the transaction space. The operator $\approx$ can be used in a predicate to examine whether transaction instances are related by the closure of the synchrony relation.

Synchrony relationships between transaction instances can be inserted into and deleted from the relation. (The dynamic creation of a synchrony relationship between two transactions can be pictured as the insertion of an edge in the undirected graph noted above, and the deletion of a relationship as the removal of an edge.) The operation

$$Sum(i) \sim Sum(j)$$

in the action of a subtransaction creates a dynamic coupling between transaction instances $Sum(i)$ and $Sum(j)$, where i and j have bound values. If i equals j, the insertion is simply ignored. If two instances are related by the synchrony relation, then

$$(Sum(i) \sim Sum(j))\dagger$$

deletes the relationship. Note that both the synchrony relation $\sim$ and its closure $\approx$ can be tested in a query, but that only the base synchrony relation $\sim$ can be directly modified by an action. Initial synchrony relationships can be specified by putting appropriate insertion operations into the initialization section of the Swarm program.

Figure 3 shows a version of the array-summation program which uses synchronic groups. The subtransactions of $Sum(j)$ have been separated into distinct transactions $Sum(k, j)$ coupled by the synchrony relation. For each phase j, all transactions associated with that phase are structured into a single synchronic group. The computation's effect is the same as that of the earlier program.

4 Programming Logics

The Swarm computational model is similar to that of UNITY [4]; hence, a UNITY-style assertional logic seems appropriate. However, we cannot use the UNITY logic directly because of the differences between the UNITY and Swarm frameworks.

This paper follows the notational conventions for UNITY as used in [4]. Properties and inference rules are written without explicit quantification; these are universally quantified over all the values of the free variables occurring in them. This paper also introduces the notation "$[t]$" to denote the predicate "transaction instance t is in the transaction space," **TRS** to denote the set of all possible transactions (not a specific transaction space), and *Initial* to denote the initial state of the program.

First we review the proof rules for the subset of Swarm without the synchrony relation then look at how these rules can be generalized to support the synchrony relation. (For more detail on the proof rules see [5] and on the formal operational model see [15]). The Swarm programming logics have been defined so that the theorems proved for UNITY in [4] can also be proved for Swarm.

```
program ArraySumSynch(N, A : [∃p : p ≥ 0 :: N = 2ᵖ], A(i : 1 ≤ i ≤ N))
tuple types
    [i, s : 1 ≤ i ≤ N :: x(i, s)]
transaction types
    [k, j : 1 ≤ k ≤ N, 1 ≤ j < N ::
        Sum(k, j) ≡
                    v1, v2 : x(k − j, v1)†, x(k, v2)†  ⟶  x(k, v1 + v2)
            ‖       k ≠ N  ⟶  (Sum(k, j) ∼ Sum(N, j))†
            ‖       j < N, k mod (j ∗ 4) = 0
                        ⟶      Sum(k, j ∗ 2),
                            Sum(k, j ∗ 2) ∼ Sum(N, j ∗ 2)

    ]
initialization
    [i : 1 ≤ i ≤ N :: x(i, A(i))];
    [k : 1 ≤ k ≤ N, k mod 2 = 0 :: Sum(k, 1) ; Sum(k, 1) ∼ Sum(N, 1)]
end
```

Fig. 3. A Parallel Array Summation Program Using Synchronic Groups

The "Hoare triple"

$$\{p\} \, t \, \{q\} \tag{1}$$

means that, whenever the dataspace satisfies the precondition predicate p and transaction instance t is in the transaction space, all dataspaces which can result from execution of transaction t satisfy the postcondition predicate q.

We define Swarm's **unless** relation with an inference rule similar to that given for UNITY's **unless** in [13]:

$$\frac{\langle \forall t : t \in \mathbf{TRS} :: \{p \wedge \neg q\} \, t \, \{p \vee q\} \rangle}{p \text{ unless } q}. \tag{2}$$

The premise of this rule means that, if p is *true* at some point in the computation and q is not, then, after the next step, p remains *true* or q becomes *true*.

Stable predicates and invariants are important for reasoning about Swarm programs. For a predicate p to be **stable** means that, if p becomes *true* at some point in a computation, it remains *true* thereafter. On the other hand, a predicate p is **invariant** if p is *true* at all points in the computation.

$$\textbf{stable } p \; \equiv \; p \text{ unless } false \tag{3}$$

$$\textbf{invariant } p \; \equiv \; (Initial \; \Rightarrow \; p) \wedge (\textbf{stable } p). \tag{4}$$

Following UNITY's definition in [13], we define Swarm's **ensures** relation with an inference rule:

$$\frac{p \text{ unless } q, \langle \exists t : t \in \mathbf{TRS} :: (p \wedge \neg q \Rightarrow [t]) \wedge \{p \wedge \neg q\} \, t \, \{q\}\rangle}{p \text{ ensures } q}. \tag{5}$$

The premise of this rule means that, if p is *true* at some point in the computation, then (1) p will remain *true* as long as q is *false*, and (2) if q is *false*, there is at least one transaction in the transaction space which can, when executed, establish q as *true*. The "$p \wedge \neg q \Rightarrow [t]$" requirement generalizes the UNITY definition of **ensures** to accommodate Swarm's dynamic transaction space.

The **leads-to** relation, written

$$p \longmapsto q \tag{6}$$

means that, once p becomes *true*, q will eventually become *true*. (However, p is not guaranteed to remain *true* until q becomes *true*.) As in UNITY, the assertion $p \longmapsto q$ is *true* if and only if it can be derived by a finite number of applications of the following inference rules:

$$- \quad \frac{p \text{ ensures } q}{p \longmapsto q} \qquad \qquad \textbf{(basis)}$$

$$- \quad \frac{p \longmapsto q, \; q \longmapsto r}{p \longmapsto r} \qquad \qquad \textbf{(transitivity)}$$

$-$ For any set W,   **(disjunction)**

$$\frac{\langle \forall m : m \in W :: p(m) \longmapsto q \rangle}{\langle \exists m : m \in W :: p(m) \rangle \longmapsto q}$$

Unlike UNITY programs, Swarm programs *terminate* when the transaction space is empty, that is

$$Termination \equiv \langle \forall t : t \in \mathbf{TRS} :: \neg [t] \rangle. \tag{7}$$

How can we generalize the above logic to accommodate synchronic groups? We need to add a synchronic group rule and redefine the **unless** and **ensures** relations. The other elements of the logic are the same.

We define the "Hoare triple" for synchronic groups

$$\{p\} \, S \, \{q\} \tag{8}$$

such that, whenever the precondition p is *true* and S is a synchronic group of the dataspace, all dataspaces which can result from execution of group S satisfy postcondition q.

A key difference between this logic and the previous logic is the set over which the properties must be proved. For example, the previous logic required that, in proof of an **unless** property, an assertion be proved for all possible transactions, i.e., over the set **TRS**. On the other hand, this generalized logic requires the proof of an assertion for all possible synchronic groups of the program, denoted by **SG**.

For the synchronic group logic, we define the logical relation **unless** with the following rule:

$$\frac{\langle \forall S : S \in \mathbf{SG} :: \{p \wedge \neg q\} \, S \, \{p \vee q\}\rangle}{p \text{ unless } q} \tag{9}$$

If synchronic groups are restricted to single transactions, this definition is the same as the definition given for the earlier subset Swarm logic.

We define the **ensures** relation as follows:

$$\frac{p \text{ unless } q\,,}{\langle \exists t : t \in \mathbf{TRS} :: (p \wedge \neg q \Rightarrow [t]) \rangle \wedge \langle \forall S : S \in \mathbf{SG} \wedge t \in S :: \{p \wedge \neg q\}\, S\, \{q\} \rangle \rangle}{p \text{ ensures } q} \quad (10)$$

This definition requires that, when $p \wedge \neg q$ is *true*, there exists a transaction t in the transaction space such that all synchronic groups which can contain t will establish q when executed from a state in which $p \wedge \neg q$ holds. Because of the fairness criterion, transaction t will eventually be chosen for execution, and hence one of the synchronic groups containing t will be executed. In the logic for the Swarm subset, the **ensures** rule requires that a single transaction be found which will establish the desired postcondition when executed. In the synchronic group logic, on the other hand, instead of requiring that a single synchronic group be found which will establish the desired state, the **ensures** rule requires that a set of synchronic groups be identified such that any of the groups will establish the desired state and that one of the groups will eventually be executed. If synchronic groups are restricted to single transactions, this definition is the same as the definition for the subset Swarm logic.

5 Example Proof

In Sections 2 and 3 we derived a Swarm program for summing an array from a similar program expressed with the Guarded Commands (GC) notation. Figure 3 gives the Swarm program *ArraySumSynch* which uses synchronic groups to compute the sum of an array. This section sketches a proof for this array sum program using the logic presented in Section 4.

The precondition for *ArraySumSynch*, call it *Initial*, is similar to Q, the precondition of the GC program's loop given in Section 2. Of course, modifications are needed to account for the differences in data and program representation. (As in the previous section, we assume that all assertions are universally quantified over all the values of the free variables occurring in them.) Using the predicates *pow2* and *node* defined in Section 2, *Initial* can be stated as follows:

$$pow2(N) \wedge (\, x(i,v) \equiv 1 \leq i \leq N \wedge v = A(i)\,) \wedge$$
$$(\, Sum(i,j) \equiv node(i, 2*j) \wedge j = 1\,) \wedge$$
$$(\, Sum(i,j) \sim Sum(k,l) \wedge i \leq k \equiv node(i, 2*j) \wedge k = N \wedge j = l = 1\,)$$

The second, third, and fourth conjuncts specify the structure of the tuple space, transaction space, and synchrony relation, respectively. Here the tuple and transaction forms, e.g., $x(i,v)$ and $Sum(i,j)$, represent predicates which are true when there is a matching entity in the dataspace and false otherwise. Likewise, predicates using the $\sim$ and $\approx$ connectives represent predicates over the synchrony relation.

The postcondition of *ArraySumSynch*, call it *Post*, is similar to R, the postcondition of the GC program. Using the sum_A expression defined in Section 2, it can be stated as

$$x(i,v) \equiv (\, i = N \wedge v = sum_A(0, N)\,).$$

To verify that the program satisfies this specification we must prove that, when the program begins execution in a state satisfying *Initial*, it eventually reaches a state satisfying *Post* and, once such a state is reached, any further execution will not falsify *Post*. That is, we must prove a progress property and a safety property—the Sum Completion and Sum Stability properties, respectively.

Property 1 (Sum Completion)   *Initial* $\longmapsto$ *Post*

Property 2 (Sum Stability)   stable *Post*

To prove these properties, another property is needed which characterizes the unchanging relationships among the elements of the dataspace. This "structure invariant" serves a role in the Swarm proof similar to the role the loop invariant Q does in a proof of the GC program. The statement of the Structure Invariant below uses the function W_x, which is N divided by the number of x-tuples present in the dataspace, i.e.,

$$W_x = \frac{N}{\langle \# i, v :: x(i,v) \rangle}.$$

W_x represents the "width" of the segment of array A whose sum is in each x-tuple—a role served by the variable j in the GC program.

Property 3 (Structure Invariant)

> **invariant**
> $pow2(N) \wedge pow2(W_x) \wedge (x(i,v) \equiv node(i, W_x) \wedge v = sum_A(i - W_x, i)) \wedge$
> $(Sum(i,j) \equiv node(i, 2*j) \wedge j = W_x) \wedge$
> $(Sum(i,j) \sim Sum(k,l) \wedge i \leq k \equiv node(i, 2*j) \wedge k = N \wedge j = l = W_x)$

The Structure Invariant is relatively complex. This complexity arises from the mutual dependencies among the data tuples and transactions of this highly synchronous program.

¶ **Proof of the Structure Invariant.** Call this property I. To prove the invariance of I, we have to show that I holds initially and that it is stable. Since initially $W_x = N/N = 1$, *Initial* $\Rightarrow I$. Hence, I holds initially.

To prove I is stable we must show that I is preserved by all possible synchronic groups G, i.e., $\{ I \} G \{ I \}$ is true for arbitrary G. For any synchronic group which does not satisfy I, this predicate is trivially true. Thus, we only need to consider those synchronic groups which satisfy I. Since the value of N is not altered by any transaction, the $pow2(N)$ conjunct is preserved trivially. We now must show that each of the remaining four conjuncts is preserved.

To see that the second and third conjuncts are preserved, we note that each executing transaction deletes two x-tuples and inserts back a single x-tuple. The "indexes" (first components) of the deleted tuples are adjacent multiples of j (i.e., of W_x). The inserted tuple is positioned at the index of the rightmost deleted tuple—at a multiple of $2 * j$. The value (the second component) of the inserted tuple is equal to the sum of the values of the two deleted tuples. Furthermore, the precondition I guarantees that each of the transactions in the group operate upon different tuples.

We now consider the fourth conjunct. All transactions (allowed by I) have the same "phase" parameter j. Furthermore, the values of the "index" parameter i for these transactions are multiples of $2 * j$. Only half of the transactions, i.e., those whose index is a multiple of $4 * j$, insert successor transactions. The phase for all the inserted transactions is $2 * j$ (i.e., $2 * W_x$). As argued above, W_x is also doubled in value by the synchronic group's execution. Thus the fourth conjunct is preserved.

The only synchrony relationship for a transaction $Sum(i, j)$, for $i < N$, is with transaction $Sum(N, j)$. Upon execution, a transaction deletes this relationship. For each new transaction inserted (into phase $2 * j$), a synchrony relationship is created with $Sum(N, 2 * j)$. Thus the fifth conjunct is also preserved. ∎

¶ **Proof of Sum Stability.** We must show that the predicate $Post$ is preserved by all synchronic groups allowed by the Structure Invariant I. We note that $Post \wedge I \Rightarrow W_x = N$. But $W_x = N \wedge I \Rightarrow \langle \forall i :: \neg node(i, 2 * W_x) \rangle$. Thus, when $Post$ is true, because of the fourth conjunct of I, the transaction space must be empty. Therefore, $Post$ is clearly stable. ∎

Now we can now turn our attention to the Sum Completion progress property. This large-grained progress property can be proved by induction using a finer-grained progress property corresponding to the execution of a single synchronic group. The Sum Step property is stated as an **ensures** relation.

Property 4 (Sum Step)

$$W_x = k < N \quad \text{ensures} \quad W_x = 2 * k.$$

¶ **Proof of the Sum Step property.** The proof of an **ensures** property has two parts: an existential part and an unless part.

The existential part requires us to prove that, whenever $W_x = k < N$, there is a transaction in the transaction space such that any synchronic group containing that transaction will establish $W_x = 2 * k$. But, in accordance with the Structure Invariant I, at most one synchronic group exists at a time. (Particularly, $W_x = k < N \wedge I \Rightarrow Sum(N, W_x)$.) As argued in the proof of the Structure Invariant, this synchronic group will double W_x, i.e., decrease the number of x-tuples by half.

The unless part requires us to prove $W_x = k < N$ **unless** $W_x = 2 * k$. That is, we must show for all synchronic groups G,

$$\{ W_x = k < N \wedge I \} \quad G \quad \{ W_x = k \vee W_x = 2 * k \}$$

is valid. As argued above, the only synchronic groups allowed by I will double W_x. Therefore, the **ensures** property holds. ∎

¶ **Proof of Sum Completion.** To prove Sum Completion, we must show that $\neg Post \longmapsto Post$. We note that $\neg Post \wedge I \Rightarrow W_x < N$ and $W_x = N \wedge I \Rightarrow Post$. We choose the well-founded metric $\frac{N}{W_x} - 1$. ($\frac{N}{W_x}$ is the count of the x-tuples present in the dataspace. The metric is similar to the variant function vf in the GC program proof.) Using this metric, the Leads-to Induction Principle [4] applied to the Sum Step property allows us to deduce that $W_x < N \longmapsto W_x = N$. Therefore, we deduce that $\neg Post \longmapsto Post$ by the Leads-to Implication Theorem [4] and the Leads-to transitivity rule. ∎

We have thus proved the Sum Stability and Sum Completion properties of the Swarm program $ArraySumSynch$. Therefore, the program satisfies its specification. Also it is true that $Post \wedge I \Rightarrow Termination$ (as we argued in the proof of Sum Stability). $ArraySumSynch$ terminates immediately upon completing the computation of the desired sum.

6 Discussion

Content-based access to data, dynamic statements (i.e., transactions), and the synchrony relation are three key features which distinguish Swarm [5, 15] from UNITY [4]. Previous papers justified the first two extensions on three grounds. First, even though the Swarm programming logic is more complex than the UNITY logic, the additional complexity is not evident in proofs unless the new features are actually used. The Swarm inference rules reduce to those employed in UNITY if we restrict the usage of Swarm to a UNITY-like subset. In such a subset, we can represent UNITY's variables as tuples, UNITY's assignments as transactions which delete and reinsert these tuples, and UNITY's static set of statements as transactions which reproduce themselves without introducing additional transactions into the dataspace. Second, for problems whose precise structure and space requirements (in terms of number of variables and statements) cannot be determined a priori, Swarm allows one to tailor the dataspace appropriately. Scaling all the values of a sparse matrix in parallel, for instance, does not require the presence of tuples and statements for the zero entries. Third, Swarm was the first notational system to make assertional-style proofs of rule-based programs feasible [9]. Moreover, since tuples can easily simulate both variables and messages, Swarm makes it possible to write and prove programs that employ these three programming paradigms.

Why introduce the synchrony relation? Consider UNITY's synchronous composition operator. The ||-operator binds a group of assignments into a single statement; the assignments in the group are executed synchronously as a single atomic action. Syntactically, the || is placed between the assignments making up the UNITY statement. Swarm's ||-operator is similar both syntactically and semantically. However, the Swarm model generalizes the notion of synchronous execution. While UNITY statements are static, anonymous entities, Swarm transactions are dynamically created entities which have unique identifiers (i.e., the type name and parameter values). This led to a more dynamic notion of synchronous execution: the atomic execution of a group of *related* transactions where the *relation* between transactions is an entity subject to examination and modification by the program. As a result, Swarm separates the definition of statements (i.e., state transformations) from the specification of their processing mode (i.e., synchronous or asynchronous). The former appears in the transaction type definitions while the latter is captured by the synchrony relation present in the dataspace. Finally, the syntactic restriction regarding the use of the ||-operator (i.e., no simultaneous assignments to the same variable) had to be removed to allow for synchronous execution of any group of transactions. This was accomplished by giving precedence to dataspace insertions over deletions.

Among all these changes, the ability to alter the definition of the synchrony relation is clearly the most radical departure from UNITY. Thus, the static synchrony offered by UNITY is augmented in Swarm by dynamic synchrony. This processing mode is unique to Swarm and cannot be simulated easily in UNITY. There are strong indications that dynamic synchrony will be helpful in modeling reconfigurable or heterogeneous computer architectures and will lead to new kinds of solutions to a variety of programming tasks. A related concept is also proving useful in parallel program refinement. Liu and Singh [12] have subsequently applied a complementary concept, the asynchrony relation, to the problem of refining a UNITY program toward architectures with different synchrony structures.

The capacity to model a variety of computer architectures makes Swarm attractive as a specification language for software which, because of performance considerations, is targeted to a specific and often heterogeneous hardware organization. In such cases, the software designer first derives a software specification expressed in the Swarm notation— verifying that it is correct with respect to the application's requirements and is compatible with the chosen architecture. Subsequently, programmers use the specification as the basis for implementing the software modules allocated to the individual architectural components. To illustrate the kinds of architectures envisioned, let us consider an application in which a three-dimensional geometric model is created, manipulated, and displayed. Furthermore, let us assume that the underlying architecture consists of a producer, a transformer, and a mapper. The producer, which could be a typical workstation, runs asynchronously, generating various objects in the 3D model. The transformer is a processor pipeline that can be dynamically reconfigured and activated by the producer. When active, the transformer takes objects from the producer's memory, applies a series of transformations to them, and places the result in a very large buffer accessible to the mapper. The mapper, in turn, is an SIMD machine whose task is to copy sections of the buffer to the refresh memories of a number of display units. In Swarm, the producer activities would be specified as a set of transactions which are asynchronous with respect to each other and to the other components. The pipeline reconfiguration would involve the formation of a synchronic group consisting of transactions which manipulate, object by object, the geometric model. Finally, the SIMD machine might be captured by yet another synchronic group, one that is not subject to change. Although the sketch of the solution might be overly simplistic, this example illustrates that the synchrony relation is a convenient construct for modeling certain kinds of architectures.

Turning now to programming considerations, the first thing that must be noted is the use of the synchronic group to control the granularity of the computation. Because each synchronic group execution represents an atomic transformation of the dataspace, by adjusting the size of each group the programmer can switch between fine-grained and course-grained operations or can combine the two in a single program. Let us consider, for instance, the earlier 3D model and let us assume that it depicts a platform which holds several machines with moving parts. At each moment the position of a point in the model is affected by the combined movement of the platform, the machine to which the point belongs, and the moving part involved. Any parallel implementation of the 3D model dynamics must maintain proper consistency in the model, i.e., the effects of each movement must be perceived as a series of small atomic changes in the positions of all points on some part, on some machine, or on the entire contents of the platform. An obvious Swarm solution associates with each point three transactions, each a member of a different synchronic group. The platform group includes one transaction for each point in the model and ensures the atomicity of the coordinate transformation resulting from the platform movement. Similar synchronic groups are formed for each machine and part.

The solution is elegant because it separates the implementation of the three independent movements and requires no synchronization code. Could we have the same solution in UNITY? If the contents of the platform does not change and if moving parts do not fall off, the answer is yes. Swarm, however, can accommodate without loss of elegance the materialization and dematerialization of machines or parts, and, in general, any arbitrary structural changes in the 3D model. This is accomplished by means of appropriate restructuring of the synchronic groups. The ability to mold the computation to the changing structure of the problem at hand, through the creation and restructuring of arbitrary atomic transformations, is yet another reason for introducing synchronic groups in Swarm.

Often the capability to exchange some information among the constituent transactions of a synchronic group would make programming more convenient. Toward this end, five special predicates have been added to Swarm: **OR**, **AND**, **NOR**, **NAND**, and **TRUE**, meaning *any*, *all*, *none*, *not-all*, and *no-matter-how-many*, respectively [15]. Upon execution, each regular query (i.e., a query not containing special predicates) makes it's success/failure status available to other queries in the synchronic group. When a query which contains a special predicate is executed, this set of boolean values is accessed to determine its outcome. The result is the convenient capability to detect certain kinds of "consensus" [7] among the subtransactions of a synchronic group. Since many common programming problems involve agreement among a set of participants, this capability can be very useful. For example, quiescence within a synchronic group involving only regular queries can be detected by introducing a **NOR** query into the group. The **NOR** succeeds only when all the regular queries have failed and, therefore, no further activity can originate within the group. Of course, an **OR** query is needed to recreate the synchronic group when quiescence is not yet reached. The definition below shows the basic code structure for transactions participating in some quiescence detection activity:

$$Worker(n) \equiv$$
$$any\_work\_for\_me? \longrightarrow do\_the\_work$$
$$\| \quad \textbf{OR} \qquad\qquad \longrightarrow Worker(n)$$
$$\| \quad \textbf{NOR} \qquad\qquad \longrightarrow follow\text{-}up\_activities$$

In contrast to the Swarm solution, classical quiescence detection algorithms are quite complex.

The updating of local clocks in a distributed simulation is another example of the use of special queries. All local clocks are placed in the same synchronic group and execute the following logic:

$$Clock(n) \equiv$$
$$is\_current\_step\_completed? \longrightarrow \textbf{skip}$$
$$\| \quad t: \textbf{AND},\ local\_time(n, t)\dagger \longrightarrow local\_time(n, t{+}1)$$
$$\| \quad \textbf{TRUE} \qquad\qquad\qquad \longrightarrow Clock(n)$$

Components that complete their simulation early can terminate by simply removing their clock from the synchronic group. The addition and removal of one clock is hidden from all others; the only interactions among the clocks are through the special predicate "consensus" mechanism.

Although experience indicates that the synchronic group is a useful concept, a number of questions remain open. Among them, three are of immediate concern. First, does the programming convenience arising from the synchronic group feature compensate for the additional complexity of proofs of programs that employ them? Although proofs involving synchronic groups have shown, in general, to be more difficult than initially expected, drastic simplifications in program logic brought about by the use of synchronic groups may ultimately ease the verification task. Second, will the study of dynamic synchrony lead to interesting new distributed algorithms for some classical problems? Finally, how can Swarm's apparent ability to model complex architectures be put to practical benefit? On-going research will likely yield at least partial answers to these questions.

7 Conclusions

The Swarm programming logic was the first axiomatic proof system for a shared data-space "language." Subsequently to and independently from this work, Waldinger and Stickel developed a proof theory for rule-based systems [17]. Banâtre and Le Métayer have done the same for GAMMA [1]. As far as the authors can determine, no axiomatic-style proof systems have been published for Linda.

The Swarm programming logic exploits the similarities between the Swarm and UNITY computational models. It uses the same logical relations as UNITY, but the definitions of the relations have been generalized to handle the dynamic nature of Swarm, i.e., dynamically created transactions and the synchrony relation. This paper has shown how one can extend the proof logic to accommodate the dynamic formation of synchronic groups specified by the runtime redefinition of the synchrony relation.

Acknowledgements

This work was supported by the Department of Computer Science, Washington University, Saint Louis, Missouri. The first author was also supported in part by the National Science Foundation under the Grant CCR-9015677. The Government has certain rights in this material. The second author thanks the Department of Computer and Information Science at the University of Mississippi for enabling him to continue this work.

References

1. J.-P. Banâtre and D. Le Métayer. The GAMMA model and its discipline of programming. *Science of Computer Programming*, 15:55–77, 1990.
2. L. Brownston, R. Farrell, E. Kant, and N. Martin. *Programming Expert Systems in OPS5: An Introduction to Rule-Based Programming.* Addison-Wesley, Reading, Massachusetts, 1985.
3. N. Carriero and D. Gelernter. Linda in context. *Communications of the ACM*, 32(4):444–458, April 1989.
4. K. M. Chandy and J. Misra. *Parallel Program Design: A Foundation.* Addison-Wesley, Reading, Massachusetts, 1988.
5. H. C. Cunningham and G.-C. Roman. A UNITY-style programming logic for shared data-space programs. *IEEE Transactions on Parallel and Distributed Systems*, 1(3):365–376, July 1990.
6. E. W. Dijkstra. *A Discipline of Programming.* Prentice-Hall, Englewood Cliffs, New Jersey, 1976.
7. M. J. Fischer, N. A. Lynch, and M. S. Paterson. Impossibility of distributed consensus with one faulty process. *Journal of the ACM*, 32(2):374–382, April 1985.
8. N. Francez. *Fairness.* Springer-Verlag, New York, 1986.
9. R. F. Gamble, G.-C. Roman, and W. E. Ball. Formal verification of pure production system programs. In *Proceedings of the Ninth National Conference on Artificial Intelligence (AAAI-91)*, pages 339–334, July 1991.

10. W. D. Hillis and G. L. Steele Jr. Data parallel algorithms. *Communications of the ACM*, 29(12):1170–1183, December 1986.
11. C. A. R. Hoare. Communicating sequential processes. *Communications of the ACM*, 21(8):666–677, August 1978.
12. Y. Liu and A. K. Singh. Parallel programming: Achieving portability through abstraction. In *Proceedings of the 11th International Conference on Distributed Computing Systems (ICDCS-11)*, pages 634–640. IEEE, May 1991.
13. J. Misra. Soundness of the substitution axiom. Notes on UNITY 14–90, Department of Computer Sciences, University of Texas at Austin, Austin, Texas, March 1990.
14. M. Rem. Associons: A program notation with tuples instead of variables. *ACM Transactions on Programming Languages and Systems*, 3(3):251–262, July 1981.
15. G.-C. Roman and H. C. Cunningham. Mixed programming metaphors in a shared dataspace model of concurrency. *IEEE Transactions on Software Engineering*, 16(12):1361–73, December 1990.
16. L. Sterling and E. Shapiro. *The Art of Prolog*. MIT Press, Cambridge, Massachusetts, 1986.
17. R. J. Waldinger and M. E. Stickel. Proving properties of rule-based systems. Technical Note 494, SRI International, 333 Ravenswood Avenue, Menlo Park, CA 94025-3493, December 1990.

(In memory of Csongor Juhasz)

An Industrial Experience in the Use of UNITY

Antonio Pizzarello

BULL Phoenix Products Division

Abstract

This paper presents the history of the use of UNITY in
the development of a portion of a large mainframe class
operating system. The emphasis is on the practical
aspects of the problem of using a formal discipline such as
UNITY in an industrial environment. The process of
introducing the technology is sketched and the currently
available data about the project are also presented.
UNITY has been shown to be remarkably suitable for
resolving the practical problem of rewriting a portion of
an existing system. However there are still serious
difficulties, mostly of organizational and educational
nature, that must be overcome. The reward for the use of
UNITY is very high since in the particular experiment
described here no errors have been discovered so far.
This is an indication of the enormous potential of an
appropriate formal method for these kind of applications.

0. Introduction

A major problem in the computer industry is the cost of developing
system software. The main reason for this high cost is that, for producing a
new release of a system, a long period of integration and system test is
necessary. During this period, the system is "tested" usually through the use
of standardized test cases, in order to determine whether or not the new
features have caused any "regression" with respect to the previous release.
The new release, at least, must satisfy the same correctness criterion before
the system can be deployed.

In a well organized development process, a separate group is responsible for the integration of all the software created by separate development groups. The resulting system undergoes a series of tests and with the help of some quantitative criterion measuring its "stability", the suitability for its shipment is evaluated. This period of test is usually very long (for large systems it is usually many months) during which the error rates (fatal error reports per week) oscillate but slowly converge toward the number considered acceptable for stability.

Once the system is deployed, a similar (although mitigated) pattern is shown for each site. An initial flurry of errors is followed by a rather low frequency of fatal error per site. This frequency is usually so low that satisfies even very stringent availability requirements of the particular site. However the supplier of the system faces a totally different situation, because even a very low and perfectly satisfactory error rate per site must be multiplied by the number of sites to obtain the number of errors that the software producer must repair. This number is usually sufficiently high to cause serious cost concerns.

Since before integration/system tests all the software parcels making up the new release are individually tested and declared correct by their own developers, the large number of errors detected during the system tests and deployment are presumably the consequence of sloppiness on the part of the developers in their unit tests or the result of unpredictable interactions between the various software parcels. Another reason is the ineffectiveness of testing as a mechanism for error discovering, together with the enormous latency [1] of software errors. However it is very likely that errors difficult to discover via testing and with very long latency are also those caused by unpredicted interactions among the separately developed software parcels.

Another phenomenon familiar to anyone who has worked with large systems, is that the continuous process of code modification for the purpose of adding new functions as well as for the error correction process contributes to the "degeneration of the system structure" [2]. What the above term means is hard to quantify even though every practitioner would agree on its effect on system maintainability. In essence what one can objectively observe is that the size of the code grows at a rate not justified by the increased number of functions. Naturally this is a subjective judgment and the only reason to consider it here is that it is universally accepted by the practitioners.

All of the above seem to indicate the failure of discovering and taking into account the interactions of the various software parcels that constitute the new software release. This failure should be traced to the system design phase. Usually during this phase the new software capabilities are discussed among the system architects (the ones who are supposed to look at the whole system) and the component developers (the ones supposed to produce the various software parcels). As a result of this discussion the developers produce the components that, once integrated, will present many errors. It is therefore reasonable to think that formalization of the design phase and a rigorous form of design verification would reduce the duration of the integration and system test phase.

1. The I/O Subsystem of GCOS8

GCOS8 is a mainframe class operating system. Once installed and stabilized a GCOS8 software release has an availability greater than 99.9%. The "kernel" (i.e,, that is that portion of the system dedicated to hardware management, resource scheduling and allocation, configuration management etc.), of GCOS8 is about 2 million lines of code, mostly written in the assembly language. Most of this code is the result of continous modifications of the original software which was written more that twenty years ago. At that time the system kernel was about one tenth of the current size.

The original structure of the kernel is now recognized as particularly cumbersome for supporting modern hardware features. The system I/O configuration, which in mainframe class system as GCOS8 can be a rather complex network, is represented in a set of tables where only the network end points are represented. These end points are channels and devices, and the information stored in these tables is used by the I/O subsystem for allocating the resource necessary to execute an I/O operation, by the peripheral allocator to allocate devices and by a plethora of other modules requiring information about the I/O subsystem. By using an automatic tool it was found that about 500 system modules made references to these tables. These modules represent about 50% of all the system kernel code.

By inspection it was easy to realize that most of these references are for obtaining static information like the name of a device. Others however, frequently modify values of data that can be used by modules whose failure would certainly be fatal for the whole system operation.

The fact that so many system modules interacted through the I/O table was considered to be the main cause of the high rate of errors for these modules. This conclusion followed the presumption that most changes were for error correcting purposes. Because of this high rate of error, most people in the GCOS8 development community would agree that some form of restructuring of the I/O tables was needed.

The perception of the I/O tables as a major cause of system fatal errors was but one of the reasons to consider the restructuring of this portion of the system. Another pressing reason was the lack of description of the details of the I/O configuration. In the hardware systems supported by GCOS8, a channel can be connected to a device via many paths which may include various hardware boxes. These hardware boxes can change state (e.g., from working to failed) or can become the object of the operation of special programs such as test/diagnostics or firmware loading, etc. The realization of these capabilities was not easy and the resulting software error prone. Other limitations existed in the size of some fields which were too small for supporting the ever increasing capabities of the hardware.

For all these reasons, the motivation for restructuring the I/O subsystem was very strong. In spite of it, the decision for doing this work was not easily made. The reasons militating against the restructuring work were many, all essentially falling within two categories. One that can be synthetically described by "how do I know that the new software will be better" was supported by past examples of restructuring which did not pay off in terms of lowering the software error rate. Another was the fear of the magnitude of the task. It was not clear how all those interactions could be detected and controlled thus suggesting a high probability of failure for a restructuring project of this complexity. The essential difficulty in making a decision about restructuring was the impossibility to quantify the gain versus costs of such type of work. To make things even more difficult for the decision makers, and in spite of all the folklore, there was no indication that the effort necessary to develop a new release was really growing with time. Therefore, although the development cost was high it was a known quantity while the risk of restructuring could have been a cause of a major increase in the next release cost. However the limitation of capabilities was not acceptable. Thus the need for adding substantial new capabilities was the motivating force for funding the rewriting of the I/O subsystem.

2. Type of Errors

There is a considerable number of case histories in the literature evaluating the software development process through a taxonomy of errors. Errors are often classified as coding or design errors and at times also as requirement errors. The meaning of these classifications is uncertain and therefore I am not going to refer to any of those in what follows. Furthermore since this paper describes a particular experience within a specific development environment, it is proper to refer to the events of this experience as observed by its participants.

Whenever a new function is to be added to the GCOS8 system, the developers must define algorithms and data structures (or modifications to existing algorithms and data structures) that realize the new desired functions. To this end the new function as seen from the outside needs to be clearly understood as well as the interactions of the new algorithms and data structures with the rest of the system. Then the algorithms can be coded. In the case of low level functions where performance priorities and hardware interactions are dominant, this needs often to be done in assembly language. This in turn requires the perfect understanding of how the hardware works.

Errors can be created during the phase described above but they are detected primarily by executing the code either mentally during the various design and code inspection phases, or during system tests and during deployment. It is here impossible to point out when errors are introduced, but it is possible to group together the causes of error according to how they are perceived by the developers.

a)   Ignorance about the working of the existing software. This type of error is reputed as the most frequent one.

b)   Misinterpretation of the hardware specifications. This usually happens for exceptional conditions which are not clearly or completely described in the hardware specifications.

c)   Algorithmic difficulties. These are mostly related to the asynchronous interplay of different software parts executing on may different processors (GCOS8 supports up to 6 CPU's) or the interactions of other separate system components such as channels, maintenance computers, operator actions, etc.

d)   Erroneous use of the programming language or violation of system conventions.

It is worth noting that case c) and d) are reputed as being much less frequent than a) and b). It is also interesting that most of the methods of computer science address the problems in c) and d) and very little is suggested to the practitioner for coping with the problem indicated in a) and b).

Classification of errors is always a bit deceiving. In fact all errors are the description of a wrong algorithm for the desired purpose. The above classification attempts to point out what are the factors causing the creation of a wrong algorithm in the opinion of the developers, . Any development method should be evaluated with respect to its ability help a development organization in minimizing these causes of error.

3. Formal Methods

The idea of introducing a formal method for the redesign of the I/O subsystem was motivated by the consideration that the new product should be much less error prone than the previous one. Obviously since many errors are caused by the ignorance of some subtle interaction with the rest of the system the addition of a formal design phase did not look as effective as desired. On the other hand, the I/O subsystem would be redesigned entirely and therefore it would be worthwhile to spend sufficient time to make the new design a showcase of correctness. At the time when the decision of redesigning the I/O subsystem was made, the UNITY design methodology had been published. One of the authors of the monograph describing UNITY [3] held a short course to a selected group of GCOS8 developers. As a result of this first exposure it was decided to use UNITY. This decision was motivated not only by the suitabilitiy of UNITY for this particular project needs, but also as an attempt to make a first step toward the introduction of a formal design method in the organization.

The characteristics of the UNITY method are described in detail elsewhere [3]. Here we briefly discuss those features which have had impact on the decision to use UNITY in practice.

The first feature that appeared to be of the greatest practical importance was the basic UNITY philosophy that the design is a sequence of refinements of specifications (expressed in the UNITY specification language) rather than layer of code. This idea solves the problem of gradually attacking the description of the system without implying that all the design steps are to be faithfully reproduced in the implementation. This is important because some (actually most) of the functions specified during the design cannot be implemented as desired, for the simple reason that they are already coded and the implementation would be only a few changed lines of code. Another important feature is the "union theorem" which states what properties must be expected by the union of two UNITY programs once the properties of the two parts are known. In practice the union theorem models the reasoning for designing the integration of new modules within an existing system.

The introduction of such drastically new approach to a very important and risky project may appear reckless to some, and in a sense it is. On the other hand any lesser project would not produce the same impact and therefore it would be a much weaker argument in favor of the use of formal methods (or of the not-use if the project failed) in the future. To minimize the risk however another experiment was performed prior to the decision of using UNITY for the I/O subsystem. This experiment consisted in the formalization (using UNITY) of an already implemented piece of software (also in the nucleus of GCOS8). This experiment was particular instructive because it permitted the comparison of the new design with the historical record of the already implemented software. The formalization was instrumental in discovering several flaws which, in the implemented version, were discovered only after the system was undergoing system tests or was already in use at customer sites. This was a sufficiently strong argument to convince the organization of the value of applying the methodology to an ambitious project such as the rewriting of the I/O subsystem.

4. The GCOS8 I/O Subsystem Project

The I/O subsystem requires considerable parallel processing not only because GCOS8 is a multiprocessor system but also because channels can change the state of certain cells in the main memory independently from the CPU's. In the original code, and to a greater extent in the new design, the hardware configuration can be changed (by changing state of peripherals, adding or removing new equipment) without suspending the operation of the I/O subsystem. The system also allows the on-line test and diagnostic of any hardware box in the I/O hardware. This inherent parallelism is a historic cause of errors in the modification work of the I/O subsystem.

The introduction of changes in the current I/O subsystem is deemed very difficult. Actually it is considered the most expensive system modification task for the development organization. This high level of expense is due to the very long period needed to identify the particular lines of code to be changed and the even longer period of time necessary to assure a reasonable level of stability once the changes are integrated in this system.

The new design differs drastically from the existing one. Instead of one configuration table three sets of data structures were defined. One contains all the configuration data (including all intermediate hardware boxes and connections) and it is used by all modules involved in configuration management or the ones needing access to the configuration data. Another set is used by the I/O subsystem itself for starting/terminating I/O operations.

These structures represent only the possible end points of all the I/O paths. The last one contains only device information and it is used by the peripheral allocation modules. This reorganization required a very accurate analysis of the existing software as well as the design of a protocol for the interaction of these new groups of modules (configuration management, I/O modules and allocation). This analysis is a long process regardless of the use of a formal design discipline.

Consequently the process of formal design took a long period of time (approximately 12 months) mostly because of the trial and error process necessary for the discovery of all the possible interactions of the rest of the system with the the new software. Conversations with developers, supported by code reading, were used as input, and once formal specifications were written they were checked with the developers again. A first set of formal specifications were written in about a month on the basis of an informal design document prepared by the author of this paper and other developers, and then checked against the currently existing software. As a consequence of these tests, formal specifications underwent continuous changes in order to accommodate the reality of the current system. Since UNITY specifications are layered and the consistency between layers is subject of formal proof, the proof process was instrumental in clarifying many obscure points as well as, in a few instances, discovering inconsistencies in the existing code. Note that these inconsistencies were still present in the system in spite of many design and code reviews, system tests and many months of deployment.

The proofs however needed to be repeated quite a few times. The resulting specifications were used to derive a UNITY program which was then used to guide the implementation.

The code (about 5000 lines of both new code and changes) was then written in less than a week and it ran without any error throughout all the testing period. The size of the new code represents a very substantial reduction when compared to the old software even though the new software implements more sophisticated functions.

The final report describing the details of the whole design, including specifications, proofs and the UNITY program represent a total of 76 pages. The formal work was done by Mark Staskauskas, U.T. Austin [4] and the implementation was done by Jeff Behm (Bull Phoenix Product Division) who completed the implementation only four months after he was first introduced to the UNITY methodology.

5. Summary of the Experience

The most rewarding result, for its long term impact, is the demonstration that the process of producing formal specification is a powerful tool for organizing the acquisition of the knowledge about existing software. This knowledge is buried in the code, unclear and non-updated documentation and, above all, in the minds of few experts. The process of formalization is a powerful synthesizing mechanism for producing a clear unambiguous description of the "rest of the system". On the other hand this is not a short process, and is far from being a one shot operation. In fact the formal specifications needed to be changed several times because of the discovery of something that was forgotten and of some existing flaw in the current software. These discoveries are a result of the formalization process. Because the specifications in UNITY are constructed in refining layers, and each layer is to be proven consistent with the preceding one, the discovery of a flaw in the code or of something forgotten caused several redoing of the proofs (with considerable chagrin for Mark Staskauskas who had to redo the proofs).

Another factor of concern is that there is the danger to keep the design at too high a level of abstraction and therefore neglecting essential details. In the I/O project this was avoided by the insistence of GCOS8 developers to include all the peculiarities and special cases of the I/O specifications. This insistence had to overcome the desire for elegance and simplicity on the part of the persons dedicated to the formalization of the design. For example, in an initial attempt to specifications the exception processing and test and diagnostic functions were represented as a single program. Since this was not the real situation but only a convenient abstraction the developers demanded the specifications to be rewritten to represent faithfully the system.

The whole process of formalization can be described as a struggle between the desire of the practitioners to introduce all the details and the specifier who needs to keep the specifications sufficiently simple to facilitate the formal manipulation. The motivation for adding details is a good one. Experience has shown that errors are caused by neglecting some detail. However in this experience we have learned that appropriate abstractions are indispensable for the feasibility of the proofs but creating abstractions without neglecting essential details is not an easy task. In fact the resulting proofs were at the limits of the specifier power of comprehension. Since the project has been successful we may state that the amount of details included was sufficient. A related problem that still requires solution, is a technique to "modify" a proof when something "minor" is changed, without undergoing the whole painful process of redoing all proof steps.

Another lesson of general interest that has been learned from this experience is that proofs, even though are difficult to generate, are essential for problems presenting this type of difficulties. After the specifications, a UNITY program was written to be used as the main source of guidance for the implementation. This program was not derived from the specification via a rigorous method nevertheless it was considered correct. After this, two simultaneous lines of work began. The specifier went through the effort of proving the program while the implementor realized (both by writing and modifying existing code) several sequential programs representing the UNITY program. Testing did not show any problem but the proving exercise showed a flaw in the design which needed to be corrected.

It is possible that this error would have appeared much later possibly during the system deployment phase. It is now this authors conviction that for critical software (such as the I/O subsystem) the cost of proving is fully justified. What is not yet clear however is if all (or most) practical problems can be practically subjected to the currently available proving process.

6. Concluding Remarks

The I/O subsystem experience has demonstrated the practicality of the use of an appropriate formal design method to its full extent. From the point of view of the industrial developer the results are incredibly good. In fact the method has proven its effectiveness in reducing to zero the number of errors in a design where we could have expected many because of the intricacy of its interactions with the rest of the system and the inherent parallelism of the hardware.

Of course some difficulties also emerged. The art of balancing details with abstraction is not an easy one to master. Also progress in the proving techniques is certainly needed if UNITY is to be applied routinely to practical problems.

Acknowledgements

The author is greatful to Professor Forouzan Golshani of Arizona State University for his reading of the manuscript and many valuable suggestions, and to Kathy Palmer-Davison for her patience and skill in typing this paper.

References

[1] H. Mills; Verbal presentation at the 9th International Conference on Software Engineering, Monterey, CA 1987

[2] L.A. Belady, M.M. Lehman: The Characteristics of Large Systems in "Research Directions in Software Technology" (P. Wagner ed.) MIT Press, Cambridge, MA 1979

[3] K. Mani Chandy, J. Misra: Parallel Program Design: A Foundation, Addison Wesley 1988

[4] M. Staskauskas: An Exercise in Verifying Concurrent Programs in Industry: The I/O Subsystem, Proceedings of the 10th IEEE Annual International Phoenix Computer and Communication Conference 1991

On the UNITY Design Decisions

Beverly Sanders
Institut für Computersysteme
Swiss Federal Institute of Technology, (ETH Zürich)
ETH Zentrum
CH-8092 Zürich, Switzerland
sanders@inf.ethz.ch

Abstract

UNITY, a surprisingly simple programming method for parallel programs comprising a program notation, specification language, and proof theory was described by Chandy and Misra [CM88] in their book, which appeared in 1988. Since then it has been applied to a wide variety of problems and has been generalized in several different ways. Further, a fair amount of research on the theoretical foundations has been carried out.

In this paper, we examine some of the original design decisions in light of these experiences and gain insight into the consequences of particular choices and an understanding of some of the ways the theory can be generalized without losing its desirable characteristics.

1   Introduction

The specification language and programming notation comprising UNITY are unusual in their simplicity. For example, the specification language is essentially a small fragment of linear temporal logic, and a UNITY program consists of variable declarations, initial conditions, and a set of multiple, deterministic assignment statements. However, experience has shown that the method can be fruitfully applied to a wide variety of problems, ranging from distributed algorithms to resource allocation in a mainframe operating system to programs for the connection machine, suggesting that Chandy and Misra have captured what is important for the design of parallel programs. On the other hand, one may still want to modify the approach in some way for special purposes. UNITY also has proved valuable in several cases by providing a basic framework. Because this original method is easy to understand, it can be modified in such a way that the consequences of the modifications are understood and much of the theory and techniques remain applicable.

In this paper, we look at some of the decisions that were made in the definition of UNITY with the goal of understanding the impact on the usefulness and elegance of the method, and also to identify easy generalizations. The scope of the discussion is limited to the design decisions "in-the-small"; we do not consider completely different approaches such as algebraic or traced based (e.g. CSP). The set of particular points addressed is, of course, incomplete. It would be impossible to claim that we had carefully considered all possible choices that went into UNITY, or all possible combinations of choices. What is discussed here are those issued which seem most fundamental, biased by what has proved interesting in our work, primarily using UNITY in the design and study of distributed algorithms.

2 Description of UNITY

In this section, we give a brief overview of UNITY. For the sake of brevity, an (in my opinion, improved) exposition of the basic theory and semantics which takes advantage of recent work on the foundations will be given directly, rather than first presenting an original definition and then suggesting modifications. Less fundamental issues will be pointed out, then discussed more thoroughly in later sections.

2.1 Program Notation and Computation Model

For our purposes, a UNITY program consists of 3 sections: the declare section consists of a list of variable names and their types, an initially section containing predicates defining allowed initial values of the variables, (when unspecified, a variable may initially have any value allowed by its type) and an assign section containing a set of multiple, deterministic assignment statements, separated by "□".[1] The expressions determining the value to be assigned may be conditional expressions. For example, with x and y variables of type integer, we might have the following "$x, y := y, x$ if $y < x$". Here, all components on the right hand side are evaluated, then the assignments to x and y are performed. Multiple conditions are also possible, provided that there is always a single well defined value for the expression. It is also required that the computation of the the value of the expression terminate. In the case that none of the conditions hold (e.g. $x \leq y$) then the effect of the assignment is to give the variables the values they currently had. At each step during program execution, a statement is chosen nondeterministically and the assignment is atomically performed. Formally, a program does not terminate, although it may reach a state (fixed point) which will remain the same thereafter. The only constraint on the nondeterminism is *unconditional fairness* which means that all statements must be chosen infinitely often.

The resulting computational model is that a program generates a set of execution sequences (sequences of states). If the program were actually implemented on a parallel processes, some statements would be performed concurrently, however, we assume *interleaving semantics*. This means that formally we view the execution of two statements concurrently as if one had happened before the other. Interleaving semantics is

---

[1]An additional section, called the always section is defined in [CM88] and allows the value of certain variables to be defined in terms of others. This provides a convenient way to make programs and specifications clearer and shorter. Since any program with an always section can be turned into an equivalent one without, this need not concern us in this paper.

an extremely fundamental aspect of UNITY. The advantage is the proof theory, the disadvantage is that this model is not convenient for reasoning about events which have a duration, or where partial orders are important such as distributed algorithms which use notions of causality. [BJ87]. It is useful to also consider the semantics to be invariant under finite stuttering, where stuttering occurs when an assignment does not change the state. In other words, we don't care about the difference between the following two execution sequences: $e_0 = x_0 x_1 x_2 \alpha$ and $e_1 = x_0 x_1 x_1 x_1 x_2 \alpha$.

Design choices which will be discussed in more detail later include the lack of sequencing of assignments and the absence of any concept of a process; the restriction to deterministic, total assignments; the requirement for unconditional fairness.

2.2 Specifications

A Unity program is specified by stating properties that the program must satisfy. There are two basic safety properties, **invariant** and **unless**; and a liveness properties, $\mapsto$ (read leads to). An additional liveness property, **ensures**, is used in proofs.

invariant p, where p is a predicate on the state space of the program, means that in every execution sequence that can be generated by the program, p holds initially and remains true during the entire execution of the program. For example, if we were to specify a program to allocate a resource among several users, we would have, for example, **invariant** $\neg(i.allocated \wedge j.allocated)$, i.e. that it is always true that not both user i and j simultaneously have simultaneously been allocated the resource. p **unless** q means that if at some point during the execution of the program, p holds while q does not, then p will continue to hold at least until q does. If q never holds, then p will hold forever. In the resource allocation program, for example, we might require $i.allocated$ **unless** $allocator.allocated \wedge \neg i.allocated$ which means that if i has been allocated the resource, then the next step is to return it to the allocator. This rules out, for example, passing it on to some other user. An important special case of **unless** is **stable**, where **stable** p is defined as p **unless** $false$ and means that once p becomes true, it remains true forever. (There is no state where false holds.)

The **invariant** and **unless** properties can be satisfied by a program that never does anything. $\mapsto$ properties allow us to specify that a program eventually does a required action. $p \mapsto q$ means that if at some point p holds, then eventually q must be established. For example, we may require in the resource allocation problem, $i.requesting \mapsto i.allocated$ and $i.allocated \mapsto \neg i.allocated$. The first property says that if i requests the resource, it will eventually be allocated. The second is a requirement on the user which says that the allocated resource must eventually be returned. p **ensures** q means p **unless** q, that if p holds, eventually q will hold, and that there is a single statement in the program which when executed will establish q. Obviously, the last requirement is not the type of requirement one would put in a specification, however **ensures** is important because it is used to prove $\mapsto$ properties.

These four properties form the basis of the UNITY specification language. They have proved to be adequate for a large variety of problems, and of course can be supplemented with new properties as required. For example, p **detects** q is defined as **invariant** $p \Rightarrow q$

and $q \mapsto p$. invariant, unless, and $\mapsto$ all can be expressed in linear temporal logic, but not the converse, but not everything expressible in temporal logic can be expressed in UNITY. For example, one cannot say $p \mapsto q$ unless r. However, in [Mis90a], it is shown how some of the properties expressible in temporal logic but not in UNITY can be indirectly expressed with the help of auxiliary variables. In these cases, no additions to the theory presented in the next section are required.

2.3 Logic

In the previous subsection, we gave the semantic definitions of the properties used in specifying UNITY programs. In this section, we describe the theory that is used to prove that a particular program satisfies a given property. The particular definitions given are from [San91a] and have certain advantages over the original ones given in [CM88], and later clarified in [Mis90b].

A complete description of the notation and conventions used for predicate calculus and proofs can be found in [DS90]. However, it should, for the most part be self explanatory. One exception is the everywhere operator, denoted with square brackets and means universal quantification over the state space. For example, consider $[p \Rightarrow q]$ with p and q predicates. Here, $p \Rightarrow q$ gives a new predicate which has the value false for states where p holds but q does not and true elsewhere. Applying the everywhere operator gives the scalar value true if $p \Rightarrow q$ is everywhere true, and false otherwise. Similarly, $[p \equiv q]$ has the scalar value true if p and q have the same value at all points.

2.3.1 Invariant

Recall that an invariant is a predicate that is true initially and holds throughout the execution of the program. It can be shown that for every legal UNITY program, there is a unique *strongest invariant*.[2] We call this predicate SI, and note that it is true exactly for those states which are reachable during some possible execution of the program. Since we have SI is the strongest invariant of the program, any predicate implied by SI is also invariant, i.e.

$$\text{invariant } p \equiv [SI \Rightarrow p] \tag{1}$$

In particular, the predicate *true* is an invariant of every program.

2.3.2 Unless

To give a rule for unless, we make use of the notion of weakest precondition originally given by Dijkstra to define the semantics of sequential programs. $\mathbf{wp}.s.q$ (weakest precondition of s) is defined as the predicate, say p, which is true on exactly those states where executing s from that state will terminate, and the final state will satisfy q. For our

---

[2]We say that a predicate p is stronger than predicate q and conversely that q is weaker than p, if $[p \Rightarrow q]$.

purposes, s will be an assignment statement in the program, and these are required to terminate by definition.[3]

$$p \text{ unless } q \equiv$$
$$\langle \forall s : s \text{ is a statement in the program} : [p \wedge \neg q \wedge SI \Rightarrow \mathbf{wp}.s.(p \vee q)) \rangle \qquad (2)$$

To see why this works, we see that starting in a reachable state where p holds and q does not and executing any statement in the program, will result in a state where either p still holds, or where q has been established. This is precisely what we wanted for **unless**. It is important to note that showing $\langle \forall s :: [p \wedge \neg q \wedge I \Rightarrow \mathbf{wp}.s.(p \vee q)) \rangle$ for any predicate I known to be invariant, including the predicate *true*, will imply the right hand side of 2 and thus the **unless** property. It is not necessary (and usually impractical) to actually determine SI. An alternative characterization of invariants can be given in terms of unless:

$$\text{invariant } p \equiv p \text{ unless } false \text{ and } [init \Rightarrow p] \qquad (3)$$

2.3.3 Ensures

To prove $p \text{ ensures } q$, we need to show $p \text{ unless } q$, as described above. The additional requirement, that q is eventually established and there is a single statement which does the job can be demonstrated by showing that for some statement in the program, starting in a state satisfying p will result in a state satisfying q. Since the program is required to be unconditionally fair, this statement will eventually be chosen for execution. Thus we have:

$$p \text{ ensures } q \equiv p \text{ unless } q \wedge \langle \exists s :: [p \wedge \neg q \wedge SI \Rightarrow \mathbf{wp}.s.q] \rangle \qquad (4)$$

A similar remark can be made here as well: if the conditions holds with SI replaced by any invariant, including *true* which holds for any program, then the required conclusion can be drawn.

2.3.4 Leads-to

Leads-to properties can be proved using the following three rules:

$$\frac{p \text{ ensures } q}{p \mapsto q} \qquad (5)$$

$$\frac{p \mapsto r, r \mapsto q}{p \mapsto q} \qquad (6)$$

$$\text{for any set W:} \frac{\langle \forall m : m \in W : p(m) \mapsto q \rangle}{\langle \exists m : m \in W : p(m) \rangle \mapsto q} \qquad (7)$$

---

[3]In the study of sequential programs, s may represent an entire program, and of course termination of programs containing loops or statements that could result in the program aborting cannot be taken for granted

The rule in 5 states that if an **ensures** property holds then the corresponding $\mapsto$ property holds as well. The rule in 6 states that leads-to is transitive while the rule in 7 states that it is disjunctive. For example if we know $p_0 \mapsto q$ and $p_1 \mapsto q$, then we can conclude $(p_0 \lor p_1) \mapsto q$. The rule given above allows disjunction over infinite sets, thus the more complicated statement.

2.3.5 Meta-theorems

One of the more useful features of UNITY is a wealth of meta-theorems that are of enormous practical importance. For example, the following rule is called consequence weakening:

$$\frac{p \text{ unless } q, [q \Rightarrow r]}{p \text{ unless } r} \tag{8}$$

The proof is short and illustrative:

Proof:
  {for all statements in the program:}
  $p \text{ unless } q, [q \Rightarrow r]$
$\Rightarrow$ {using 2}
  $[p \land \neg q \land SI \Rightarrow \mathbf{wp}.s.p \lor q]$
$\Rightarrow$ {predicate calculus and $[q \Rightarrow r]$}
  $[p \land \neg r \land SI \Rightarrow \mathbf{wp}.s.p \lor q]$
$\Rightarrow$ {**wp** monotonic and $[q \Rightarrow r]$}
  $[p \land \neg r \land SI \Rightarrow \mathbf{wp}.s.p \lor r]$
$=$ {using 2}
  $p \text{ unless } r$

The logic above differs from that given in [CM88, Mis90b] in two ways. First, we *define* the properties according to the semantics instead of as what can be proved with a particular rule. This allows issues of soundness (only properties that hold can be proved) and completeness (if a property holds, one can prove that it holds) to be addressed. These issues are addressed in [San91a, Pac90, Rao91a, GP89]. Second, the original description of UNITY logic had no mention of the strongest invariant, but did include an axiom called the substitution axiom which allowed invariants to be replaced by *true* in properties of programs. This results in weaker rules: the original rules are obtained from 2 and 4 by eliminating the SI conjunct, and replacing "$\equiv$" with "$\Leftarrow$". Thus, the first step in the proof above (after all references to SI have been removed) would not be valid. Fortunately, it is possible to prove a meta-meta-theorem which fixes up the problem, but in any case, proofs using the version with SI are more straightforward and there is the additional benefit that the substitution axiom becomes unnecessary; the ability to replace invariants with *true* and vice-versa can be proved as a meta-theorem. This is desirable since the role of the substitution axiom in the Unity logic has been widely misunderstood; several theoretical studies of the UNITY logic have simply omitted it, with the result that the results do not actually apply to the "real UNITY". As a practical matter, the difference in formulation of the logic has little effect on the process of deriving programs.

3 Discussion of Design Decisions

3.1 Processes and Sequential Control

The essential difference between a UNITY program and a similar looking program in some imperative programming language such as Pascal, or Dijkstra's Guarded Commands language, is that the statements in the assign section form a *set*. The order in which they are listed does not matter. The lack of sequencing has the effect that statements can easily be mapped in various ways onto different processes for execution. However, formally, no notion of a process is necessary, and the design can be carried out more or less independently of the final architecture, at least in the initial stages. A program that is of form particularly convenient for particular architectures are also possible to express using the notation already defined, without the need for additional language constructs for interprocess communication. For example, a variable of type sequence where values the only operations used are appending and removing the head can easily be mapped into message passing, where the sequence variable corresponds to the communication channel and send and receive correspond to append and remove the head, respectively.

The lack of sequencing and processes can be seen as the major departure that was made in UNITY when compared with earlier attempts to generalize the Dijkstra/Hoare approach to reasoning about sequential programs with pre- and post-conditions to parallel programs [OG76, LS85]. These, inspired by the may multiprocess programs are implemented, generalized the programming notation to allow multiple processes instead of just one, and added constructs for interprocess communication. This resulted in a modification of the proof theory which turned out to be rather awkward to use in practice. One would first annotate each individual process and show that the annotation was valid, then show an additional property (or properties) non-interference. Unfortunately, non-interference can only be shown for some of the many possible ways of annotating the individual processes. The difficulty lies in guessing which one. Another problem is that one may need to express the position in the program in an annotation. The underlying problem here is that the program counter, which is part of the state, is hidden and the relevant information must be recovered in some way (usually with auxiliary variables). Often, the annotation of one process will refer to variables in another. Due to the complexity of dealing with the part of the state hidden in the program counters and the need to anticipate the non-interference proofs, there is little hope of success without a very thorough understanding of what is going on in the entire program.

UNITY, almost paradoxically, can be viewed as a restriction of Dijkstra's Guarded Command notation, allowing only programs containing a single loop [4], where all guards are *true* and the commands in the loop are multiple assignments. How the statements are mapped onto processes is irrelevant for a proof, which is much easier once we have eliminated an artificial separation of the proof into annotations of different processes which may fit an implementation but not correspond to a natural partitioning of the

---

[4]Recall a loop in GC do $b_0 \rightarrow s_0 \square \cdots b_n \rightarrow s_n$ od is executed by nondeterministically choosing a guard, say b_i that evaluates to true and performing the corresponding command s_i. The loop is terminated when none of the guards are true. Unlike UNITY, in GC, there is no fairness requirement.

problem. Finally, whatever precedence constraints are required must be explicitly stated using program variables. There is no part of the state which is hidden, and also no spurious precedence constraints which arise simply because program statements must be written in a linear order. This results in a more uniform logic. Of course, the price to be paid is in the complexity of writing a program that does happen to have many necessary precedence constraints. For many situations, however, the rather radical departure of UNITY from earlier, more obvious approaches has clear benefits.

3.2 Deterministic, Total Assignments

A very important restriction in UNITY is the requirement that all assignment statements be deterministic and total (i.e. defined and "enabled" from every state). The requirement that assignments be total is not a major issue since we have unconditional fairness and the basic semantics are invariant under finite stuttering. If an expression on the right hand side of an assignment is undefined or the assignment is "not enabled" in some state, then simply modify the statement so that executing it does not change the state. This idea is already built into the program notion. Recall that, for example, "$x := e$ if b" is a shorthand for "$x := e$ if $b \sim x$ if $\neg b$" rather than an indication that the statement cannot be executed unless b holds.

The disadvantage of requiring deterministic statements is one of expressibility. It might be convenient, for example, to have a statement which removes some element from a set. The advantage which comes from deterministic assignment statements, and to some extent from the totality requirement is that the predicate transformers on which the logic are based are well behaved. A predicate transformer is a function from predicates to predicates (**wp**.s. is a predicate transformer) and a rather rich theory, originally developed to study the semantics of sequential programs, has been developed for such functions. A description of this theory can be found in [DS90]. Fortunately, a small number of concepts suffice for our purposes.

As a pragmatic matter, **wp** for deterministic assignments is easy to define and calculate.

$$\mathbf{wp}.\text{"}x := e_0 \text{ if } b_0 \sim \cdots \sim e_n \text{ if } b_n\text{"}.q =$$
$$(b_0 \Rightarrow (x := e_0)q) \wedge \cdots \wedge (b_n \Rightarrow (x := e_n)q) \wedge ((\neg b_0 \wedge \cdots \wedge \neg b_n) \Rightarrow q) \qquad (9)$$

where

$(x := e)q = q$ after all occurrences of x have been replaced by e

For example, $\mathbf{wp}.\text{"}x := x + 2 \text{ if } y < 0 \sim x - 2 \text{ if } y > 0\text{"}.x > 0 = (y < 0 \Rightarrow x > -2)$ $\wedge (y > 0 \Rightarrow x > 2) \wedge (y = 0 \Rightarrow x > 0)$.

However, there are more fundamental properties of **wp** which are guaranteed by the restriction to deterministic, total assignment statements and which are essential for the basic logic and the meta-theory. Identifying these properties allows us to state conditions under which the restrictions to deterministic assignments can be relaxed without damaging the logic.

First, we introduce a few important properties of predicate transformers. Let f be a predicate transformer. We say

f is *monotonic* if for all predicates p and q: $[p \Rightarrow q] \Rightarrow [f.p \Rightarrow f.q]$ (10)

In other words, if p is stronger than q, then the result of applying f to p (this is a predicate) will be stronger than the result of applying f to q. Recall that this property of **wp** was used in the proof of consequence weakening for **unless** given in section 2.3.5. Thus we see that in order for this theorem to remain valid in a generalized theory, we would want to make sure that the new **wp** is monotonic.

A second property of interest is called *universally conjunctivity*.

f is *universally conjunctive* if $[f.\langle \forall X : X \in V : X \rangle \equiv \langle \forall X : X \in V : f.X \rangle]$ (11)

In the above, V can be any bag of predicates, including those that infinite or empty. This means that taking the conjunction of all the predicates in V and applying f gives the same result as first applying f to each individual predicate in V and then taking the conjunction of these results. By requiring the property only when V is finite and nonempty, we get a weaker property called *finite conjunctivity*. It can be shown that any predicate transformer that is universally conjunctive is also monotonic, and that universal conjunctivity implies that the predicate transformer is *truth preserving*, i.e. $[f.true \equiv true]$. One final property is called the *law of the excluded miracle*.

f satisfies the law of the excluded miracle if $[f.false \equiv false]$ (12)

In section 2.3.1, it was asserted that the strongest invariant SI exists and is unique for each legal UNITY program. In fact, as is shown in [San91a], it suffices for the **wp** for each statement in the program to be monotonic. A systematic study of the UNITY meta-theorems as given in chapter 3 of [CM88] shows that the meta-theorems about **unless** hold if **wp** is monotonic, truth-preserving, and finitely conjunctive. Thus universal conjunctivity suffices for SI to exist, and for the meta-theorems for **unless** to remain valid. A similar study of the meta-theorems for **ensures** gives the result that universal conjunctivity plus the law of the excluded miracle for the predicate transformer on the right hand side of the implication (in standard UNITY, this is just **wp**) suffice for these theorems to remain valid. The theorems for $\mapsto$ are derived from those for **unless** and **ensures**. Thus, we have an important result for generalizing UNITY: After checking that the necessary predicate transformers satisfy universal conjunctivity and the law of the excluded miracle, one can conclude that the strongest invariant, SI, exists and is unique, and the meta-theorems for **unless** and **ensures** remain valid.

Similar results were presented by Rao in [Rao91b] where the goal of the work was to generalize UNITY to allow reasoning about probabilistic algorithms. Non-deterministic statements were added (a statement has k modes, and executing the statement implies making a random choice between the modes), the properties of the new **wp** checked, allowing the conclusion that the previously described theory remained valid.

Another extension to UNITY to incorporate the idea of knowledge-based protocols [HM90, HF89] was presented in [San91b]. The idea is that in a distributed system, a process only "knows" what can be concluded from its local state, and a special logic has been developed based on these ideas. (A "process", for the purposes of that paper, was characterized by a subset of the program variables that were considered to be accessible by the process. No sequencing was introduced). Knowledge-based protocols allow actions made by a process to explicitly depend on its knowledge, for example statements such as $x := e$ if $K_i p$ ($K_i p$ is read process i knows p). What is interesting here, is that the resulting predicate transformers did *not* satisfy the needed monotonicity properties. This negative result led to the discovery of additional new results about knowledge-based protocols and has since spurned additional research in that area.

As a final example, we mention the Swarm model [CR90, RC90], a generalization to UNITY especially designed for shared data-space programming. The data space contains tuples which may be inserted and removed from the space. The analogue of executing a statement is executing a transaction which involves making a nondeterministic choice between all tuples that satisfy a given criterion. The definition of **wp** can be easily seen to satisfy the necessary properties for existence of SI and for the **unless** meta-theorems to remain valid, thus providing additional justification for the authors' claims. The meta-theorems about **ensures** are also preserved. This is discussed in more detail in the next section.

3.3 Constant, Finite Programs, and Fairness

In UNITY, the set of assignments that makes up a program is required to be fixed. The notation does have some syntactic sugar in the form of quantifications. For example instead of writing $x_0 := e_0 \square x_1 := e_1 \ldots \square x_N := e_N$, one could write $\langle \square i : 0 \leq i \leq N : x_i := e_i \rangle$. This convenient shorthand requires, however, that the range in such a quantification be computable ahead of time, thus guaranteeing that the set of statements making up the program is fixed.

The most obvious disadvantage of this restriction is that it is difficult to model anything that resembles dynamic process creation and deletion in UNITY. Although, formally, UNITY has no processes, one could still imagine situations where allowing groups of statements to come and go depending on the course that the execution of the program took would be a natural way to model a program that would later be implemented with a dynamic set of processes.

The biggest problem with relaxing the restriction that a program must consist of a finite and constant set of assignments is defining an appropriate notion of fairness. With this constraint, unconditional fairness, i.e. that every statement is chosen infinitely often, provides a rule that is both easy to implement and results in a simple theory which is embodied in the rule for **ensures** (4). It is difficult to imagine an appropriate fairness rule with an infinite number of statements. In the case where the statements come and go from a fixed set, we essentially have the situation where, instead of begin total, assignments can be enabled or disabled. In this case the value of **wp**.s.*false* is true for all states where s is not enabled. A concept from temporal logic which could be applied is called strong fairness and means that any assignment enabled infinitely often must be chosen infinitely often. Other methods allow such things as partitioning statements into fairness classes and requiring some sort of fairness between the classes, and then between the statements in a class. Obviously, this generality makes the theory, the actual work of constructing proofs of liveness properties, and constructing an implementation that satisfies the fairness constraint more difficult.

Although these generalizations of the UNITY fairness requirement do not seem worthwhile, two simpler alternatives have proven useful. The first has as its main goal allowing a more natural modeling of situations where the set of statements in the program is dynamic, the second is even simpler and is useful for modeling programs with actions, for example failures or some possible input from a user, that may, but need not ever happen.

The first example is found in Swarm logic, the generalization of UNITY to facilitate reasoning about programming with a shared data-space model already mentioned in the previous section. For the purposes of discussion of its fairness properties, we consider Swarm to be a modification that allows particular statements (transactions), taken from a finite set to become enabled or disabled, but which must satisfy the following requirements: Once a statement becomes enabled, it remains enabled at least until it is executed, and every enabled statement will eventually be chosen. Statements may be enabled at any time. Although the analogue of statements in Swarm may also be nondeterministic, there are no fairness constraints on the alternatives belonging to individual statements. The rule for the Swarm version of ensures is given below, the rules for unless and $\mapsto$ are essentially unchanged.

$$\frac{p \text{ unless } q, \langle \exists s :: [p \land \neg q \land SI \Rightarrow s \text{ enabled} \land \text{wp}.s.q] \rangle}{p \text{ ensures } q} \tag{13}$$

The rule in 13 is taken from [CR90] with a change in notation to make it consistent with what is used in this paper, and has been strengthened by conjoining SI with the left hand side of the implication in the rule, as was done for standard UNITY. The soundness of the rule is intuitively obvious. If p holds, but q does not, then from the unless property, p will continue to hold at least as long as q does not. On the other hand, we are guaranteed that if p holds but q does not, then there is some enabled statement that, when executed, will establish q. Since any enabled statement must remain enabled until it is chosen, and every enabled statement will eventually be chosen, eventually q will be established. The complication here is that we have the additional obligation to prove $[p \land \neg q \Rightarrow s \text{ enabled}]$, which is essentially an invariant property. It is easy to see that this requires that predicates be able to refer to whether or not individual statements are enabled, and also requires that the definition of wp be formulated to take into account the fact that executing a statement may cause it to be disabled. In order to claim that the meta-theorems for ensures still hold, it suffices that the predicate transformer on the right hand side of the implication satisfy the law of excluded miracle condition, i.e. $[s \text{ enabled} \land \text{wp}.s.false \equiv false]$.

An even simpler generalization to the requirement of unconditional fairness for all statements is to allow the fixed, finite set of statements to be partitioned into two sets: a non-empty set of those that are chosen according to an unconditional fairness rule, and those that have no fairness requirement associated with them at all. The statements without a fairness requirement need never be chosen. This approach is found in for example [LS90] and has two benefits when adopted in UNITY. The first is that it is often desirable to include events in a program that need not ever happen, such as failures or the occurrence of a particular input event. The second is that a UNITY program may be considered to be a high level specification which will later be refined in such a way as to preserve all its **unless**, **invariant**, and $\mapsto$ properties [San90]. In practice, it turns out that requiring unconditional fairness for all statements in a specification often results in overspecification because the program happens to satisfy $\mapsto$ properties that are not really necessary and need not hold in refinements. The revised rule for **ensures** is given below:

$$p \text{ ensures } q \equiv p \text{ unless } q \wedge \langle \exists s : s \in \text{fair set} : [p \wedge \neg q \wedge SI \Rightarrow \text{wp}.s.q] \rangle \qquad (14)$$

It is required that the set of statements with unconditional fairness be non-empty. This fits well with the intended application of unfair statements to represent failures and inputs, and allows us to avoid introducing a special case in the rule for the case when none of the statements are fair, but presumably something must eventually happen. The only difference between this and the original rule for **ensures** as given in 4 is that the range in the quantification is the set of statements with unconditional fairness rather than the complete set of statements in the program. The process of constructing a proof is not harder than before. Chandy and Misra have justified the decision to require unconditional fairness of all statements by pointing out that unconditional fairness can be simulated in standard UNITY as follows: A statement "s" where fairness is not required is replaced by "s if b", and an additional statement "$b := \neg b$" is added to the program. Thus execution sequences where the statement "s if b" is always chosen when b is false are possible. However, since this approach makes the program considerably less clear, and the modification to the proof system to avoid the problem altogether is trivial, it seems that this particular generalization would be worthwhile to incorporate into the "standard".

One final generalization that should be pointed out is found in Rao's work on probabilistic algorithms. Statements may have a finite number of different modes that are probabilistically chosen. Individual statements are chosen according to unconditional fairness, individual modes are chosen subject to the constraint of extreme fairness. Extreme fairness with respect to a predicate x means that if the statement is executed infinitely often from a state satisfying x, then each mode is executed infinitely often from a state satisfying x. An execution is extremely fair if it is extremely fair with respect to all predicates. It is interesting here that for deterministic properties like **ensures** and $\mapsto$, the exact same rules as in standard UNITY still apply. (Of course **wp** must be defined appropriately for the probabilistic statements). The value of the generalization is in defining new types of liveness properties, for example $\models\Longrightarrow$, read probabilistic leads-to. $p \models\Longrightarrow q$ means that if at some point p becomes true, then q will eventually become true *with probability 1*.

The primary problem with eliminating the constraint of constant programs is finding an appropriate notion of fairness along with a definition of **wp** that accounts for the enabling and disabling of statements. The temptation to adopt very general fairness notations should be avoided lest one end up with a yet another proof theory that is studied but never used. The Swarm system is an example where the requirement of constant programs has been eliminated under fairly strict restrictions on the way that statements may become enabled and disabled. This does make proofs more difficult as can be seen from the examples in the Swarm literature. It is also the case that different kinds of fairness may allow a more natural modeling of the problem. One approach is the idea of allowing the set of statements to be partitioned into fair and unfair statements, where the unfair statements model events that need not happen. Finally, we saw that adding extremely fair probabilistic statements where the individual statements are still chosen according to unconditional fairness did not invalidate any of the UNITY proof theory, but allowed new, probabilistic properties to be defined.

4 Conclusion

The wide variety of problems to which UNITY has been applied, and also the ease in which it has been modified and extended for special purposes, indicate that the engineering tradeoffs made in its design were on the mark. In this paper, we have taken advantage of these experiences and recent research into its theoretical foundations to suggest an improved formulation of the underlying theory, and to identify fundamental concepts which are useful when extending the method. It should be pointed out that compositionality, an extremely important aspect of UNITY has not been discussed in this paper. This is also arguably the least satisfactory part of the theory and research on this problem is likely to motivate additional modifications and extensions in the future.

References

[BJ87]   K. Birman and T. Joseph. Reliable communication in the presence of failures. *ACM Transactions on Computer Systems*, 5(1):47–76, February 1987.

[CM88]   K. Mani Chandy and Jayadev Misra. *Parallel Program Design: A Foundation.* Addison-Wesley, 1988.

[CR90]   H. C. Cunningham and G.-C. Roman. A UNITY-style programming logic for shared data-space programs. *IEEE Transactions on Parallel and Distributed Systems*, 1(3):365–376, July 1990.

[DS90]   Edsger W. Dijkstra and Carel S. Scholten. *Predicate Calculus and Program Semantics.* Springer-Verlag, 1990.

[GP89]   R. Gerth and Amir Pnueli. Rooting UNITY. In *Proceedings of 5th International Workshop on Software Specification and Design*, Pittsburgh, 1989.

[HF89]   Joseph H. Halpern and Ronald Fagin. Modelling knowledge and action in distributed systems. *Distributed Computing*, 3:159–177, 1989.

[HM90]   Joseph Y. Halpern and Yoram Moses. Knowledge and common knowledge in a distributed environment. *Journal of the ACM*, 37(3):549–587, July 1990.

[LS85]   Leslie Lamport and Fred Schneider. Formal foundation for specification and verification. In M. Paul and H. J. Siegert, editors, *Distributed Systems: Methods and Tools for Specification*, pages 203–286. Springer-Verlag, 1985. Lecture Notes in Computer Science 190.

[LS90]   Simon S. Lam and A. Udaya Shankar. A relational notation for state-transition systems. *IEEE Transactions on Software Enginnering*, 16(7):755–775, July 1990.

[Mis90a] Jayadev Misra. Auxiliary variables. Notes on UNITY: 15-90, 1990.

[Mis90b] Jayadev Misra. Soundness of the substitution axiom. Notes on UNITY: 14-90, 1990.

[OG76]   Susan Owicki and David Gries. An axiomatic proof technique for parallel programs I. *Acta Informatica*, 6(1):319–340, 1976.

[Pac90]   Jan Pachl. Three definitions of leads-to for UNITY. Notes on UNITY: 23-90, 1990.

[Rao91a] Josyula R. Rao. On a notion of completeness for the leads-to. Notes on UNITY 24-90, 1991.

[Rao91b] Josyula R. Rao. Reasoning about probabilistic algorithms. In *Proceedings of 9th ACM Symposium on Principles of Distributed Computing*, 1991.

[RC90]   G.-C. Roman and H. C. Cunningham. Mixed programming metaphors in a shared data-space model of concurrency. *IEEE Transactions on Software Engineering*, 16(12):1361–1373, December 1990.

[San90]   Beverly Sanders. Stepwise refinement of mixed specifications of concurrent programs. In M. Broy and C.B. Jones, editors, *Proceedings of the IFIP Working Conference on Programming Concepts and Methods*, Israel, 1990. Elsiever Science Publishers.

[San91a] Beverly Sanders. Eliminating the substitution axiom from UNITY logic. *Formal Aspects of Computing*, 3(2):189–205, 1991.

[San91b] Beverly Sanders. A predicate transformer approach to knowledge and knowledge-based protocols. In *Proceedings of the 10th ACM Symposium on Principles of Distributed Computing*, Montreal, 1991.

Flexible Program Structures for Concurrent Programming

Ambuj K. Singh* and Ying Liu*

Department of Computer Science
University of California at Santa Barbara
Santa Barbara, CA 93106

Abstract

Current programming languages and models fix the structure of concurrent programs. This hinders the portability of programs across architectures. In this paper, we propose flexible program structures through which the synchrony relation of a program can be changed in accordance with the underlying architecture without compromising correctness.

1 Introduction

Omission of irrelevant details is a basic tenet of programming. In specification of programs, the principle permits a user to utilize an implementation in several situations and provides greater freedom to the designer in choosing a particular implementation. In derivation of programs, the principle allows a designer to solve a problem at an abstract level and postpone design decisions concerning efficiency of the program. The principle manifests itself in programming languages and methodologies through nondeterministic constructs [3]. Essentially, a nondeterministic program is an abstraction of several deterministic programs, and therefore, a particular deterministic program that is efficient can be isolated later in the design process.

Achieving the right level of abstraction in programming becomes even more important in the domain of concurrent programs. This is mainly because of the existence of diverse architectures (SIMD vs. MIMD, shared-variable vs. message-passing) to which a program may have to be mapped. Specifying the structure of programs as little as possible permits programs for different architectures to share much of the initial development. For example, the *Unity* model of parallel programming [1] eschews control flow altogether. A Unity program consists of a set of multiple-assignment statements and any fair selection of the statements is an acceptable execution of the program. The success of the Unity methodology stems from the fact that the initial program development proceeds independent of any architectural concerns and all the necessary choices for efficiency can be made late in the design process.

---

* Work supported in part by NSF Grant CCR-9008628 and a grant from Lawrence Livermore National Laboratory.

Motivated by the ideas of nondeterminism and absence of control flow, we extend the principle of omission of irrelevant details to a new direction in this paper. We explore the under-specification of the structure of concurrent programs. A concurrent program usually has a fixed set of primitive statements that are organized by means of control flow mechanisms. Some languages have elaborate control flow (conditionals, loops, etc.) whereas some like Unity have minimal control flow (a program consists simply of a set of assignment statements). However, in all the approaches the primitive steps (e.g., the assignment statements in Unity) cannot be changed. This means that the underlying synchrony relation of a program that defines the composition of the primitive steps is fixed once for all when a program is written down. This makes it difficult to change the structure of the program on the fly without compromising its correctness. We investigate mechanisms by which a program can be written down by stratifying only that part of its structure that is needed for its correctness. We refer to such a program as an *abstract program*. Just as determinism is viewed as a special case of non-determinism, we view a completely stratified program as an abstract program for which the entire synchrony relation has been fixed. An abstract program represents an entire class of completely stratified programs and consequently, the correctness of an abstract program implies the correctness of all the completely stratified programs that it represents.

A number of alternatives are possible in the definition of abstract programs. One possibility is to extend the approach of pomsets [7] and event structures [9] and define an abstract program by a partial order on the primitive steps. Primitive steps that are ordered are executed in the indicated order and primitive steps that are unordered may be executed in any order including simultaneously. However, a major distinction from the pomsets (or the event structures) approach is that instead of a partial order on *events* we now have a partial order on *actions* themselves. Some operators such as concurrence, and orthocurrence [7] can be extended to abstract programs with little difficulty, while others such as concatenation and Kleene star require considerable rethinking.

In this paper, our definition of abstract programs is motivated by two basic notions in concurrent programming: synchrony and asynchrony. A specific implementation of a program defines, for every two primitive steps of the program, whether they are executed synchronously or asynchronously. However, there is no need to completely define this relationship at the level of abstract programs. An *abstract program* only defines which primitive steps *cannot* be executed synchronously; all other steps can be executed either synchronously or asynchronously. For convenience, we adopt the Unity model where synchrony is modeled by grouping primitive steps into the same assignment statement and asynchrony is modeled by grouping primitive steps into different assignment statements. An abstract program consists of a set of primitive steps along with an *asynchrony relation* [5]. This under-specification of the synchrony structure allows implementations for different architectures to share the initial steps of program development and provides a basis for a much more flexible and portable program design.

The rest of paper is organized as follows. Section 2 gives a brief introduction to the Unity syntax and logic. In Section 3, we present the idea of abstract programs. In Section 4, we illustrate the concept of abstract programs through an example of sorting an array. Finally, Section 5 contains some concluding remarks.

2 A Brief Introduction to Unity

A Unity program [1] consists of four sections: a **declare** section that declares the variables used in the program, an **always** section that consists of a set of proper equations defining certain variables as functions of other variables, an **initially** section that describes the initial values of the variables, and an **assign** section that consists of a non-empty set of assignment statements.

An assignment statement contains one or more assignment components separated by ||. An assignment component is either a quantified assignment or an enumerated assignment. A quantified assignment specifies a quantification and an assignment that is to be instantiated with the given quantification; a quantification names a set of bound variables and a boolean expression satisfied by the instances of the bound variables. An enumerated assignment has a variable list on the left, a corresponding expression list in the middle, and a boolean expression on the right:

$$\langle variable\text{-}list \rangle := \langle expression\text{-}list \rangle \ \textbf{if} \ \langle condition \rangle.$$

An assignment component is executed by first evaluating all expressions and then assigning the values of evaluated expressions to the appropriate variables, if the associated boolean is true; otherwise, the variables are left unchanged.

The set of assignment statements in **assign** section is written down either by enumerating every statement singly and using $[\![$ as the set constructor, or by using a quantification of the form $\langle \, [\![\ var : range : statement \rangle$. A program execution starts from any state satisfying the initial conditions and goes on forever; in each step of execution some assignment statement is selected nondeterministically and executed. Nondeterministic selection is constrained by the following fairness rule: every statement is selected infinitely often.

There are five relations on predicates in Unity theory: *unless, stable, invariant, ensures,* and *leads-to.* The first three are used for stating safety properties whereas the last two are used for stating progress properties. In the following description, s is an arbitrary statement in a given program and p, q are predicates.

- $p \ unless \ q \ \equiv \ (\forall s :: \{p \wedge \neg q\} \ s \ \{p \vee q\}).$
- $stable \ p \ \equiv \ p \ unless \ false.$
- $invariant \ p \ \equiv \ initially \ p \wedge p \ unless \ false.$
- $p \ ensures \ q \ \equiv \ p \ unless \ q \wedge (\exists s :: \{p \wedge \neg q\} \ s \ \{q\}).$
- The relation *leads-to*, denoted by $\mapsto$, is defined by following three rules.
  1. $p \ ensures \ q \ \Rightarrow \ p \mapsto q,$
  2. $(p \mapsto q \wedge q \mapsto r) \ \Rightarrow \ p \mapsto r,$ and
  3. For any set W,
     $$(\forall m : m \in W : p.m \mapsto q) \ \Rightarrow \ ((\exists m : m \in W : p.m) \mapsto q).$$

The *fixed point* of a program, represented by FP, describes the state of the program upon termination. It is defined to be the conjunction of the fixed point of the statements of the program. The fixed point of a statement is in turn obtained by replacing the assignment symbol := by the equality symbol =. In other words, for any program P,

- $FP\text{-}P \ \equiv \ (\forall s : s \in P : FP\text{-}s),$
  where for any $s :: X := E \ \textbf{if} \ B \ , \quad FP\text{-}s \ \equiv \ B \Rightarrow (X = E).$

3 Abstract Programs

An *abstract program* F consists of a *primitive statement* set S that describes the primitive actions and an irreflexive, symmetric *asynchrony relation* A that constrains the execution of the statements in S. Each primitive statement is an assignment statement of the form defined in the previous section. Relation A over S specifies the asynchrony relationship of the primitive statements: $A(s_1, s_2)$ implies that statements s_1 and s_2 can only be executed asynchronously. If $A(s_1, s_2)$ does not hold, statements s_1 and s_2 can be executed in any order, either $s_1 \parallel s_2$ or $s_1 \, \| \, s_2$.

Given an abstract program $F = (S, A)$, a *compound statement* v of F is defined to be a multiple assignment statement composed of the primitive statements and complying with the restrictions of A. In other words, v is a compound statement of F iff for any pair of primitive statements s_1, s_2 in v, there is no asynchrony relation between them, i.e., $\neg A(s_1, s_2)$. We use $[v]_F$ to denote the set of primitive assignment statements constituting v, i.e.,

$$[v]_F \equiv \{s \; : \; s \in S \land s \text{ is a component of } v\}.$$

The fixed point of a compound statement is defined to be the conjunction of the fixed points of the component statements.

As an example, consider an abstract program F with $S = \{s_1, s_2, s_3, s_4\}$ and $A = \{(s_1, s_4), (s_4, s_1)\}$. Then $v = s_1 \parallel s_2 \parallel s_3$ is a compound statement of F, and $[v]_F = \{s_1, s_2, s_3\}$. The fixed point of compound statement v is the conjunction of the fixed points of statements s_1, s_2, and s_3. Compound statement $v' = s_1 \parallel s_2 \parallel s_4$ is an invalid compound statement as $A(s_1, s_4)$ holds in F. Note that a Unity program is an abstract program where each statement is a primitive statement and all statements are restricted to be executed asynchronously (i.e., the asynchrony relation contains all possible pairs).

We define $\mathcal{M}(F)$ to be the set of all possible compound statements of abstract program F, i.e.,

$$\mathcal{M}(F) \equiv \{v \; : \; v \text{ is a compound statement of } F\}.$$

Observe that for a Unity program $F = (S, A)$, $\quad \mathcal{M}(F) = S$.

A number of design decisions concerning the target architecture have to be made during the implementation of a program on a target architecture. One of these decisions involves refining the synchrony relation of the program to suit the architecture. The idea of implementation of abstract programs defined below provides us with the necessary theory for such implementations. Given an abstract program $F = (S, A)$, we say that another abstract program $F' = (S', A')$ is an *implementation* of F if and only if the following three conditions hold.

1. The set of primitive statements in S' are obtained from the compound statements of F, i.e., $S' \subseteq \mathcal{M}(F)$.
2. Every primitive statement in S is included in some primitive statement in F', i.e.,
   $$(\forall s : \; s \in S : (\exists t : t \in S' : \; s \in [t]_F)).$$
3. The asynchrony relation of F' obeys the asynchrony relation of F, i.e.,
   $$(\forall s_1, s_2, t_1, t_2 : \; s_1, s_2 \in S \land t_1, t_2 \in S' \land s_1 \in [t_1]_F \land s_2 \in [t_2]_F :$$
   $$(s_1, s_2) \in A \Rightarrow (t_1, t_2) \in A').$$

In other words, abstract program F' contains the same set of assignments as abstract program F, but is possibly more specific about the asynchrony relation among the statements. Observe that if F' is an implementation of F, then $\mathcal{M}(F') \subseteq \mathcal{M}(F)$. Moreover, $S = \bigcup_{t \in S'} [t]_F$.

Now, we extend the logic of Unity to accommodate abstract programs. We redefine the primary relations *unless, ensures,* and the fixed point for an abstract program $F = (S, A)$. The secondary relations, such as *stable, invariant,* and *leads-to,* are defined as in Section 2.

- p *unless* $q \equiv (\forall t : t \in \mathcal{M}(F) : \{p \wedge \neg q\} \, t \, \{p \vee q\})$
- p *ensures* $q \equiv (p$ *unless* $q) \wedge$
  $$(\exists s : s \in S : (\forall v : v \in \mathcal{M}(F) \wedge s \in [v]_F : \{p \wedge \neg q\} \, v \, \{q\}))$$
- $FP\text{-}F \equiv (\forall s : s \in S : FP\text{-}s)$.

(The above definition of *ensures* is similar to that presented by Cunningham and Roman for *synchronic groups* [2].) Observe that all theorems about *unless* (and consequently, *stable* and *invariant*), *ensures, lead-to,* and the fixed point in [1] also hold for abstract programs.

The union of two abstract programs $F = (S, A)$ and $G = (T, B)$, written as $F \, \| \, G = (R, C)$, is composed of all primitive statements in S and in T, i.e., $R = S \cup T$. The asynchrony relation C for $F \, \| \, G$ inherits the restrictions of A and B, and imposes asynchronous executions on statements between S and $T - S$, as well as T and $S - T$:
$$C = A \cup B \cup (S \times (T - S)) \cup ((T - S) \times S) \cup (T \times (S - T)) \cup ((S - T) \times T))$$
Following the definition, the set of compound statements of $F \, \| \, G$ is a subset of the union of the compound statements of F and G, i.e., $\mathcal{M}(F \, \| \, G) \subseteq \mathcal{M}(F) \cup \mathcal{M}(G)$. Based on this fact, the Union Theorem in [1] can be modified as follows:

1. $(p$ *unless* q *in* $F \wedge p$ *unless* q *in* $G) \Rightarrow p$ *unless* q *in* $F \, \| \, G$
2. $((p$ *ensures* q *in* $F \wedge p$ *unless* q *in* $G) \vee (p$ *ensures* q *in* $G \wedge p$ *unless* q *in* $F)) \Rightarrow$
   p *ensures* q *in* $F \, \| \, G$
3. $FP\text{-}(F \, \| \, G) = FP\text{-}F \wedge FP\text{-}G$

When statement sets S and T are disjoint, $\mathcal{M}(F \, \| \, G) = \mathcal{M}(F) \cup \mathcal{M}(G)$. The implications in the above theorem can then be substituted by equivalences.

4 An Example

In this section, we illustrate the usefulness of abstract programs through an example of sorting an array. We are given an input array $X[1 \cdots N]$ that is to be sorted in an increasing order by exchange sort and the result has to be stored in an output array $y[1 \cdots N]$. In our algorithm, array y is initialized to array X, and any two neighboring elements in y that are not in an increasing order are exchanged until the array is sorted. The following is the formal specification of the solution strategy as defined in [1].

(1) **invariant** y is a permutation of X
(2) $FP \equiv (M = 0)$
(3) $\langle \forall k : k > 0 : M = k \ \mapsto \ M < k \rangle$,
    where $M = \langle + \, i, j : 0 \le i < j < N \wedge y[i] > y[j] : 1 \rangle$.

Now, we need to design a program to meet this specification. Since all exchange operations can be executed asynchronously, the following program P (from [1]) which includes $N - 1$ statements, one for each pair of neighbors, may be written down and proved correct.

Program P
  initially $y = X$
  assign
    $\langle \; [] \; i : 1 \leq i < N : y[i], y[i+1] := sort'(y[i], y[i+1]) \rangle$
end

Here $sort'$ is a function that takes two arguments and returns them sorted in an increasing order. Program P is very simple (in fact, it is hard to imagine a simpler program). However, it can not be efficiently mapped to synchronous architectures. This is because all the exchange operations in P have been constrained to be executed asynchronously. In order to obtain an efficient program for synchronous architectures, we have to go back to the formal specification of the solution strategy and rewrite another program. Program Q follows from these considerations. In this program, all statements that can be executed concurrently are gathered into one multiple-assignment statement. Of course, this program has to be proved correct again.

Program Q
  initially $y = X$
  assign
    $\langle \| \; i : 1 \leq i < N \; \wedge \; even(i) : y[i], y[i+1] := sort'(y[i], y[i+1]) \rangle$
    $[] \; \langle \| \; i : 1 \leq i < N \; \wedge \; odd(i) : y[i], y[i+1] := sort'(y[i], y[i+1]) \rangle$
end

Although program Q is more suitable than P for synchronous architectures with an unlimited number of processors, it is difficult to map it to machines with a fixed number of processors. This is because the exchange statements of the program may need to be partitioned differently to reflect the number of processors. Thus, if the target architecture is not completely known at the initial stage of program implementations, then writing down a Unity program hinders (on account of its fixed synchrony structure) the portability of program development across different architectures.

The introduction of an abstract program overcomes these problems since its flexible synchrony structure avoids over-specification. We illustrate this by designing an abstract program $F = (S, A)$ for the above sorting problem. From the specification, a basic statement set S and an asynchrony relation A may be written down as follows.
  $S = \{t_i : 1 \leq i < N\},$
  $A = \{(t_i, t_j) : |i - j| = 1\},$
where $t_i :: y[i], y[i+1] := sort'(y[i], y[i+1])$.

As shown below, the proof of correctness of F is not any more difficult than the proof of P or Q. The proof obligation is to show that F satisfies conditions (1), (2), and (3).

Proof of (1): Straightforward and omitted.

Proof of (2):

  $FP\text{-}F$
  $\equiv$ {definition of fixed point}

$$(\forall i : 1 \leq i < N : y[i], y[i+1] = sort'(y[i], y[i+1]))$$
$\equiv$ {definition of $sort'$}
$$(\forall i : 1 \leq i < N : y[i] \leq y[i+1])$$
$\equiv$ {definition of M}
$$M = 0$$

Proof of (3): It is straightforward to see that the metric M never increases and that the reordering of any two neighboring elements can only decrease it. Therefore,
$$M = k \ \wedge \ y[i] > y[i+1] \ unless \ M < k.$$
Let i be any index for which the neighbors $y[i]$ and $y[i+1]$ are not in the right order, i.e., $y[i] > y[i+1]$. Consider the basic statement t_i that exchanges these two elements and any compound statement r containing t_i (i.e., $r = t_i \parallel \cdots$). Then, the execution of r will interchange $y[i]$ and $y[i+1]$ and reduce the metric, i.e.,

$\{M = k \ \wedge \ y[i] > y[i+1]\} \ r \ \{M < k\}$
$\Rightarrow \{M = k \ \wedge \ y[i] > y[i+1] \ unless \ M < k\}$
$M = k \ \wedge \ y[i] > y[i+1] \ ensures \ M < k$
$\Rightarrow$ {replacing $ensures$ by $\mapsto$ and taking disjunction}
$M = k \ \wedge \ (\exists i : 1 \leq i < N : y[i] > y[i+1]) \ \mapsto \ M < k$
$\Rightarrow \{M = k \ \wedge \ k > 0 \Rightarrow \ (\exists i : 1 \leq i < N : y[i] > y[i+1])\}$
$M = k \ \wedge \ k > 0 \ \mapsto \ M < k.$

This concludes the proof of correctness of the proposed abstract program F. Program F can be easily implemented on a variety of architectures and represents the abstraction of a number of Unity programs. In particular, programs P and Q are easily seen to be implementations of F.

5 Discussion

Stepwise development of programs is a well-known technique for programming [3, 4, 10]. It encourages a style in which much of a program's derivation is independent of any particular architecture; thus, alternatives can be retargeted during the later refinement stages without substantial program modification [1]. Stepwise development usually consists of two phases: property refinement and program refinement. During property refinement, a property of the specification is successively refined to a stronger property that is less abstract or closer to a machine architecture. Property refinement usually continues until it is clear as to how a program meeting the refined specification can be drawn up. This program forms the starting point for program refinement. During program refinement, a program is continuously refined until a complete running program on the target architecture is obtained. The issues addressed by program refinement include implementation of abstract data types, division of program into processes, and interprocess synchronization [8]. We expect the idea of abstract programs to be useful in the program refinement phase of program development. Support of flexible program structures in programming languages and design tools for concurrent programs may also alleviate some of the problems associated with mapping a program to different architectures.

The idea of abstract programs as discussed here first appeared in [5]. Abstract programs are partly motivated by the idea of *synchronic groups* proposed by Cunningham and Roman [2]. In their formalism, a program contains a set of transactions and a synchronic group is defined to be a subset of transactions that are executed synchronously.

However, as in Unity, a program in [2] has a completely specified synchrony structure; it is not possible to delay the specifics of statement composition until the target architecture is completely known.

Our work also has similarities with the *Conditional Rewriting Logic* proposed by Meseguer [6]. This logic models concurrency by term-rewriting and allows for concurrent rewriting of disjoint terms. The synchrony relation between rewritings of disjoint terms is not specified and may proceed in any order. Intuitively, we are modeling the same phenomenon through the idea of abstract programs.

References

1. Chandy, K. M., and J. Misra, Parallel Program Design: A Foundation, Reading, Massachusetts: Addison-Wesley, 1988.
2. Cunningham, H. C., and Roman, G., A Unity-Style Programming Logic for Shared Dataspace Programs, *IEEE Transactions on Parallel and Distributed System*, 1(3), 1990.
3. Dijkstra, E. W., A Discipline of Programming, Englewood Cliffs, New Jersey: Prentice-Hall, 1976.
4. Gries, D., The Science of Programming, New York: Springer-Verlag, 1982.
5. Liu, Y., and Singh, A. K., Parallel Programming: Achieving Portability Through Abstraction, *11th International Conference on Distributed Computing Systems*, 1991.
6. Meseguer, José, Conditional Rewriting Logic as a Unified Model of Concurrency, *SRI International Technique Report*, Feb. 1991.
7. Pratt, V., Modeling Concurrency with Partial Orders, *International Journal of Parallel Programming*, 15(1), Feb. 1986, pp. 33 – 71.
8. Singh, A. K., and Overbeek, Ross, Derivation of Efficient Parallel Programs: An Example From Genetic Sequence Analysis, *International Journal of Parallel Programming*, 18(6), December 1989.
9. Winskel, G., An Introduction to Event Structures, Workshop on Linear Time, Branching Time, and Partial Orders in Logics and Models for Concurrency, *Lecture Notes in Computer Science 354*, 1989, pp. 364 – 397.
10. Wirth, N., Program Development by Stepwise Refinement, *Communications of the ACM*, 14(4), April 1971, pp. 221 – 227.

Part 2: Linda

Current Research on Linda

David Gelernter

Department of Computer Science, Yale University, New Haven, CT 06520

Linda is a coordination language based on a shared, associative object memory—a "tuple space." This memory is directly accessible to all processes in an ensemble, whether they have access to a physically shared memory or (the more usual case) they are executing on memory-disjoint processors, in a distributed-memory parallel computer or a network of autonomous machines. The objects in this memory are tuples, either passive or active; an active tuple is a process, destined to turn into an ordinary passive tuple upon completion. Objects are removed using an associative matching protocol that resembles the "select" operation in a relational database. Commercial Linda systems (from Scientific Computing Associates[1]) support a single global tuple space; certain research implementations support multiple, first-class tuple spaces, and this is clearly the evolutionary direction of choice for Linda systems generally.

To the extent that Linda has been successful—a recent article in the trade publication *Digital Review* calls Linda "perhaps the best-known parallel-processing language available today,"[2] which may or may not be true, but is at least arguable—this success is based on four factors, two fairly abstract and two pragmatic.

Abstractly, Linda provides a radically *uncoupled* model of parallel computing, and it is a language design that places *simplicity* uppermost. "Uncoupling" has a space-wise and a time-wise aspect. Processes may communicate in Linda although they are mutually anonymous—a sender may generate data without knowing or caring about the identity of the recipient. This is "space-wise uncoupling." Processes may communicate although their lifetimes are disjoint—this is "time-wise uncoupling." The same characteristics might be claimed for any shared-memory system, but Linda takes matters a step further: in a conventional shared-memory system, your communication partners *are* constrained, in the sense that (at least) they must have access to the same address space that you do, and they must share your interpretation of memory addresses. Linda's shared memory on the other hand may encompass arbitrarily many separate computers without any physically-shared memory. Nor does a conventional shared memory blend smoothly into a file system or persistent object store, as a tuple space does. In practice, Linda-style uncoupling has tended to simplify the parallel programmer's task. It's no more possible to "prove" that Linda is simple than to prove that a Zen garden is simple. Empirically, many people do find Linda notably simple, and simplicity was the major design goal.

Pragmatically, Linda is a coordination language, designed to be mated with, not to supercede, a conventional sequential programming language. The typical parallel appli-

---

[1] New Haven, CT, USA; Linda is a registered trademark of Scientific Computing Associates.
[2] Oct. 21, 1991

cation begins life as a serial program that runs too slowly; retaining as much of the original, serial code as possible is obviously desirable. Retaining the expertise, tools and implementations centered on the serial language are desirable even in those cases where we build parallel applications *ab initio*. Finally, and the key ingredient so far as Linda's practical successes in commercial applications are concerned, highly efficient Linda implementations have been achieved on virtually all classes of asynchronous multiprocessors and networks. (These implementations are generally based on Nicholas Carriero's original work on efficient Linda systems.)

The papers gathered in this section are a good example of the range of current research on Linda. Linda research falls into three broad areas: extensions to the model itself, new implementation techniques and application studies.

The first category is the most "radical" in a sense; although Standard Linda exists (in the form of the commercial Linda implementation), Linda can also be understood as a "paradigm," like "Lisp" or "object-oriented programming," although of course on a far smaller scale. The basic ideas in Linda are so simple that they lend themselves to interpretations, extensions and refinements of all kinds. Fine-grained parallelism, databases and logic programming are three domains where Linda is arguably useful and appropriate, but they aren't supported in the "standard Linda" model. Three papers by Jagannathan, Anderson and Shasha, and Ciancarini explore alterations and additions to the basic Linda paradigm to make it useful in these three significant areas. Papers by Butcher and Zedan and by Zenith explore other instantiations of the Linda paradigm, in the framework of a more integrated type system and of a somewhat different notion of a tuple space (called a "context"). These last two are particularly heterodox (they are focussed respectively on "Problems with current Linda implementations" and "What's wrong with Linda," and in both cases—particularly the latter—the keepers of the current Standard Linda implementation would dispute the list of allegations). Both papers would be tossed out of the Linda church immediately, if there were a Linda church. (Luckily there isn't. And we, at any rate, have no plans to start one...)

Faasen's paper falls into the "implementation" category; this is in a sense the classical genre for Linda papers. Since the first papers describing the model, Linda has been regarded as a challenge to implementors at best, and unimplementable at worst. In fact, Scientific Computing Associate's commercial Linda system achieves efficiencies that are competitive with message passing on representative problems. It's pleasant to be able to report that the long-standing contention that Linda is necessarily inefficient has been carefully investigated and proven false. (There are implications here for *all* high-level parallel languages.) Nonetheless, Linda implementation in new hardware environments continues to pose interesting problems, and Faasen's paper describes one example.

Padget, Broadbery and Hutchinson's paper is an example of another extremely important category: how do you do X with language Y? (X in this case is Time Warp.) This last category is crucial as the language research community attempts to come to grips with the strengths and weaknesses of competing models. There aren't many published studies of this sort; there ought to be a lot more. The Carriero *et. al.* paper describes another appliction domain, applications that are "distributed" as opposed to "parallel."

The Linda research effort at Yale has gained immeasurably from research of the sort reported in these papers. In fact, Linda research is no longer a centralized resource; it's distributed, as appropriate. It's unlikely that any single approach to parallel programming will dominate the field any time soon. It *is* likely that a fairly small number of alternatives will hold sway over the next several years; we don't know the precise composition of the list, but we do know that Linda will be on it. Research of the sort reported here will contribute much to our understanding of what exactly this "Linda" ought to look like. Speaking more generally, Linda's success is one instance of the success of high-level parallel languages in general. As the design, construction and analysis of software ensembles comes to dominate research in software systems, this area will continue to be vitally important to the future of computing.

This article was processed using the LaTeX macro package with LMAMULT style

Expressing Fine-Grained Parallelism Using Concurrent Data Structures

Suresh Jagannathan

NEC Research Institute, 4 Independence Way, Princeton, NJ 08540

1 Introduction

Efficient support for fine-grained parallelism on stock hardware has been the focus of much recent research interest[1, 18]. The realization of this goal involves the design of linguistic devices for expressing concurrency, compile-time analysis techniques for constructing efficient implementations of shared data objects, and a runtime support system for managing lightweight threads. In this paper, we examine one specific approach to realizing fine-grained parallelism based on this general strategy. Our starting point is an explicitly parallel language that relies on *concurrent data structures* for expressing synchronization and communication constraints. We argue that given a toolbox of compile-time analyses for optimizing the representation of these structures, and a robust runtime system tailored for managing dynamically instantiated lightweight processes, fine-grained parallel applications can be made to run efficiently on stock multiprocessor hardware.

A concurrent data structure (CDS) is an abstraction that serves as a communication and synchronization repository for a collection of asynchronously executing processes. Explicitly parallel languages such as FCP[16], Concurrent Smalltalk[9, 11], C-Linda[5], MultiLisp[10] etc. permit many producers and consumers simultaneously to modify and read the contents of shared CDS objects. Consumers that access a component of such an object block until a producer provides a value. Advocates argue that programming with CDS objects leads to a methodology in which low-level process synchronization concerns are abstracted to high-level algorithmic design issues involving data structure access and generation.

There are several requirements that must be satisfied by any system intended to support fine-grained parallelism. First, synchronization must be cheap; in order to sustain acceptable performance in the presence of a large number of dynamically instantiated asynchronous processes, latencies introduced by context-switching must be very small. Second, linguistic mechanisms must be provided to express dynamic process creation and synchronization. Third, the communication medium used for process synchronization must be robust and highly concurrent; the semantics of this medium must impose no serialization requirements other than what is specified by obvious data and control flow dependencies.

On the surface, one would expect that the flexibility provided by CDS-based systems would make them an ideal device for expressing fine-grained parallelism. This has not been the case, however, for two reasons. First, the generality afforded by the semantics of most CDS proposals makes generating efficient representations difficult in the absence of either (a) advanced compile-time analysis or (b) specialized hardware[9, 14]. No system to our knowledge has seriously pursued the former approach; the latter alternative suffers from lack of portability and high cost. Consequently, many languages that implement some form of concurrent data structure do so by requiring user annotations to aid the compiler in generating a more optimal representation (*e.g.*, [2, 7, 13]). Requiring user annotations compromises abstraction, however; to take advantage of any annotation-based optimizations, users must be aware of the underlying machine topology and often require knowledge of the compiler implementation. Second, explicitly parallel languages such as C-Linda or FCP typically rely on low-level OS kernel support for process management and scheduling. The fact that synchronization and context switching is managed by the kernel means that fine-grained parallel programs written in these languages incur significant performance penalties; all scheduling decisions and thread management schemes must be implemented outside the purview of a dedicated runtime system sensitive to the language's semantics.

In this paper, we consider compile-time analysis techniques and runtime support mechanisms that offer the possibility of making concurrent data structures a viable tool for expressing fine-grained parallelism. To answer questions regarding how shared concurrent objects should be represented and partitioned, we define a suitably structured type inference system; the "type" of a concurrent data structure contains information regarding its patterns of usage and sharing. The runtime kernel effectively manages and schedules dynamically instantiated lightweight threads of control at the user level; the design of the runtime system makes it easy to control the amount of concurrency generated, and to dynamically load-balance available work among a processor ensemble.

The type system permits the construction of customized implementations of first-class concurrent data structures even in the presence of higher-order functions and recursive data structures. The manner in which structures are shared, the kinds of operations performed on a CDS object, the input-output behavior of these objects, and the communication structure of processes are all attributes that can be derived by this interpretation. The representations chosen for such structures reflect their use – thus, different instantiations of the same (high-level) structure may entail different (low-level) implementations.

The scheduling policies of the runtime system permit users to define a "lazy" process evaluation strategy. In the context of fine-grained parallelism, this permits users to create many more processes than exist physical processors *without* inducing any performance degradation. Processes are evaluated only if resources are available, or if their results are required. In the latter case, the process may be executed within the same context as the accessor; no separate thread of control need be created. In addition to lazy scheduling, users can specify various priority schemes for evaluating threads; the priority scheme chosen is influenced by information gleaned from the type system.

2 The Context

Our discussion is based on a semantics for concurrent data structures that is a significant generalization of Linda's tuple-space abstraction[5]. The sequential core of the kernel language (called $\mathcal{TS}^k$) used in this paper forms a higher-order strongly-typed strict functional language.

Tuple-spaces in $\mathcal{TS}^k$ are first-class objects. By way of introduction, a first-class tuple-space is a synchronization repository that may be bound to variables, passed as an argument to (or returned as a result from) functions, or embedded within data structures or tuples. A tuple-space defines a content-addressable shared associative memory. Its elements are ordered set of heterogeneous typed values or processes known as *tuples*. Fields in tuples can be retrieved using a simple pattern-matching procedure; failure to procedure a satisfactory substitution causes the initiating process to block. Such a process may resume only after a matching tuple is deposited into the specified tuple-space. The $\mathcal{TS}^k$ type system constrains all elements found in a given tuple-space to have the same length and type.

The paper is organized as follows. The next section describes the kernel language and provides further motivation for the problems addressed. Section 5 gives an overview of the type system and details how it can be used to optimize the representation of tuple-spaces. Section 7 provides a description of the runtime kernel on which $\mathcal{TS}^k$ runs; we develop some scheduling policies for $\mathcal{TS}^k$ processes that can be used to effectively realize fine-grained parallelism.

3 The Language

$\mathcal{TS}^k$ is a higher-order parallel programming language whose grammar is shown in Fig. 1. Its sequential core forms a simple higher-order lexically-scoped functional language with abstraction (λ), recursion (letrec), conditionals ($\rightarrow$), and sequencing (begin). $\mathcal{TS}^k$ also supports five operations for creating and manipulating tuple-spaces.

Creating a Tuple-Space

The expression, (make-ts), returns a reference to a new tuple-space object[1]. Since (make-ts) yields a reference to a tuple-space (and not the tuple-space itself), it follows that a tuple-space can never directly contain another tuple-space object. The semantics of tuple-spaces in this regard resembles the treatment of complex data structures in Lisp and similar heap (or reference) based languages.

---

[1] Throughout this paper, we will blur the distinction between a tuple-space object and its reference when clear from context.

$$
\begin{array}{lll}
\text{E} & ::= & \text{true} \mid \text{false} \mid c \mid x \mid s \mid \\
& & (\lambda \ (x_1 \ x_2 \ldots x_n) \ \text{E}) \mid (\text{E}_1 \ \text{E}_2 \ldots \text{E}_n) \mid \\
& & \text{letrec} \ x_1 = \text{E}_1, x_2 = \text{E}_2 \ldots x_n = \text{E}_n \ \text{in} \ \text{E} \mid \\
& & (\text{begin} \ \text{E}_1; \text{E}_2; \ldots; \text{E}_n) \mid \\[4pt]
& & \text{E}_b \rightarrow \text{E}_t \ ; \ \text{E}_f \mid \\[4pt]
& & (\text{make-ts}) \mid \\
& & (\text{put} \ \text{E} \ (\text{E}_1, \ \text{E}_2, \ \ldots, \ \text{E}_n)) \mid \\
& & (\text{spawn} \ \text{E} \ (\text{E}_1, \ \text{E}_2, \ \ldots, \ \text{E}_n)) \mid \\
& & (\text{rd} \ \text{E} \ (\text{T}_1, \ \text{T}_2, \ \ldots, \ \text{T}_n) \ \text{E}_b) \mid \\
& & (\text{get} \ \text{E} \ (\text{T}_1, \ \text{T}_2, \ \ldots, \ \text{T}_n) \ \text{E}_b) \\[12pt]
\text{T} & ::= & \text{E} \mid ?x
\end{array}
$$

Fig. 1. Grammar for TS^k.

Generating New Tuples

There are two operators that are used to deposit tuples. Given expressions $e_1, \ldots, e_n$ and an expression E_t that yields a tuple-space object T, the operation

$$(\text{put} \ E_t \ (e_1, e_2, \ldots, e_n))$$

evaluates (in the current evaluation environment) E_t to get T and similarly evaluates $e_1, e_2, \ldots, e_n$ to get values $v_1, v_2, \ldots, v_n$. A value is either a constant of base type (*e.g.*, an integer, Boolean or string), a list whose elements are all values, a function closure, or a tuple-space object. The tuple yielded by replacing each e_i with v_i is deposited into T The value of put is unspecified; it is executed for effect, not value.

Spawn is the *non-strict* counterpart of put. Evaluating the expression

$$(\text{spawn} \ E_t \ (e_1 \ e_2 \ \ldots \ e_n))$$

deposits a tuple containing a process for each of the e_i; the processes found in this tuple are evaluated in arbitrary order. The issue of whether processes are evaluated lazily or eagerly is left unspecified.

Processes in a **spawn**-generated tuple can communicate only via the tuple-spaces accessible to them. This is the sole form of inter-process communication available in the language – there are no side-effecting operations in the language other than those that manipulate tuple-spaces. Thus, processes do not transmit information by mutating non-tuple-space shared variables.

Retrieving Tuples

Get and **rd** are used to remove and read elements from a tuple-space. Consider the expression:

(rd E_t (e_1, e_2, ..., e_n) *body*)

Unlike tuple-generator expressions, each of the e_i may be either an ordinary TS^k expression *or* an identifier prefixed by a "?"; such an identifier is referred to as a *formal*. The evaluation of the above expression takes place in three steps. First, E_t is evaluated to yield a tuple-space object T. Second, every TS^k expression is evaluated to a value. The resulting object is known as a *tuple-template*: it consists of values and formals.

This template is pattern-matched against the passive tuples found in T. A successful pattern-match results in each of the "?"-prefixed identifiers in the template obtaining as their binding-value the value of the corresponding field in the tuple to which this template was matched. A template T successfully matches a tuple t if (a) T and t are of the same length, (b) all non-formal fields are pairwise equal and (c) the type of all formal fields in T are pairwise the same as the types of the corresponding fields in t.

The binding values associated with these formals are used in the evaluation of *body*. The value of the expression is the value yielded by *body*. Free references in *body* not defined by any of the formals are resolved relative to the **get** or **rd**'s lexical environment.

If the pattern-matching operation fails, the executing **rd** or **get** blocks. The evaluation of the expression resumes when a matching passive tuple is deposited into the requisite tuple-space. If there are several tuples that match a template, only one is chosen (non-deterministically) to establish the binding-values of the template's formals.

The **get** operation is semantically identical to **rd** except that the tuple chosen for the match is removed from the given tuple-space after the bindings for its formals have been established.

4 Motivation

First-class tuple-spaces are a flexible tool for specifying parallelism, but this flexibility comes at a price. In a naive implementation, matching a tuple template against the tuples found within a tuple-space T would require an exhaustive search of T's contents. The cost of such an operation limits the utility of tuple-spaces for expressing fine-grained concurrency.

Carriero[6] describes an approach to limit the overhead of tuple-space access in C-Linda that involves constructing partitions of the global tuple-space object; this construction is based on an examination of the structure and type of tuples found within a C-Linda program. Partitions are constructed by syntactic analysis and from type declarations. Tuple operations whose tuple arguments are type and length consonant get placed within the same partition; the representation of individual partitions is therefore customized to the structure of the tuples that occupy it.

Partitioning of this kind is unnecessary in TS^k since all components of a given tuple-space must have the same type signature; the length of the tuples occupying a tuple-space T contribute to T's type. On the other hand, the fact that tuple-spaces are now denotable (first-class) objects embedded within a higher-order language means that sharing and aliasing analysis is more complicated; simple textual examination of a program will not reveal all operations performed on a given tuple-space object. The inference system given below provides a basis for implementing these analyses in purely type-theoretic terms.

The type system gives information on the structural attributes of tuples and tuple-spaces, but it does not address important runtime issues such as dynamic process scheduling or protocols for fast context switching. We take the position that these issues are best tackled at runtime by a robust kernel that permits fast creation of lightweight processes, and whose data structures are chosen to make context switching cheap. One way that process creation costs are minimized is by deferring the evaluation of lightweight threads of control. Creating a thread[2] does not involve a system trap, or initial allocation of storage. Deferred or "lazy" threads can execute within the context of processes that require their results. Furthermore, since storage for these threads are acquired only when they are run, cache and page locality is improved. Optimizations of this sort on runtime data structures are designed to realize efficient fine-grained parallelism using conventional hardware. The compiler and runtime system are closely integrated; the compiler suggests priority schemes for managing threads within a given TS^k program based on process communication patterns it detects via type inference.

To motivate these techniques, we consider two simple examples. The first is a TS^k implementation of a memory cell (shown in Fig. 2); the second is a fine-grained parallel matrix multiplication procedure (shown in Fig. 3).

```
make-cell =
  (λ (initial-value)
       let cell = (make-ts)
       in
        (begin
           (put cell (initial-value));
           cell))

read-cell =
  (λ (cell)
       (rd cell (?v) v))

write-cell =
  (λ (cell v)
       (get cell (?old-v)
            (put cell (v))))
```

Fig. 2. A cell abstraction using first-class tuple-spaces. A cell contains exactly one element – before a new element is written, the old element is removed. The let form used in make-cell is syntactic sugar for application.

In the case of the memory cell abstraction, the following information can be deduced by the type system described in Sect. 5:

---

[2] A thread is the system representation of a process; it is a lightweight independent locus of control executing within the same address space as the process which created it.

1. A cell contains only tuples of length one whose type is that of **v**.
2. Cells that are read but never written do have not have any **get** operations performed upon them, and thus do not need read locks.
3. There are no constant-valued fields in a cell.
4. There are no processes that execute within the tuple-representation of a cell.

Flow analysis on this program would further reveal that every **put** operation either occurs after a **get** or after a (**make-ts**); furthermore, a **rd** never precedes a **put**. Thus, a cell can never contain more than one element and can never be read while empty.

Using this information, we can construct a suitable representation for the cell abstraction. Cell instances can be implemented as a single word object; write operations require the cell to be locked, whereas no locks are necessary on reads. In the absence of any structural or flow information on the tuples inhabiting a tuple-space, the representation must be chosen with no assumptions on the kind of operations performed, or the structure of the tuples read and deposited.

The matrix multiplication code is a straightforward (albeit naive) generalization of the simple sequential algorithm. Unfortunately, implementations of this code using conventional hardware and compilation techniques would exhibit poor performance. Most (efficient) parallel implementations of this problem often use a more complex program structure (*e.g.*, master-slave[4]) in which the number of processes generated is manually determined by the programmer, rather than automatically inferred by the compiler/runtime system.

The type inference system described below will deduce that A, B, and C should be implemented in terms of a matrix object with suitable locks associated with its elements (*e.g.*, if the result matrix is never mutated by **put** or **get** operations, it need not be locked before it is read). However, the inference system can make no judgments regarding optimal scheduling policies for the processes generated within **innerloop**. In a naive system where each **spawn** generated process creates an active thread of control, performance may be significantly compromised – many processes may compete for the same limited resources, leading to reduced throughput and increased contention.

Consider, therefore, the following implementation scheme for **spawn**. Each tuple field t found in a **spawn** operation evaluates to a *lazy thread*. A lazy thread has no associated storage (such as stack or heap). **Spawn** generated tuples are deposited into a tuple-space just as **put** generated ones are. No thread storage is allocated, but the resulting tuple (containing process-value fields) is deposited within the tuple-space.

A tuple operation that reads t initiates the evaluation of all of t's process-valued fields needed to determine if a successful match exists. The evaluation of these fields takes place either within the dynamic context of the process executing the read operation or within a new evaluation context. Having one process evaluate the code associated with another is known as *stealing*. Stealing a thread does not require the allocation of a new process context; new processes can run within the same context as the processes that demand their value.

Other implementations are conceivable that evaluate processes in a more eager fashion. We discuss some of these alternative strategies in Sect. 7. The choice of scheduling pol-

```
matrix_multiply =
  (λ (A B m n k)
     let C = (make-ts)
        build-vectors =
          (λ (A-row B-col)
              rec loop = (λ (i dot)
                               i > n →
                                 dot;
                                 (loop
                                   (1+ i)
                                   (+ dot (* (rd A (A-row i ?a) a)
                                             (rd B (i B-col ?b) b)))))
                in (loop 1 0))

     in rec loop = (λ (i)
                         i > m → C;
                         (begin
                           rec innerloop = (λ (j)
                                                 j <= k →
                                                 (begin
                                                   (spawn C
                                                    (i j
                                                    (build-vectors i j)))
                                                   (innerloop (+ j 1))))
                           in (innerloop 1);
                           (loop (+ 1 i))))
         in (loop 1))
```

Fig. 3. A fine-grained parallel matrix multiplication routine. The function takes two matrices with dimension m x n and n x k resp. and computes their product. Matrices are represented as tuple-spaces whose elements are triples, i,j,v, where (i,j) denotes a matrix index, and v is the value found at that index.

icy depends on the application; in the runtime system envisioned, programmers have flexibility in specifying the policy implementation of their choice.

5 The Type System

The type language is shown in figure 4. ι ranges over primitive types, α ranges over tuple-space type variables (TSVars), and β ranges over type variables representing other types. Besides tuple-space and tuple types, there are two other type constructors in our type language: $\to$ builds function types, and $\times$ builds cross products.

The type language subsumes an attribute language used to characterize tuple-space objects. The base elements in the attribute language consist of the "null" attribute (written ϕ), primitive kinds (*e.g.*, READ, WRITE, etc.), pairs of the form: $< process - id, kind >$, triples of the form: $< process - id, integer, type >$, and four-tuples of the form: $<$

process → *id, integer, expression, type* >. *Process-id* ranges over a set of unique identifiers denoting process labels.

Complex attributes are built from a sum constructor (+). Attributes capture specific properties of a tuple-space. Thus, $\mathcal{K}$ ranges over pairs consisting of kinds and the process labels of those processes that perform tuple-operations associated with this kind on the tuple-space; $\mathcal{F}$ ranges over structures containing the tuple indices of all formals (*i.e.*, "?" prefixed variables) occurring in **rd** and **get** operations, their types, and the process labels of those processes that perform **rd** and **get** operations on the tuple-space; $\mathcal{A}$ ranges over structures containing the non-formal expressions, their locations, types, and the process labels of those processes that perform tuple operations containing non-formal expressions on this tuple-space.

τ	::=	$\sigma \mid \iota \mid \tau \rightarrow \tau \mid \gamma$
σ	::=	$\alpha \mid \beta$
γ	::=	$(\delta, \mathcal{K}, \mathcal{F}, \mathcal{A})$
δ	::=	$\tau \mid \delta \times \delta$
S	::=	$\phi \mid$ READ $\mid$ WRITE $\mid$ REMOVE $\mid$ FORK
L	::=	an infinite set of unique identifiers
$\mathcal{K}$	::=	$\phi \mid (\mathbf{L}, \mathbf{S}) + \mathcal{K}$
$\mathcal{F}$	::=	$\phi \mid (\mathbf{L}, \mathbf{N}, \tau) + \mathcal{F}$
$\mathcal{A}$	::=	$\phi \mid (\mathbf{L}, \mathbf{N}, E, \tau) + \mathcal{A}$

Fig. 4. The Type Language.

For any tuple-space type γ and sum type, $\beta_1 + \beta_2 + \dots \beta_n$ associated with attribute A found in γ, there exists a predicate $\downarrow_A$ such that $\gamma \downarrow_A \beta_i$ is true for $1 \leq i \leq n$ and false otherwise. We also adopt a canonical reduction that eliminates duplication of elements in a sum type: $\tau + \tau = \tau$.

5.1 An Inference System

We define an inference system that associates a type expression with every $\mathcal{TS}^k$ syntactic construct. Let $\rho[a \mapsto \tau]$ denote the usual extension operation on partial functions. We write

$$\rho, \psi \vdash e : \tau$$

to indicate that $\mathcal{TS}^k$ expression e has type τ given assumptions ρ and process label ψ[3].

(Identifier)

$$\rho, \psi \vdash x : \tau \qquad \rho(x) = \tau$$

---

[3] The inference rules for conditionals and sequencing is straightforward and omitted here.

(Type Variable Instantiation)

$$\frac{\rho, \psi \vdash e : \tau}{\rho, \psi \vdash e : \tau[\sigma/\tau_1]}$$

(Abstraction)

$$\frac{\rho[x \mapsto \tau], \psi \vdash e_b : \tau_b}{\rho, \psi \vdash (\lambda\,(x)\,e_b) : \tau \to \tau_b}$$

(Application)

$$\frac{\rho, \psi \vdash e_1 : \tau_1 \to \tau_f \qquad \rho, \psi \vdash e_2 : \tau_1}{\rho, \psi \vdash (e_1\,e_2) : \tau_f}$$

(Recursion)

$$\frac{\rho[x \mapsto \tau], \psi \vdash e_1 : \tau \qquad \rho[x \mapsto \tau], \psi \vdash e_b : \tau_b}{\rho, \psi \vdash \text{letrec } x = e_1 \text{ in } e_b : \tau_b}$$

(Tuple-Space)

$$\rho, \psi \vdash (\mathbf{make-ts}) : \gamma$$

(Generate)

$$\frac{\begin{array}{c} \rho, \psi \vdash e_1 : \tau_1 \\ \rho, \psi \vdash e_T : \gamma \\ \gamma = (\tau_1, \mathcal{K}, \mathcal{F}, \mathcal{A}) \\ \gamma \downarrow_{\mathcal{K}} (\psi, \text{WRITE}) \\ \gamma \downarrow_{\mathcal{A}} (\psi, 1, e_1, \tau_1) \end{array}}{\rho, \psi \vdash (\mathbf{put}\ e_T\,(e_1)) : \gamma}$$

(Read – Non-Formal)

$$\rho, \psi \vdash e_1 : \tau_1$$
$$\rho, \psi \vdash e_T : \gamma$$
$$\gamma = (\tau_1, \mathcal{K}, \mathcal{F}, \mathcal{A})$$
$$\gamma \downarrow_{\mathcal{K}} (\psi, \text{READ})$$
$$\gamma \downarrow_{\mathcal{A}} (\psi, 1, e_1, \tau_1)$$
$$\rho, \psi \vdash e_b : \tau_b$$
$$\overline{A \vdash (\mathbf{rd}\ e_T\ (e_1)e_b) : \tau_b}$$

(Read – Formal)

$$\rho[x \mapsto \tau], \psi \vdash e_b : \tau_b$$
$$\rho, \psi \vdash e_T : \gamma$$
$$\gamma = (\tau, \mathcal{K}, \mathcal{F}, \mathcal{A})$$
$$\gamma \downarrow_{\mathcal{K}} (\psi, \text{READ})$$
$$\gamma \downarrow_{\mathcal{F}} (\psi, 1, \tau)$$
$$\overline{A \vdash (\mathbf{rd}\ e_T\ (?x)\ e_b) : \tau_b}$$

(Spawn)

$$\rho, \psi_1 \vdash e_1 : \tau_1 \qquad \psi_1 \text{ fresh}$$
$$\rho, \psi \vdash e_T : \gamma$$
$$\gamma = (\tau_1, \mathcal{K}, \mathcal{F}, \mathcal{A})$$
$$\gamma \downarrow_{\mathcal{K}} (\psi, \text{FORK})$$
$$\gamma \downarrow_{\mathcal{A}} (\psi, 1, e_1, \tau_1)$$
$$\overline{\rho, \psi \vdash (\mathbf{spawn}\ e_T\ (e_1)) : \gamma}$$

6 Using Type Information to Build Implementations

We can use type information to generate efficient compiled code. The representation chosen for a tuple-space is a reflection of the structure of the operations performed; the evaluation strategy used to schedule $\mathcal{TS}^k$ processes is predicated (partially) on the kinds of tuple-space operations executed by these processes.

For example, a tuple-space whose elements are never read or removed need not be shared among processors; a **spawn** operation executed for effect is a case in point.

Spawn operations performed on a tuple-space T can be compiled to take advantage of the structure of operations on T that read and remove tuples. Thus, if all **rd** expressions on T are of the form:

    (rd T (x,?y) y)

it is reasonable to defer the evaluation of E_2, and to proceed with the evaluation of E_1 in the expression:

(spawn T (E_1, E_2))

This is because the value of the formal in the rd operation is required only if the value of the first field (x) matches the value yielded by E_1. Insofar as the type system gives information about which fields serve directly in the matching process, and which fields do not, it can be used as a tool that provides a first approximation for determining process priorities.

Consider another simple priority scheme derived from type analysis. In this scheme, the order in which processes are evaluated depends on the kind of tuple operations they execute. Processes that do not manipulate or access tuple-space have higher priority than those that do. A process that makes no use of tuple-spaces is guaranteed not to block. Similarly, processes that manipulate tuple-spaces only via put and spawn never block while executing these operations; these processes should have higher priority than those that read or remove tuple-space elements. The type system associates each tuple space with a type; associated with each potential process is a union of the types of all tuple-spaces it accesses.

Tuple-space that have non-empty $\mathcal{F}$ components are associated with a set of *search keys*. The set of search keys for a given tuple-space define exactly those fields that are involved in a match. If the search keys for a given tuple-space denote tuple indices whose contents are all of homogeneous type, the tuple-space can be represented as an n dimensional matrix where n denotes the number of search keys for the tuple-space. The structure of this matrix is given by allocating a dimension for each tuple index corresponding to a search key; the contents of the nth dimension contains a parallel queue to hold the binding-values for the formals found in rd or get expressions that access this tuple-space. A concurrent array (*e.g.*, the matrices defined in the matrix multiplication example) or a homogeneous stream would satisfy these constraints.

Tuple-spaces that are read, but not removed need not have read locks. Such tuple-spaces also can be replicated; put operations entail a broadcast, but rd operations can use the local image of the tuple-space. This is a valid optimization since there are no global synchronization constraints imposed within this programming model.

7 Runtime Support

The inference system described in the previous section has its limitations – while it can be used to transform amorphous tuple-spaces into well-structured concurrent data objects, it does not implement or manage lightweight processes. To address this concern, we have developed a runtime kernel built on top of Scheme[15] called sos that we intend to use as a high-level operating system kernel for implementing fine-grained parallel programs written in $\mathcal{TS}^k$ and related dialects. $\mathcal{TS}^k$ operations on tuple-spaces are implemented in terms of sos operations on threads. The detailed design of sos is described elsewhere[12]; we list the salient properties of the system relevant to our discussion below:

1. Threads are treated as a Scheme abstraction with a well-defined representation. As a result, most thread management routines are expressed in terms of ordinary

Scheme procedures. The implementation relies heavily on Scheme's efficient support for higher-order lexically-scoped procedures, and makes few demands on the underlying OS kernel. Because threads are integrated into the base language, it is straightforward to customize or extend their implementation; unlike thread packages built on top of particular operating systems (such as CThreads/Mach[8, 17] or FastThreads/Topaz[1, 3, 18]) our implementation makes *no* assumptions on the availability or efficiency of particular OS services. Thus, there is no interface specification between our augmented Scheme system and the underlying operating system that must be upheld in order to effect any modifications to the thread abstraction.

2. The design provides flexibility to define new scheduling policies (*e.g.*, FIFO, LIFO, round-robin, priority, realtime, etc.). The SOS scheduler is implemented by a virtual processor (VP) that defines the high-level kernel for the thread system. A VP runs on top of a lightweight OS-managed (low-level kernel) thread. Each VP runs a dedicated scheduler responsible for providing thread-related services. All thread management structures used by the scheduler are represented in terms of Scheme objects. The heart of the scheduler is defined by a straight-line code procedure that allocates no storage.

3. Thread creation is cheap since SOS permits deferred or "lazy" evaluation of thread objects. Allocating a thread does not involve trapping into the system kernel, nor does it require initial allocation of storage. It is straightforward to implement storage allocation policies for threads in which stack and heap allocation is delayed until the thread is actually scheduled to run; the ability to express such a policy permits possible reuse of storage created by previously executed threads. This strategy lead to better cache and page utilization. It also allows users to experiment with a variety of different execution regimes – from *fully delayed* to *completely eager* evaluation.

The virtual machine on which $\mathcal{TS}^k$ processes execute consists of a number of queues responsible for holding threads in various states (runnable, suspended, etc.) The most interesting of these queues is the delay queue used to hold lazy threads. A lazy thread is a thread template – it contains information about the environment within which the process is to be run, but has no associated storage (*i.e.*, stack or heap). Lazy threads are an important innovation in SOS because they contribute directly to the efficient implementation of lightweight $\mathcal{TS}^k$ processes.

A lazy thread is executed only when one of the following conditions are satisfied:

1. When the virtual processor has no runnable threads on its ready queue, it may choose to evaluate a thread object found on its lazy queue.

2. When a virtual processor has no local runnable or lazy threads, it may choose to migrate a lazy thread from another VP. Note that because lazy threads have no associated storage, this migration operation does not entail significant data movement of stack or heap.

3. When a process P requires the value yielded by a lazy thread T, it can execute T's code within its own context. To do so, we need only swap P's dynamic environment information (*e.g.*, exception handler codes etc.) with T's. T can now run using P's stack and heap; no new process state is created. When T completes, P's dynamic context is restored and execution proceeds using T's result.

These options can be used to implement lazy process evaluation in $\mathcal{TS}^k$. To support fine-grained parallelism, we specify that the expression

(spawn T (E_1, E_2, ..., E_n))

creates n lazy threads. Each thread is a closure over the E_i. The effect of executing spawn is to deposit a tuple containing these threads into T. A rd or get operation that is subsequently performed on T which extracts this tuple can be implemented by either:

1. Transforming each of these lazy threads to "eager" ones, and then proceeding to examine other tuple elements.
2. Evaluating only those lazy threads corresponding to the E_i whose value is needed to determine if a match exists. These threads are evaluated in some sequential order within the execution environment of the process in which the rd or get operation is found. The lazy threads matched to formals are eligible for stealing only after it has been determined that a match exists.
3. Evaluating one thread in the execution environment of the current process, and transforming the others to eager threads. The current process blocks until the value of these threads is determined.
4. Ignoring the tuple altogether, allowing the runtime system to determine when the lazy thread components should be executed.

All these implementations help throttle the creation of new threads; delaying thread creation minimizes the time used by the runtime system to context switch and manage storage. sos permits programmers to choose their own scheduling policy; thus, different applications can be executed using scheduling disciplines tailored to their particular runtime requirements.

Consider the matrix multiplication example given earlier. The inner loop of the procedure generates $3 * (m * k)$ processes; there are $m * k$ processes responsible for computing the value of a field in the result matrix. Implementing spawn-created tuples in terms of lazy threads builds a result matrix defined as a tuple-space containing $m * k$ tuples – these tuples contain lazy threads that are initiated either when their values are demanded or when free processors remove them from the lazy queue and evaluate them. Thus, evaluating the rd expression in the following program fragment:

```
result = (matrix_multiply A B m n k);
(rd result (1,1,?v) v)
```

causes a tuple to be read from result; this tuple consists of three lazy threads. The first two processes compute indices of the result entry; the last process computes the value of this entry. At the time the above rd expression accesses such a tuple, the component fields of the tuple are either:

1. Lazy threads that have been transferred to the ready queue of some virtual processor and are currently under evaluation.
2. Threads that have finished evaluating.
3. Lazy threads that have not been allocated to a virtual processor and have not been stolen.

In the first case, the executing rd blocks on the appropriate threads and waits for their results. In the second case, the values generated by evaluating the lazy thread are retrieved from the thread's local state. In the last case, the operation can either (a) block waiting for the remaining threads to be evaluated, (b) look for another matching tuple, or (c) steal one of the lazy threads and evaluate it within the dynamic context of its process. The decision taken is based on the scheduling policy specified by the application, and runtime conditions at the time the operation executes.

Note that the third field need only be evaluated if a successful pattern-match is deemed to exist. Since the result computed by instantiating a lazy thread is cached within the thread's descriptor, subsequent rd 's on this tuple do not require establishing new thread contexts to evaluate these processes.

The type system can provide information useful in building a priority queue for lazy threads. By analyzing the type of result, it can be determined that the first two fields of result 's tuples are always used in matching operations whereas the third field is not. By building a priority queue structure for lazy threads in which these fields have higher priority than the third, we can increase the likelihood that any given rd will encounter fully evaluated matching fields when a matrix element is accessed.

8 Conclusions

A major criticism of concurrent data structures has been that efficient implementations are difficult to construct. To some extent, these criticisms have been valid particularly when considered in the context of fine-grained concurrency. Previous implementations of tuple-space languages, for example, have by and large ignored issues of runtime scheduling and storage management, and have not fully addressed the implications of using semantic-based compile-time analysis for building optimal representations of tuple-space structures.

This paper has focused on both concerns. Type analysis is used to infer structural properties of concurrent data structures. Generating efficient representations for tuple-spaces becomes tractable once their type structure is derived. A runtime kernel that permits deferred evaluation of thread objects makes it possible for programs to generate many fine-grained processes; resources for these processes are allocated only when the values they produce are required. Thus, the creation of active threads is dictated wholly by a program's runtime dynamics.

We expect these techniques will make concurrent data structures a natural linguistic device within which to efficiently exploit fine-grained parallelism in a variety of applications. Implementation of these ideas is currently underway.

References

1. Thomas Anderson, Edward Lazowska, and Henry Levy. The Performance Implications of Thread Management Alternatives for Shared Memory MultiProcessors. *IEEE Transactions on Computers*, 38(12):1631–1644, December 1989.

2. Rajive Bagrodia and Sharad Mathur. Efficient Implementation of High-Level Parallel Programs. In *Proceedings of the Fourth International Conference on Architectural Support for Programming Languages and Operating Systems (ASPLOS)*, pages 142–151, 1991.

3. A.D. Birrell, J.V. Guttag, J.J. Horning, and R. Levi. Synchronization Primitives for a Multiprocessor: A Formal Specification. In *Proceedings of the 11th Symposium on Operating Systems Principles*, pages 94–102, November 1987.

4. Nick Carriero and David Gelernter. How to Write Parallel Programs: A Guide to the Perplexed. *ACM Computing Surveys*, 21(3), September 1989.

5. Nick Carriero and David Gelernter. Linda in Context. *Communications of the ACM*, 32(4):444 – 458, April 1989.

6. Nick Carriero and David Gelernter. Tuple Analysis and Partial Evaluation Strategies in the Linda Precompiler. In *Second Workshop on Languages and Compilers for Parallelism*. MIT Press, August 1989.

7. Marina Chen, Young-Il Choo, and Jingke Li. Compiling Parallel Programs by Optimizing Performance. *Journal of Supercomputing*, 2:171–207, 198.

8. Eric Cooper and Richard Draves. C Threads. Technical Report CMU-CS-88-154, Carnegie-Mellon University, June.

9. William Dally *et. al.* The J-Machine: A Fine-Grain Concurrent Computer. In *Proceedings of the 1989 IFIPS Conference*, 1989.

10. Robert Halstead. Multilisp: A Language for Concurrent Symbolic Computation. *Transactions on Programming Languages and Systems*, 7(4):501–538, October 1985.

11. Waldemar Horwat, Andrew Chien, and William Dally. Experience with CST: Programming and Implementation. In *ACM SIGPLAN '89 Conference on Programming Language Design and Implementation*, pages 101–109, June 1989.

12. Suresh Jagannathan and Jim Philbin. A foundation for an efficient multi-threaded scheme system. Technical Report 91-009-3-0050-2, NEC Research Institute, 1991.

13. Charles Koelbel and Piyush Mehrotra. Supporting Shared Data Structures on Distributed Memory Machines. In *Second ACM Symposium on Principles and Practice of Parallel Programming*, pages 177–187, March 1990.

14. Greg Papadopolus and David Culler. Monsoon: An Explicit Token-Store Architecture. In *Proceedings of the 1990 Conference on Computer Architecture*, pages 82–92, 1990.

15. Jonathan Rees and William Clinger, editors. The Revised[3] Report on the Algorithmic Language Scheme. *ACM Sigplan Notices*, 21(12), 1986.

16. Ehud Shapiro, editor. *Concurrent Prolog : Collected Papers*. MIT Press, 1987. Volumes 1 and 2.

17. A. Tevanian, R. Rashid, D. Golub, D. Black, E. Cooper, and M. Young. Mach Treads and the UNIX Kernel: The Battle for Control. In *1987 USENIX Summer Conference*, pages 185–197, 1987.

18. Charles Thacker, Lawerence Stewart, and Edward Satterthwaite, Jr. Firefly: A Multiprocessor Workstation. *IEEE Transactions on Computers*, 37(8):909–920, August 1988.

Persistent Linda: Linda + Transactions + Query Processing*

Brian G. Anderson[1] *and Dennis Shasha*[2]

[1] Teradata Corp., 1919 Addison Ave., Berkeley CA 94704 USA
[2] Courant Institute, New York University, 251 Mercer Street NY, NY 10012 USA

1 Review of Linda

Since other papers in this book describe Linda in depth, we content ourself with a brief review of the essentials. Linda is a small set of extensions to an otherwise sequential language, like C or Pascal, allowing the construction of programs that perform computations in parallel. Communication between the cooperating processes is accomplished by using a globally accessible *tuple space* composed of *passive* and *active* tuples. A passive tuple is merely a sequence of values of various types similar to a Pascal record or C structure. Each value and type is call a *field* of the tuple and the acceptable data types include basic types (integer, float, etc.) as well as arrays and records of data types. Active tuples are also sequences like passive tuples, but include unevaluated function calls with a statically typed result in addition to values. An active tuple cannot be accessed until it becomes passive, when all functions in tuples fields have terminated and resulted in a value. Tuple space is heterogeneous; two tuples in the space can have different types and numbers of fields. Tuple space can contain multiple copies of a tuple, unlike mathematical sets or database relations.

Linda allows the programmer to access tuple space using four basic operations: two that place new tuples into tuple space and two that retrieve passive tuples from tuple space.

Out and **Eval**. These create active tuples and transform them into passive ones. The **out** command specifies some sequence of values and functions that are placed into tuple space:

```
out("example", f(x+y), 2, i)
```

The **out** command takes a sequence of constants, language variables, and unevaluated functions called a *pattern*. The expressions in the pattern's fields are called *actuals* since each has a static type and results in a value that is placed in the tuple. We differentiate between compile time constant expressions called *constant actuals* and expressions that must be evaluated at run time called *variable actuals*. In the previous example, fields one and three contain constant actuals while fields two and four contain variable actuals.

* This work is supported by the National Science Foundation grants ICI-89-1699 and CCR-9103953, and the Office of Naval Research grants N00014-90-J-1110 and N00014-91-J1472.

The process that created the active tuple by executing the above command would then transform the active tuple to a passive one by replacing each function with the value returned after evaluating the function. The **eval** command differs from **out** only in that a new process is created to transform the functions into values. This is how Linda dynamically creates new concurrent processes.

In and **Rd**. These bring a single passive tuple into a process' memory space. Retrieval is associative using an exact match mechanism. Like **out** and **eval** the pattern argument has a sequence of actuals, however, it also contains formals that retrieve tuple data. Formals can bind tuple field values to language identifiers (*binding formals*) or specify the type of the tuple field without binding the data (*projection formals*). An example retrieval command,

```
in("example", i, ?j, ? char *),
```

has actuals in the first two fields, a binding formal in the third field that binds the field value of the tuple to identifier j, and, a projection formal in the fourth field. The projection field specifies that the field must have type **char** but does not bind the data to any variable. The number of fields and each of their types must be derivable at compile time. A pattern and a tuple (or two patterns) are *pattern-similar* if the number of fields and type of each field in one is identical to the number of fields and type of each field in the other. PLinda can determine if a pattern and a tuple are pattern-similar at compile time. A tuple in tuple space matches the pattern if the two are pattern-similar and actuals in the pattern are equal to values in the corresponding fields of the tuple. If two or more tuples in tuple space match a retrieval operation's pattern then one is chosen arbitrarily. The **in** and **rd** operations differ in that **in** removes the matching tuple from tuple space after copying it to process memory while **rd** leaves the tuple in tuple space. If there are no matching tuples then the operations will block until a matching tuple appears in tuple space for retrieval. This blocking behavior is used to coordinate the different processes working concurrently on different parts of the overall task. A non-blocking predicate version of each retrieval command is available (**rdp** and **inp**) which returns true if a matching tuple is found and false otherwise.

A much more detailed description of basic Linda concepts (global tuple space, patterns, the semantics of the six Linda commands, and using Linda to write parallel programs) is contained in the original Yale papers [1] [2] [3] [4].

2 Motivation for Persistent Linda

In a world that is fairly groaning under the babel of new programming models, a new model must give a convincing justification for its existence. In this section, we will discuss our reasons and goals for extending Linda and how this new model improves existing environments.

Persistent Linda attempts to unify two different kinds of parallelism.

- *Cooperative parallelism* — multiple processes run concurrently to solve a single unit of work.
  In this environment, the cooperating processes need facilities to share intermediate results and synchronize their activities.

– *Competitive parallelism* — multiple processes run concurrently, but each performs a separate piece of work competing with other processes for shared resources.

In this environment, processes need facilities to ensure that they see only the completed work of other processes. That is, they do not wish to share intermediate results. The basic correctness goal is that each process appears to execute in isolation (in the jargon, serializably and in an all-or-nothing manner).

2.1 Making Linda Even More Beautiful

One of the attractive aspects of Linda is that it doesn't try to convert programmers to a new language. It provides a virtual shared memory model and a set of language extensions that can be applied to any language. Furthermore, the model is very general and enables the programmer to use different parallel programming strategies to solve a problem.[3]

Persistent data manipulation is an important programming tool that most existing languages fail to provide. Rather than develop a new language incorporating persistence, as many have done, we sought simple, language-independent extensions, similar to Linda's, that would enable an existing program language to work with persistent data.

Happily, Linda already provides the core of a persistent system. A distributed persistent system provides a way to store data without requiring the programmer to know where data is located; all programs have a global view of the persistent store. Access should also be associative so that the programmer need not know how data is stored. Linda's global tuple space is very close to what we wanted, but lacks persistence. In Linda, tuple lifetimes end when the programs that manipulate them end. From the database perspective, Linda also lacks sufficient associative retrieval power and transactional semantics. We created Persistent Linda by using Linda as a starting point and adding extensions that transform it into a tool for manipulating persistent data.

Specifically, Persistent Linda extends Linda by providing:

1. a transaction notion (i.e. serializability, crash recovery, and persistence).
2. extended tuple patterns to allow non-equality matching and relational database join semantics.
3. in-place updates
4. hints (pragmas) to be supplied by the programmer so that data organization and process scheduling is more efficient.

We tried to make the extensions mutually orthogonal whenever possible. We wanted PLinda to be nearly as simple to learn as Linda.

Transactions, however, are a form of competitive parallelism. Linda, by contrast, is a tool for cooperative parallelism. Persistent Linda resolves this tension by allowing many *processes* to cooperate within one *transaction*. That is, a transactional moat surrounds a cooperative castle if you will forgive a metaphor inspired by this workshop's surroundings.

Besides adding persistence and transactions to the model, we also include constructs that are useful in manipulating the large amounts of data that are likely to arise in persistent applications. While a simplified extended model with only persistent tuples and transactions could perform these functions, we include bulk manipulation primitives

---

[3] See [4] for a discussion of how Linda supports *result*, *specialist*, and *agenda* parallelism.

in PLinda to ease the coding burden of the programmer and to present a higher level target for optimization. For example, programs often retrieve a tuple, modify one of the fields and place the tuple back in tuple space. One can express such modifications in Linda, but if the tuple contains large array fields, retrieval into processor memory followed by placement back into stable storage can be very expensive. The preprocessor could be modified to recognize such sequences of commands and optimize them, but this can be difficult and the programmer usually has update-in-place in mind when coding. The benefits warrant a special modify access command. Similar arguments led us to add syntax allowing access to sets of tuples and more powerful pattern matching.

2.2 How is PLinda better?

Persistent Linda borrows ideas from both the original Linda model and from database management systems (DBMS). As a result, a user of original Linda and a user of a traditional DBMS will find familiar features in Persistent Linda and may wonder what advantages it provides over their current systems. We will examine each of these existing systems and attempt to identify PLinda's niche.

Linda with Files. The Linda programmer usually needs persistent storage and has to implement it manually. For example, initialization data and result data are external to the program and must be copied into and out from Linda's shared tuple space. This tedious transfer step is not needed for PLinda programs because PLinda has persistent tuple spaces.

But tedium is the least of the problems. In the Linda model, the programmer has two ways of implementing persistence: use the normal file mechanism supplied by the underlying programming language or extend Linda to periodically checkpoint its shared tuple space. Let us examine each in turn.

- A programmer using the Linda model with files must explicitly do all transfers between the file data format and Linda tuples. In Linda's parallel environment, the programmer must implement concurrency control, so that one process does not accidentally overwrite the changes of another process. All this can be implemented, but the result may be awkward if it forces the programmer to use one mechanism for manipulating persistent data and another for manipulating the shared tuple data. Persistent Linda presents a unified model to the programmer as well as concurrency guarantees.
- Another alternative that might occur to the Linda programmer is to extend Linda by periodically checkpointing the shared tuple space, i.e., writing it all out as of some moment in time. This can prove punishing to performance if done often. If done too seldom, then much work is lost after a failure. In either case, the work that is lost is hard to identify precisely (e.g. do you remember exactly what files you have modified in the last three days?). PLinda provides transactions which are a finer-grained mechanism that saves changes as they are committed. Programmers are likely to remember what transactions they are running at the time of a crash. Finally, PLinda's transaction mechanism provides the atomicity and concurrency control for competative parallelism that checkpointing, by itself, does not.

DBMS with Multiprocessing The other system, a traditional DBMS, already has transaction facilities and persistent data. What does PLinda add? The two word answer is cooperative parallelism. Let us enumerate the features such parallelism requires on asynchronous hardware.

1. Allow each of a set of cooperating processes to access and partition a shared collection of work items. That is, we want to ensure that each work item is eventually done by exactly one process.

   In a DBMS, such a description would have to be in the database. A transaction that accessed the shared data, deleted some work item, and then performed some work could easily block other transactions from doing useful work until it completed, however. For example, if the work items are held in a table and transaction T scans the table for the first work item w available, then T will prevent other transactions from scanning past w. In Persistent Linda as in pure Linda, one can use "to do" tuples and perform simple "in" commands. Two such commands on different tuples do not lock one another out.

2. Allow cooperating processes to communicate.

   Since communication requires a write by the sender and a read by a receiver, performing communication through a database will require that the sender commits before the receiver can read the sent data.[4] One might call this *post-mortem communication*. In Persistent Linda, cooperating processes can use the normal Linda in and out commands.

3. Provide synchronization mechanisms (barriers, semaphores, etc.) to coordinate collections of cooperating processes [5].

   Encoding a barrier with its associated semantics (no one continue until everyone has reached this point) into a DBMS seems challenging to say the least. (The least ugly solution would use a trigger that would fire when everyone had incremented some shared variable. The variable would likely suffer from concurrency control contention, however.) Most practical applications would probably use operating system facilities. However, this would increase the code complexity. Again, Persistent Linda can use the pure Linda facilities.

Traditional Linda is designed for cooperative parallelism, while a traditional DBMS is designed for competitive parallelism. Persistent Linda tries to combine the two. Applications that need parallel cooperation, persistence, all-or-nothing updates, and concurrency control should at least consider PLinda. In following sections, we define our extensions in more detail. All examples in this document use a "C" flavor of PLinda.

3 Tuple Patterns

As previously explained, a *pattern* is a sequence of *actuals* and *formals*. A tuple matches a pattern if the two are pattern-similar and any actual values in the pattern match the

---

[4] Most commercial database systems allow certain locks to be released before a transaction ends. These are usually read locks, but sometimes write locks. Such locks might make communication possible between ongoing transactions. Since using this option jeopardizes the recovery of the concerned data items, however, use of these locks might cause mysterious errors in a complicated application.

corresponding values in the tuple. In a database sense, a match is simply a selection on equality among the tuples of the tuple space.

Formals are used to bind data in the retrieved tuple to language identifiers. PLinda extends Linda's pattern matching capability by adding non-equality matching, intra-field comparisons, projection of array fields, and joining of tuples. A formal is compared to a range of values by appending a suffix to the formal, using the following notation borrowed from mathematics:

- :$[x, y]$, the closed interval of values i such that $x \le i \le y$.
- :(x, y), the open interval of values i such that $x < i < y$.
- :$(x, y]$, the interval of values i such that $x < i \le y$.
- :$[x, y)$, the interval of values i such that $x \le i < y$.

where x and y are either constant actuals, variable actuals, or binding formals of the same type as the modified formal. The pattern (`"count"`, `?int *:(-2,6]`) is matched by the tuples (`"count"`, `6`) and (`"count"`, `-1`), but not (`"count"`, `-2`) or (`"count"`, `7`). If either range limit value is omitted from the range (i.e. `( ,y]`) then the range is unrestricted for that limit. Only PLinda types that support ordering are allowed ranges; structures, unions, arrays, and identifier types may not have range modifiers.

The placement and retrieval of arrays in tuple fields use the same mechanisms as Linda. A limitation of Linda is that the entire array must be retrieved into memory in order to access any part. This can be inefficient if the array is very large and the amount accessed is very small. A PLinda pattern may specify that only a projection of the array be retrieved when a tuple is read or removed for tuple space. A *slice* modifier appended to the variable formal indicates the portion of the field array the user requires:

```
int *ptr, ary[] = {1,2,3,4,5,6,7,8,9,10};
.
/* put array into tuple space */
out("array", ary);
.
/* retrieve only the 3rd through 7th element */
in("array", ?ptr:{3..7});
```

The slice limit values are constant (as above) or variable actuals. However, only one of the integer types, **int**, **short**, or **long**, may limit a slice. Clearly the array matched must have at least as many elements as the upper limit index. Note that slice modifiers and range modifiers are mutually exclusive.

All occurrences of binding formals with the same base language variable retrieve the same value in a PLinda pattern. For example, the formal "`?i`" appearing in field two and in field three implies that these two fields are equal:

```
in("example 1", ?i, ?i).
```

The **rd** and **rdp** operations accept sequences of patterns called *multiple patterns* whose component patterns are referred to as *sub-patterns*. The semantics of a multiple pattern are those of a relational join. That is, those elements of the cross-product of tuples matching each sub-pattern are chosen whose values are the same in positions corresponding to formals having the same variable names. For example,

```
("day", ?num, "Friday")("month", ?num,
                              ?name, ?year)
```

will match the pair

```
("day",5,"Friday") ("month",5,"May",1948),
```

and the pair

```
("day",4,"Friday")("month",4,"April",1951),
```

but not

```
("day",5,"Friday") ("month",4,"April",1951).
```

If a **rd** accepts the first match, num will get the value 5, name will get "May", and year will get 1948. A multiple pattern may, in general, contain any number of sub-patterns. Fields with binding formals of the same identifier are equal even between sub-patterns.

The PLinda operations **rd** or **rdp**, including the **all** variations discussed later, can take multiple patterns. Tuple removal commands (**in**, **inp**, and their variants) may not have multiple patterns since any conceivable definition for tuple removal is unsatisfactory. (The problem is similar to the view update problem for views defined by joins in relational query languages.) **Out** and **eval** are also only allowed a single pattern with the additional requirement that they cannot contain any binding formals.

4 Transactions

In order to implement persistence, concurrency control, and crash-resilience, databases use transactions. Transactions require the existence of stable storage, i.e. storage assumed to survive failures (perhaps by being replicated). For PLinda, stable storage is associated with the persistent tuple space.

Transactions have three properties:

1. Crash recovery. If a transaction T commits, then all updates of T are guaranteed to be on stable storage. If T aborts, then any updates done by T to stable storage are undone.
2. Serializability. A concurrent execution of committing transactions behaves as if the transactions executed one at a time.
3. Permanence of effect. Data on stable storage will remain there until deleted by a transaction.

In most database systems, these two requirements are implemented by a protocol known as strict two phase locking[5]

The transaction notion is often useful in programming systems, since one may want to know that something has completed and is safely stored. For example, assume there is a collection of tuples with English text and tuples with translated French text are being created. If only half the tuples were translated, the tuple space would be inconsistent

---

[5] A lock (read or write) is acquired on every data item before the item is accessed and all locks are released at the point of commitment. Releasing all locks at the end prevents other transactions from reading uncommitted updates.

since there would be no way to refer to some tuples in French that can be referred to in English.

There are two mechanisms provided in PLinda for using transactions. Like **eval**, **xeval** adds an active tuple to tuple space and creates a new process to convert the active tuple to a passive one. All PLinda operations executed during the conversion — including the creation of the final passive tuple — are included in a transaction. If the active-to-passive tuple conversion is successful then all changes to tuple space are made permanent and recoverable. The conversion can fail because of a spontaneous abort operation, **xabort**, or because of a lock conflict that results in a deadlock; in that case, any modifications are rolled back and the active tuple is destroyed. The **xeval** command can take an optional argument, **on abort**, and a second pattern. After abort, the process creates a new active tuple based on the second pattern and converts it to a passive tuple. However, this conversion is not part of any transaction. The **on abort** pattern allows the programmer to take some action if the transaction aborts.

The second transaction mechanism does not create a new process for the transaction. A transaction begins when a **xstart** command is executed and ends with a **xcommit** or **xabort** command. Any PLinda operations executed between a transaction's beginning and end are included in the transaction. If the transaction ends with **xcommit**, then all modifications to tuple space are written to safe storage and all updates will be recoverable; if the transaction ends with **xabort**, then all transaction modifications are rolled back and execution resumes by returning at the **xstart** command that began the transaction. A false return value indicates the command is restarting. By checking the value returned by **xstart** the program can detect a spontaneous abort and do special processing.

If there are hardware failures (processor failure, communication failure, etc.), transaction semantics for both constructs are preserved; however, the *entire* program is aborted if a hard failure occurs for any child thread. The program must be restarted by the user.

The **xeval** construct is easier to use than **xstart** because the transaction automatically ends when the active tuple to passive tuple conversion is complete. A transaction started with **xstart** must have a matching **xcommit** or **xabort** operations in every thread of control. If the programmer erroneously omits a termination, then later operations will inadvertently be included in the transaction. **xeval** is also a better construct for the purpose of implementing robust parallel computation (section 5). The **xeval** process is easier to restart because all initial data for the process is contained in the pattern argument. The **xstart** construct is provided to support programs that create many transactions without suffering the overhead of creating a new process each time.

No process will read dirty (uncommitted) updates because processes modifying tuples hold write locks on those tuples until the transaction ends. No nesting of transactions is allowed; a process must end an active transaction before beginning a new transaction.[6] An **xcommit** or **xabort** of a transaction that has already terminated is ignored by PLinda which allows a program to have multiple termination statements for a transaction.

The following two examples use transactions to convert English month tuples to French month tuples. (The "all" construct, to be explained later in detail, applies to all matching tuple instead of just a single one. The curly brackets following "all" indicate a statement that will apply to all matching tuples.) The first example uses **xeval**:

---

[6] We are currently enhancing PLinda to allow nested transactions to support a prototyping language under development at NYU.

```
/* convert English to French */
int translate() {
    /* transaction begins when this function is
       invoked in an xeval() */
    static e_to_f[12] = {"Janvier", ..., "Decembre" };
    int i = 0;
    inp("month", ?number, ? char*, ?year) all {
        if (number < 1 || number > 12)
            xabort;         /* an invalid tuple was found.  all previous
                               inp and out operations are rolled back. */
        else
            out("mois", number, e_to_f[number-1], year);
                            /* if condition was false then this is still
                               a member of transaction. */
        i++;
    }
    return i;
}

char *name, *nom;
rd("month", 1, ?name, 1990); /* not part of transaction */
xeval("committed", translate()) on abort ("aborted");
rd("mais", 1, ?nom, 1990); /* not part of transaction */
```

The second example uses **translate()** from the previous example and **xstart**. The result is the same as in the first example, but no new process is created for the transaction:

```
int translate() {
    ...
}

char *name, *nom;
rd("month", 1, ?name, 1990); /* not part of transaction */
if(!xstart) {
    /* caught a spontaneous abort */
    out("aborted");
} else {
    /* transaction begins */
    out("committed", translate());
    xcommit;        /* end transaction */
}
rd("mois", 1, ?nom, 1990); /* not part of transaction */
```

Since any PLinda operation, including **eval**, can be included in a transaction, many threads can work on a transaction. However, all the child threads must terminate before the transaction commits; otherwise, the transaction is aborted. Any thread can abort the transaction. For transactions started using **xstart**, however, only the thread that began the transaction can commit it; a commit by another thread causes the transaction to abort. When a transaction aborts, all child threads are terminated.

By default, all PLinda operations in the scope of an active transaction are members of that transaction and are accompanied by implicit locks. In an environment where tuples are being used for communication among cooperating processes, some tuple operations *should not* acquire transaction locks. For example, if a counter tuple used to assign work is locked by a transaction, then only one work item can execute at a time since the lock on the counter tuple would be held until the end of the transaction. PLinda allows an operation to be excluded from the transaction by enclosing it in a **nolock()** wrapper; for example, in

```
int sum = 0;
.
tid = xstart;
nolock(rd( "example 8","work count",?count)all
   {sum += count;});
.
out("example 8", "other work", ...);
```

"**nolock(rd("example 8", "work count", ...)all)**" is not a member of the transaction. If the transaction aborts, the **rd(...)all** operation is *not* rolled back, but the **out** operation is. **nolock** does respect locks already present on tuples so that programs expecting to maintain data consistency using locks are not surprised by other processes modifying a tuple using **nolock**.

We should point out that PLinda has no protection against phantom tuples. An example of a phantom occurrence is in a database of assets and liabilities that must always be kept in balance: every time an asset is added, so is a liability. Suppose one program checks that the balance is maintained by separately totaling all assets and liabilities using **rdp(...)all**, and then comparing the totals. If a new asset and liability pair is added to the database after the assets are totaled, but before the liabilities are totaled, then the check program will detect a false out-of-balance condition. The phantom asset tuple is visible before the matching liability tuple could be added. In PLinda it is the programmer's responsibility to prevent phantom tuples from affecting the desired computation. The out of balance error can be avoided if the check program uses a tuple to signal other processes that addition of assets and liabilities should be suspended.[7]

5 Slowdown Failures

Like database management systems, Persistent Linda tries to guarantee that any concurrent execution of transactions will have the same effect as a sequential execution of those transactions that commit during execution, while aborted transactions have no affect. To make this guarantee most systems must assume that all failures are *soft fail-stop*. This

---

[7] It is possible to extend the model to handle phantoms by adding predicate locking. The checking program would begin a transaction and issue:

```
lock(<asset pattern>);
lock(<liability pattern>);
```

All access (**rd**, **in**, **eval**, or **out**) to tuples matching this pattern by processes not in the transaction is prevented until the transaction ends. We are considering adding predicate locking to a later version of PLinda.

means that a process fails by halting and that, while main memory is lost, there is a portion of memory (usually implemented on redundant disks) called *stable storage* that is reliable and will survive the failure. An additional implicit (and critical) assumption is that such failures can be reliably diagnosed by using timeouts.

The fail-stop failure assumption is valid for hardware failures on many systems. Vendors sell systems that detect malfunctions within a few machine cycles and halt by announcing failure. When the system is repaired, the processor "knows" that it has failed and performs special recovery activities when it is restarted. However, in a distributed processing environment, even if all the individual processors are running properly, some processors may be unable to communicate with other processors due to a network failure or some other temporary failure, rendering the assumption that timeouts are a reliable diagnosis tool invalid. In this case, no processor will halt and announce failure.

We can extend PLinda to survive a more general class of failures: *slow-down* failures. We assume that our model system can support multiple threads of control called processes. A process can fail by either stopping (it will never execute another instruction) or by slowing down (it may eventually speed up again). We do not assume that we can distinguish between the two types so we call either a slow-down failure. Notice that slow-down failures contain the class of fail-stop failures. Network congestion and cycle stealing by high priority jobs are better modeled by slow-down failures.

An algorithm that tolerates slow-down failures was first presented by Shasha and Turek [6]. A unit of work to be done is a *transaction* and a thread of control working on the transaction is an *actor*. Shasha and Turek's algorithm overcomes slow-down failures at client sites by dispatching new actors to complete the work left unfinished by the slow actor. The new actor is created dynamically as soon as the system detects that the slow actor has slowed down. The algorithm does not assume that any actor can be reliably killed. It is possible for actor a to slow-down fail; actor a' is dispatched to begins to redo the work; and, then, a speeds up again. All actors working on the same transaction share locks, but do not read one another's updates. An actor that continues to execute after another actor for the same transaction commits does not update any pages. Using two-phase locking and a form of no undo/no redo recovery, the algorithm is able to guarantee the following correctness criteria:

1. If a transaction commits, then the effect is as if exactly one actor for that transaction commits.
2. Committing actors will behave serializably with respect to other committing actors.
3. The failure of any actor will not prevent other actors from making progress.

Shasha and Turek assumed a multi-processor reliable shared memory system supporting the atomic hardware primitive "compare&swap" for their computational environment. It is straightforward to extend the algorithm to distributed reliable memory, but distributed unreliable memory requires randomization to achieve consensus.

Persistent Linda provides protection, called *robust processing*, from slow-down failures at client sites. Little or no modification to the actual language is needed because the unit of work, the transaction, is conveniently specified using the existing **xeval** construction.

The model could make every **xeval** statement a robust transaction and no language change would be necessary. However, we feel it is better to give the programmer the choice of having robust processing, so the system provides the facility only when the pragma "**robust**" appears before an **xeval**. The system identifies slow **xeval** actors[8] and dispatches redundant actors to ensure that the transaction completes. Of course, the redundant actor could slow down also and a new redundant actor could be dispatched. Redundant actors will be dispatched until the transaction commits. As in the Shasha and Turek algorithm, all actors for the same transaction share locks.

Once an actor for some transaction t commits, the PLinda server(s) will

- ignore future update requests from other actors executing on behalf of t and will attempt to kill those actors; and
- remove the locks held on behalf of t.

6 Set-based constructs

Since many applications, particularly database ones, are expressed naturally in sets, we expect operations that iterate through sets of tuples to be useful. In vanilla Linda, a **rd** may repeatedly return the same tuple, even if several other tuples match. In PLinda, retrieval operations (**in**, **inp**, **rd**, **rdp**, and their combination commands) have an **all** variation. Each takes a pattern (multiple patterns are allowed with **rd** and **rdp** only) and an instruction block as arguments:

```
/* sum the count field of all tuples matching the
   tuple pattern.
*/
int i, sum = 0;
.
inp("example 8","count",?i)all {sum += i;};
```

The above example would sum the third field of every tuple in tuple space matching the pattern.

Instead of returning one tuple, the **all** variation of the command returns *every* tuple matching the pattern including duplicates. The code in the block of the command is executed, with variable formals bound to the returned tuple's values, each time a new tuple is retrieved. Except for a guarantee that each tuple is retrieved only once, the semantics are that of a loop with the tuple operator at the head and the code block as the body:

```
while(<command> <pattern>){
   <code block>
}
```

where <command> is the command the **all** is modifying. All variables, global or local to this block's scope, and functions are accessible allowing calculations of functions such as total or average. The code block of an **all** variation is any sequence of base-language or PLinda commands. The **all** variation for a combination command (see section 7) uses the code block of the combined command as the iteration code block.

The **all** variation of a command is *not* atomic; the set of tuples that match the pattern can change before the command completes. We could have used "snapshot" semantics

---

[8] For our discussion, an actor is some client evaluating the **xeval** operation.

requiring that when the command is issued all tuples currently matching the pattern are retrieved, but we felt that this was too difficult to implement efficiently. We are interested in the reactions of potential users.

Another example creates a collection of month tuples with all strings in French without destroying those in English.

```
rdp("month", ?number, ?char *, ?year)all {
    static e_to_f[12] = {"Janvier", "Fevrier", "Mars",
                         "Avril", "Mai", "Juin",
"Jullet", "Aout","Septembre",
"Octobre","Novembre",
         "Decembre" };

    out("mois", number, e_to_f[number-1], year);
}
```

If the month tuples are partitioned across several machines, then we can partition the rdp(...)all using **eval** to create sub-processes to convert each month concurrently:

```
main(){
for(i=1; i<=12; i++)
    eval("done",convert(i));

for(i=1; i<=12; i++)
    in("done",i);
}
.
int convert(month)
int month;
{
    char *e_to_f[12] = { "Janvier", ..., "Decembre" };

    rdp("month", month, ?char *, ?year)all {
        out("mois", month, e_to_f[month-1], year);
    }
}
```

When using the **all** modifier with multiple patterns, we do not specify if the joins are computed before execution of the command block or if they are incrementally computed each iteration of the loop. The reason is similar to the one used for choosing weak **all** semantics: allow a greater choice in selecting the most efficient implementation strategy. This will make an **all** command that has its source tuples modified during computation behave differently depending on the underlying implementation. Suppose the following example is run:

```
int i, j, k;
```

```
rdp("example1", ?i, ?j)("example2", ?i, ?k)all
{
    printf("example, %d, %d, %d\n",i,j,k);
    inp("example1", i, j);
    inp("example2", i, k);
}
```

and the following tuples are the tuple space:

```
"example1", 1, 2 "example2", 1, 10
"example1", 2, 4 "example2", 1, 20
                 "example2", 2, 30
```

If the join is computed before execution then the following is printed:

```
"example", 1, 2, 10
"example", 1, 2, 20
"example", 2, 4, 30
```

The removal of the source tuples does not affect the join. However, if the join is incrementally computed then the following is printed:

```
"example", 1, 2, 10
"example", 2, 4, 30
```

Removing the source tuple prevents calculation of the join tuple ("example", 1, 2, 20). Better practice is to write programs that do not modify source tuples as these will not be affected by the underlying implementation of the **all** variation.

7 Combination Commands

A common command sequence occurring in Linda programs is retrieval of a tuple from tuple space, modification of one or more field contents, and replacement of the tuple back into tuple space. The canonical example in Linda programs is a work tuple that controls other processes: the tuple, containing a count field, is removed, the counter field incremented, and the tuple replaced in tuple space. What the programmer intends is atomic modification of the tuple contents; removing and replacing the tuple, though inefficient, is the only way to accomplish this in Linda. Because PLinda has persistent tuple spaces on stable storage, the cost can be even greater. The tuple can contain large array fields, so physically moving it from stable storage to processor memory can be prohibitively time consuming. In-place modification of tuples is essential for performance.

The structure for the combination variant of a command is retrieval, manipulation of tuple contents, and replacement. We have introduced this structure into PLinda by allowing the combination of a retrieval command (**rd**, **rdp**, **in**, or **inp**) with a placement command (**out** or **eval**) into one command. The syntax is the retrieval and placement command separated by -, a pattern argument and a code block. For example,

```
in-out("example", ?i) {i++;};
```

retrieves a tuple matching the pattern, increments the value in the second field and puts the tuple back in tuple space. In general, the contents of the code block can be any valid sequence of PLinda and base-language commands. Only single patterns are allowed for combination commands, even for **in** and **inp**, since an in-place update of a join result is not defined.

A combination command is any one of the following:

> **in-out   in-eval   in-xeval**
> **inp-out inp-eval inp-xeval**
> **rd-out   rd-eval   rd-xeval**
> **rdp-out rdp-eval rdp-xeval**

The blocking versions of a combination command waits for a matching tuple before executing. The non-blocking version returns true and executes if a tuple is found, but returns false and *does not* execute the code block or tuple placement if no tuple for retrieval is found.

A combination command uses one pattern for both retrieval and placement. However, some transformations are performed during execution since binding formals are not allowed in placement patterns. For our discussion, a pattern is a collection of constants, actual variables, functions of actual variables and formal variables. Let an assignment to a base-language variable be a pair (v, value). The steps for the combination command

> **in-out**(pattern)code-block

are the following:

1. Perform **in**(pattern). Keep the assignments of actual variables.
2. Perform code-block. This yields an assignment to the formal variables.
3. **out**(pattern-instantiated), where pattern-instantiated is the result of replacing the actuals in pattern by the assignments from 1 and the formals in pattern by the assignments from 2.

In general, any PLinda retrieval and placement can be used. The effect is an in-place update; only fields with binding formals are changed.[9]

The reader might ask why the combination commands are introduced at all. Clearly efficiency is a consideration, but it is conceivable that an optimizer could scan user code looking for the retrieval-modification-replacement sequence of commands and replace them with a low-level in-place update. However, by introducing the combination commands we allow the user to explicitly indicate modification and help the compiler. Since the programmer usually has modification in mind when coding the retrieval-modification-replacement sequence, it is natural to use the combination construct during coding.

8 Summary

An important reason for Linda's attractiveness is its simplicity and universality. Great expressiveness and power is contained in a few simple constructions. Many different

---

[9] The rules make a combination command using **eval** equivalent to the similar combination using **out**. We provide the **eval** version in order to preserve orthogonality.

parallel programming strategies can be implemented using Linda. Furthermore, the Linda model is portable across many different languages. Linda encapsulates the mechanisms needed for distributed computing — synchronization and data interchange — in simple constructs orthogonal to the underlying programming language.

This paper has presented extensions to Linda creating a model powerful enough for persistent data storage in addition to distributing computing. A major goal during the design of Persistent Linda was to preserve the virtues of Linda: simplicity, expressiveness, and universality.

We added persistent tuple spaces to support long-lived data. These tuple spaces are manipulated using parallel transactions to preserve consistency and enhance availability. We also added constructs that would provide good targets for optimization:

- *Multiple patterns* will do a multi-way join of tuples.
- *Set operations* provide a mechanism to retrieve a collection of tuples.
- *Combination operations* allow the programmer to achieve in-place updates of tuples.

Whenever possible, we kept the different features orthogonal in order to preserve the simplicity of the model. The following table illustrates the new language constructions and how they extend the Linda model:

operations	multiple patterns	set ops	combine ops	extended matching
rd	✓		✓	✓
rdp	✓	✓	✓	✓
in			✓	✓
inp		✓	✓	✓
out			✓	✓
eval			✓	✓
xeval				
xstart				
xcommit				
xabort				
nolock				
robust				

✓ = added query power

new operations (xeval, xstart, xcommit, xabort, nolock, robust)

We have implemented a prototype Persistent Linda system that runs on a network of SUN workstations. The prototype supports persistent tuple spaces and transactions. Our design is a single threaded server process that accepts requests from many client processes. A client request tells the server to perform some operation on the behalf of the client. This design was straightforward to implement and provides a core upon which to build a larger system. We designed the single server to be easily expandable to a multiple server design.

References

1. S. Ahuja et al. Linda and friends. *IEEE Computer*, August 1986.
2. N. Carriero. *Implementation of Tuple Space Machines*. PhD thesis, Yale University, December 1987.

3. N. Carriero and D. Gelérnter. Applications experience with linda. In *Proceedings of the ACM/SIGPLAN PPEALS*. ACM, 1988.
4. N. Carriero and D. Gelernter. How to write parallel programs: A guide to the perplexed. *ACM Computing Surveys*, 21(3), September 1989.
5. Harvey M. Deitel. *An Introduction to Operating Systems*. Addison-Wesley, 1984.
6. D. Shasha and J. Turek. Beyond fail-stop: Wait-free serializability and resiliency in the presence of slow-down failures. *New York University Computer Science Technical Report 514*, September 1990.

This article was processed using the LaTeX macro package with LMAMULT style

Parallel logic programming
using the Linda model of computation

Paolo Ciancarini*

University of Pisa and Yale University
New Haven, Connecticut
E-mail: ciancarini@cs.yale.edu

Abstract

In this paper we study the relationship between Linda programming and parallel logic programming. We define *PoliSpaces* (PoliS) as an extension of Linda with Multiple Tuple Spaces. PoliS is introduced as a framework for designing multiparadigm systems, *i.e.*, systems where code written in different languages can coexist. Our first test for PoliS is logic programming. We describe syntax and semantics of PoliS Prolog, a new parallel logic language based on PoliS. A parallel semantics for PoliS Prolog is given defining a multilevel abstract machine based on a chemical interpretation of the basic logic programming execution mechanism. The multilevel abstract machine is the basis for an implementation where the key idea consists of introducing a meta tuple space as a communication kernel across different tuple spaces.

1 Prologue: Linda Prolog?

In the design of new parallel languages the idea of coordination language [6] is useful because it allows to neatly separate the issues pertinent to concurrency and communication from the issues pertinent to data structures and sequential control flow. Linda [11] is an example of coordination language: it consists of a small set of mechanisms that in principle can be embedded in any traditional sequential language.

In this paper we study the problem of defining a Linda-based logic programming language. Even leaving aside concurrency and communication mechanisms, Linda (actually we refer now to the most known Linda dialect, *i.e.*, C-Linda) is apparently very different from a logic language like Prolog. The main data structures in Prolog are typeless terms; Linda's tuples are manipulated by type checking. Prolog uses unification to access clauses in the knowledge base; Linda uses typed pattern matching to access tuples in the Tuple Space. All Prolog procedures are predicates; Linda's predicates on the Tuple Space, *i.e.*, operations readp and inp, are not supported in all the implementations, for both theoretical and implementative reasons. Linda is different also from the family of parallel logic languages described in [20]; most of these cannot be classified as coordination languages because no sequential component is clearly defined.

*This work is partially supported by a N.A.T.O. grant, and by C.N.R. Progetto Finalizzato Sistemi Paralleli, and M.U.R.S.T.

On the other side, Linda has also some points in common with logic languages. In fact, very early in its history, Linda programming was compared to parallel logic programming [10]. In that paper Gelernter suggested that the Linda model of concurrency could be an interesting alternative to the programming approaches explored with parallel logic languages. The relationship between Linda and parallel logic languages was explored also in [19]. Shapiro showed how a structure called "blackboard" could be handled in a number of dialects of Flat Concurrent Prolog, with the implicit assumption that a blackboard is very similar to a Tuple Space. He suggested that Linda is easily "embedded" in parallel logic programming. Shapiro however said that current implementations of parallel logic languages are not comparable to Linda implementations from the point of view of performance.

In this paper we study the problem of developing a logic language inspired by Linda, introducing in Prolog a small set of coordination mechanisms, trying to keep the language simple and declarative, and aiming at a reasonable performance of its parallel implementations.

We believe that the relationship between Linda and the logic programming community would be advantageous for both by developing a "Linda Prolog" language. Such a language could be defined in at least four different ways:

- Adding the Linda primitives (in, inp, read, readp, out, eval) to Prolog as non backtrackable built-in predicates, and upgrading the Linda's typed pattern matching to full unification of logic terms. This solution is not trivial to implement, and from a theoretical point of view it seems difficult to integrate with traditional logic programming semantics. A Linda Prolog defined in this way would have new Linda-like built-ins whose semantics would be declaratively obscure and difficult to merge with the semantics of Prolog.

- Adding backtrackable Linda primitives to Prolog. This solution consists of defining backtrackable communication primitives. An approach of this kind was followed in the definition and implementation of DeltaProlog [16], whose communication primitives were borrowed from Hoare's CSP: they were backtrackable communication events. To define the semantics of DeltaProlog it was necessary to introduce a temporal logic framework. Moreover, backtracking of communications among distributed logic processes was very complex to implement. Similar problems would be encountered in the definition of really backtrackable Linda-like primitives.

- A more viable alternative consists of the definition of a new abstract machine for Prolog based on the Linda model. Such a solution would imply to build a parallel interpreter for sequential Prolog using Linda's distributed data structures and mechanisms. A possible model for such a language design could be an OR-parallel Prolog, like Aurora [15].

- A last but not least possibility is the definition of a brand new parallel logic language having a "Linda flavor". This is what we did when we defined Shared Prolog [5], a logic language based on a logic tuple space called "blackboard".

When, about five years ago, we started our researches on parallel logic programming we developed the basic computing model of Shared Prolog independently from Linda. When, subsequently, we realized the similarities between the two languages, we started an attempt to close the gap between their theoretical and implementative bases.

In this paper we describe a solution centered around PoliS, a Multiple Tuple Spaces coordination language designed as a general multiparadigm framework for Linda-like programming languages. One main contribution of the paper is the description of PoliS; the second contribution is PoliS Prolog, a logic programming instance of PoliS. We give syntax and semantics of both PoliS and of PoliS Prolog, and describe an implementation.

This paper has the following structure: Section 2 describes PoliSpaces, *i.e.*, a coordination model embedding Multiple Tuple Spaces for multiparadigm programming. Section 3 describes PoliS Prolog as a logic programming counterpart of PoliS. Section 4 describes an operational semantics for PoliS Prolog, introducing the chemical interpretation of logic programming. Finally, Section 5 describes the current implementation of PoliS Prolog, based on a meta Tuple Space.

2 PoliSpaces (Multiple Tuple Spaces)

Although Linda's strength derives mainly from its expressive simplicity and efficient implementations, from the point of view of a programmer it shows some drawbacks. A first issue is information hiding in the Tuple Space. The monolithic Tuple Space offers no mechanisms for structuring or partitioning the tuples it contains: every process can in principle access every tuple. Suppose we want to use the Tuple Space to build a database of tuples shared among several users: security issues in such a framework are expensive to deal with, because it is difficult for instance to forbid accessing a specific subset of the Tuple Space. Also from the point of view of multiparadigm programming the monolithic Tuple Space is unsatisfactory, because different languages need different protocols to represent and access shared data in the Tuple Space.

Multiple Tuple Spaces were suggested by Gelernter [12] as a possible solution to these problems. Languages based on Multiple Tuple Spaces should maintain all the features of Linda, introducing the possibility of structuring a system as a set of separate Tuple Spaces.

PoliS is a coordination language based on Multiple Tuple Spaces. The main idea in PoliS is that a distributed system is seen as a "city", *i.e.*, as a set of *places* each containing several *agents*. Places are organizational mechanisms that structure activities taking place in the "city". The relationship between PoliS and Linda is very close, because a PoliS place simply a multiset of tuples, *i.e.*, it is a Linda Tuple Space.

A tuple is an ordered collection of fields that can be treated as a unit. In PoliS we do not assume any type structure on fields; these can represent either data objects, or unbound values. More important is that PoliS tuples can be active - they represent agents - or passive - they represent messages deposited in the place by some agent. Agents are independent computing processes that are bound to their place: they cannot migrate to another place, and they react to the contents of their place, possibly consuming some tuples.

We remark that agents' I/O behavior is asymmetric. They can output tuples in any place they know, but they can only look inside their own place for input. Communication in PoliS is modeled using electronic mail systems as an inspiration guide: an agent can send tuples to any mailbox it knows, but it can only look for tuples inside its mailbox, that is shared with other agents.

In the following subsections we develop syntax and semantics of PoliS.

2.1 A syntax for PoliS

We introduce PoliS giving its syntax in fig. 1.

A PoliS place is a named multiset of tuples, and a tuple is either a normal tuple or a program tuple. A program tuple is a pair: the first component is a normal tuple, the second component is a pattern, *i.e.*, a program composed of four sections: a set of *tests*, a set of *consumptions*, a *local evaluation*, and an set of *outs*.

Such a syntax reflects the fact that a coordination language is composed of two components: a *coordination* component and a *computation* component. In fact, the PoliS grammar is parametric, *i.e.*, some non-terminals are not specified, but are left as degrees of freedom to instantiate the model. The syntax is parametric insofar as we leave out of PoliS the choice of the name system for places, of the type system for data fields in the tuples, of the invocation mechanism of the sequential components, and of the set of predefined tests that can be tried in a place.

2.2 PoliS semantics

PoliS is intended as a language for programming "coordination". In PoliS we can program many different levels of coordination:

- the structure of the "city". Semantically, a PoliS program defines a "landscape", *i.e.*, a set of named places. Such a set is structured if names are structured. For instance, if we have names structured as Unix pathnames we have a tree of places. Such a structure could own specific semantics properties: *e.g.*, , a number of special scope rules could be associated to the name system. For simplicity, in this paper we will always assume a flat name system where different names points to different places, and no structure is given, *i.e.*, there is a unique global space name.

- the activities among different places; these include place creations and communications between places. A place is created by an agent when it executes a tsc() (*i.e.*, tuple space create) operation. An agent in a place can output a tuple in another place executing a non-local out operation (see below). Such non-local communications are possible only if the agent "knows" the name of the target place. Place names are thus also communication capabilities that can be passed around to other agents. Figure 2 shows a set of places containing agents; arrows represent communication capabilities.

- the activities inside a place; the unit of activity is the agent (or *thread*). Each place is both a container and a communication channel. A place contains agents and resources, both represented by tuples. In fact, there are two basic kinds of tuples: normal-tuples and program-tuples. A *normal – tuple* is simply a collection of fields. A *program – tuple* is a pair ⟨*heading, pattern*⟩: the first element has the syntax of a normal-tuple, whereas a pattern is composed by four 'sections': *test, consume, loc_eval,* and *out*. Instead of a normal-tuple, some program-tuples have as a first element the keyword invariant. These tuples represent special activities that are associated to the place itself; for instance, only these tuples can terminate the activities inside the place. Invariant program tuples are also useful for reasoning about PoliS programs.

- the activities encompassing different agents in the same place. Agents do not know each other: PoliS strictly follows the Linda model of communication. An agent can only get or

⟨place ⟩ ::⇒
    ⟨p_name ⟩ { ⟨multiset_of_tuples ⟩ }

⟨tuple ⟩ ::⇒
    ⟨normal_tuple ⟩ | ⟨program_tuple ⟩

⟨normal_tuple ⟩ ::⇒
    (⟨seq_of_fields ⟩)

⟨program_tuple ⟩ ::⇒
    (⟨heading ⟩ : ⟨pattern ⟩) | (invariant⊔: ⟨pattern ⟩)

⟨heading ⟩ ::⇒
    ⟨normal_tuple ⟩

⟨pattern ⟩ ::⇒
    (⟨test ⟩ ; ⟨consume ⟩ ; ⟨loc_eval ⟩ ; ⟨out ⟩)

⟨test ⟩ ::⇒
    test⊔ ⟨tuple ⟩ | ⟨predefined_test ⟩ | ⟨test ⟩ ; ⟨test ⟩

⟨consume ⟩ ::⇒
    consume⊔ ⟨tuple ⟩ | ⟨consume ⟩ ; ⟨consume ⟩

⟨loc_eval ⟩ ::⇒
    loc_eval⊔ ⟨call_seq_program ⟩

⟨out ⟩ ::⇒
    out⊔ ⟨tuple ⟩ | ⟨p_name ⟩ .out⊔ ⟨tuple ⟩ |
    ⟨p_name ⟩ .tsc | ⟨out ⟩ ; ⟨out ⟩

⟨p_name ⟩ ::⇒

⟨seq_of_fields ⟩ ::⇒

⟨call_seq_program ⟩ ::⇒

⟨predefined_test ⟩ ::⇒

Figure 1: *PoliS syntax*

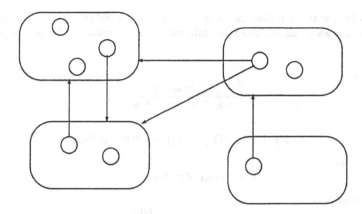

Figure 2: *A PoliSpace (rounded boxes represent places, circles represent agents, arrows represent communication capabilities)*

put tuples in the place; it cannot communicate directly with another agent.

- the activities carried out by an agent. An agent is "reactive": it reacts to the contents of its place. Such a reaction is described by the pattern in a program-tuple. The first two sections of a pattern, *i.e.*, *test* and *consume*, are abstractions of the Linda operations read/readp and in/inp, respectively. In other words, *test* is a set of tests on the place contents, whereas *consume* denotes a set of tuple deletions from the place. The *loc_eval* is the invocation of a sequential program (*i.e.*, no side effects on the place are allowed in such an evaluation). The *out* defines the "output" of the pattern: it consists of a set of tuple creations (like Linda's out) and/or places' creations. In fact, to create a place we introduce an operation that is not present in Linda: *place_name*.tsc(). Production of tuples in outside places also has its own syntax: *place_name*.out. Note that if the target place does not exist, the tuple "waits" somewhere for its creation. Thus this operation keeps a generative communication flavour, insofar as its semantics remains similar to Linda's out semantics. We remark that a PoliS program-tuple is very similar to a Linda program that satisfies the following syntactic constraint: all read/readp operations precede all in/inp operations; these precede all the operations that have nothing to do with the Tuple Space; only at the end there out and/or tsc operations. This constraint simplifies the semantics of a PoliS program-tuple with respect to a Linda program: a pattern takes all its inputs at the beginning of the evaluation, then computes locally something, then outputs the results. We note that such a structure reminds also rule clauses in parallel logic programming languages [17], and we will discuss such a resemblance in section 4.

There is no eval operation in PoliS (we remind that eval is used in Linda to create a process). In PoliS we define a "reactive" activation mechanism: if the place contains both a program-tuple (say (A : (T;C;B;O))), and a normal-tuple (A) that matches the heading of the program-tuple, a process starts.

Semantically,.for the activities inside a place P we can define a transition system where configurations are whole places, and rules determine transformations of places in places:

activation)

$$\frac{(T : Prog) \in P}{P \uplus T \longrightarrow P \uplus Prog}$$

test)

$$P \uplus T \uplus (test(T); Prog) \longrightarrow P \uplus T \uplus Prog$$

consumption)

$$P \uplus T \uplus (consume(T); Prog) \longrightarrow P \uplus Prog$$

local evaluation)

$$P \uplus (loc\_eval(B); Prog) \xrightarrow{L(B)} P \uplus Prog$$

out)

$$P \uplus (out(T); Prog) \longrightarrow P \uplus T \uplus Prog$$

Here P is a place, T is a normal-tuple, and Prog is a pattern. The operation $\uplus$ denotes multiset construction; the symbol is overloaded for multiset union and insertion. To simplify the presentation, we do not take into account fields' matching; however, such an aspect is discussed in [7].

The semantics of B inside the local evaluation is given when the programming language L for sequential computations is chosen; we label the transaction with L(B) simply to state that "something has to be done" using L semantics. We could use a transition system for describing the semantics of the evaluation of B as well, so that PoliS semantics would be based on a two level transition system; for an example of this technique, see [5].

Finally, we note that it is possible that the place contains several program-tuples having the same heading: this is the way of expressing non-determinism in PoliS. In other words, if a place contains a normal-tuple that matches the first element of several program-tuples, one is chosen non-deterministically.

3 PoliS Prolog

In this section we define the logic instance of PoliS, that we call *PoliS Prolog*. According to the PoliS definition given in Sect. 2, to introduce a PoliS instance we need to specify a name system for places, a type system and access method for tuple fields, a language for sequential components, and a set of predicates on the contents of a place.

In the following discussion we assume some familiarity with Prolog terminology. Place names in PoliS Prolog are ground terms (*e.g.*, a place could be called foo(1,[a,b,c])); no structure is assumed in this name system. Places are multisets of terms, that we see simply as named tuples. The sequential language for local evaluations is Prolog, with the restriction that predicates of the assert/retract family are not allowed: agents do not have a local state, a part from variables in the heading. The predefined tests are mostly inherited from Prolog;

for instance, we can ask if a field X inside a tuple is a variable (var(X)) or a non-variable (nonvar(X)).

Syntactically, a PoliS Prolog program is composed of a set of theories. A *theory* has the following syntax:

```
theory name(V1,...,Vn):-              % theory heading
eval pattern₁ # ... # patternₖ        % theory interface
with Prolog_program                   % theory implementation.
```

The theory patterns can be considered as the interface of a module, because only through such an interface the sequential program, *i.e.*, the theory implementation, can be activated. A PoliS Prolog pattern has the following structure:

$$Guard \rightarrow Prolog\_Goal \; \{Success\_Out\} \; ; \; \{Failure\_Out\}$$

where *Guard* is a goal evaluated with respect the contents of the place; it is a combination of logic *test* and *consume* operations. Syntactically, terms to be consumed from the place are bracketed. The *Prolog_Goal* is locally evaluated with respect the *Prolog_program* following the keyword with; finally, *Success_Out* and *Failure_Out* specify a set of terms to be written back in the place or in other places, or some place creations (*i.e.*, they are PoliS *out* operations). *Success_Out* is executed if the *Prolog_goal* is successful, else *Failure_Out* is executed.

For instance, the following is a simple theory including one pattern.

```
theory eval_f(State):-
eval
        {tuple(Input)}                           % consume
        →
        f(Input, State, Output, NewState)        % Prolog_Goal
        {tuple(Output), eval_f(NewState)}        % Success_Out
with
        f(I,S,O,NS):- ...                        % Prolog_program
```

Such a theory defines an agent eval_f that if it can consume a tuple tuple(Input), then it computes a function f, it produces a result tuple(Output), and it invokes again itself.

A PoliS Prolog theory is easily compiled in a number of PoliS program-tuples. Each logic *pattern_i* corresponds to a program-tuple having as first component a tuple including the theory name and input parameters. For instance, the above eval_f theory corresponds to the following PoliS program-tuple:

```
(eval_f(S): (consume tuple(I); loc_eval f(I,S,O,N); out tuple(O); out eval_f(N)))
```

Logic program-tuples use for *test* and *consume* operations a control strategy based on backtracking. The idea is that in a program-tuple the pair $< test, consume >$ is a guard atomically executed as a transaction. Such a transaction concerns a subset of the place that is defined as follows: it contains exactly one program-tuple, exactly one normal-tuple matching with the first component of the program-tuple, and a multiset of normal-tuples as defined in the *consume* part C of the program-tuple.

Given a logic place P, and a program-tuple (A : (T;C;B;O))), operationally we have a transition system that operates on configurations that are multisets of tuples as follows:

$$\frac{(A:(T;C;B;O)) \in P, \quad (A) \in P, \quad P \Rightarrow T, \quad C \subseteq (P \setminus \{(A)\})}{P \overset{prolog(B)}{\longrightarrow} (P \setminus (C \uplus \{(A)\})) \uplus O}$$

A configuration P that include a program-tuple (A: (T ; C ; B ; O)) is transformed if a) P includes a matching normal-tuple (A), and b) from P we can infer T (*i.e.*, the *test* is satisfied by the current contents of P), and c) C is a subset of P\{(A)}.

After executing the local evaluation of goal B according to Prolog semantics, that we denote labeling the transition with *prolog(B)*, the result is a new configuration where tuple (A) and the multiset of tuples C have been "consumed", and the mutliset of tuples O has been produced.

The above semantics is very coarse-grained, because conceptually there is only one thread of control per place. In the following section we study a parallel abstract machine for PoliS Prolog.

4 The chemical interpretation of logic programming

The development of the family of parallel logic languages described in [20] was based on the definition of a new interpretation of logic programming, called the *process interpretation*. According to the process interpretation, that was inspired by the Kahn and MacQueen model of concurrency [14], a logic goal $G_1, \ldots, G_n$ is mapped on a hypergraph whose nodes are a set of processes $P_1, \ldots, P_n$, whereas the hyperedges are a set of bidirectional communication channels C_j. The mapping associates each atomic goal G_i with a process P_i, and each variable V_j with a channel C_j. The logic program is then a set of rules that transform the graph structure. For instance, the Concurrent Prolog goal

    a(X, Y), b(Y, Z), c(Z, W)

starts three processes named *a*, *b*, and *c* that communicate using streams represented by the logical variables Y (by which *a* and *b* communicate) and Z (by which *b* and *c* communicate). Logic clauses that define the behavior of a process have the following structure:

    process-invocation :- guard → body

where both the guard and the body are networks of processes - they are logic goals.

In this framework logic processes are very short lived: when a clause fires, the process dies and it is replaced by a network of new logic processes as described in the body. It is worth noting that this interpretation is non-declarative insofar as the outputs of a program do not include all possible solutions of a goal. In fact, if a process can choose more than one clause, one is arbitrarily chosen by local non backtrackable non determinism. We say that the process has *committed* itself to that clause. The process interpretation is the basis of both first-generation parallel logic languages, like Parlog, Flat Concurrent Prolog and GHC, and second-generation parallel logic languages, like Strand [9], and Janus [18]. From a pragmatic point of view these languages mainly differ for the special kind of unification constraints that they enforce, whereas from a semantic point of view they are so close that they have been collected in a general theoretic model called "Concurrent Constraint Logic Programming" (CCLP) [17]. According to Saraswat, the guard should be composed of two separate sets of tests: *ask* tests and *tell* tests. CCLP *ask* tests are very similar to PoliS *test* operations: they cannot alter the global state of the system. CCLP *tell* tests can alter such a global state, imposing some new constraints on the global variables included in the goal; so *tell* tests are similar to PoliS *consume* operations, the main difference being that CCLP *tell* tests are allowed only if they are monotonically compatible with tests carried by other processes.

PoliS Prolog, like Shared Prolog, is based on a different operational semantics, that here we will formalize as the "chemical interpretation of logic programming". In the chemical interpretation of logic programming the scope of variables is a key issue. Suppose we have the following terms inside a place:

```
a(X), b(X)
```

Is there any relationship between variable X in the first term and variable X in the second term? In the chemical interpretation the answer is no: scope of variables spans only for the term to which they belong. So actually the above place is completely equivalent to the following one:

```
a(Y), b(Z)
```

where variables have been renamed.

In the chemical interpretation each term inside a place is completely independent from other terms. The logic languages based on the process interpretation take the opposite view, as demonstrated by Flat Concurrent Prolog [20]. In every logic language of this family the goal can be seen as a set of processes that share variables. A logic goal

```
a(X,Y), b(X,Y)
```

has the following declarative reading in the process interpretation:

$$\neg(\exists x(\exists y(a(x,y) \land b(x,y))))$$

Shared logic variables complicate the language semantics and its distributed implementation as well. Conversely, a place containing the same terms has the following declarative reading:

$$(\forall x(\forall y(a(x,y)))) \lor (\forall x(\forall y(b(x,y))))$$

It is easy to see that this is the same declarative reading of a Prolog knowledge base. With the chemical interpretation a logic place is very similar to both a Linda's Tuple Space and a Prolog knowledge base. The key idea in PoliS Prolog is to have an "active" knowledge base, where computation is carried on by a "magic" chemical mechanism. There is an important difference between logic processes in the chemical interpretation and logic processes in the process interpretation: since there are no variables that are shared among the terms in the place, no global environment is necessary.

In figure 3 we have defined a simplified abstract syntax for a logic place (l_place) that will be the basis of the chemical interpretation. A logic program is a set of rules that define the

⟨l_place⟩ ::⇒ { ⟨multiset_of_terms_and_rules⟩ }

⟨term⟩ ::⇒ ⟨constant⟩ | ⟨functor⟩ (⟨list_of_terms_and_variables⟩)

⟨rule⟩ ::⇒ ⟨term⟩ :- ⟨l_place⟩ ↦ ⟨l_place⟩

⟨molecule⟩ ::⇒ ·⟨l_place⟩ | < ⟨l_place⟩ , ⟨l_place⟩ , ⟨l_place⟩ >

Figure 3: *Abstract syntax of a logic place for the chemical interpretation*

behavior of a place. Inside a rule the scope of variables ranges over all components of the rule itself.

The dynamic behavior of a place under the chemical interpretation is defined by a chemical abstract machine (CHAM for short) [4]. Using the metaphor proposed by Berry and Boudol a logic place can be seen as a chemical solution in which some "molecules" float, interact and change according to some "reaction" rules. A CHAM is specified by defining the concepts of *solution* and *molecule*, and by introducing a number of *transformation rules*. It is easy to see logic places as solutions. A molecule is either a logic place, or a triple containing three logic places.

If $(A :- I \mapsto O)$ is a rule in a place P, the basic transformation rules are the following:

---

start-firing)

$$\frac{(A :- I \mapsto O) \in P}{A \longleftrightarrow < \{A\}, I, O >}$$

cont-firing)

$$\frac{}{< L, \{I'\} \uplus I'', O >, I' \longleftrightarrow < L \uplus \{I'\}, I'', O >}$$

commit)

$$\frac{}{< L, \emptyset, O > \longrightarrow O}$$

Rules *start − firing* and *cont − firing* are reversible: they take care of backtracking consumptions. The *commit* rule produces a multiset of tuples that will be "dissolved" in the logic place. These rules determine the basic computing step in this interpretation; parallelism follows from the application of the chemical laws (metarules) described in [4]. Let us see an example: given the place

{p1, p2, ping}

and the program composed of the following rules (not included in the place only to facilitate the reader's task):

```
p1 :- {pong} ↦ {ping, p1}
p2 :- {ping} ↦ {pong, p2}
```

we have the following sequence of "reactions":

$$\{p1, p2, ping\} \longrightarrow \{p1, p2, pong\} \longrightarrow \{p1, p2, ping\} \longrightarrow \dots$$

This sequence is infinite: no termination is specified for the two agents p1 and p2. Moreover, it represents a sequential system, in which only one molecule can react; no parallelism is present. The situation would be completely different if we should add another term to the initial place:

```
{p1, p2, ping, pong}
```

Now agents p1 and p2 run in parallel.

In the simplified CHAM described above we have left aside all the unifications of logic variables. We should generalize the above discussion to terms including variables, and introduce matching rules based on unification. For lack of space we are not going here to develop all the related theory; however, in [7] the reader can find a treatment of these topics in the context of Linda's pattern-matching.

We also did not show how *test* operations and local evaluations are executed. A simple and inefficient solution for *test* operations consists of systematically transform every atomic *test* in a *consumption* and a successive *out* of the same term. This reduces the degree of parallelism that can be exploited by the above abstract machine. Local evaluations can be treated invoking a lower-level transition system in the *commit* rule immediately before the Out production.

Finally, we should show how the creation of a new place, and the production of tuples in an outside place are dealt with. Place creation is enabled if a place with the same name does not exist. Production in another place (that here we call *extra-production*) can have two different results: if the target place does exist, the tuple "pops in" such a place; contrariwise, if the target place does not exist, the tuple should "wait" somewhere for the place creation.

In order to deal with these operations, we introduce a higher-level chemical abstract machine (we intend such a concept in a way similar to multilevel transition systems), where solutions consist of set of named places. An empty place named *name* is written *name*{}, while a place containing something is written *name*{_}. Operations that create a new place, *i.e.*, `name.tsc`, or communicate with an external place, *i.e.*, `name.out(Term)`, simply "pop out" from the place where they were issued into the higher-level abstract machine molecules *tsc*(*name*) and *out*(*name*, *Term*), respectively.

Unfortunately, creating a place requires dealing with negative information ("if such a place does not exist, then …"). Negative information is very expensive to deal with within a distributed framework; for instance, this is the case also for Linda operations readp and inp, that when they report a failure actually they say something negative about the Tuple Space. To simplify the semantics of place creation, we postulate that initially in the higher-level abstract machine we have for every allowed place name *name* a molecule representing a relationship *allowed*(*name*). The p_creation rule states that, as soon as a place P has been created, the tuple *allowed*(P) is substituted by the tuple *exists*(P).

p_creation)	$tsc(name), allowed(name) \longrightarrow name\{\}, exists(name)$
p_nocreation)	$tsc(name), exists(name) \longrightarrow exists(name)$
extra-production)	$out(name, T), name\{\_\} \longrightarrow name\{\_\} \uplus \{T\}$

Finally, we must deal with place termination. We define this operation too at the level of the higher-level abstract machine. When a place has to terminate, it pops out a `terminate(name)` molecule.

$$p\_termination) \qquad terminate(name), name\{\_\}, exists(name) \longrightarrow allowed(name)$$

This completes the description of the general structure of PoliS Prolog. An interesting aspect of this three-levels structure (one level for the local evaluations, one level for activities inside a place, and one level for activities outside the place) is that it partially justifies the asymmetry between tuple consumptions, that happen only inside a place, and tuple productions, that can cross the place boundaries. A non-local consumption can be obtained outputting in the external place an agent that sends back an answer when the tuple is found.

5 Implementing PoliS Prolog

The abstract machine described above has been a useful guide in the design of a PoliS implementation developed by the author. A distributed prototype of an interpreter for PoliS Prolog has been implemented using Network C-Linda and Prolog by BIM over an internet network of workstations.

The prototype has a structure that mirrors the multilevel abstract machine described in section 4. Communications between places are handled by a *Meta Tuple Space* (MetaTS). Network C-Linda is used as a distributed communication kernel and support for the whole landscape of places. The MetaTS is a C-Linda program that handles a set of processors. Figure 5 depicts the current implementation.

Place names are Prolog ground terms. When a request to create a new place is issued by an agent in the MetaTS, there is a check that such a name is not used for an existing place; if this is the case, a processor is chosen among those available, and a new place is activated. A PoliS Prolog place is actually a separate Prolog process where logic agents are light-weighted; their concurrency is simulated.

For technical reasons (Network Linda uses a special linkage-editor) in the current implementation logic places are processes created not by Linda's distributed `eval`, but launching a remote evaluation. The remote Prolog process then starts a connection with a true Linda worker that is the representative of the remote place inside the MetaTS. Sockets are used for communications between the representatives inside the MetaTS and the corresponding places. Using the procedural interface, Prolog has been extended with a number of non backtrackable built-ins that implement the main Linda predicates.

We are testing this implementation on several benchmarks. It is too early to draw any conclusions on performance, that will be the subject of another paper.

6 Conclusions

In this paper we have introduced PoliS, a coordination language based on Multiple Tuple Spaces. We have defined PoliS semantics using a multilevel abstract machine that mirrors the idea of coordination based on the separation of the parallel language component from the sequential language component. We have shown how PoliS can be used as the basic framework for PoliS Prolog, a new parallel logic language. We have introduced a chemical interpretation

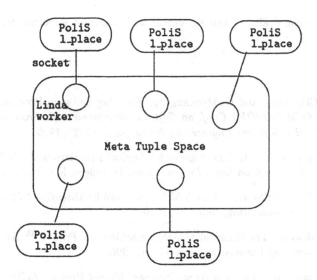

Figure 4: *Implementing PoliS with a Meta Tuple Space*

for logic programming, that is the basis for a Linda-like execution mechanism of logic agents. We have implemented a prototype of PoliS Prolog, and in another paper we will describe more extensively such implementation and its performance.

What kind of applications are best realized with PoliS and Multiple Tuple Spaces? It is too early to give an answer to such a question. However, currently a group at the University of Pisa is using ESP, a variant of PoliS Prolog based on hierarchical PoliSpaces, in the construction of Oikos, a multiuser distributed environment [1]. There are also many points of contact between our multiple tuple space programming model and the GAMMA model of parallel programming [3], that we are currently exploring. Moreover, a logic-based tuple space seems promising even from the point of view of a logic of programming, aiming at proving poperties of parallel programs, as it is shown by the SWARM programming notation [8], that is very similar to a monospace PoliS Prolog.

The main theoretical problem that remains open in PoliS Prolog is its declarative seman-tics. Its computing model is very different from parallel logic languages of the family of Flat Concurrent Prolog, and it is impossible to give it a declarative semantics based on classic first order logic. This is because it is impossible to specify in first order logic dynamic situations, *e.g.*, where resources are consumed and produced. Interestingly, recently a new kind of logic, called Linear Logic, was introduced to deal with dynamic situations [13]. This logic promises to offer a new theoretical basis to parallel logic programming, as was shown in [2], where a new logic language called LO was introduced. LO has some points in common with PoliS Prolog, and we intend to explore this relationship.

Acknowledgements The author is very grateful to T.Castagnetti, D.Gelernter, and

N.Carriero, that read some drafts of this document and discussed its contents, helping to improve the paper.

References

[1] V. Ambriola, P. Ciancarini, and C. Montangero. Enacting Software Processes in Oikos. In *Proceedings of ACM SIGSOFT Conf. on Software Development Environments*, volume 15:6 of *ACM SIGSOFT Software Engineering Notes*, pages 12–23, 1990.

[2] J.-M. Andreoli and R. Pareschi. Linear Objects: Logical Processes with Built-In Inheritance. In *Proc. 7th Int. Conf. on Logic Programming*, Jerusalem, May 1990. MIT Press.

[3] J.-P. Banatre and D. LeMetayer. The GAMMA model and its Discipline of Programming. *Science of Computer Programming*, 15:55–77, 1990.

[4] G. Berry and G. Boudol. The chemical abstract machine. In *Proc. 17th ACM Conf. on Principles of Programming Languages*, pages 81–94, 1990.

[5] A. Brogi and P. Ciancarini. The concurrent language Shared Prolog. *ACM Transactions on Programming Languages and Systems*, 13(1):99–123, 1991.

[6] N. Carriero and D. Gelernter. Coordination languages and their significance. *Communications of the ACM*, 1991, to appear.

[7] P. Ciancarini and D. Yankelewich. Inside Linda. Technical Report RR YALEU/DCS/RR-831, Yale University, Dept. of Computer Science, October 1990.

[8] H. C. Cunningham and G.-C. Roman. A Unity-Style Programming Logic for Shared Dataspace Programs. *IEEE Transactions on Parallel and Distributed Systems*, 1(3):365–376, July 1990.

[9] I. Foster and S. Taylor. *Strand: New Concepts in Parallel Programming*. Prentice Hall, 1990.

[10] D. Gelernter. A Note on Systems Programming in Concurrent Prolog. In *Proc. Int. Symp. Logic Programming*, February 1984.

[11] D. Gelernter. Generative Communication in Linda. *ACM Transactions on Programming Languages and Systems*, 7(1):80–112, 1985.

[12] D. Gelernter. Multiple tuple spaces in Linda. In *Proceedings of PARLE '89*, volume 365 of *Lecture Notes in Computer Science*, pages 20–27, 1989.

[13] J. Y. Girard. Linear Logic. *Theoretical Computer Science*, 50:1–102, 1987.

[14] G. Kahn and D. MacQueen. Coroutines and Networks of Parallel Processes. In B. Gilchrist, editor, *Information Processing 77: Proc. IFIP Congress*, pages 993–998. North Holland, 1977.

[15] E. Lusk, D. Warren, and alii. The Aurora OR-parallel Prolog System. In *Proc. Int. Conf. on 5th Generation Computer Systems*, pages 819–830. ICOT, 1988.

[16] L. Pereira and R. Nasr. Deltaprolog: A distributed logic programming language. In *Proc. of the Int. Conf. on Fifth Generation Computer Systems*, pages 283–291, 1984.

[17] V. Saraswat. *Concurrent Constraint Programming Languages*. PhD thesis, Carnegie Mellon University, 1989. (To be published by MIT Press).

[18] V. Saraswat, K. Kahn, and J. Levy. Janus: A step towards distributed constraint programming. In *North American Conference on Logic Programming*, 1990.

[19] E. Y. Shapiro. Embedding Linda and other joys of concurrent logic programming. *Communications of the ACM*, 33(10):1240–1258, October 1989.

[20] E. Y. Shapiro. The family of concurrent logic languages. *ACM Computing Surveys*, 21(3), September 1989.

Lucinda — A Polymorphic Linda

Paul Butcher[*] & Hussein Zedan
Department of Computer Science, University of York
Heslington, York, YO1 5DD, England

{paulb, zedan}@uk.ac.york.minster

Abstract

This document describes the courting of Linda (a co-ordination language) by Russell (a computation language), and the subsequent conception of their child Lucinda. Mother and baby are both doing well.

A number of deficiencies of the standard Linda dialect, C-Linda, are identified, and a new language, Lucinda, is proposed to overcome them. Lucinda provides dynamically created multiple tuple spaces and polymorphism via the type system of Russell. A formal semantics and proof rule system is given in a categorical framework.

1. Introduction

There is no doubt that during the past two decades or so, the design of languages for parallel machines has increasingly become an important and popular area of research and development. Many languages have emerged, including CSP[17], DP[3], Concurrent Pascal[4], Path Pascal[21], Ada[12], occam[25] *etc.*

One of the fundamental design differences of these languages has been in the way communication and synchronisation is achieved between two "building blocks" (be they processes, tasks, modules *etc.*). At one end of the spectrum, we find communication is point-to-point and is tightly synchronous (*e.g.* occam and CSP). Communication and synchronisation are treated in a single command considered as a primitive of the language. At the other end of the spectrum, we find languages such as Linda[6, 8, 14] where synchronisation is hidden from the programmer and the communication philosophy is based on the notion of having a globally available "tuple space".

---

[*] This work is supported by a SERC Studentship

When developing a concurrent/distributed language, there are some criteria and features that are desirable. These include:

Simplicity The language should be based upon as few "basic concepts" as possible.

Regularity The basic concepts of the language should be applied consistently, and universally.

Orthogonality Independent functions should be controlled by independent mechanisms.

Abstraction Mechanisms should be available to allow recurring patterns in the code to be factored out.

Clarity The mechanisms used by the language should be well defined, and the outcome of a particular section of code easily predicted.

Information Hiding Each "basic program unit" should only have access to the information that it requires.

Explicit Interfaces Interfaces between basic program units should be stated explicitly.

Safety Mechanisms should be available to allow semantic errors to be detected.

Expressivity The language should allow us to construct as wide a variety of programs as possible.

Efficiency The language should not preclude the production of efficient code. It should allow the programmer to provide the compiler with any information which may improve the resultant code.

1.1. Linda

Linda provides a number of advantages over existing parallel, distributed languages, in particular simplicity and portability. In addition, it encourages the construction of *uncoupled* programs. Unfortunately, current Linda implementations have a number of deficiencies. This paper examines these deficiencies, and proposes a new language, Lucinda, to overcome them.

1.2. Problems with current Linda implementations

Linda only addresses the problem of Inter-Process Communication (IPC), and doesn't provide any control structures. As a result, all current implementations treat Linda as a *co-ordinating language*[8], i.e. a "host" language is selected (usually C[20], but in principle any language could be used) to provide those features not supported by Linda. Unfortunately, embedding Linda into a host language contradicts a number of the principles outlined above. We will examine some of these problems with reference to C-Linda, the most common Linda variant. Most of the points made are relevant to other Linda embeddings as well.

Simplicity Linda is certainly simple, providing only four (six if you include the predicate forms) primitives. Similarly, the host language may be simple. Unfortunately, as we will see below, several of the "basic concepts" of most popular sequential languages conflict with the concepts upon which Linda is based, resulting in a significantly more complex language than might be hoped for.

Orthogonality Proponents of the co-ordinating language model argue that communication and computation are orthogonal and that therefore the use of Linda as an IPC mechanism is independent of the host language. There are a number of problems with this approach. Firstly, as Linda relies heavily on type matching, the type system of the host language has a dramatic effect. Most current C-Linda implementations have to extend the type system of C to overcome some of the problems thus caused (see [22]).

Secondly, Linda is not solely an IPC mechanism. As well as transferring information between processes, Linda may be used as a data storage and structuring mechanism. The programmer therefore has a difficult choice to make; when does he store data in tuple space, structured as tuples, and when does he use the native data structuring techniques of the underlying language.

Regularity The points mentioned above also have an impact on the regularity of the language. How can we ensure that all the concepts of the language are applied regularly if they are in conflict?

Information Hiding In its current form, Linda provides little or no information hiding; any process may access any tuple.[1]

Explicit Interfaces There is no means, in any Linda implementation known to the author, to specify how two processes will interact.

Safety Tuple space accesses, in all Linda implementation known to the author, are untyped. There is no means of checking that only tuples of the correct form are inserted into a tuple space (*i.e.* that there is a process somewhere expecting a tuple of that form).

Efficiency Embedding Linda into a sequential language has a number of implications for efficiency. Many of the assumptions made by a sequential language are invalid in a distributed environment. To mention just one of the more obvious problems, global variables have no obvious implementation.

In the opinion of the authors, the above problems are of such a magnitude that the design of a new language, specifically intended to support Linda, is warranted. This paper presents the design of such a new language, Lucinda.

---

[1]There are proposals to overcome this problem. See [15, 18].

2. The Design of Lucinda

Given that a new language is called for, it is necessary to determine what features would be desirable in a language based on Linda. Firstly, the principles of simplicity, regularity and orthogonality mean that not only should Linda be the sole IPC mechanism, but also that the language should use tuple spaces as its sole data storage and structuring mechanism. Therefore the language should not directly support the "variable" abstraction. Similarly, tuples should be supported directly in the language.

The principles of safety and explicit interfaces are slightly more difficult. As Linda stands there is no means of type-checking tuple space accesses, nor is there any way of specifying which forms of tuples will be accepted by a particular tuple space. Such mechanisms, if provided, should not decrease the power of Lucinda in any way. As a result it has been decided to incorporate a polymorphic type system into Lucinda.

2.1. Polymorphism

Type systems have been a part of programming languages ever since their conception. Initially they were introduced to improve efficiency (e.g. to allow a compiler to distinguish between integers and floating point values), but it was soon realised that a type system could be used to improve the safety of programs by allowing many varieties of programmer error to be detected. It is the safety properties of type systems that we are interested in here.

Type systems fall into two broad categories; those which allow static type checking and those that require run-time type checking. In static type checking, the program source is statically analysed (usually at compile time), and if no errors are detected during this analysis, we may guarantee that no type errors will occur at run time. The improved safety properties of static type checking mean that we will only concern ourselves with static systems here.

All type systems restrict the programmer in some way (indeed that is their purpose). A "good" type system will allow a wide variety of programs to be compiled (i.e. it will be expressive), while at the same time it will detect a wide variety of programming errors. Polymorphism is one means of increasing the expressivity of a type system while retaining strong static type checking.

Two main classes of polymorphic type system were considered for Lucinda. The most often used, which we have chosen to call "set based", views a type as a set.[2] A number of basic types are provided (e.g. Int, Real, etc.), and a number of combinators (e.g. cartesian product, function construction, etc.). Polymorphism is introduced via quantifiers, both universal($\forall$), which

---

[2]In fact, a restricted set known as an ideal.

may be used to define functions which range over a number of types, and existential (∃), which may be used to define *abstract data types*[27]. A good exposition of this form of type system is given in [7]. Languages based on this system include ML[26] (which uses type inference, rather than an explicit type expression sublanguage) and Ten15[11].

Set-based polymorphism certainly fares well with respect to the criteria given in section 1.1. It is both simple and regular, depending upon only a few well understood and consistently applied mathematical concepts. Quantifiers provide a powerful abstraction mechanism, expressivity and, by retaining static type checking, safety. It is not, however, as regular as it might be. Not all language elements are "first class", in particular it is not possible to implement first class *types* in a set-based type system. A type system which overcomes this problem is the type system of the language Russell.

Russell[2, 13] takes an alternative view of what constitutes a type. Rather than regarding a type as a set of values, Russell assumes the existence of an untyped *value space*, of which every value manipulable by a Russell program (including the program itself) is a member. An example of such a value space would be the set of all bit strings which may be held within the memory of a particular computer. Given a particular bit string, we have no means of determining its type. The best that we may do is to say "If this bit string were to be interpreted as an integer, it would represent the integer n", or "If this bit string were to be interpreted as a set of instructions, it would represent a bubble sort" *etc.* As a result, Russell defines a type as follows;

A data type is a collection of named operations that provide an interpretation of values and variables of a single universal value space.

One advantage of this approach is that types can themselves be values (they are, after all, simply collections of functions), and may be passed to functions, returned from functions and stored in variables. Polymorphism is therefore realised by passing the type of the arguments together with the arguments themselves.

Type checking is simply a matter of ensuring that any given value is not *misinterpreted*. In Russell this is achieved by associating a *signature* with each value, and defining a signature calculus which determines whether a program is type-correct.

Figure 1 shows the Russell definition of the polymorphic identity function. The parameter T is an unconstrained type (shown by the empty 'curly brackets' after the keyword type) demonstrating that this function may act on values of any type. Figure 2 shows the Russell definition of a generic "swap" function, which given two variables of type T swaps their values (using a temporary variable of the same type). The type T is constrained to include functions to create a new variable of type T (the

```
Identity ==
   func[T : type{}; x : val T] val T
   {
      (* return *) x;
   }
```

Figure 1. The polymorphic identity function in Russell

```
Swap ==
   func[T : type t {New : func[] var t;
                    V   : func[var t] val t;
                    :=  : func[var t; val t] val t};
        x, y : var T]
   {
      let z == T$New[] in
         z := V[x];
         x := V[y];
         y := V[z];
      ni
   }
```

Figure 2. A generic swap function in Russell

function New), extract the value of a variable (V) and assign a value to a variable (:=).

Russell also fares well with respect to the criteria mentioned in section 1.1. It is simple and extremely regular (*everything* is first class including types). Abstraction and information hiding are provided through the type structure, and interfaces to types are explicit (the types themselves *are* the interfaces!). The language is both expressive and safe. Finally, Russell's view of types closely matches the underlying hardware representation, allowing Russell programs to be compiled extremely efficiently.

It is this type system that has been chosen for Lucinda.

2.2. Multiple Tuple Spaces

A number of proposals have been made for introducing multiple tuple spaces into Linda. Cogent Research have produced a Linda variant called Kernel Linda, which incorporates multiple tuple spaces[23]. The Advanced Technology Group at Apple have also produced a multiple tuple space version of Linda[1]. Both of these proposals treat tuple spaces purely as a data structuring mechanism. No consideration is given to handling active tuples, type checking of tuple space access *etc.*

A more complete treatment of possible semantics for multiple tuple spaces is given in [15] and expanded upon in [18]. This allows the dynamic creation of tuple spaces with the tsc() construct, and defines more accurately the meaning of an active tuple. We may remove active tuples from tuple space, resulting in the suspension of the processes associated with them and we receive an *image* of the computation. This image may be reanimated at a later time, opening up the interesting possibility of archiving processes. Tuple spaces in this proposal form a strict hierarchy, which may be traversed in a manner similar to the UNIX™ filing system.

For Lucinda, it has been decided to adopt a mechanism similar in many ways to the above, with the exception that we do not organise tuple spaces into a hierarchy. Instead tuple spaces are created on a 'heap', and their structure represented by references (pointers). Tuple spaces may be garbage collected when no references to them are left (an active tuple is considered to have a reference to the tuple space in which it resides). No explicit deletion operator is provided for tuple spaces (in the same way that no explicit variable deletion operator is provided in most programming languages, including Russell) so we do not have to consider the 'liveness condition' for a tuple space discussed in [18].

Lucinda introduces the concept of *typed tuple spaces*. A type constructor `tuplespace` is provided, which given a set of types returns the type of a tuple space which may store tuples of those types. For example, the type;

```
tuplespace {
  foo == actual Short;
  bar == tuple{actual Float; formal Short};
}
```

defines a tuplespace which may accept two classes of tuples. The first of which consists of tuples of a single element of type `Short`, where that element is constrained to be an actual value. The second class consists of tuples of two elements, the first an actual value of type `Float`, the second a value of type `Short` which may be either formal or actual. Tuples of one class may not match tuples of another class.

1 Tuple space operations may be type-checked, allowing two classes of errors to be detected. Firstly *unintended alasing* (different parts of the program unintentionally interfering with each other through use of tuples with similar signature) may be eliminated. Secondly accidentally placing tuples of a form unrecognised by their intended recipient into tuple space is impossible.

2 The addition of 'extra' fields to tuples simply to distinguish between them may be eliminated. For example, we may wish to manipulate two conceptually separate integer values. In 'standard' Linda we would have to use tuples of the form;

("name1", value1) and ("name2", value2)

In Lucinda we simply define the type of the tuple space as follows;

```
tuplespace {
  name1 == formal Short;
  name2 == formal Short;
};
```

Tuples of class `name1` cannot match tuples of class `name2`, so no distinguishing fields are necessary. None of the power of Linda is lost through this mechanism — most Linda optimisers perform similar partitioning of tuple signatures at compile time[9], we simply make such partitioning explicit.

3 As the above may suggest, optimisation is facilitated by the introduction of typed tuple spaces. At present it is necessary to perform extensive static analysis to determine the tuple space access patterns of a Linda program. This mechanism, in making such patterns explicit, allows a number of powerful optimisations to be performed almost trivially. In addition, separate compilation is easier as we need not analyse the complete text of a program to determine its tuple space access patterns.

2.3. Syntax and Semantics

Russell is a modern language with a clean syntax and a large applicative subset (indeed it is possible to write purely functional programs in Russell). As a result is has been decided to retain the syntax and semantics of Russell for Lucinda wherever possible. In order to overcome the problems associated with orthogonality described earlier, those elements of Russell which would conflict with Linda have been removed. In addition Russell's syntax has been slightly changed.

1 Variables and references have been removed from the language. These provide a means of storing and structuring data, a feature already provided by Linda's tuple spaces.

2 Most of Russell's type constructors have been removed, as we wish to encourage the programmer to use tuple space as a data structuring mechanism. This should result in finer grain tuple space accesses.

3 Two new type constructors have been added, `tuple` and `tuplespace`. The first of these is a slightly modified version of the Russell type constructor `Prod`. The second constructs tuple spaces as described above.

4 The syntax of a Russell `let ... in ... ni` block has been changed (for obvious reasons!) to `let ... |[ ... ]|`. Values may be declared as either `actual` or `formal` (rather than `val`).

It can easily be shown that none of the power of Russell has been lost by removing variables from the language, as variables may be emulated completely by tuple spaces (see figure 3). Similarly we may define other state-encapsulating entities, such as *iterators* (see figure 4).

134

```
let var == func[T : type{}] {
  tuplespace {
    theValue == formal T
  } with S {
    := == func[x : actual S; v : actual T] actual T {
      in[x, ?];
      out[x, v];
      v
    };
    V == func[x : actual S] actual T {
      rd[x, ?]
    };
    New == func[v : actual T] actual S {
      let x = S$New[] |[
        out[x, v];
        x
      ]|
    }
  } export {:=; V; New}
}
```

Figure 3. Variables in Lucinda.

```
let iterator == func[initial : Short] {
  tuplespace {
    theValue == formal T;
  } with S {
    Next == func[x : actual S] actual Short {
      let y == in[x, ?]; |[
        out[x, y + 1];
      ]|
      y;
    };
    V == func[x : actual S] actual Short {
      rd[x, ?]
    };
    New == func[v : actual Short] actual S {
      let x = S$New[] |[
        out[x, v];
        x
      ]|
    }
  } export {:=; V; New}
}
```

Figure 4. Iterators in Lucinda.

3. Example

As an example of Lucinda code, we shall examine a parallel, polymorphic matrix multiplication routine. Figure 5 shows the first part of the matrix multiplication example, and defines what we mean by a matrix.

```
let
  Matrix == func[T : type{}; n, m : actual Short] {
    tuplespace {
      Element == tuple {x, y : actual T; e : formal T}
    } with TS {
      New == func [initial : actual T] {
        let
          M == TS$New[];
          i == Iterator$New[0, 1];
          j == Iterator$New[0, 1]
        |[
          do i < n ==>
            do j < m ==>
              out[M, Element$Mk[i, j, initial]];
              Next[j]
            od
            Next[i]
          od;
          M
        ]|
      };
      V == func[M : actual TS; x, y : actual Short] {
        e[rd[M, Element$Mk[x, y, ?]]]
      };
      := == func[M : actual TS; x, y : actual Short;
                  e : actual T] {
        in[M, Element$Mk[x, y, ?]];
        out[M, Element$Mk[x, y, e]]
      }
    } export {New; V; :=}
  };
```

Figure 5. Definition of a matrix in Lucinda.

We define a matrix to be a tuple space which may contain tuples of the form Element, *i.e.* containing a pair of coordinates (of type Short) and a value of type T (the value of the matrix at those coordinates). The coordinates are constrained to always be actual, but the element may be either actual or formal. Three functions are defined on matrices, New (which creates a new, initialised, matrix), V (which returns the value of a particular element of a matrix) and := which assigns a value to a particular element of a matrix.

Next we define the multiplication routine. This is shown in figure 6.

The function * takes the two matrices to be multiplied as its arguments. The other arguments to * may be inferred from the first three, and need not therefore be explicitly given. Note that the type system allows us to represent the relationships between the matrices that must hold if they are to be multiplied (*i.e.* that the number of columns in the first matrix must be equal to the number of rows in the second). The "0", "*" and "+" inside the curly brackets after the keyword type indicate that the type of the matrix elements

```
*  ==  func[arg1 : actual Matrix[T, p, q];
          arg2 : actual Matrix[T, r, p];
          T : type{0, *, +}; p, q, r : actual Short] {
   let
     result == Matrix[T, r, p]$New[T$0];
     workerSig === func[arg1 : actual Matrix[T, p, q];
                        arg2 : actual Matrix[T, r, p];
                        result : actual Matrix[T, r, q];
                        this : actual Workspace;
                        T : type{0, *, +};
                        p, q, r : actual Short] actual Void;
     Workspace == tuplespace {
       Next == formal Short;
       Worker == WorkerSig
     };
     worker == WorkerSig {
       do rd[this, Next$?] < (r * q) ==>
         let next == in[this, Next$?] |[
           out[this, next + 1];
           let
             x == next / r; y == next % r;
             i == Iterator$New[0, 1]
           |[
             do i < p ==>
               [result, x, y] := (V[result, x, y] +
                 (V[arg1, i, y] * V[arg2, x, i]))
             od
           ]|
         ]|
       od
     };
     NumWorkers == Iterator[10, -1]$New[];
     TS == Workspace$New[]
   |[
     out[TS, Next$0];
     do NumWorkers > 0 ==>
       eval[TS, worker[arg1, arg2, result, TS]]
     od;
     rd[TS, (r * q) - 1];
     result
   ]|
}
```

Figure 6. A parallel, polymorphic matrix multiplication routine.

must be one which has a zero element and the multiplication and addition operators defined upon it.

Inside the body of the function, we define a new matrix result to hold the return value. This is returned by the function. We also define a Workspace tuple space, in which working values will be stored (these are Next, the next value of the result to calculate, and Worker, the class of active tuples containing the worker processes). The function worker contains the code for each worker process[3]. This is the "standard" Linda matrix multiplication algorithm in which each worker grabs an element of the result to calculate, performs the calculation, and then grabs another element until all elements have been calculated. Finally, the function $*$ itself creates 10 worker processes (with `eval`), sets the Next tuple to zero, and blocks until the calculation is finished.

4. Formal Semantics of Lucinda

This section is devoted to giving a mathematical framework upon which we develop a formal semantics and proof rule system for Lucinda. Presenting "semantic equations" for the language constructs is done in a categorical setting. We begin by considering the purely logical forms of specification, and derive semantic valuations for any category of possible worlds. Following this, we present proof rules using an axiomatic approach. We do not attempt to show the soundness and completeness of the system — this is left for a subsequent paper.

4.1. Categorical Insight

In this section an attempt to derive a semantic definition of Lucinda applying Category Theory[16] is given.

4.1.1. Functor-category semantics

Consider a phrase Z, for which we require an interpretation. Conventionally, $[\![Z]\!]$ is given by

$$Env \xrightarrow{[\![Z]\!]} M$$

where Env and M are suitable domains of Environment and meaning respectively.

Suppose that x is an object that specifies some local properties (*e.g.* an aspect of storage of tuple space). It is know that, in logic, such an object is called "possible worlds". Then both the valuation function and semantic domain must be parameterised by x. This is written as;

$$Env(x) \xrightarrow{[\![Z]\!]x} M(x)$$

This has the advantage that environment and meaning should be tailored to whatever constraint on the local states might be appropriate.

We note however that the valuation functions and semantic domains for different possible worlds can not, and should not, be different. To achieve

---

[3]The `===` form of definition is akin to the C pre-processor `#define` statement, *ie.* the text after the `===` is inserted verbatim wherever the identifier before the `===` is found.

the required uniformity, let us assume the existence of another possible world y and that

$$f : x \to y$$

specifies how the changes from x to y are made. For example if the possible world is the cardinality of a tuple space then there would be a (unique) function f for every y such that $x \le y$.

It is also reasonable to require that for any possible world x, there is a 'null' change of possible world. This is to say

$$id_x : x \to x$$

and that if $f : x \to y$ and $g : y \to z$ then compositionality of possible worlds is also required, i.e.

$$f \circ g : x \to y$$

Therefore, possible worlds and the change-of-possible-worlds form a category. We shall denote such a category as an X-category.

It is now clear that every X-morphism

$$f : x \to y$$

induces a change of meaning

$$M(f) : M(x) \to M(y)$$

For example, if f specifies again the increase of the cardinality of a tuple space than M(f) for commands will map every command meaning c for the "shorter" tuple space to a command meaning for the "longer" one.

In the same way, Env(f) should do the same thing component-wise for the environments, i.e.

$$Env(f) : Env(x) \to Env(y)$$

Moreover it is reasonable to assume that, as for f, M(f) and Env(f) should preserve identities and composites for all possible worlds. I.e. Env and M are functors from the category of possible worlds (i.e. X) to a suitable category of semantic domains i.e.

$$
\begin{array}{ccc}
x & Env(x) & M(x) \\
{\scriptstyle f}\downarrow & {\scriptstyle Env(f)}\downarrow & {\scriptstyle M(f)}\downarrow \\
y & Env(y) & M(y)
\end{array}
$$

To ensure uniformity of the valuations, $[\![Z]\!]$ must be a *natural transformation* from Env to M. This is to say that the following diagram must commute for every phrase Z and every X-morphism $f : x \to y$.

$$x \quad Env(x) \xrightarrow{\ [Z]x\ } M(x)$$

$$f \downarrow \quad Env(f) \downarrow \qquad\qquad M(f) \downarrow$$

$$y \quad Env(y) \xrightarrow{\ [Z]x\ } M(y)$$

So what we have done is to move from the categories of domains and functions to functor categories $X \Rightarrow Y$ (where objects are now the functors from the category of possible worlds, X, to the category of semantic domains, D) whose morphisms are the natural transformations of these functors.

One way of constructing a category of possible worlds is to consider objects X, Y, ... as sets that can be interpreted as sets of states allowed by the reasoning context; the morphisms from X to Y are injective functions from Y to X. Simply, this means that every element in Y is mapped to an element of X that it represents; elements of X not in the range of the function are called "unreachable" when executing in the more restricted possible world. Composition of the morphisms is the normal function composition.

4.1.2. Semantic Valuation

This section deals with presenting "semantic equations" for Lucinda. But first let us look how these equations are written within our functor category semantics given previously. Throughout we use x to denote an object in the category of domains, u is an element in the environment appropriate to x and to the free identifiers of the phrase, and $f : x \to y$ is a morphism with a domain x.

For example is Z_1 and Z_2 are two phrases then

$$[Z_1 \cap Z_2]xuf = [Z_1]xuf \cap [Z_2]xuf$$

Note also that from topos theory we shall have

$$[Z_1 \Rightarrow Z_2]xuf = \forall g{:}y{\to}z\bullet \text{ if } [Z_1]xu(f{\circ}g) \text{ then } [Z_2]xu(f{\circ}g)$$

In order to define the meaning functors for a phrase Z of type T we need to identify two functors: value and state functors. For all X-objects x, $V_T(x)$ defines the set of functions of datatype T (e.g. $V_{Bool}(x) = \{$True, False, And, Or, etc.$\}$). The functor S(x) defines the set of all states allowed in possible world x. Therefore, if Z is an assertion (in an if ... fi or do ... od clause) then $[Z]$ is given as $S \to V_{Bool}$; and if Z is an expression of datatype T then

$$[Z] : S \to V_{T_\perp}$$

Now we are in a position to give semantic equations for these Lucinda phrases that form the integral part of the language.

The empty phrase

$$[\{\}]xuf = id_{S(y)}$$

Sequential Composition

$$[\![Z_1 \fbox{;} Z_2]\!]xuf = [\![Z_1]\!]xuf \circ [\![Z_2]\!]xuf$$

where $\circ$ represents composition of partial functions.

Conditional phrase

Let IF = $\fbox{if}$ g $\fbox{==>}$ A $\fbox{fi}$, then

$$\forall y_0 \in S(y) \bullet [\![IF]\!]xuf = \begin{cases} [\![A]\!]xufy_0, & \text{if } [\![g]\!]xufy_0 = \text{True}[] \in V_{\text{Bool}}(y) \\ id_{S(y)}, & \text{otherwise} \end{cases}$$

If the conditional phrase is of the form IF = $\fbox{if}$ g $\fbox{==>}$ A $\fbox{;}$ $\fbox{else}$ B $\fbox{fi}$ then we have:

$$[\![IF]\!]xufy_0 = \begin{cases} [\![A]\!]xufy_0, & \text{if } [\![g]\!]xufy_0 = \text{True}[] \in V_{\text{Bool}}(y) \\ [\![B]\!]xufy_0, & \text{otherwise} \end{cases}$$

Loop phrase We treat loop phrases as recursive definition of conditional ones.

Let W = $\fbox{do}$ α $\fbox{==>}$ P $\fbox{od}$ $\equiv_{\text{def}}$ α $\fbox{==>}$ P $\fbox{;}$ W $\fbox{;}$ $\fbox{else}$ {};

Therefore, for all $y_0 \in S(y)$

$$[\![W]\!]xufy_0 = \begin{cases} [\![P]\!]xufy_0 \circ [\![W]\!], & \text{if} [\![\alpha]\!]xufy_0 = \text{True}[] \in V_{\text{Bool}}(y) \\ id_{S(y)}, & \text{otherwise} \end{cases}$$

once again $\circ$ denotes partial function composition.

4.2. Axiomatic Semantics

4.2.1. Introduction

In this section we derive an axiomatic semantics for Lucinda. Such a semantics allows us to derive proof rules for correctness. We shall not attempt to show the completeness of the derived proof system. The purpose of defining a total correctness theory T for a language L is to allow us to infer theorems of the form

$$P\{c\}Q$$

about the behaviour of a given program c in L. The interpretation of the above is taken to be "if P is true, then c terminates in a state in which Q is true" (this is of course different from the non-interference axioms formed in some logic programming, *e.g.* P#C, which is interpreted as being P is always true before, after and during C).

Let us now denote $\mathcal{A}$ to be the assertion language used in defining the semantics of L. The set of all valid assertions of $\mathcal{A}$ forms the axioms of L.

4.2.2. Proof Rules

The empty command

$$\frac{P \Rightarrow Q}{P\{\}Q}$$

Sequencing rule

$$\frac{P\{c_1\}R, \ R\{c_2\}Q}{P\{c_1 \boxed{;} c_2\}Q}$$

Conditional rule

$$\frac{P \wedge b\{c_1\}Q, \ P \wedge \neg b\{c_2\}Q}{P\{\boxed{if}\,b\,\boxed{==>}\,c_1\,\boxed{else}\,c_2\,\boxed{fi}\}Q}$$

Bounded loop rule

$$\frac{P \wedge (V \leq 0) \Rightarrow \neg b, \ P \wedge b(V=t)\{c\}P \wedge (v < t)}{P\{\boxed{do}\,b\,\boxed{==>}\,c\,\boxed{od}\}P \wedge \neg b}$$

Note that v denotes a monotonically decreasing integer valued function, which for given values of a program alphabet yields an upper bound on the number of iterations still to be performed.

Developing logical systems for proving assertions about programs (written in a given language) in the style of Hoare's triple consistently deviate from a purely denotational approach. In every case, this ideal approach has been deemed inconvenient and has been compromised in favour of operational foundations, notably in explaining inference rules for calls of recursive procedures and for declarations of local variables. This is due to the fact that the denotational semantics of local storage for blocks has never adequately been worked out. The axiomatic semantics given here fall into this category. One approach, that is under investigation, is to formalize the assignment of semantics to a Lucinda program in two steps:

(a) a purely syntactic translation from Lucinda to a fully-typed λ-calculus; and

(b) assignment of semantics to the λ-calculus in the standard way (programs simply inherit their semantics directly from the λ-calculus into which they translate.

5. Further and Related Work

This paper has presented a preliminary design for a polymorphic, distributed programming language, Lucinda based upon Linda. Implementation of

Lucinda is proceeding, both on a network of transputers and a network of Sun workstations. A prototype is hoped to be completed by the second quarter of 1991.

There has, to the best of the author's knowledge, been little research into polymorphic, parallel, distributed programming languages in the past. There are some signs that this will change in the future. Bruce[5] is looking at the construction of parallel systems with a strongly typed language, but this work has been started only recently. An Eiffel-Linda[19] variant has been constructed recently, which gains polymorphism through the type system of Eiffel. Unfortunately, Eiffel's type system is not perfect (although work is under way to remedy this[10]). It is also not clear how well the object-oriented style of programming language and Linda co-exist. Linda's matching seems to require that we break encapsulation.

Lucinda is not the only new language based upon the ideas found in Linda. Ease[28] is aimed at low level applications, and as a target for formally derived programs. To this end it combines features of both CSP and Linda.

References

[1]   Abarbanel, R. & Janin, A. *Distributed Object Management with Linda.* Advanced Technology Group, Apple Computer Inc. Technical Report, September 1989.

[2]   Boehm, H., Demers, A. & Donahue, J. *An Informal Description of Russell.* Department of Computer Science, Cornell University. Technical Report TR 80–430, October 1980.

[3]   Brinch Hansen, P. *Distributed processes: A concurrent programming concept.* Communications of the ACM, 21(11) pp 934–940, November 1978.

[4]   Brinch Hansen, P. *The programming language Concurrent Pascal.* Transactions on Software Engineering, 1(2) pp 199–207, June 1975.

[5]   Bruce, D. *A Strongly-Typed Approach to Parallel Systems.* Royal Signals and Radar Establishment, Malvern. Position paper, 1991.

[6]   Butcher, P. *A Behavioural Semantics for Linda-2.* Department of Computer Science, University of York. Technical Report YCS–137, July 1990. To appear in IEE Software Engineering Journal.

[7]   Cardelli, L. & Wegner, P. *On Understanding Types, Data Abstraction, and Polymorphism.* Computing Surveys, 17(4), December 1985.

[8]   Carriero, N. & Gelernter, D. *Coordination Languages and their Significance.* Yale University, Department of Computer Science. Research Report YALEU/DCS/RR–716, July 1989.

[9]   Carriero, N. & Gelernter, D. *Tuple analysis and partial evaluation strategies in the Linda precompiler.* In Proceedings, Second Workshop on Languages and Compilers for Parallelism, August 1989.

[10]   Cook, W. *A proposal for making Eiffel type-safe.* Computer Journal 32(4) pp 305–311, August 1989.

[11]   Core, P. & Foster, J. *Ten15: An Overview.* Royal Signals and Radar Establishment. Technical Report 3977, September 1986.

[12]   Dawes, J. *The Professional Programmer's Guide to Ada.* Pitman, 1988.

[13]   Donahue, J. & Demers, A. *Data Types Are Values.* Transactions on Programming Languages and Systems 7(3) pp 426–445, July 1985.

[14]   Gelernter, D. *Generative Communication in Linda.* Transactions on Programming Languages and Systems, 2(1) pp 80–112, January 1985.

[15]   Gelernter, D. *Multiple tuple spaces in Linda.* In Odijk, E., Rem, M. & Syre, J.-C. ed. PARLE '89: Parallel Architectures and Languages Europe. Volume II: Parallel Languages. LNCS 366, pp 20–27. June 1989.

[16]   Goldblatt, R. *Topi, the categorical analysis of logic,* North-Holland, 1984.

[17]   Hoare, C. *Communicating Sequential Processes.* Communications of the ACM, 21(8) pp 666–677, August 1978.

[18]   Hupfer, S. *Melinda: Linda with Multiple Tuple Spaces.* Yale University, Department of Computer Science. Research Report YALEU/DCS/RR-766. February 1990.

[19]   Jellinghaus, R. *Eiffel Linda: An object-oriented Linda dialect.* SIGPLAN Notices 25(12) pp 70–84, December 1990.

[20]   Kernighan, B. & Ritchie, D. *The C Programming Language,* Second Edition. Prentice Hall, 1988.

[21]   Kilstad, R. & Campbell, R. *Path Pascal User Manual.* Sigplan Notices, 15(9) pp 13–24, September 1980.

[22]   Leichter, J. *Shared Tuple Memories, Shared Memories, Buses and LAN's — Linda Implementations Across the Spectrum of Connectivity.* Yale University, Department of Computer Science. Research Report YALEU/DCS/TR-714, July 1989.

[23]   Leler, W. *Linda Meets UNIX.* Computer, 23(2) pp52–76, September 1990.

[24] MacLennan, B. *Principles of Programming Languages: Design, Evaluation, and Implementation*, Second Edition. Holt, Rinehart and Winston, 1987.

[25] May, D. *occam-2 language definition*. Inmos, Technical Note. February 1987.

[26] Milner, R. *A Proposal for Standard ML*. University of Edinburgh, Department of Computer Science. Technical Report CSR-157-83, December 1983.

[27] Mitchell, J. & Plotkin, G. *Abstract types have existential type*. In Proceedings, 12th Annual Symposium on the Principles of Programming Languages, pp37-51, January 1985.

[28] Zenith, S. *Programming with Ease: Semiotic definition of the language*. Yale University, Department of Computer Science. Research Report YALEU/DCS/RR-809, July 1990.

Appendix — An EBNF Syntax for Lucinda

Program

Program	::= Denotation

Denotations

Denotation	::= Signature | PrimaryList
DenotationSeq	::= Denotation $\boxed{;}$ [DenotationSeq]
DenotationList	::= Denotation $\{\boxed{,}$ Denotation$\}$
PrimaryList	::= Primary {Primary}
Primary	::= FuncConstruction
	| Selection
	| Pimary TypeModifier
	| $\boxed{(}$ DenotationSeq $\boxed{)}$
	| $\boxed{if}$ GuardedList $\boxed{fi}$
	| $\boxed{do}$ GuardedList $\boxed{od}$
	| $\boxed{let}$ DeclarationList $\boxed{[}$ DenotationSeq $\boxed{]}$
	| $\boxed{use}$ DenotationList $\boxed{[}$ DenotationSeq $\boxed{]}$
	| $\boxed{[}$ [DenotationList $\boxed{]}$

Constructions

FuncConstruction	::= FuncSignature $\boxed{(}$ DenotationSeq $\boxed{)}$
ParameterList	::= Parameter $\{\boxed{;}$ Parameter$\}$
Paramter	::= [IdList $\boxed{:}$] Signature
TypeConstruction	::= Enumeration | Tuple | TupleSpace

Enumeration	::=	`enum` `{` IdList `}`
Tuple	::=	`tuple` `{` ParameterList `}`
TupleSpace	::=	`tuplespace` `{` DeclarationList `}`

Type Modifications

TypeModifier	::=	WithClause | ExportClause
WithClause	::=	`with` [Id] `{` DeclarationList `}`
ExportClause	::=	(`export` | `hide`) [Id] `{` ExportList `}`
ExportList	::=	ExportElement `{` `;` ExportElement}
ExportElement	::=	Id [SigClause] [ExportList]
		| `constants`

Signatures

Signature	::=	(`actual` | `formal` | `active`) PrimaryList
		| FuncSignature
		| `type` [Id] `{` ParamterList `}`
FuncSignature	::=	`func` `[` [ParamterList] `]` [Signature]

Declarations

DeclarationList	::=	Declaration `;` {Declaration}
Declaration	::=	IdList [`:` Signature] `==` Denotation
		| IdList `===` Denotation

Guards

GuardedList	::=	GuardDenotation `{` `#` GuardDenotation}
GuardDenotation	::=	Denotation `==>` Denotation

Selections

Selection	::=	Primary `$` Id [SigClause]
		| Primary `$` String
		| Id [SigClause]
		| String
SigClause	::=	`<<` Signature `>>`

Identifiers

IdList	::=	Id `{` `,` Id}
Id	::=	WordId | OpId | QuotedId
WordId	::=	Alpha {AlphaNum}
OpId	::=	OpChar {OpChar}

QuotedId	::=	`'` Character {Character} `'`
String	::=	Number | QuotedString
Number	::=	Digit {AlphaNum}
QuotedString	::=	`"` Character {Character} `"`
AlphaNum	::=	Alpha | Num
Alpha	::=	`a` | ... | `z` | `A` | ... | `Z`
Num	::=	`0` | ... | `9`
Character	::=	AlphaNum | OpChar | SpecialChar
OpChar	::=	`!` | `@` | `%` | `^` | `&` | `*` | `_` | `-` | `+` | `=` | `|` | `\` | `` ` `` | `~` | `.` | `?` | `/` | `<` | `>`
SpecialChar	::=	`;` | `,` | `(` | `)` | `[` | `]` | `{` | `}` | `:` | `#` | `"` | `'` | `$`

A Rationale for Programming with *Ease*

Steven Ericsson Zenith

Ecole Nationale Supérieure des Mines de Paris
Centre du Recherche en Informatique
35 rue Saint-Honore 77305 Fontainebleau FRANCE*.

1 Introduction

Message passing has proven a difficult addendum to existing programming practices primarily because it preoccupies the programmer with issues of data distribution.

The Linda model proposes a solution to data distribution issues by providing a global associative memory and simple interaction primitives. However, the implementation of Linda is complex, heavily dependent on either optimization or efficient matching protocols. Intuitive predictions about the performance behavior of a Linda program are difficult to make leading to subliminal effects on the way programs are developed.

This paper presents a new model (*Ease*) for parallel programming which evolves from and refines these earlier models.

Ease is a simple and integrated model for the development of efficient parallel systems, regardless of the underlying memory architecture.

A program is described as a collection of processes which execute concurrently, constructing and interacting via strictly typed distributed data structures called *contexts*.

The paper does not attempt to cover the full detail of the language. The motivating arguments which lead to the development of *Ease* are discussed. The introduction, part one and two discuss problems in related models, section five onward provides an overview of the new model.

2 Interaction Models

The construction of programs as a collection of behavior patterns called *processes* and some mechanism by which they *interact* is evolving as a positive engineering solution to programming parallel machines. Whilst much work has been done on understanding process models, the models by which processes interact remains today a subject of great debate.

Message passing has, for sometime, been a favored interaction model on the basis that it is simple and readily understood. In several quarters (primarily in the European

* Funding for this work was provided in part by the Association pour la Recherche et le Développement des Méthodes et processus Industriels (ARMINES). This paper derives from a thesis in preparation and remains copyright of the author.

Computer Science community) the message passing model is being put forward as a general purpose programming model for parallel machines.

Yet message passing is unsuitable as a general purpose model for parallel programming. Programmers using the model become preoccupied by issues of data distribution.

Forget for the moment issues of mapping programs to hardware topology. The programmer using a message passing model is forced to consider, in some detail, multiplexing and routing issues when distributing data among groups of processes.

Further, the model does not map well onto the range of parallel machine architectures for a general set of applications. In applications with medium to coarse data granularity the model compels an implementation to copy data that might otherwise be passed by reference.

Linda[Gelernter 85] provides a solution to the problems of data distribution which preoccupy programmers of the message passing model. However, the Linda model is flawed since performance semantics in the model are unpredictable and still applications are compelled to copy data that might otherwise be passed by reference.

The strategy[Carriero 88][Zenith 90/794] used by Linda optimizations cause a program's performance characteristics to alter widely during the course of development.

There is a *semiotic effect*[2] Empirical analysis leads the programmer to write code based on an *understanding* of how the optimizer or underlying matching protocol behaves - thus subverting any meaningful portability.

Interest in the Linda model is driven by the richness of the *shared data space model*. This model provides a uniform mechanism for constructing and *addressing* shared data.

Linda addressing is by *associative matching* based on the value and type of *tuples*. Shared objects are created, read, and removed by simple primitives.

The Linda interaction model possesses several desirable characteristics as a programmers model. In particular it alleviates the problems observed in message passing – that is, the programmer need no longer be concerned by issues of data distribution, and is free to focus on algorithmic issues i.e. solving the problem and not fighting or mastering integral characteristics of the programming model.

Since the addressing mechanism is conceptually distinct from the linear address space, or distributed disjoint address space associated with current machine architectures, novel implementation techniques can be considered.

However, use of the Linda programming model requires many contrivances on the part of the programmer to construct shared data structures and provides no guaranteed call–reply semantics between processes. Message passing languages like Occam aand C with extensions are better suited to topology dependent embedded systems and realtime.

---

[2] Semiotic: This term is more usually found in linguistics or philosophy and refers to "a general philosophical theory of signs and symbols that deals esp. with their function in both artificially constructed and natural languages and comprises the three branches of syntactics, semantics, and pragmatics"(Webster's Third New International Dictionary). In the manner used here semiotics considers the effect the language has upon the programmer, and in particular, the pragmatic statements required for the programmer to make consistent and efficient use of the language.

3 What's Wrong with Message Passing?

If it isn't clear yet it is important here to understand the distinction between message passing as a component of parallel machine architecture and *generalized message passing* as a programming model.

Concern for the characteristics of communication between nodes of a machine is an important and significant issue in computer architecture. Operating systems and VLSI must provide internodal connectivity, in part by message passing, to support higher level models such as *Ease*. These are not the issues being addressed here.

The issues here concern the programming model. How programmers may conceive and construct parallel programs whose performance semantics may be well understood and remain efficient regardless of the architecture of the machines memory subsystem.

The Occam model[INMOS 88/Occ] of message passing enables simplicity in implementation. However, this simplicity has a cost, and the cost is a significant one.

The primary goals of the Occam model were

1. Simple implementation
2. Message passing as the basis of a general purpose parallel programming model
3. Efficiency

The first goal was undoubtedly achieved in 1985 with the manifestation of the transputer [INMOS 88/Tra]. However, the remaining goals are incompatible and both fail as a result.

The failure of the model as general purpose has already been highlighted in the previous section. The efficiency failure occurs in the context of this generalization and is in essence caused by the copying of data which might otherwise be passed by reference.

The criticism here does not apply in such cases where the model is tied closely to specialized machine architecture. Specialized applications of message passing, such as systolic algorithms for systolic arrays are simply outside this criticism.

Generalized message passing implements communication between processes in the same address space as a memory to memory copy operation. This increases traffic in the most significant bottleneck in modern machine architecture – the memory subsystem. Indeed, modern cache memory and load and store CPU architecture conspire against the efficiency of memory to memory copy operations.

The model does not map well across the range of MIMD parallel machine architectures for this reason. A message passing program on a shared memory multi-processor would certainly pay a performance penalty for these copy operations and other programming models, which do allow the exchange of data by reference, would be (indeed are) preferred on such machines.

4 What's Wrong with Linda?

In addition to the work described here, several other groups have been prompted to examine the ideas behind this loosely defined model.

Most notable among the recent work – and representative of the broad spectrum of interest – are the UNITY like SWARM[Roman 90] and Orca[Bal 90], a component of the Amoeba[Tanenbaum 90] distributed operating system.

The important fundamentals introduced by Linda are a distinct shared data space and simple operations to change the state of that space.

Linda has changed the understanding of how data objects can be *addressed* in parallel machines.

Linda concepts are powerful. However, they are too abstract in the context of the common host language C.

The model cannot be applied to a broad spectrum of applications on parallel machines.

The model is unsuitable for programming real-time or embedded systems since the performance semantics of tuple space operations are difficult to predict. Linda programming is heavily dependent on program optimization. So much so it leads programmers to develop techniques and conventions founded on an understanding of the behavior of a particular optimizer or underlying matching protocol. Linda programs written in this way possess a hidden, and undesirable performance semantic.

All modern compilers utilized optimization and these optimizations have performance effects. However, the Linda optimizations are of a radical nature, with such different performance characteristics, ranging from the cost of a simple counting semaphore to the complex cost of a distributed hash table and exhaustive searching. The introduction to a program of a single new tuple type may cause the optimizer to change strategy with remarkable effects, invalidating any earlier empirical analysis by the programmer.

Linda does not provide opportunities for exchanging data by reference. Each operation may involve several more copy operations than the equivalent operations in the message passing model. The value matching overhead, which can be significant in systems dependent on it, has been ignored here.

The expression of distributed matrices cannot be achieved simply, demanding the programmer contrive a tuple structure to meet the requirement. This is a serious problem in scientific computing applications.

Processes in the Linda model are disjoint, making it necessary for programmers to contrive naming schemes within tuple space to allow an (uncertain) association between processes. This disjointness makes it difficult to consider well formed process structures. For example, such as those which might describe the behavior of robots.

5 *Ease* – a New Model Arises

The remainder of this paper gives an overview of the *Ease* model[Zenith 90/809]. This section concentrates on those aspects of the model which distinguish *Ease* as a unique model for programming parallel machines.

Ease is a general purpose, high level, imperative programming language designed to enable the simple expression of concurrent algorithms.

The language provides a type associative storage model which can be efficiently implemented on a range of machine memory architectures.

The model is sufficiently distinct to be added to a conventional language in the same way as message passing primitives and, indeed Linda primitives, have been in the past. A full *Ease* language compiler is in advanced stages of development and work is currently underway on implementation of C–with–Ease.

The model enables simpler implementation and thus greater efficiency than Linda type/value associativity by obviating all runtime matching.

The model maintains, and enhances, the richness of shared data space as the basis for expressing interactions between processes.

The *Ease* model can be implemented efficiently since the model encapsulates a mechanism for exchanging data by reference.

This encapsulation enables the model to be implemented independent of machine memory architecture, yet remain efficient when compiled for either shared or distributed memory machines.

A program is described as a collection of processes which execute concurrently, constructing and interacting via strictly typed distributed data structures called *contexts*.

Ease is novel in the following regard: a *context* provides a *priority* oriented and strictly typed intermediary in which shared/distributed data structures are constructed and by which processes may interact. Though priority aspects of the model are not considered here.

The model provides simple and symmetric operators (read and write, get and put). The process model provides constructions for both cooperative and subordinate concurrency and a mechanism for building statically reusable and virtual resources on parallel and distributed machines.

6 Contexts – Shared Data Structures

Data concepts

- **Local data** – *Variables* which are named sets of values totally ordered over time. May be acted upon by only one, sequential, process.
- **Shared data** – *Contexts* which are named sets of values partially ordered over time. May be acted upon by several processes concurrently.
- **Scope** – the process in which a name is valid.
- **Environment** – a set of scopes whose names are valid in a process.

These data concepts capture the changing nature of (for example) variables by viewing them as the set of all the values held by the variable during its existence. Similarly, a context is the set of values held during its existence. Each value held by a variable is, in effect, indexed (defined) by the action which assigned the variable that value. Similarly, each value held by a context is indexed (defined) by the action which assigned the context that value. Since variables are assigned strictly in sequence the values held by a variable are totally ordered, we can say that in an expression "a variable has the value *most recently* assigned to it".

A context value is assigned to a variable by an *input* action (which will be described shortly). The value of a context may have one of three *properties* it may be

- a **singular value** (like a variable) – an input value is the *most recent* value assigned to it.
- a **stream of values** – an input value is the *least recent* value assigned to it.
- an **unordered set of values** – an input value is one of the values *previously* assigned to it.

Here the terms *most recent*, *least recent* and *previous* are used in the sense of the partial order obtained by the interleaving of all the concurrent processes acting upon the context.

Contexts are unlike variables however, since a context value has a partial order defined by the concurrent processes which act upon it and they may themselves be sets of values, i.e. an assignment (output) to a context may not "overwrite" the previous value but simply add the value to the set of values assigned to it. Conversely an input may not just read a value in the set but also delete it.

A value is added to a context by an *output* action. The values output to a context inherit an ordering determined by the composition of the processes in which the outputs appear. Thus two outputs in a sequential composition place the values into a context with a total order. How that order is interpreted is determined by the *property* (described above) specified for the context. Thus a context is either

- a *singleton* – a single distinct object or array of such objects which may be selected by subscription.
- a *stream* – a serially ordered set of some type where the least recently output value is the value input.
- a *bag* – an unordered set of some type.

In addition, a further type is useful for resources.

- a *call–reply* – a type providing guaranteed call reply semantics

Contexts of distinct types may be gathered under a single name enabling a single shared *space* of multiple types to be constructed. Operations on a context space are type associative (name equivalent), that is, operations are valid if the type of the value or variable is one of the types specified for the space.

7 Operations – Actions on Shared Data

There are four simple, symmetric, operations on contexts. They are

- **write (c, e)** – copies the value of the expression **e** to the context **c**.
- **read (c, v)** – copies a value from the context **c** to a variable **v**.

- **put (c, n)** – moves the value associated with the name **n** to the context **c**.
- **get (c, n)** – moves a value from the context **c** and binds it to the name **n**.

Write and read are copy operations. Put and get are binding operators. The synchronization characteristics of the operations are similarly symmetric

- get and read block if data is not existent
- write and put are non-blocking.

Consider how these operations change the state of a program.

Write changes the state of a context, leaving the local state unchanged. Read changes the local state whilst leaving the context state unchanged.

Put changes both the context state and local state, i.e. subsequently the value associated with the variable name used in the operation is undefined. Get also changes both the context state and the local state, i.e. the value bound to the variable name used in the operation is removed from the context.

8 Uniformly Building and Using Resources

The construction of and interaction with resources has special requirements. To enable the simple and uniform view of resources in parallel and distributed environments, *Ease* provides *combinations*.

A *combination* provides guaranteed call-reply semantics via some context. A process which outputs a request to some resource which has access to a shared context is guaranteed to receive the corresponding reply to the *request*. Thus two particular processes synchronize.

A combination consists of two associated operations.

- a *call* – behaves like an output followed by a get
- a *resource* – behaves like a get, a process and subsequently an output

The value output by the resource is guaranteed to satisfy the corresponding get of the associated call.

This call-reply guarantee allows the simple creation of *statically reusable* and *virtual resources*.

A *statically reusable* resource is a process which manages direct access to the actual resource. A vector processor may be considered a *statically reusable* resource since the user process must await its turn before use. A simulation of the resource behavior may not be useful.

A *virtual resource* is a process which *pretends* to be the actual resource. A disc cache can be considered to provide *virtual resource* since it returns to the user immediately as though the requested action had been completed on the actual resource.

9 The Process Model

Process concepts

- An **action** is an assignment to a variable or shared data structure.
- A **process** is an action or combination of processes such as a sequence, conditional, loop or parallel.

Ease provides two forms of process creation which differ in their synchronization characteristics and the rules for access to local data.

9.1 Cooperating Processes

A cooperation, creates some number of *cooperating* parallel processes.

$$\|p()\|q();$$

creates two processes $p()$ and $q()$. The cooperation terminates when all the processes have terminated.

All interaction between processes is isolated to shared data structures (contexts). Thus processes may operate on contexts but cannot use free variables in their body. Variables are strictly local data objects belonging to a single sequence.

Cooperations thus represent processes which cooperate closely since they share a mutual barrier synchronization.

A special shorthand, a *replication*, allows many similar processes to be created

$$||i \text{ for } n \text{ from } b : P(i);$$

creates a cooperation of n processes where each has an index i in its scope.

9.2 Subordinate Processes

A subordination, creates one or more *subordinate* processes.

$$//p();$$

creates a single process $p()$. Unlike cooperation subordination terminates immediately – the subordinate process is created and the creating process continues.

Again, a replication allows many similar processes to be created

$$//i \text{ for } n \text{ from } b : P(i);$$

creates n processes, each of which has an argument index i with a distinct value from b to $n - 1$.

10 An Example

To give a feel for the nature of *Ease* an example is presented. The example is an implementation of the well known "Sieve of Eratosthenes"[3]

The object of the program is to sum all the primes from the first prime 2 to LIMIT.

Begin by defining a context type stream called "ordered". A stream of integers. Contexts of this type will connect processes in a pipeline.

type ordered context stream int

In addition a singleton type is required to hold the final summation.

type one context single int

The algorithm is well known. Briefly, a stream of candidate prime numbers is passed through a pipeline of filters. The first number in the stream is a new prime. Each filter looks for numbers which are not multiples of the prime the filter represents – such numbers are potentially prime and are passed on to the next filter in the pipeline.

Consider the following implementation of a filter process.

---

[3] The language used here is according to the revised language definition. The revised definition is the first complete definition of the language first presented as a Yale University Research Report (809) in July 1990.

```
procedure filter (pipe, sum)
  let next := ordered
  let prime, candidate := int :
{
  pipe ?* prime
  pipe ?* candidate
  test (prime*prime) < LIMIT : {
      let sum = sum+prime :
      // filter (next, sum);
      while candidate <> NULL
        test (candidate % prime)=0 : pipe ?* candidate
        else {next !* candidate
             pipe ?* candidate};
      next ! NULL
      }
  else let result := sum+prime :{
      while candidate <> NULL {
          result := result + candidate
          pipe   ?* candidate
          }
      sigma ! result
      };
}
```

A filter process begins by allocating a context next. This will be used to pass data to the next stage in the pipeline. A new pipeline stage, a copy of the filter process itself, is created as required. The operators !, !*, ? and ?* represent write, put, read and get respectively.

Next a procedure which writes into the head of the pipe a sequence of odd numbers.

```
procedure source(pipe)
{
 {i for LIMIT/2-1 from 3 by 2 : pipe ! i}
 pipe ! NULL
}
```

Two is considered a "found" prime. The final program can be expressed by the following.

```
let sum   := int
let sigma := one
let pipe  := ordered :
{
  //filter(pipe, 2) //source(pipe) ;
  sigma ? sum
  printf("Sum of primes: %d.\n", sum)
}
```

Here there are three processes. The two subordinate processes, the first stage filter process and the source process writing odd numbers. The creating process waits and presents the final result.

11 Conclusion

It is reasoned that for a broad range of parallel programming applications *Ease* is a more efficient model than either message passing or Linda, since it elegantly encapsulates the expression of shared data exchanges by reference.

Efficiency remains – regardless of a parallel machine's memory subsystem architecture. Subverting the copy overhead compelled by message passing implementations and obviating any need for the run time matching required by Linda. Thus providing for greater portability of parallel programs.

Other features of the model, in particular those which enable the simple construction of resources, enable the construction of large multifaceted programs to be considered.

Ease maintains the simple elegance of a shared data space with a few simple interaction primitives in a manner that is readily accessible to the broad range of existing applications programmers.

Implementations of the language and model are at advanced stages of development, and several other implementation projects have already begun at other centers around the world.

References

[Bal 90] H.E.Bal et.al *Orca: A language for distributed Programming*, Report IR 140, Dept Maths and CS, Vrije Universiteit, Dec 1987.

[Carriero 88] N. Carriero, *The Implementation of Tuple Space Machines*, Ph.D Thesis Yale University

[Gelernter 85] David Gelernter, *Generative Communication in Linda*, ACM Transactions 1985.

[Hoare 85] C.A.R.Hoare. *Communicating Sequential Processes*, Prentice-Hall 1985.

[INMOS 88/Occ] INMOS Ltd (Steven Ericsson Zenith and David May). *Occam 2 Reference Manual*, Prentice-Hall 1988.

[INMOS 88/Tra] INMOS Limited, *Transputer Reference Manual*, Prentice-Hall 1988.

[Roman 90] Roman and Cunningham, *Mixed Programming Metaphors in a Shared Dataspace Model of Concurrency.*, IEEE Transactions on software engineering, Dec 1990.

[Tanenbaum 90] Tanenbaum and Mullender et.al. *Amoeba – a distributed operating system for the 1990s*, IEEE Computer Magazine, May 1990.

[Zenith 90/809] Steven Ericsson Zenith. *Programming with Ease; Semiotic definition of the language*, Yale Technical Report RR 809, July 1990.

[Zenith 90/794] Steven Ericsson Zenith. *Linda coordination language; subsystem kernel architecture*, Yale Technical Report RR 794, May 1990

This article was processed using the LaTeX macro package with LMAMULT style

INTERMEDIATE UNIFORMLY DISTRIBUTED TUPLE SPACE ON TRANSPUTER MESHES

Craig Faasen[1]

Perihelion Software Limited, The Maltings, Charlton Road
Shepton Mallet, Somerset, BA4 5QE England
E-Mail : craig@perisl.uucp

Abstract

Linda is a paradigm for high-level parallel programming that offers a novel alternative to conventional models of process coordination and communication. The basis of the Linda model is a global, logically shared tuple space through which process interaction and synchronization are achieved, providing a conceptually simple approach to parallel programming. There is evidence that suggests a need for a new programming methodology to support transputer-based applications, and Linda, as an attractive and elegant alternative to existing methodologies, has great potential for this role. This paper describes the implementation of a particular tuple space model, intermediate uniform distribution, on transputer meshes and discusses the nature of the overheads inherent in the implementation. It is concluded that although the specific tuple space model is not ideally suited to transputer-based systems and the implementation, as it stands, is too inefficient to be of practical use, the approach requires further exploration in order to exhaust its full research potential.

1.0 INTRODUCTION

Linda is a paradigm for high-level parallel programming, the basis of which is a global, logically shared *tuple space* (TS). TS is a form of associative memory that is accessible to all processes running within a parallel program. These processes communicate by manipulating the TS – i.e. by inserting and retrieving data objects (*tuples*). Processes therefore have no direct interaction with each other. Instead, process synchronization and communication are achieved via tuple space operations. Inherently, a shared-memory architecture appears most suited to supporting Linda efficiently and there are a number of such implementations in existence [Carriero 1987]. However, distributed-memory architectures are not excluded from the sphere

---

[1]This research was conducted in partial fulfilment of the requirements for the degree of Master of Science at the University of the Witwatersrand, Johannesburg. Funding for this research was provided by the Foundation for Research Development and the University of the Witwatersrand

of potential Linda target machines and are indeed regarded as an important area of application [Ahuja *et al.* 1988].

The transputer is representative of such distributed-memory architectures, offering supercomputer performance for a fraction of the cost. There is a close relationship between the transputer and its programming model, occam. This means that problems to be solved using the hardware can be expressed naturally and elegantly (and efficiently) in occam [Pountain 1989]. However, because of the close relationship between the hardware and the software formalism, the style of programming is closely coupled to the specific hardware topology. Consequently, the underlying processor configuration plays a prominent role in algorithm design. This suggests a need for a new programming paradigm to support transputer-based applications. Linda, as an elegant and conceptually simple alternative to existing methodologies, is a strong candidate for this role. The implementation of a globally accessible tuple space on transputers does, however, pose a number of problems. The transputer is a message passing distributed-memory architecture, with processor interconnection via point-to-point synchronous links. Hence, there is the problem of maintaining distributed data over independent local memories, and also having to deal with a potential communications bottleneck.

A particular tuple space methodology, intermediate uniform distribution, has been implemented on transputer meshes [Faasen 1991]. This was done in order to investigate the communication overheads imposed by the model, and hence evaluate the feasibility of the approach. This paper reviews the above research, and gives a concise overview of the design and implementation of the system (which is termed *X-Linda*). It should be pointed out that X-Linda is not a fully-fledged Linda implementation. The design and functionality of the model are restricted to meet the needs and requirements of the research.

This paper presumes some familiarity with the Linda paradigm and does not attempt to introduce the underlying concepts (i.e. tuples and TS, the semantics of the TS primitive operations and the associated programming methodology). Detailed descriptions of these issues are given (among others) by Ahuja *et al.* [1986], Carriero [1987], Gelernter [1988] and Carriero and Gelernter [1988]. Issues pertaining to the implementation of TS on distributed-memory systems are considered in section 2, focussing on a particular TS model, *viz.* intermediate uniform distribution. The X-Linda implementation is described in section 3, re-emphasizing the need for an alternative transputer-based programming methodology as motivation for the research direction in general. The fundamental design and specification of X-Linda are outlined, and the design of the individual nodes within the system examined. The influence of the design of the Linda Machine on X-Linda is made apparent, and it is shown that, essentially, the X-Linda node can be regarded a software implementation of the Linda node. The implementation of the TS operations under X-Linda is described in some detail. Finally, some observations regarding the nature of the overheads inherent in the implementation and the resultant lack of efficiency are given. It is concluded that although the specific tuple space model is not ideally suited to transputer-based systems, the approach requires further exploration in order to exhaust its full research potential.

2.0 TUPLE SPACE ON DISTRIBUTED-MEMORY SYSTEMS

Implementing tuple space on a machine that lacks physically shared-memory poses a number of implementation problems [Gelernter 1985, Carriero 1987]. Various approaches to implementing a logically shared tuple space across distributed-memories have been proposed, the most significant of which are hashing and uniform distribution. This section focuses on a derivative of uniform distribution, *viz. intermediate* uniform distribution. The applicability and elegance of this model is illustrated in the context of the Linda Machine – a custom-built distributed-memory system, designed specifically to support intermediate uniformly distributed tuple space.

2.1 HASHING

Carriero *et al.* [1986] describe a scheme based on *distributed hash tables*. Tuples are stored on unique nodes in the system, where the identity of the node responsible for any given tuple is hashed from the tuple's fields. Hashing is economical [Bjornson *et al.* 1987] since tuples do not need to be replicated, and there is never a need to broadcast data over the network. Hash-based approaches are described in more detail by Carriero [1987] and Ahuja *et al.* [1988].

2.2 UNIFORM DISTRIBUTION

Gelernter [1985] and Ahuja *et al.* [1988] describe a technique that attempts to distribute the TS evenly over the nodes in the system. Each node has an "out-set" and an "in-set". Tuples to be inserted into TS are sent to the nodes that make up the out-set, and tuple requests (templates) are broadcast to those in the in-set. Uniform distribution covers a wide range of implementation possibilities. At the one extreme, tuples injected into TS are passed to and subsequently stored in *every* node in the system. An in or rd operation would therefore necessitate a requesting node to perform a search of its own tuple memory. Note, however, that tuple deletion requires a network-wide operation. At the other extreme, tuples could be stored only in the memories of the nodes performing an out operation. In this case, although a global network search is necessary in order to locate a specific tuple, the maintenance of TS consistency is considerably simpler.

2.3 INTERMEDIATE UNIFORM DISTRIBUTION

This scheme is mid-way between the above extremes. Assuming that there are k nodes in the system, both the in-set and out-set comprise $\sqrt{k}$ nodes and must intersect. Since the number of nodes involved in the insertion and withdrawal of a tuple is only $2\sqrt{k}$ ($\sqrt{k}$ for an out and $\sqrt{k}$ for an in), "the intermediate scheme is provably optimal even if we consider the entire spectrum of uniform distribution schemes" [Ahuja *et al.* 1988]. An interesting description of how TS operations are implemented under the intermediate uniformly distributed scheme is given using the concepts of *tuple beams* and *inverse beams* [*ibid.*]. Tuples in TS (injected using an out statement) are represented as a tuple "beam" across a row of nodes (i.e. the out-set). When a node requires to locate a tuple (executing an in command), it "flashes an inverse beam along a column". If two matching beams intersect, the tuple is returned to the requesting node, and both beams disappear. The intermediate uniform distribution scheme suggests itself as an effective way of sharing the communication load among the nodes in the system [Ahuja *et al.* 1988]. Furthermore, it may be generalizable to bigger systems and is an extremely effective way of implementing tuple space over distributed-memory systems [Bjornson *et al.* 1987].

Hardware Topology

Intermediate uniform distribution lends itself to a particular topology – a wrap-around mesh of processors. Using this topology, a node's out-set is defined as the nodes on its row of the grid and the in-set as the nodes that make up a column. Each node maintains a store of tuples and tuple requests. An out operation causes a tuple to be sent to all nodes along a row and an in or rd operation causes a template to be sent to the nodes in a column. A tuple match occurs when a particular node is in possession of both a tuple and a matching template. The tuple is sent to the requesting node and, in the case of an in operation, the tuple is deleted from TS.

2.3.1 The Linda Machine

The Linda Machine is a custom-built distributed-memory architecture designed to support intermediate uniformly distributed tuple space over a mesh of processors. The design of the Linda Machine was first comprehensively detailed by Ahuja *et al.* [1988] who described the system as "a parallel computer that has been designed to support the Linda parallel programming environment in hardware". A brief description of the system is given below since this design was very influential in the construction of X-Linda (this aspect is further addressed in section 3.2.2). The system comprises a grid of *Linda nodes*. These nodes in turn consist of a computation processor and a Linda co-processor (termed the *Linda Engine*) that is responsible for TS communication and management. The nodes are connected via broadcast buses – as a result, tuples can be sent to their respective in- and out-sets in a single operation.

2.3.1.1 The Linda Engine

The Linda engine comprises a tuple memory, a working store, an operations controller (consisting of an IN- and OUT-processor) and interfaces to the buses and computation processor. This is illustrated in Figure 2.1.

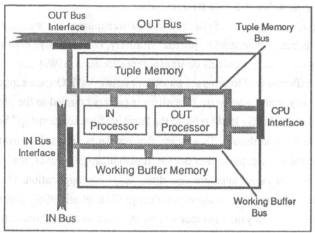

Figure 2.1 : Structure of the Linda Engine

The tuple memory, working store and operations controller are very briefly described below.

Tuple Memory – the tuple memory stores the data fields of the tuples and also, for the purpose of tuple matching, information pertaining to the size and type of these fields.

Working Buffer Memory – the working store holds two queues – the *in-request*, which stores pending in requests (either from the computation processor or from other nodes), and the *out-request* which stores out requests from the computation processor.

Operations Controller – the operations controller comprises the IN-processor and the OUT-processor which operate on the in-request and out-request queues respectively.

2.3.1.2 *Maintaining TS Consistency*

In any Linda system, the maintenance of TS consistency is a key issue [Gelernter 1985]. With respect to an intermediate uniformly distributed TS, the biggest problem is with regard to the in operation – if two nodes simultaneously issue identical tuple requests, only one must succeed in retrieving the data and deleting the tuple. Network protocols must be implemented in order to make certain that TS operations are carried out correctly and to ensure TS consistency. Ahuja *et al.* [1988] discuss the network protocols that are proposed in the design of the Linda Machine. The protocols are based on *distributed arbitration* and although they have been formalized with broadcast buses in mind, the concepts are both important and generalizable.

3.0 THE X-LINDA IMPLEMENTATION

As indicated in section 1, X-Linda was created as a means of investigating the communication overheads associated with the implementation of a particular tuple space methodology on networks of transputers. This section describes the X-Linda implementation – i.e. an intermediate uniformly distributed tuple space implemented in occam 2 on transputer meshes.

3.1 THE NEED FOR A NEW PARADIGM

Since their inception in the mid-1980s, the use of transputers has steadily become more widespread in industrial and academic spheres. Similarly, occam enjoys high regard as an effective vehicle for expressing problems on transputers (Pountain [1989] describes occam as "a safe, elegant, and efficient way to program transputer networks"). Occam supports the process model of concurrency, and the software formalism is closely coupled to the physical architecture of the transputer (INMOS [1988] refer to the "architectural relationship" between the programming model and the hardware). This means that problems to be solved using the hardware can be simply and naturally expressed in occam. It also means, however, that the programmer must have a clear idea of the architecture underlying a specific application. The hardware configuration plays a prominent role in algorithm design [Rabagliati 1990]. Not only is the programmer restricted by the physical number of communication links [Pountain 1990], there is the added burden of having to explicitly identify source and destination processors involved in communication, and the responsibility of processor synchronization and coordination. Furthermore, algorithms designed for specific hardware topologies are not easily portable to different configurations [Rabagliati 1990]. The occam model is based on that of CSP [Hoare 1978]; i.e. process communication occurs via synchronous message-passing. Consequently, the sending process is blocked until the receiver is ready to accept the message. This conflicts with the notion of temporal uncoupling addressed by Gelernter [1985] (that a producer's progress should not be restricted by that of a consumer). Bal et al. [1989] state that the synchronous model of communication has a "major impact" on the style of programming. Finally, Bjornson et al. [1987] criticize the tight binding of parallel processes within the occam model.

There is a need to tear down the process / processor coupling inherent in the style of programming, and unburden the programmer from the restrictions imposed by the model of communication – i.e. a need for a programming methodology that will complement the power and availability of transputers. This, of course, is where Linda comes in. It may be argued that there is no need to specifically use occam to program transputers. There are a variety of other languages that can be used for this purpose, and there are a number of operating systems running on transputers that effectively "hide" the underlying hardware configuration from the user. Nonetheless, it is maintained that there is a need for a programming methodology that is conceptually simple, portable, and, from the programmer's point of view, topology independent. X-Linda was consequently constructed with the intent of investigating the feasibility of a particular tuple space implementation on transputer networks.

3.2 DESIGN AND SPECIFICATION

The fundamental design and specification of X-Linda are described below, illustrating the storage and structure of tuples within the TS model, and the choice of TS primitives provided. The structure of the individual nodes within the system is also described, highlighting the influence of the Linda Machine on the overall design.

3.2.1 Tuple Space Model

Tuple space is implemented under the intermediate uniformly distributed scheme on a mesh of transputers. Intermediate uniform distribution is discussed in detail in section 2.3 – all the concepts described in that section apply directly to X-Linda (e.g. the definition of in- and out-sets and the hardware topology are unchanged). This particular scheme was chosen for the reasons that it is

- simple and elegant
- featured in a "state-of-the-art" Linda implementation (the Linda machine)
- unique within the sphere of existing transputer-based Linda implementations.

X-Linda was developed on a 16-processor Parsytec SuperCluster, and the tuple space model implemented on meshes of 4, 9 and 16 transputers.

3.2.1.1 Tuple Storage

A major influence of the Linda Machine on X-Linda is seen in the way that individual tuples are stored in the *same* TS addresses of all the nodes within a specific out-set. This technique was taken a step further and also applied to templates which are also stored in the same locations over the nodes in the in-sets. The need for this strategy is evident with regard to maintaining TS consistency – most notably with respect to tuple / template deletion (using this technique, only an address is required for deletion – otherwise, a search would have to be made for the required tuple or template). Given that there are k nodes in the mesh, each in- and out-set comprises $\sqrt{k}$ nodes. The tuple and template queues on each node are sub-divided into $\sqrt{k}$ "buckets" – i.e. every node maintains a bucket that belongs to each of the other nodes in its respective in- or out-set. As a result, it is possible to ensure that every tuple or template issued from a specific node will occupy the *identical* location in the tuple and template request queues within *all* of the nodes in the sets.

3.2.1.2 Tuple Structure

This research is concerned only with the communication overheads associated with the implementation of TS – it was desired that the intricacies and added complexity of tuple matching not be included in the investigation. It is therefore required that

- the tuple matching process be kept as simple as possible (a simple linear search is utilized for this purpose)
- tuple fields be able to assume different lengths for the purpose of ascertaining the overheads with respect to the size of the tuple.

To meet this specification, tuples and templates need only comprise two fields – a tuple name (for matching) and a data field (of modifiable length). For ease of implementation, the tuple name is defined as a single 32-bit integer, and the data field comprises an array of integers. Notice that the name is *always* an *actual* parameter; it always contains some physical value, irrespective of whether it pertains to a tuple or a template. Tuple matching is therefore performed against a single key field. A tuple's data field is likewise always an actual parameter. Conversely, the data field for a template is always *formal* (i.e. a variable name that is assigned a value when the template name is successfully matched against a corresponding tuple). The above specification may appear overly restrictive. Indeed, under X-Linda it is not possible to capture the full flavour of the Linda programming methodology (keeping in mind, of course, that this was never the intention). However, as illustrated by Faasen [1991], it is still possible to program algorithms in a fairly elegant and expressive way.

3.2.1.3 TS Operations

In order to investigate the communication overheads of the model, it was only necessary to provide the out, in and rd operations. Eval and the predicate operations were not implemented, as discussed below :

eval – the presence of this primitive would achieve little with regard to ascertaining the communication overhead of the implementation.

inp, rdp – similarly, the predicate operations, inp and rdp, were not considered. The feasibility of providing these operations within a distributed environment is, in fact, highly debatable. Leichter [1990] argues against the implementation of inp and rdp in a distributed environment, claiming that their inclusion in such systems either causes inefficiency or introduces "bizarre semantics".

3.2.2 X-Linda Node

Each transputer within the mesh executes a number of inter-communicating, concurrent processes, each of which is dedicated to some specific function. For the sake of clarity, the transputers are referred to as *X-Linda nodes* to make a distinction between them and the *Linda nodes* that are specific to the Linda Machine. Recall that the Linda node comprises a Linda Engine and a computation co-processor, and that the Linda Engine has dedicated hardware components that are responsible for tuple memory, TS management and the processing of TS operations. The Linda Engine also has interfaces to the in- and out-buses. This arrangement was very influential in the design of the X-Linda node, to the extent that it can, in a sense, be regarded as a *software* implementation of the Linda node. The X-Linda node features dedicated software processes which are responsible for the functions of computation, tuple storage and TS management, the processing of primitive operations and providing an interface into the in- and out-sets. The structure of the X-Linda node is shown in Figure 3.1.

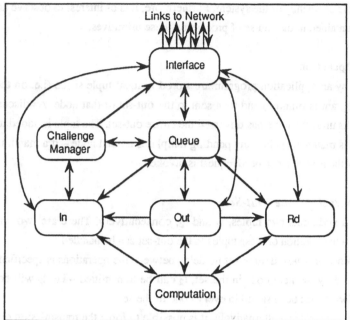

Figure 3.1 : Structure of the X-Linda Node

Linda programs are launched within the Computation process – i.e. the primitive operations are invoked from here. The In, Out and Rd processes control the processing of the TS operations, received both locally (from the Computation process) and externally (received via the Interface process). Tuple space (i.e. the tuple and template queues) is stored on the Queue process – all tuple space addition, deletion and matching is done here. The Interface process is responsible for :

1. receiving tuples and templates from the In, Out and Rd processes, and distributing them to the in- and out-sets

2. the reverse operation – i.e. receiving information from the in- and out-sets, and sending it on to the internal processes.

Finally, the Challenge Manager is an extra process dedicated to handling the requests for tuple ownership and subsequent deletion associated with the satisfaction of an in operation. The intention here is only to outline the structure of the X-Linda node, and to illustrate the influence of the Linda Machine on its design. A detailed account of the internal structure and operation of the X-Linda node is given by Faasen [1991].

3.3 IMPLEMENTATION OF THE TS PRIMITIVES

This section describes the design considerations regarding the specification and implementation of the TS primitive operations. It is important to note these considerations as they have a direct influence on the efficiency of the system. Furthermore, it is of interest to observe how TS consistency is maintained in the course of processing these primitives.

3.3.1 Out Operation

Tuples outed by an application program are stored in local tuple space (i.e. on the processor where the program is running) and then sent to the out-set of that node. As discussed below, the node blocks until the tuple has traversed the entire out-set. The tuple is added to each node in the set and is matched against any pending templates on that node – if a match is found, the satisfaction of the associated in or rd request is invoked.

3.3.1.1 Traversal of the Out-Set

Assume that a node outs two tuples, t_1 and t_2, consecutively. There are two ways [Faasen 1990] in which the addition of these tuples to the out-set can be handled :

1. *no delay between transmissions* – if no delay between the operations is specified, as soon as t_1 is received by the next node in the set, t_2 can be transmitted – i.e. t_2 will be sent to the out-set *before* t_1 has been stored in every node in the set.
2. *blocked transmissions* – alternatively, it is possible to force the transmission of t_2 to be delayed until t_1 has been stored in every node in the out-set – i.e. to wait until the tuple returns to the node that invoked the out.

Both strategies satisfy Linda's semantic specifications equally well. The first approach was implemented in earlier phases of X-Linda. However, this unrestrained form of transmission understandably resulted in the out-set becoming saturated, and consequently caused deadlock. Hence, the second strategy was adopted. The effect of forcing the processor to block *does* have a significant effect on the efficiency of the out operation – however, proposals for reducing the effects of blocking are discussed by Faasen [1991].

3.3.1.2 Processing the Out Request
Locally Invoked

A locally invoked out request can be either a normal out operation (i.e. invoked by an application program) or the restoration of a tuple satisfying an in request (a single in request may be satisfied at more than one location, resulting in multiple tuples being returned to the requesting node – as detailed in section 3.3.3.4, the "extra" tuples must be re-inserted into TS). In either case, the processing of the request is the same. The tuple is added to local TS and matched against pending templates in the request queue. If no match is found, the tuple is forwarded to the out-set. In the case of a match against a rd request, the tuple is *still* forwarded to the out-set – rds are non-destructive, and the tuple must as usual be added to TS – and the satisfaction of the request invoked. A successful match against an in request causes the tuple to be deleted from the local TS before it is returned to the application program that is requesting it.

Externally Invoked

Nodes receiving external out requests add these tuples to their TS and attempt to match them against their local request queues. If no match is found, the tuple is passed to the next node in the in-set – otherwise, the associated tuple is sent via the in-set to the node that issued the request.

3.3.1.3 Matching Tuples against Templates
Rd Requests

As stated above, a tuple added to a local TS must be matched against the templates in the request queue. It is worth noting that if a match is found against a rd request (as opposed to an in request), it is necessary to test for further matches. Rds are non-destructive; hence, a single tuple may match *all* pending rd requests in the request queue. Therefore, on successfully locating a rd request, the matching process must be successively repeated until all matching rd templates have been located, or until a matching in request is encountered. Successful matches are satisfied as discussed in section 3.3.2.2 below.

In Requests

Obviously, the procedure regarding an in request is different – only one matching in request in the request queue can be satisfied by a tuple. These requests are satisfied as described in section 3.3.3.3.

3.3.2 Rd Operation

A rd operation causes a template to be stored in the local memory of the node from which it is invoked, and then to be transmitted to all nodes that make up the in-set. The template is added to the request queues within these nodes, and is matched against the tuples present in the tuple space. A successful match causes the associated tuple to be returned to the requesting node, and the request to be deleted from the nodes within the in-set.

3.3.2.1 Processing the Rd Request
Locally Invoked

Local rd requests are appended to the request queue of the processor invoking the operation and matched against the tuples resident in the local TS. If no match is found, the request is then transmitted to the other nodes in the in-set. If a match is found, the request obviously need not be sent to the in-set as the request can immediately be satisfied (this procedure is different with respect to an in request).

Externally Invoked

Nodes receiving external rd requests add these templates to their request queues and attempt to match them against their local TS. If no match is found, the template is passed to the next node in the in-set – otherwise, the associated tuple is sent via the in-set to the requesting node.

3.3.2.2 Satisfying the Request

When a template is successfully matched, that template is deleted from the local request queue. If the request was invoked locally, no further action is necessary. On the other hand, the satisfaction of an external request necessitates the deletion of the request from the entire in-set and the return of the associated tuple to the requesting node via the in-set. The node satisfying the match must transmit a delete command to the nodes in the in-set. On receipt of this command, these nodes remove the template from their request queues. Notice, however, that this is slightly more complicated than simply deleting the entry. It is possible that a match may be found *before* the template has traversed the in-set. The command to delete the template that is subsequently issued may therefore be received by a node in the in-set before the template is itself received. Consequently, before a template can be deleted, a check must be made that it actually exists. If not, the state of the entry in the queue corresponding to that template is set to "delete pending" – when the template finally arrives and is added to the queue, it will immediately be destroyed.

Satisfaction by an Out Operation

A pending template present in the request queue can be matched by a tuple added to the processor's local TS. If the template was locally invoked the request is satisfied locally – otherwise, the tuple is passed via the in-set to the requesting processor.

3.3.2.3 Multiple Satisfaction of Requests

It is possible that a rd request may be satisfied at more than one node. Consider a situation whereby a node invokes a rd request, and transmits a template to all of the nodes in its in-set. If two nodes in different out-sets subsequently issue matching tuples, the request will be satisfied at two different locations. Both of the nodes that locate the match will then return the associated tuple to the requesting node, which obviously will receive both tuples. It must accept only the first tuple it receives, and discard all others. A simple sequencing strategy is used to associate templates with the tuples that are received, providing the means to detect and subsequently discard multiple request satisfies.

3.3.3 In Operation

The processing of an in operation is similar to the rd in that the template is stored locally and in the memories of nodes in the in-set, and is matched against the tuples in the respective tuple spaces. However, on a successful match, the associated tuple is deleted from the entire out-set before it is returned to the requesting node. Nodes requiring to satisfy an in request must contend for the tuple in question. If there is more than one request on the same tuple, only one of these may succeed in deleting the tuple and returning it to the requesting processor. When a request has been satisfied, the template is removed from the nodes in the in-set.

3.3.3.1 Processing the In Request
Locally Invoked
Local in requests are appended to the request queue of the processor invoking the operation and matched against the tuples resident in the local TS. If no match is found, the request is then transmitted to the other nodes in the in-set. Notice that, in the case of a successful match, the template must *still* be transmitted to the in-set. It is possible that another node may also request the tuple in question; hence templates must *always* be sent to the in-set as the node invoking the request may lose a tuple challenge and have to find another tuple elsewhere. When a match is found, the tuple cannot be simply deleted from TS and consumed. The node must "challenge" the other nodes in the out-set in case they too are attempting to satisfy a request on the same tuple.

Externally Invoked
Nodes receiving external in requests add these templates to their request queues and attempt to match them against their local TS. If no match is found, the template is passed to the next node in the in-set – otherwise, the satisfaction of the request can be invoked. As indicated above, the node must invoke a challenge before it may delete and return the tuple.

3.3.3.2 The Challenge Process
The issue of tuple contention was briefly mentioned above. This is a very real problem. If two nodes simultaneously issue a request for, and successfully locate the same tuple, only one may be permitted to retrieve that tuple and delete it from TS; the other must withdraw from contention and seek another tuple. Take the example whereby a tuple is present in a row of the mesh. Now, if two nodes in different in-sets simultaneously issue requests for that tuple, a match will succeed in two locations. On finding a match, a node must "fight" for ownership of the associated tuple before it can be deleted from TS and returned to the requesting node. This is implemented using a simple and efficient strategy. When a match is found, the node sends to the out-set a *challenge token*, which essentially contains the address (i.e. location in TS) of the tuple to be deleted and the identity of the node invoking the challenge. A node receiving a token from a foreign processor tests whether or not it itself is attempting to satisfy an in request on the same tuple. If not, it deletes the tuple from its local TS and passes the token on. On the other hand, if it too is satisfying a request on the same tuple, it must contend the challenge – i.e. one of the nodes must lose out and withdraw from contention. The strategy used in determining the outcome of a challenge is simple. The node with lowest identity wins the challenge; if the identity of the node receiving the token is *less* than that of the node that issued the token, it wins the challenge; otherwise it loses. The procedure associated with winning or losing challenges is outlined below :

* *winning a challenge* – if the node wins the challenge, it consumes the token (i.e. the losing node's challenge "dies").

- *losing a challenge* – conversely, on losing the challenge, the node deletes the tuple from its local TS, passes the token on, and then re-attempts to find a match for the unsatisfied template. Effectively, the node has now withdrawn from contention with regard to the tuple that it originally tried to claim.

Once a token returns to the node that issued it, it is guaranteed that the associated tuple has been deleted from TS, and can now be returned to the requesting node. The contention strategy (i.e. based on the identity of the conflicting nodes) is somewhat arbitrary, and obviously favours nodes with low processor identities. The strategy is, however, simple to implement and, since this issue does not directly relate to the objective of the research, was considered acceptable to use. Other possible challenge strategies are discussed by Faasen [1991].

3.3.3.3 Satisfying the Request

When a template is successfully matched, that template is deleted from the local request queue. It must also (even in the case of a local request) be deleted from the entire in-set (as was seen previously, in requests are *always* sent to the entire in-set). Furthermore, the associated tuple must be either returned to the application program in the case of a local request, or, if the request is external, to the requesting node via the in-set. The same procedure for deleting templates that was described for the rd operation is utilized here. Notably, care must again be taken against deleting a template that has not yet been added to the request queue, and the "delete pending" state is used in this regard.

Satisfaction by an Out Operation

Pending templates present in the request queue that are matched by a tuple added to the processor's local TS are processed as described above.

3.3.3.4 Multiple Satisfaction of Requests

With respect to the rd operation, it was described how a request could be satisfied at more than node – obviously, the same applies to in requests. The same sequencing strategy as used for rd requests is employed. Notice, however, that a tuple that has already been received can no longer merely be discarded – instead, it must be *restored* back into TS. A tuple that matches an in request is deleted from TS. Consequently, a node receiving multiple tuples must re-out the extra tuples as these have been (incorrectly) removed from TS. Tuple restoration does have an interesting side-effect. If the requesting node requires to obtain another tuple with the same name (the term "name" being used in its broadest sense), it will find this tuple locally – i.e. the tuple will be resident in local TS as a result of being restored.

3.3.4 Discussion

The design considerations detailed in this section have illustrated that the implementation of the TS operations was far from trivial. The greatest factor contributing to the overall complexity stems from the need to maintain TS consistency, a problem obviously common to all systems that are required to maintain distributed data. It is relevant to note that, given the design considerations outlined in this section, the implementation of the predicate operations (inp and rdp) would be exceedingly difficult, justifying the comments in section 3.2.1.3 regarding their unsuitability to distributed-memory implementations.

3.4 EFFICIENCY

The communication overheads associated with X-Linda are examined in detail by Faasen [1991]. This is done by means of a comprehensive series of tests and experiments designed to measure the extent of these overheads (relative to message passing performance on native transputer networks). Specific details regarding the design, implementation and results of these experiments are not included here. Instead, some general observations regarding the nature of the overheads and the resultant lack of efficiency are given.

3.4.1 Communication Overheads

The analysis of X-Linda's communication overheads (i.e. the overheads associated with the processing of out, rd and in operations) covers various performance issues. These include :
- the overheads of inter-processor communication via TS, relative to native occam 2 implementations of the same operation
- the effects of network traffic on the performance of the TS operations
- the extra processor utilization associated with processing the operations.

Issues specific to individual TS operations such as the blocking of the out operation and the effect of the challenge process on the in operation were also investigated.

It was found that, although X-Linda does impose a significant cost on the processing of TS primitive operations, this overhead is not necessarily prohibitive. Given the fact that, according to the Linda philosophy, it is acceptable to trade some processing performance against the gains provided by the programming paradigm [Ahuja *et al.* 1988], it can be argued that the communication overheads are reasonable. This is not to say that X-Linda is the answer to programming transputer networks. Apart from the communication costs, there are a host of other overheads associated with the implementation. These are discussed briefly below in the context of X-Linda's overall inefficiency.

3.4.2 Discussion

A number of additional overheads were isolated and investigated in the course the analysis. These include :
- process scheduling – the overhead of scheduling the 40 odd concurrent processes resident on each X-Linda node.

- synchronization – strict synchronization of the above processes is necessary to ensure atomicity of operations and to prevent concurrent access to the contents of TS. A process requesting the service of another may therefore be required to block until the latter has completed processing both its current operation and the requested service.
- set-up – the overhead associated with invoking TS operations, attributable to the delays incurred in the transmission of tuple and control information via the various internal sub-processes resident on each node.
- TS search – as indicated in section 3.2.1.2, tuple matching is implemented by means of a simple linear search. The time to search TS is naturally O(size of TS) – obviously, a linear search is not an optimal way of locating a specific tuple. It is important to note that, given an empty TS, the overhead of tuple or template addition includes this extra expense.

The inefficiency of TS search is probably the most significant of the above overheads, and it is reasonable to assume that, together, TS search and communication are responsible for the vast majority of the overall overhead. The cumulative effect of the above overheads is excessive, and their impact on the overall efficiency of the system severe. In addition, there are various aspects specific to the implementation design and environment that directly influence the performance of the system. However, as discussed below, this research is concerned primarily with the communication overheads imposed by the model, and aspects such as the optimization of TS search do not fall within the scope of the implementation.

4.0 CONCLUSIONS

The X-Linda implementation suffers significant communication overheads and the system, as it stands, is too inefficient to be of practical use. It is concluded that the communication capabilities of the transputer are not well suited to the efficient implementation of in- and out-sets. The magnitude of the design effort associated with the implementation of the TS primitive operations is immediately indicative of this unsuitability, and the extent of the overheads inherent in the implementation illustrates this point in a more obvious way. It is important to keep in mind, however, that X-Linda is not intended to be a fully-fledged Linda system, but was created to provide a means of investigating the communication overheads pertaining to a specific TS model. This is especially relevant with regard to the TS search strategy, the inefficiency of which is commented on above.

Therefore, is a full Linda implementation based on the X-Linda approach feasible ? In favour of this evaluation, there is the elegance of a design that is modelled on the successful Linda Machine project, and the fact that, as a result of this research, it is known that the design can be applied to transputer networks. The communication costs imposed by the model are not necessarily prohibitive, and it is not unreasonable to assume that a redesign of the system, taking into account the enhancements proposed by Faasen [1991], may yield "acceptable" performance. The answer to the question posed above is reservedly affirmative. The system undoubtedly has the potential for development into an efficient and usable product; however, extensive effort would be required to achieve this. Nevertheless, the X-Linda approach requires further exploration in order to exhaust its full research potential; personal opinion favours further development of the system, and, in particular, investigating the use of dedicated hardware support in this regard.

Acknowledgements

I extend my thanks to Conrad Mueller and Scott Hazelhurst for their valuable contributions to many fruitful discussions during the course of this research. Thanks also to Nick Carriero, Jerry Leichter, Steven Ericsson Zenith and Venkatesh Krishnaswamy for answering various questions and providing access to a significant amount of literature.

REFERENCES
S. Ahuja, N. Carriero and D. Gelernter [1986], *Linda and Friends*, IEEE Computer, 19 (8), August, 26-34
S. Ahuja, N. Carriero, D. Gelernter and V. Krishnaswamy [1988], *Matching Language and Hardware for Parallel Computation in the Linda Machine*, IEEE Trans. Computers, 37 (8), August, 921-929
H. Bal, J. Steiner and A. Tanenbaum [1989], *Programming Languages for Distributed Computing Systems*, ACM Computing Surveys, 21 (3), September, 261-322
R. Bjornson, N. Carriero, D. Gelernter and J. Leichter [1987], *Linda, The Portable Parallel*, Yale Univ. Dept. of Computer Science Research Report 520, February
N. Carriero [1987], *Implementing Tuple Space Machines*, Yale Univ. Dept. of Computer Science Research Report 567, December (also a 1987 Yale Univ. Ph.D Thesis)
N. Carriero, D. Gelernter and J. Leichter [1986], *Distributed Data Structures in Linda*, Proc. ACM Symp. Princ. Prog. Lang., (January 13-15, St. Petersburg, Fla.), 236-242
N. Carriero and D. Gelernter [1988], *How to write Parallel Programs : A Guide to the Perplexed*, Yale Univ. Dept. of Computer Science Research Report 628, November
C. Faasen [1990], Subject : *Out-Set Protocol*, Linda Users Group Bulletin Board, 11 May
C. Faasen [1991], *Implementing Tuple Space on Transputer Meshes*, Research report submitted in partial fulfilment of the requirements for the degree of MSc, Dept. of Computer Science, Univ. of the Witwatersrand, February
D. Gelernter [1985], *Generative Communication in Linda*, ACM Trans. Prog. Lang. Syst., 7 (1), January, 80-112
D. Gelernter [1988], *Getting the Job Done*, BYTE, 13 (12), November, 301-309
C. Hoare [1978], *Communicating Sequential Processes*, Comm. ACM, 21 (8), August, 666-677
INMOS [1988], *The Transputer Databook*, INMOS Limited
INMOS [1989], *Transputer Handbook*, INMOS Limited
J. Leichter [1990], Subject : *re : Linda Semantics Question*, Linda Users Group Bulletin Board, 18 May
D. Pountain [1989], *Occam 2*, BYTE, October, 279-284
D. Pountain [1990], *Virtual Channels : The Next Generation of Transputers*, BYTE, April, 3-12
A. Rabagliati [1990], Subject : *New Electronics Article, Sept 1990*, North American Transputer User's Group Bulletin Board, 23 October

Mixing Concurrency Abstractions and Classes

*Julian Padget, Peter Broadbery, David Hutchinson**

School of Mathematical Sciences
University of Bath
BATH, Avon, United Kingdom
E-mail: jap,pab@maths.bath.ac.uk, dh@hermes.mod.uk

1 Introduction

We report experience with the construction of a system supporting several concurrent programming abstractions (futures, Linda, CSP, time-warp and paralations) and of an experiment (in an earlier system) in which time-warp was modelled in Linda. As a result of this work we can now cast these competing abstractions in a common framework by the use of classes. This leads to the concept of the generic scheduler. As an application of these techniques, we discuss a railway simulation which uses Linda and time-warp.

The central theme of this paper is process control structures, also known as concurrency abstractions. Our concerns are two-fold: how the abstractions support the various algorithmic classes of concurrency and the degree of abstraction provided. We start with a brief review of algorithmic models since these are the principal behaviours the abstractions need to reflect (section 2) and continue with a short summary of some of the process control structures currently in use (section 3). Our first experiment in mixing paradigms is described in section 4 where we discuss the modelling of time-warp using Linda. In a desire to organise our implementation of multiple concurrency abstractions better we turned to object-oriented programming—although it is no accident that our experimental environment, EuLisp, described in section 5 is an object-oriented language—and realised that these abstractions were not very different from each other and could easily be expressed as specializations of the process class and, more importantly, could be controlled by generic schedulers. Our second experiment in mixed paradigms is not incestuous, being a simulation which uses both Linda and time-warp (section 6): the former for handling persistent object and as a communications medium and the latter for the actual simulation.

2 Algorithmic Models

This brief description of algorithmic models establishes the background for the linguistic abstractions, since to be effective they must be capable of expressing some or all of these patterns of behaviour. Most parallel algorithms can be classified against one of the

---

* Present address: Royal Signals and Radar Establishment, St. Andrews Road, Great Malvern, WORCS, WR14 3PS, UK.

following four descriptive categories. Whilst there is a danger of pigeon-holing limiting us from novel solutions, the focus this classification provides can be very helpful—although many programs will often contain several of these paradigms.

master-slave describes an organisation where a central process (the master) breaks up the problem into smaller pieces and distributes them to a set of processes (the slaves) which return results for the central process either to combine into the final result or to generate further subproblems. The latter case is akin to divide-and-conquer, but using only a finite number of resources. As an example, consider the combination of s-polynomials in Gröbner bases [Melenk & Neun, 1988].

producer-consumer describes an organisation of one process generating information which is the input to another. This generalises into streams of communicating processes.

divide-and-conquer has some similarities to master-slave, as one process breaks up the problem into smaller pieces and distributes it. However, whilst the master-slave organisation is flat, divide-and-conquer is recursive, in that each of the processes handling a subproblem may decide to split the problem further and create yet more processes for those subproblems.

data-parallel is orthogonal to the other classifications, which can be viewed primarily as a number of processes each doing a different task, because here the operation is the same but is applied simultaneously across vast data sets, such as happens with vector and array operations.

These terms describe the behaviour of *algorithms* and are largely architecture independent, although classifying some algorithm as data-parallel does suggest that is is probably only practical to execute it on an array machine. In order to express the concurrency we need some means to describe processes (either explicitly or implicitly), their creation and their interaction in a programming language. The next section surveys this issue.

3 Linguistic Abstractions

A number of abstractions of processes have been proposed over the last several years. A distinguishing feature of these abstractions has been the disregard of each for the existence of the others. Some of the abstractions have been designed to be added to existing languages and others have formed the basis for whole new languages. Here we consider: futures [Halstead, 1985], [Gabriel & McCarthy, 1984], [Kranz et al, 1989], Linda [Carriero & Gelernter, 1989], communicating sequential processes (CSP) [Hoare, 1985], Gamma [Banâtre & LeMetayer, 1986], time-warp [Jefferson, 1985], UNITY [Chandy & Misra, 1988] and paralations [Sabot, 1988]. Intentionally omitted are monitors, serializers and actors.

The plethora of means for expressing concurrency in different languages via different abstractions is akin to the fad for designing language syntax and, in particular, loop constructs which afflicted language design in the 1960's—and is still occasionally seen today. There are two primitive operations to be expressed when writing concurrent programs:

1. that some expression be evaluated concurrently—typified by the construction of a new thread;

2. that some resource be accessed in an orderly manner—controlled by some synchronisation mechanism.

Thus, the basic elements of parallel processing are a means of allocating multiple threads of control (alternatively called task, light-weight process (LWP) or thread), a means of synchronising access to shared resources (such as semaphores or critical regions) and a means of controlling these threads so that the primary resource, the CPUs, is shared between them (the scheduler). These primitives appear in many systems with a number of different names, but, we believe, the principles we have listed here are uniform. Being primitives they are sufficient to express any MIMD parallel program we wish to write, but also, being primitive means they are prone to abuse, misuse and errors in protocol. For all these reasons these mechanisms are too crude to be used directly for safely and effectively expressing concurrency, which is the motivation for packaging them in abstractions.

The degrees of abstraction provided by the different models listed in the opening paragraph vary quite widely as does the support for formal reasoning. The simplest is probably the future, but there are too many criteria to allow a reasonable selection of its opposite. Only CSP and UNITY offer any means for program analysis. Linda, Gamma and UNITY share a common view of concurrent computation, although the details vary in practice, of a collection of processes and/or processors communicating via a shared pool of packets to be reduced: when there are no packets left, the computation has terminated. Communication in these abstractions is asynchronous and unordered. CSP is the opposite, in that communications are synchronous and ordered and time-warp is different again in being asynchronous but ordered.

Applying a different criterion, it is also interesting to see how the abstractions can support the algorithmic models listed in the preceding section. All but future are essentially static in nature (unless we admit Linda's eval) and can therefore express master-slave and producer-consumer problems, but not (directly) divide-and-conquer. Unfortunately, this strength is also future's weakness since it can lead to the creation of too many processes and swamping of the system. In practice, some kind of throttle on process creation is required. Only the paralation model can handle data-parallel as well as master-slave and producer-consumer. Thus, there is no clear winner amongst these abstractions, but situations where one is better than another. We develop this theme further below.

4 Time-warp in Linda

A brief description of how time-warp works is in order before attempting to explain the Linda based implementation; a more complete description and justifications can be found in [Jefferson, 1985].

4.1 Time-warp: a brief introduction

A timewarp system is comprised of objects, which interact by sending messages. Each object has a local clock, which represents the progress it has made in its computation. An object only performs computations in response to messages it receives. All messages are stamped with the time, by the sender's clock, at which they were sent (the *virtual send time* or VST), the identity of the sender and the time at which they are to be received (the *virtual receive time* or VRT). VRT has to be strictly greater than VST to prevent logical paradoxes.

An object has local state information, which is periodically saved (with a timestamp). An object also preserves all input messages sent to it and output messages it generates, as this is necessary in the case of rollback, described below. A single unit of computation consists of reading in a message, updating the local clock with the VRT of the message, performing computation which may alter the local state, and sending zero or more messages to other objects or itself. All such output messages have VST's of the local clock—during the actual execution of the computation the local clock does *not* advance. An object causes time to advance by sending messages into its future (VRT of message). An object which does not interact with any other objects would send itself messages in the future to cause its local clock to advance.

If several messages (with identical VRT's) are sent to an object then, once all these messages have been processed, the final state of that object, and the set of messages which the object has sent must be identical regardless of order of processing. Although the order in which such messages are processed may alter the order in which new messages are sent, the overall effect must be the same. A corollary of this is that information gained as the result of receiving a message must not affect the processing of any other message with the same VRT.

The system proceeds smoothly unless an object receives a message with a VRT earlier than its current local time. In this case the object is *rolled back* to a time of the latest saved state earlier than the VRT of the late message. The computation is then re-run, with the late message being received at the correct time. During the rollback phase computation is notionally undone, with *antimessages* being sent to cancel the effects of those messages sent erroneously. An variation of this (called *lazy* rollback) does not immediately cancel all the messages. Instead it compares the new messages being generated after the rollback with the ones previously sent, and only sends antimessages for those which differ. We use this variant.

Receipt of an antimessage requires the receiver to behave as if the original message had never been received. If the message to be cancelled is in the local future this is easy, the message is simply ignored, or annihilated. If it has been processed then the receiver must itself roll back to a saved state before the VRT of the message, and then compute forward again.

The existence of rollback implies that all actions may be undone at some time in the future. However at any wall clock time in a given system there is an object whose local clock is the furthest behind of all the objects and since an object can only send messages with VRT's later than its local clock and assuming there are no messages in transit, then any action which occurred before the local clock time of the furthest behind object cannot be undone. This time is called the *global virtual time* or GVT. Irreversible actions should therefore be deferred until GVT is later than their time of execution. In addition, since no rollback can ever go back before GVT there is only a need to preserve sufficient saved states and messages to permit rollback to GVT. This only requires the last saved state at or before GVT, and the messages after the time of that saved state. The removal of earlier data is called "fossil" collection, and is necessary if the saved data is not to expand without bounds.

The system described here saves state after every input message. The choice of how often to save state is a compromise, and is known to have a significant effect on some applications [Lin & Lazowska, 1990]. Varying the state saving frequency would be possible with only minor changes in the Linda system described below.

4.2 A Linda Implementation

Linda provides a reliable unordered communication system. Through this experiment we identify where in timewarp it is necessary to preserve order of communications, and where ordering is optional.

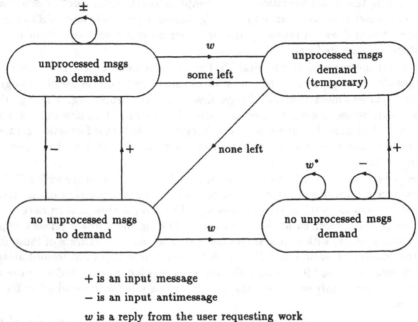

+ is an input message

− is an input antimessage

w is a reply from the user requesting work

w^* is an error (since work is already demanded)

Fig. 1. States of a timewarp task group

An early version of the Linda based system was designed to discover the various interactions which occur within a timewarp object. To force all interactions within a timewarp object to be explicit each object comprised three Linda tasks, which constitute a "task group": an input message receiver, an output message buffer, and a wrapper around the user code. For each time-warp object the user writes a single function to handle the messages. The only communication between the tasks is via tuple exchange. This makes the communication visible, and makes debugging easier. It does however impose a performance cost, due to the overheads of task swapping and tuple exchange.

Figure 1 shows the four possible states of task group: processing a message, not processing a message, an empty input queue and a non-empty input queue. The state of having a non-empty input queue and the user task not processing a message is transitory.

The storage of the input messages can be done in two obvious ways: a single queue of messages, or two queues, one for messages which have been processed, the other for messages awaiting processing. Both approaches have been used elsewhere, and after experimentation the Linda system uses a single queue. This necessitates keeping a pointer into the queue to indicate the boundary between processed and unprocessed messages. Having a single queue means that processing messages for a different time means moving the pointer, rather than transferring messages between queues.

The input queue handler must perform two major functions; insertion of new messages and supply of the next message to the timewarp object. These two functions interact via rollback.

The output queue must store old messages so that at some later time antimessages could be generated. Normal rollback does this by sending antimessages corresponding to all messages sent after a specified time (the VRT of the message causing the rollback).

The three task system could not implement lazy rollback, since keeping the input and output queues separate destroys the mapping of input message to output messages. The transfer of messages from the input queue handler to the user, and from the user to the output queue handler has to be ordered.

The basic form of interaction in a timewarp system is the exchange of inter-group messages. It is thus attractive to treat an input message and the changes it causes to the group state as a unit. This model captures the mapping needed for lazy rollback, and also simplifies the code needed considerably.

4.3 The two task Linda version

The second version has a unified queue, which stores an input message, the set of output messages produced by that input message, and the new state saved after processing the message (see figure 2). In this version the functions of the receiver and transmitter in the three task version are merged into a single queue handler task. Two tasks are used so that, whilst the user task is computing, messages addressed to the task group can be being removed from the pool and processed.

back	backwards (earlier) pointer
fwd	forwards (later) pointer
time	the VRT of the input message
in_msg	the input message
out_msgs	the list of messages generated by in_msg
state	the saved state generated by in_msg

Fig. 2. Unified queue element structure

The unified queue is ordered by virtual receive times of the input messages. All antimessages with a given VRT which have not yet cancelled are stored after any messages with the same time—that is, the anti-message has arrived before the corresponding message.

The algorithm to insert a message or an antimessage is moderately complex. It is a charactersitic of timewarp implementations that there are a great number of different cases to handle, and "off–by–one" errors are extremely easy to make. For complete details of this implementation see [Hutchinson, 1990]. It should be noted that whenever a part of the queue is to be given to the user task or some other task group then a copy must be made, since the original in the queue must not be modified.

4.4 GVT Computation

The calculation of GVT requires knowledge about all messages in transit in the system, and all objects in the system. Linda provides a reliable *unordered* unacknowledged link between timewarp objects (that is messages between task groups). It is thus impossible to compute GVT without either knowing that there are no inter-group tuples in the pool, or inspecting the VRT's of all such messages at a given instant. Without one of these pieces of knowledge there could be a tuple in the pool earlier than the estimate of GVT.

The algorithm used for GVT calculation is counter to the spirit of time-warp, as will be seen. Two special tuples are used to control and distribute GVT, which we call the *GVT-control* and the *GVT-value* tuples. In effect, these act like global variables. The control tuple contains one of three values: *drain*, *out_lvt* or *normal*. The value tuple contains the current value of GVT. The start of the calculation of GVT is signalled by changing the control tuple to *drain*. As part of the protocol obeyed by a queue handler, it first **reads** the control tuple before attempting to **in** more work. If the control value is *drain* then the queue handler proceeds normally except that it does satisfy any more requests for work from the user task. Eventually every linda task will be blocked, since the receivers (or queue handlers) will have removed all the inter-group messages, the user tasks will have no work, and the transmitters will have no pending messages. At this point a function (attached to a hook in the linda scheduler) is called. This function then removes the old *GVT-value* tuple, changes the control tuple to *out_lvt* and **outs** one dummy tuple for each group in order to unblock the receivers and allow them to reread the control tuple. The calculation of GVT is performed by a normal linda task, which is almost always blocked attempting to **in** an *LVT* tuple. With the control tuple set to *out_lvt* each receiver outputs its LVT, and **ins** the new GVT value. The GVT computation task **ins** all the *LVT* tuples, and then resets the control tuple to *normal* after **outing** the new value of GVT (being the minimum of the LVTs).

As noted above, this method of GVT calculation is contrary to the spirit of timewarp, in that synchronization occurs when GVT is calculated. This is a direct consequence of the unacknowledged nature of the inter-group message system. A more significant problem is the use of the linda scheduler to detect when all the tuples have been read in. This method works for a single processor, and requires only trivial extension for a system using a shared memory Linda pool.

On a distributed memory multiprocessor, which would have multiple pools containing unique copies of the tuples, any single Linda scheduler cannot determine that all of its tasks cannot be run without knowledge of the tuples in the other pools. In this, the use of acknowledgement for inter-object messages would be of benefit, and would permit GVT to be found as in [Jefferson, 1985]. Here GVT is the minimum over the system of the earlier (on each object) of the first unprocessed input message and the earliest unacknowledged output message.

5 An Experimental Environment

Our research is based on the dialect of Lisp called EuLisp [Padget *et al*, 1986], [Padget & Nuyens, 1991]. There is portable parallel implementation in use and under development at Bath. The system supports both true multiprocessor shared memory parallelism as well as providing primitives for communication within a distributed network of processors. A brief synopsis of the language features is: modules for separate compilation and constructing stand-alone applications, classes and generic functions, for object-oriented programming [Graube, 1989], and threads and semaphores for building concurrent processing abstractions. The primary hardware at Bath is a pair of Stardent Titan P3s (vector multi-processors) on which we have developed implementations of futures, Linda, time-warp, CSP [Padget *et al*, 1991] and (simulated) paralations in EuLisp [Padget & Merrall, 1991]. We are currently developing a version of our implemention which splits its heap to store ordinary Lisp objects on the workstation being used and links to a MasPar array processor, where its stores the paralation heap. Thus, when the MasPar based implementation is complete, we will also be able to carry out experiments in hybrid parallel processing, running part of an application on a Stardent and the other part on the MasPar. At present, we have no realistically-sized applications running concurrently, but we are actively working on problems in computer algebra, expert systems and discrete event simulation.

5.1 Processes Specialization

As we observed above, many of the linguistic abstractions are very similar. We can regard each of the abstractions as declarations about how a process is going to behave: for instance, a future is likely to be short-lived, whereas a Linda or time-warp process is not. In consequence, we have developed a hierarchy of processes, in which the different abstractions are expressed as specialisations of the primitive process class. The user is also free to specialise these classes further, so (s)he could experiment with a version of time-warp that used a different roll-back algorithm or a different state-saving strategy, debugging versions of an abstraction, profiling versions, migratable versions (which collect information to determine when and where to migrate), or the *spec-futures* of [Osborne, 1990] or the similar lazy creation mechanism of [Levy *et al*, 1990].

However, such a variety of process classes creates its own problems: one is how to schedule these different classes and the other is the management of collections of processes. We propose to handle the latter by constructing paralations of processes (or futures, etc.)[Padget & Merrall, 1991]. In this sense, the paralation is kind of process modularisation structure having some similarity to the sponsors of [Osborne, 1990], but whereas the paralation of processes is a static mechanism (in principle, it is of fixed size), the sponsor scheme is a dynamically expanding and contracting tree. In consequence, while it might be possible to scale a theory from a process class to a paralation of such processes (for example, CSP), the dynamic nature of sponsors makes this infeasable with current knowledge.

5.2 Generic Scheduling

A system only containing primitive processes has a limited number of choices to implement a "fair" scheduling policy, the most basic being round-robin.

A slight sophistication is to incorporate some priority mechanism, whereby the programmer may assign relative importance to a task at creation time or retrospectively. The scheduler too may change the priority of a process based on some fixed algorithm, using a criterion such as how long the process has existed to promote or demote. None of these is particularly satisfactory since many factors, important in shared and distributed systems, are ignored. They are also unsatisfactory because such techniques are not sufficiently adaptive—although, in large part, this is a consequence of not using a sufficiently wide set of criteria to control the choice of process to run. Classical scheduling algorithms are unsuitable because they were conceived for operating systems where the goal was the efficient use of that scarce resource the CPU. In concurrent processing, the premise is that processing power is no longer a scarce resource and the goal is to solve the problem as fast as possible. Hence the need for process class specific scheduling and also problem specific scheduling.

Another aspect of process control that has not usually been considered the province of a scheduler is process migration. However, since we are proposing to use much more information about each process, it is now reasonable for the scheduler to make the decision whether a process would benefit from being moved to another processor. Thus, load-balancing becomes a scheduling factor in a multi-processor architecture.

The issue is how can we schedule in a system with several different abstractions? The scheduling parameters of a process depend on the kind of abstraction. This organisation can be handled very elegantly by object oriented programming and generic functions: now that each of the parallel abstractions is a specialised class of the primitive process class, as described above, the scheduler simply becomes a generic function which dispatches on the class of the process and the user may define additional scheduling methods for a specialised process classes. Thus, for a future, we might ask whether the future has been touched (has another process tried to access the value), and, if not, move to the next process, giving rise to a kind of lazy evaluation. A spectacular example of how specialist scheduling for one linguistic abstraction (time-warp) paid off is described in [Burdorf & Marti, 1990]. Furthermore, if the programmer specialises the process class (or whichever process abstraction chosen) for the program being written, or we can introduce problem-specific scheduling methods for those classes. At the next level of granularity, we can schedule processes grouped together in a paralation by a similar means. In this latter case, there are some related ideas in [Osborne, 1990] for futures, but here the size of the group may expand and contract, whilst the paralation version is static.

5.3 Linda in EuLisp

Much of our research is oriented towards the design and implementation of object-oriented models for the description and control of parallelism. One goal of this work is to produce a system providing a general framework in terms of which many diverse parallel constructs may be efficiently implemented and used together with well defined interaction characteristics.

In this context we view Linda as such an integrated construct—just one of any number that could be chosen to express the parallelism inherent in some section of an algorithm we wish to implement. As such, considerations of how Linda-implemented routines interact with one another, as well as with those employing different constructs, are of great importance. We contend that within this environment, extending the basic model to support dynamically-instantiable tuple spaces is not a debatable luxury but rather a necessity in order to preserve the integrity of separate Linda-implemented routines by localising their communications.

ELLIS (a EuLisp LInda System) is our implementation of Linda, extended both to meet the requirements mentioned above and also to exploit EuLisp's object system in such a way as to provide an elegant and flexible interface to Linda. It provides an extensible system within which tuples, tuple spaces and schedulers are all first class items whose default definition and function may be altered or extended via inheritance and method specialisation. Operations such as tuple matching on specific classes of tuple may be modified to suit any peculiar properties of that class. Apart from the above mentioned extensions, ELLIS also augments the basic model with the linda-or and linda-and forms for generalised selective and aggregate tuple matching.

The ELLIS model was first implemented via a set of methods exploiting Feel's native thread-based parallelism within a shared address space. Since then a version for distributed systems (called ELSIE) has been developed and further investigation is underway in such areas as object transfer protocols and the garbage collection of distributed tuple pools.

The current ELSIE implementation seems best suited to master/slave configured problems but is likely to benefit from related research into abstract machine communication and distributed scheduling models to be built in a similarly object-oriented style.

To date, ELLIS and ELSIE have been used as a basis for parallel implementations of some simple algorithms in the areas of computer algebra, artificial intelligence and planning. ELLIS is also in use as a general purpose construct within Feel applications— one example being as the basis for a pipelining abstraction that implements the read mechanism of a persistent object system. It is also being used as a communication medium in a time-warp simulation environment which we discuss in more detail in the next section.

6 A Mixed Abstraction Simulation

The simulation is more of an exploration of techniques, rather than a realistic application. The object of the simulations is a group of trains running on a rail network bounded by Birmingham in the north, Southampton in the south, Slough in the east and Bristol in the west. This example was chosen because of its large physical size, but relative simplicity. The simulation runs distributed over a group of multi-processor machines connected by ethernet.

The network has been extracted from a flat database and stored in a database using gdbm (The GNU version of the UNIX^{TM} dbm program). There are two parts to the implementation of the simulation: the management of the database representing the network and of the objects modelling the entities in the simulation. Clearly, there is too much data for it all to be loaded into memory, and only small relatively predictable parts are needed at any time we find that the use of a pre-fetching technique is straightforward [Burdorf & Cammerata, 1991]. The database itself is changed rarely, so a simple write protocol can be used to guarantee consistency.

As with any persistent system, the illusion is created of all the elements of the network being present whenever they are accessed [Rowe, 1986], [Rowe 1988]. In practice, if a segment is not in memory, it is read from the database and instantiated by a two-stage Linda process to create access the segment and then instatiate a time-warp object representing the segment. Linda is also used as the medium for transporting messages between the time-warp simulation objects. A diagram of the structure of the simulation program is given in figure 3. Note that we are not using a time-warp based on Linda, but another implementation which uses shared memory as its default communications medium.

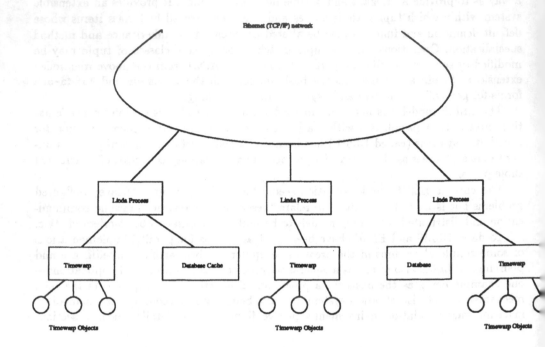

Fig. 3. Block diagram of system

The simulation consists of wagons traversing the network, trying to get to their respective destinations. As a segment of rail track can hold only a fixed number of wagons, there is competition for this resource. Therefore a wagon must locate and interact with the object representing the line segment before attempting to cross it. The very large number of lines means that, instead of creating all necessary lines at initialisation, the simulation must lazily instantiate them, and delete them when no longer required. This implies that the fossil collection part of the algorithm must be able to detect when it can destroy an object.

Most of the actions in the simulation return one of a very small number of possibilities— generally either a permission or a denial. We can use this to continue the calculation in an optimistic manner. The requesting object sends a message with virtual time $t + \epsilon$ to the server, and another message stamped $t + 2\epsilon$ to itself (ϵ is a guaranteed to be such that no message will arrive at the object in the interval $(t, t + \epsilon)$. If the server denies the request the it must send a denial message that will arrive before the message arriving at $t + 2\epsilon$, otherwise it sends no message and updates its internal state. The requesting object then checks to see if the denial has been sent, and if not, continues. This mechanism obviates the need for lazy rollback in a large number of cases. It does however mean that we need a system of stamping messages all time intervals can be split into subintervals — similar to that used in ParaTran[Tinker, 1988].

The TW interface to the database allows any host to instantiate line segments providing that this operation is atomic from both the viewpoint of the object requesting the object, and from that of the database (ie. both simulated time and real time atomicity). These conditions are sufficient to ensure that no object is replicated, and also that the interface objects never need to roll back.

Output from the program is placed in a Linda pool by the objects, and removed as it is needed by the output routines. The current implementation has 2 outputs—one displaying the perceived progress of the simulation via an X-window, and another to record simulation events on an output file.

The simulation will be used in further experiments exploring the possibility of creating a simulation which allows objects to look ahead (by simulation) and make a choice at an earlier time. Using the timewarp techniques, the network of active objects can be copied lazily rather than having to duplicate the state each time an object looks ahead. This has several potential applications in planning.

7 Conclusions

We started by describing an experiment which mixed Linda and time-warp to construct an implementation of time-warp on top of Linda. As a result of this experience and coupled with the development of an implementation of the concurrent object oriented language EuLisp we realised that the numerous concurrency abstractions could be elegantly packaged using classes and specialization to reflect the different interaction protocols whilst still permitting different abstractions to cooperate. Hence we conclude that object oriented techniques are valuable as a means of expressing and controlling concurrency and that there is more to concurrent object-oriented programming than simply viewing objects as units of concurrency. To exercise this new implementation a persistent concurrent OO simulation of a railway network has been developed.

Bibliography

[Banâtre & LeMetayer, 1986] Banâtre J-P. & Le Metayer D., *A new computational model and its discipline of programming*, INRIA Research Report, 566, 1986.

[Burdorf & Cammerata, 1991] , Burdorf C. & Cammerata S., *Prefetching Simulation Objects in a Persistent Simulation Environment*, to appear in the Journal of Object-oriented Programming.

[Burdorf & Marti, 1990] Burdorf C. & Marti J.B., *Non-Preemptive Time Warp Scheduling Algorithms* Operating Systems Review, April, 1990, ACM Press.

[Carriero & Gelernter, 1989] Carriero N. & Gelernter D., *Linda in Context*, Communications of the ACM, Vol. 32, No. 4, April 1989, pp444–459.

[Chandy & Misra, 1988] Chandy K.M. & Misra J., *Parallel Program Design: A Foundation*, Addison-Wesley, ISBN 0-201-05866-9.

[Gabriel & McCarthy, 1984] Gabriel R.P. & McCarthy J.M., *Queue-based Multiprocessing Lisp*, Proceedings of 1984 ACM Conference on Lisp and Functional Programming, published by ACM, New York, 1984.

[Graube, 1989] Graube N., *Architectures réflexives et implémentations des langages à taxonomie de classes en Lisp : Applications à ObjVlisp, Common Lisp Object System et Telos*, Thèse Doctorat de l'Université PARIS 6, December 1989.

[Halstead, 1985] Halstead, R.H., *Multilisp: A Language for Concurrent Symbolic Computation*, ACM TOPLAS 7, October 1985, pp501–538.

[Hoare, 1985] Hoare, C.A.R., *Communicating Sequential Processes*, Prentice Hall, ISBN:0-13-153289-8.

[Hutchinson, 1990] Hutchinson D.J.C., *Building Block for Parallel Programmers* School of Mathematical Sciences, University of Bath, Ph.D. thesis.

[Jefferson, 1985] Jefferson D., *Virtual Time*, ACM TOPLAS 7, pp404–425, 1985.

[Kranz *et al*, 1989] Kranz D.A., Halstead R.H. & Mohr E., *Mul-T: A High-Performance Parallel Lisp*, in Proceedings of SIGPLAN '89 Conference on Programming Language Design and Implementation, published by ACM Press, New York, pp81–90.

[Levy *et al*, 1990] Levy J-J., *et al, Management of Futures in CAML*, INRIA Rapports de Recherche, 1990.

[Lin & Lazowska, 1990] Lin Y-B & Lazowska E.D., *Reducing the State Saving Overhead for Time Warp Parallel Simulation*, Dept. of Computer Science and Engineering, University of Washington, Technical Report 90-02-03.

[Melenk & Neun, 1988] Melenk H. & Neun W., *Parallel Polynomial Operations in the Buchberger Algorithm*, Proceedings of the European Workshop on Parallelism and Algebra, Grenbole, 1988.

[Osborne, 1990] Osborne R.B., *Speculative Computation in MultiLisp*, published in the Proceedings of the 1990 ACCM Conference on Lisp and Functional Programming, ACM Press, ACM, New York, pp198–208.

[Padget *et al*, 1986] , Padget J.A. and many others, *Some Desiderata for the Standardisation of LISP*, published in the Proceedings of 1986 ACM Conference on LISP and Functional Programming, ACM Press, ACM, New York, pp54–66.

[Padget *et al*, 1991] Padget J.A., Bradford R.J., & Fitch J.P., *Concurrent Object-Oriented Programming*, to appear in The Computer Journal.

[Padget & Merrall, 1991] , Padget J.A. & Merrall S., *Bridging the MIMD—SIMD Gap*, in the proceedings of the BCS Parallel Specialist Interest Group Workshop on Abstract Machine Models, March, 1991.

[Padget & Nuyens, 1991] , Padget J.A. & Nuyens G., *The EuLisp Definition*, to be published by the Commission of the European Communities.

[Piquer, 1991] Piquer J., *Parallélisme et Distribution en Lisp*, Thèse d'école Polytechnique, Palaiseau, 1991.

[Rowe, 1986] Rowe L.A., *A Shared Object Hierarchy*, in Proceedings of the International Workshop on Object-Oriented Database Systems, published by IEEE, 1986.

[Rowe 1988] Rowe, L. A., *PICASSO Shared Object Hierarchy*, Proceedings of the First CLOS Users and Implementors Workshop, Palo Alto, Ca, October 1988.

[Tinker, 1988] Tinker P. & Katz M., Parallel Execution of Sequential Scheme with Para-Tran, in Conference Record of the 1988 ACM Symposium on Lisp and Functional Programming, ACM Press, ACM, New York, pp28-39.

[Sabot, 1988] Sabot G., *The Paralation Model*, MIT Press, 1988.

[Valiant, 1989] Valiant L.G., *The Bulk Synchronous Parallel Model*, Harvard University Department of Computer Science Technical Report TR-08-89.

Coordination Applications of Linda

Susanne Hupfer, David Kaminsky, Nicholas Carriero and David Gelernter

Department of Computer Science, Yale University, New Haven, CT 06520

1 Introduction

Much of the recent development and deployment of Linda systems has been in the context of parallel applications—where the focus is on performance enhancement through multiprocessing. We have discussed [2] parallel applications ranging from raytracing to seismology to financial modeling. And we've presented results for codes running on networks, hypercubes and shared memory machines. A pattern of straightforward coding and good performance has emerged.

But from the start it was clear that Linda was well suited to distributed and concurrent applications as well. Indeed, many of the early presentations (e.g. [7]) of Linda focussed on classic problems in this domain (readers/writers, dining philosophers), comparing and contrasting Linda solutions with other proposals. Having addressed these shibboleths, we moved on to more practical problems.

This paper will present case studies from actual code either in use or in development. We will see examples of Linda used to bootstrap Linda implementations, Linda used to implement a new execution model for some kinds of Linda programs, and a non-parallel-computation application where the emphasis is on presenting a coordinated view of distributed information with the goal of facilitating human interactions.

2 Bootstrapping Linda: The eval Server

Linda's **eval** operation presents a challenge to the Linda implementor. On shared memory machines, this challenge can usually be met via **fork()** (but see below). When implementing Linda on distributed memory architectures, we usually need some sort of remote execution facility—**fork()** won't do here.

We could (and have) patched together system-specific solutions or ignored the problem altogether (forced the user to start multiple copies, leaving **eval** out of the picture). But there must be a better way—if only we had a tool for developing portable distributed applications... . We have: Linda.

Using a combination of source to source translation and Linda operations, we have built an **eval** server that provides a portable solution—on any system for which **in** and **out** have been implemented, **eval** follows for free.

The transformation replaces an **eval** with a series of **outs** that generate tuples describing the functions to be executed and their arguments. The transformation also generates a new function, **eval_server()**, that is used as an alternate entry point to the user's executable. Multiple copies of the user's executables are started (either by a driver program or as a result of **fork()**s on a shared memory machine). One executable begins by executing the user's main route; all the rest, after initializing, begin executing at **eval_server()**. The latter simply waits on an **in** of one of the tuples generated by the **outs** used to rewrite the original **eval**. This tuple describes the function to be executed and its arguments. The **eval_server()** then executes the function. The final step fills in the appropriate slot of a vector (stored in yet another tuple) that holds data for the fields of the tuple that ultimately results from the **eval()**. If the vector is full, the **eval_server()** does the corresponding **out** using the data in the vector. An example:

```
foo(i, j) {
  return i+j;
}

bar(i) {
  return (i*i);
}

real_main() {
  int i=2, j=3;
  eval("tasks", foo(j,j), bar(i));
  in("tasks", ? i, ?j);
  printf("%d, %d\n", i, j);
}
```

This will be translated to:

```
foo(i, j) {
  return i+j;
}

bar(i) {
  return (i*i);
}

real_main() {
  int i=2, j=3;
  /* Random names generated by the transformer. */
  __lo_AWhfbc( foo ,j,j , bar ,i );
  __lo_FakHoc(&(  i),&(  j));
  printf("%d, %d\n", i, j);
}
```

The **eval()** has been replaced by an invocation of this function:

```
int __lo_AWhfbc(arg1,arg2,arg3,arg4,arg5)
```

```
int (*arg1)(), arg2, arg3, (*arg4)(), arg5;
{
  int base_id;
  CAST_UNION cu;
  CAST_UNION out_fv[2];
  TASK t;

  t.out_id = 0;
  /* Reserve 2 unique ids for labeling the tasks.*/
  base_id = __es_reserve_ids(2);
  t.out_tid = base_id;

  /* Describe the first task. */
  t.pos = 0; t.func_id = 1; t.tid = base_id++;
  t.args[0].i = arg2; t.args[1].i = arg3;
  /* out the structure. */
  __es_out_task(&t);

  t.pos = 1; t.func_id = 2; t.tid = base_id++;
  t.args[0].i = arg5;
  __es_out_task(&t);

  /* Create a tuple with a vector to hold the results
     of the function invocations. */
  __es_out_fv(t.out_tid, out_fv, 2, 2);
}
```

The generated **eval_server** (note in this version of the system, the initial in of the task descriptor has already taken place in an auxiliary routine):

```
int __eval_server(t)
      TASK *t;
{
  int        arg_count;
  if (t->func_id == 1) {
    CAST_UNION      cu;
    CAST_UNION      out_fv[3];
    int             foo();

    cu.i = foo(t->args[0].i, t->args[1].i);
    /* Update the result vector. */
    __es_in_fv(t->out_tid, out_fv, &arg_count);
    --arg_count;
    out_fv[t->pos].i = cu.i;
    __es_out_fv(t->out_tid, out_fv, 3, arg_count);
  }
  else if (t->func_id == 2) {
    CAST_UNION      cu;
```

```
CAST_UNION        out_fv[3];
int               bar();

cu.i = bar(t->args[0].i);
__es_in_fv(t->out_tid, out_fv, &arg_count);
--arg_count;
out_fv[t->pos].i = cu.i;
__es_out_fv(t->out_tid, out_fv, 3, arg_count);
}
/* If the current result completes the eval, do the
   corresponding out. */.
if (!arg_count) {
  if (t->out_id == 0) {
    CAST_UNION      out_fv[3];

    __es_in_fv(t->out_tid, out_fv, &arg_count);
    __lo_AWhfbc_out(out_fv[0].i, out_fv[1].i);
  }
}
}
```

Finally `__lo_AWhfbc_out()` is the function that actually creates the tuple resulting from the **eval**, by simply doing the equivalent of an **out** on the data returned from the **eval**ed functions.

Portability has an additional advantage: we can "port" this approach back to the shared memory systems. These traditionally handle **eval** by a simpler mechanism, again based on **fork()**, that did not enforce some of the semantics of eval. The port provides the *same* **eval** environment on shared memory machines, increasing the portability of Linda codes.

In fact, the **eval** server is now used in all of our Linda implementations.

3 Piranha

As local area networks spanning large numbers of powerful workstations become commonplace, researchers have come to realize that at most sites, many nodes are idle much of the time. Ideally there would be some way to recapture some of these lost cycles, which grow increasingly formidable in the aggregate as workstations grow more powerful. In the Piranha model, idle nodes are recycled by focusing them on explicitly-parallel programs. The user builds a parallel program, structured as a collection of worker processes sharing access to a distributed data structure in which task descriptors are stored. The *number* of worker processes (or "Piranhas") expands and contracts as the program executes. Any participating workstation has the option of joining the ongoing computation (in other words, running a worker process) when it becomes idle. When a user reclaims his workstation, it leaves the ongoing parallel computation and returns to normal duties.

The Piranha model, in the abstract, makes no assumptions about the mechanism used to express the application's parallelism. In practice, Piranha is an immediate fit to the Linda model: Linda makes it easy to structure computations as collections of workers sharing access to distributed data structures. Thus Piranha is, in practice, an execution model and support system for a certain class of Linda programs.

A Piranha program centers on a collection of tasks stored one per tuple in some data structure (an unstructured bag or an ordered structure) within a tuple space. When a node becomes free, it may start consuming tasks from the collection. When it becomes "unfree" (its user needs it again), it stops consuming tasks. Clearly, the more Piranha (i.e., the more nodes consuming tasks), the faster the computation completes, up to the number of concurrently-available tasks.

The user's Piranha program consists of three basic functions: *feeder*, *piranha*, and *retreat*. The first two correspond to the *master* and *worker* functions in a master-worker Linda program [3].

The *feeder* runs on the so-called "home node," the node belonging to the user who submitted the job. Our current implementation requires that the user who submits an application donate his node for the duration of the computation, so that the feeder is never suspended. (This and many other subsequent aspects of our current system are artifacts of the implementation; reasonable choices, we believe, but in no sense intrinsic to the model.) Its functions often include distributing tasks (creating the task collection) and collecting the results. It may also join in consuming tasks.

The *piranha* function is automatically executed on all nodes that join a computation, except for the home node. Typically, a piranha function executes a loop that reads tasks and consumes them until none remain. The code to consume a task is application-dependent. The Piranha read the parameters for the computation from tuple space.

If a node aborts a computation in the middle of a task, the *retreat* function restores the global state of the system. In the simplest case, *retreat* returns the task to tuple space. More complicated retreat functions pass accumulated state from a retreating process to some other Piranha process.

Piranha applications are written in Linda, and they differ only in minor ways from standard Linda applications (i.e., they define a function called "piranha" and not a function called "worker," they define a retreat function and so on). They are required to play by the rules (Piranha applications are a subset of Linda programs, which needn't necessarily have master-worker structures at all), but Piranha doesn't require that the user learn a new language or new operations. Piranha applications are supported by the Linda Program Builder[1].

3.1 Architecture

The Piranha software has two basic parts: a Piranha daemon (called the kernel) and the user application software. The kernels are responsible for managing each node's Piranha functions. The user applications do computations. The applications programs are linked to a run-time library that provides an interface to the kernel. There is, of course, a need to communicate between the various distributed pieces of the user's code (traditional parallel computation coordination). But in addition there is a need to communicate between the user's code and the local Piranha daemon, and between daemons. Lacking a better alternative, each of these communication needs might be met by an ad hoc collection of mechanisms. But the better way, Linda, provides a simple, uniform framework for all of these—at least in principle.

In practice, Piranha helped push the realization of Linda systems that were open and support multiple tuple spaces [4]. Initial Linda implementations depended upon a complete picture of Linda operations at link time. This information permitted optimizations that reduced much of the Linda runtime overhead—providing a level of efficiency demanded by parallel computations. This approach, however, prohibits separately built executables from talking to one another. Each lives in a tuple space closed off from the others. As we turn away from parallel codes and towards distributed applications, this tradeoff of flexibility for performance is less desirable. Open tuple spaces—tuple spaces that are accessible by any executable—combined with multiple tuple spaces allow us to construct ensembles of the sort we need for Piranha. The user's code converses with itself via a closed tuple space, and also converses with the Piranha daemons (independent executables) using an open tuple space. Similarly, the daemons exchange information between themselves via an open tuple space. We have built a prototype implementation out of these elements. Aside from providing a convenient mechanism for building the basic system, Linda will encourage elaboration via construction of related distribute data structures in tuple space.

3.2 Current Status

The prototype implementation of Piranha has proven to be an effective way to consume idle cycles of the nodes in a LAN. We have run a number of scientific and industry programs (for example: freewake, a computational fluid dynamics code, and linkmap, a genetic analysis program) [2] with encouraging results. In one roughly thirteen hour period, for example, Piranha delivered over 550 aggregate computing hours to a Physics application using an average of 43 nodes [6]. We have been able to provide a powerful computing engine with little effect on interactive performance.

4 The InfoLandscape: Coordinating Human Workers

In distributed and concurrent applications, many simultaneous, asynchronous activities focus on solving one problem. The individual threads of activity each work independently on one or more pieces of the overall task but commonly need to exchange information and coordinate their activity with other threads in order to arrive at the complete problem solution.

If we consider projects or large tasks carried out by groups of human workers, we soon realize that there are obvious similarities to the concurrent solution of problems by computer. In collaborative human work, multiple simultaneous, asynchronous *human* elements focus on solving a common problem. Again, each individual works largely independently on its assigned parts of the overall task but sometimes needs to communicate information or to synchronize its activities with the other human workers. The burgeoning multidisciplinary field of *computer-supported cooperative work* (also known as *collaboration technology*) addresses issues of how groups work on common problems and how computer-based systems can help them work together more effectively. *Groupware* is the name given to software systems which provide groups of workers with an interface to a shared environment which aids communication and coordination of activities [5].

Linda's tuple space coordination medium has proven effective in supporting uncoupled communication (through both space and time) and coordination of multiple processing threads in concurrent applications. Since human workers engaged in a common task also have a need for uncoupled communication across space and time, and for coordination, we believe that Linda can be useful in coordinating human processing agents as well. Hence, we have begun constructing a Linda-based groupware system.

4.1 The InfoLandscape System

Our "InfoLandscape" system is a software architecture (tool) for building distributed, interactive "information landscapes" through which human workers can share information and communicate. Just as Linda's uncoupled coordination model allows for great flexibility in structuring a parallel computation, we can use Linda, with support for multiple, persistent tuple spaces, to build a flexible tool for structuring ensembles of human processes and information. InfoLandscape looks to a user like a database organized by multiple, hierarchical tuple spaces and accessible to multiple workers.

The workers' interface to the InfoLandscape system is visual, iconographic, and interactive. It provides graphical representations of hierarchical tuple spaces and the tuples (data) within them. A worker can grow or shrink the information landscape, i.e. customize the database, at will. E.g., by using the mouse and buttons, the user can create and destroy tuple spaces, or in and out tuples. A user can dynamically see changes made by other workers to the system. For example, if tuple space is currently displayed on a user's screen, and another worker adds or deletes a tuple in that tuple space, the user viewing the tuple space will be able to note the change. A user can also change his viewing perspective by "hopping" into a tuple space, an arena of associated information and human processes with common interests. Once there, the worker can meet and talk to other parties and possibly leave daemon software agents behind.

The InfoLandscape system has several interesting characteristics. It supports flexible interaction among workers; both group and one-on-one communication is supported. It enables information sharing. Moreover, the system allows user-customization of the information/communication framework. No unnatural communication or information structure is imposed upon users; the workers themselves build a flexible, natural structure that best reflects how they like to organize information and communicate. Furthermore, the system features easy, dynamic adaptability; workers are permitted to reconfigure the system by creating/removing tuple space information modules as desired.

4.2 Implementation

Essentially, the InfoLandscape system has three fundamental components: multiple, hierarchical tuple spaces, support for interpreted Linda operations, and a visualization interface. Hence, in order to build the InfoLandscape system, we need the features of open Linda. One of these is multiple, hierarchical tuple spaces. Another is open access to tuple spaces: human and software agents may show up to alter tuple space at any time, so we no longer have a global, compile-time view of all Linda operations which will occur. A third Linda requirement is tuple space persistence: open access to tuple spaces means that we cannot know when a tuple space is no longer of interest, so tuple spaces must persist unless we explicitly destroy them. To support this, an open Linda implementation will need to back up these tuple spaces to file storage to achieve real persistence. Because of the functionality it provides, open Linda will play a fundamental role in the InfoLandscape system implementation.

4.3 Current Status

Implementation of the InfoLandscape software architecture is currently focusing on the design and implementation of the visualization interface component, which is X-Windows-based. The interface handles interactive events (e.g. mouse clicks) by translating them into requests to an open Linda system (e.g. requests to create or destroy tuple spaces, add, read, or remove tuples).

5 Conclusions

While the limelight has been focussed on the use of Linda to build efficient parallel programs, we have been steadily building a portfolio of successes in other areas of co-ordinated computing. It's time to make more of these efforts. They will begin to crowd center stage as open Linda systems—Linda systems that support access to the same tuple space from different executables—become more widely available, spawning a creative frenzy of coordinated programming.

From the perspective of the Linda project, these efforts emphasize the general utility of the Linda model. Few other approaches having some promise as tools for parallel computation maintain their attractiveness as tools for other sorts of distributed ensembles.

From a larger perspective, it is important to emphasize the full panoply of coordination applications. Arguably, significant future developments in large-scale systems will more often than not be members of this group. Current (over) emphasis on parallel computation risks stunting the development of the tools necessary to meet the needs of these next generation systems.

This research is supported by National Science Foundation grant CCR-8657615, by the Air Force Office of Scientific Research under grant number AFOSR-91-0098, and by NASA under NASA Training Grant NGT-50719.

References

1. Ahmed, S., Carriero, N., Gelernter, D., "The Linda Program Builder", Proc. Third Workshop on Languages and Compilers for Parallelism (Irvine, 1990), MIT Press 1991.
2. Bjornson, R., Carriero, N., Gelernter, D., Kaminsky, D., Mattson, T., and Sherman, A. "Experience with Linda", YALEU/DCS/TR-866, 8/91.
3. Carriero, N. and Gelernter, D., "How to Write Parallel Programs: A Guide to the Perplexed", *ACM Computing Surveys*, (Sept. 1989).
4. Carriero, N., Gelernter D., and Mattson T., "Linda in Heterogeneous Computing Environments", YALEU/DCS/TR-876, 10/91.
5. Ellis, C., Gibbs, S. and Rein, G., "Groupware: Some Issues and Experiences", *Communications of the ACM*, (Jan. 1991):38–58.
6. Gates, E., Krauss, L., White, M., "Solar Neutrino Data and Its Implications", YCTP-P26-91, Yale University, 8/91.
7. Gelernter, D. and Bernstein, A., "Distributed communication via global buffer," in *Proc. ACM Symp. Principles of Distributed Computing*, (Aug. 1982):10–18.

This article was processed using the LaTeX macro package with LMAMULT style

Part 3: Gamma

The chemical reaction model

Daniel Le Métayer

Irisa, Campus de Beaulieu, 35042 Rennes Cedex, France

The Gamma formalism has been proposed some years ago to allow the description of programs without artificial sequentiality (by artificial, we mean sequentiality that is not implied by the logic of the program). Gamma is a minimal language based on one data structure, the multiset, and the corresponding control structure, the chemical reaction. The language is briefly presented in the first paper. The second paper, by Louis Mussat, shows the significance of Gamma for program derivation. As an illustration, a Gamma program is derived from the specification of a general class of problems. Then it is shown that apparently unrelated problems taken from various application fields turn out to be instances of this general specification. In the third paper Christian Creveuil shows how Gamma programs can be implemented rather naturally on massively parallel machines. The fourth paper, by Rachel Harrison investigates program transformation techniques to improve the efficiency of the parallel implementations of functional languages. Gamma is used in this context as a case study.

José Meseguer and Timothy Winkler conclude with a presentation of the Maude language, which is based on a logic of actions called rewriting logic. The main goal of the Maude project is to integrate concurrent programming and object-oriented programming into the functional programming paradigm. As a consequence Meseguer and Winkler provide a unifying formal framework in which several of the parallel languages that were presented during the workshop (including Unity, Gamma and the Chemical Abstract Machine) can be compared.

Introduction to Gamma

Jean-Pierre Banâtre and Daniel Le Métayer

Irisa, Campus de Beaulieu, 35042 Rennes Cedex, France

It is now recognized that correctness should be the primary concern in program development; it is only in a second stage that provably correct solutions should be used to derive more efficient versions. In order to achieve this goal, one should be able to build in the first place an abstract version of the program in a high level language. In particular, these abstract programs should be free of artificial sequentiality. Unfortunately, to our knowledge, there is no available formalism allowing such an abstract description of programs. Let us take a simple example to illustrate this point. The problem is to find the maximum element of a non-empty set. In an imperative language the set can be represented as an array $a[1:n]$ and a possible program is:

```
maxset₁:    m := a[1];
            i := 1;
          * [i < n →
                i := i+1;
                m := max(m, a[i])]
```

While the condition $i < n$ holds, index i is incremented and a new value of m is computed. In a functional language, the set would be represented as a list and the program would be:

$$maxset_2(l) = if\ tail(l) = nil\ then\ head(l)\ else\ max\ (head(l), maxset_2(tail(l)))$$

In both cases the program imposes a total ordering on the comparisons of the elements: the first element is compared with the second, then their maximum is compared with the third, and so forth... In both formalisms one could imagine a less constraining solution involving implicit parallelism. For example, in the functional language a divide-and-conquer version of the above program would be:

$$maxset_3(l) = if \ tail(l) = nil \ then \ head(l) \ else$$
$$let \ (l_1, l_2) = split(l) \quad in$$
$$max(maxset_3(l_1), maxset_3(l_2))$$

where $split \ (l_1, ..., l_n) = ((l_1, ..., l_{n/2}), (l_{n/2+1}, ..., l_n))$. Here again a (partial) ordering is imposed on the comparisons: for example the first and last elements of the list will not be compared (except in the case where they are the maxima of their respective sublists).

In fact the maximum of a set can be computed by performing the comparisons of the elements in any order. So we would like an abstract algorithm of the form:

while *there are at least two elements in the set*
   select *two elements of the set,* **compare** *them and* **remove** *the smaller one*

This is almost a GAMMA program. In GAMMA such a statement can be written as follows:

$$maxset_4 \ (s) = \Gamma((R,A)) \ (s) \quad where$$
$$R(x,y) = x \leq y$$
$$A(x,y) = \{y\}$$

Function R specifies a property to be satisfied by the selected elements; these elements are replaced in the set by the result of the application of function A. Nothing is said in this definition about the order of evaluation of the comparisons; if several disjoint pairs of elements satisfy property R, the comparisons and replacements can even be performed in parallel. An intuitive way of describing the meaning of a GAMMA program is the metaphor of the chemical reaction: the set can be seen as a chemical solution, function R (called the reaction condition) is a property to be satisfied by reacting elements and A (the action) describes the product of the reaction. The computation terminates when a stable state is reached, that is to say when no elements of the set satisfy the reaction condition.

Let us now give a more formal presentation of GAMMA. The basic data structure in GAMMA (General Abstract Model for Multiset mAnipulation) is the *multiset*, which is the same as a set except that it may contain multiple occurrences of the same element; the multiset is sometimes referred to as a *bag*. The benefit of using multisets is the possibility of describing compound data without any form of constraint or hierarchy between its components. This is not the case for recursively defined data structures such as lists which impose an ordering on the examination of elements (function $maxset_2$ above is an illustration of this constraint). The control structure associated with multisets is the Γ operator; as we have seen on the above example, Γ reflects the absence of hierarchy in the data structure and entails some kind of chaotic model of execution. Its formal definition can be stated as follows:

$$\Gamma((R_1,A_1),...,(R_m,A_m)) \ (M) =$$

$$\begin{array}{ll} if & \forall i \in [1,m], \ \forall x_1,...x_n \in M, \ \rceil R_i \ (x_1,...x_n) \\ then & M \\ else & let \ x_1,...,x_n \in M, \ let \ i \in [1,m] \ such \ that \ R_i \ (x_1,...,x_n) \ in \\ & \Gamma((R_1,A_1),...,(R_m,A_m)) \ ((M - \{x_1,...x_n\}) + A_i \ (x_1,...x_n)) \end{array}$$

The notation $\{..\}$ is used to represent multisets. There is no ambiguity here since we never use simple sets. The basic operations on multisets are the following:

- *union*: the number of occurrences of an element in $M_1 + M_2$ is the sum of its numbers of occurrences in M_1 and M_2.

- *difference*: the number of occurrences of an element in $M_1 - M_2$ is the difference between its numbers of occurrences in M_1 and M_2 (if this difference is greater than or equal to zero, otherwise it is zero).

(R_i,A_i) are pairs of closed functions (functions whose definition does not involve global variables) specifying reactions. The effect of a reaction (R_i,A_i) on a multiset M is to replace in M a subset of elements $\{x_1,...,x_n\}$ such that $R_i \ (x_1,...,x_n)$ is true by the elements of A_i $(x_1,...x_n)$. If no elements of M satisfy any reaction condition $(\forall i \in [1,m], \ \forall x_1,...x_n \in M, \ \rceil R_i \ (x_1,...,x_n))$ then the result is M; otherwise the result is obtained by carrying out one reaction $((M - \{x_1,...x_n\}) + A_i(x_1,...x_n))$ and repeating the same process. The above definition implies that if one or several reaction conditions hold for several subsets at the same time, the choice which is made among them is not deterministic. The importance of the *locality property* of GAMMA cannot be overemphasized: R_i, and A_i are pure functions operating on their arguments (elements extracted from the multiset) and returning a result; as a consequence, if the reaction condition holds for several disjoint subsets, the reactions can be carried out independently (and simultaneously). This property is the basic reason why GAMMA programs do generally exhibit a lot of potential parallelism.

GAMMA programs can be composed using the traditional functional notation. Furthermore, functions R_i and A_i can be defined by pattern matching on the form of their arguments; pattern matching can also be used to extract elements from a multiset (for example m *where* $\{m\} = \Gamma((R,A))(G)$ is the extraction of the unique element of the result multiset). It should be noticed that the arguments of R_i and A_i must be of the same form since A_i is applied to arguments satisfying R_i. The notation used above to describe GAMMA programs is slightly awkward since it requires two separate definitions for R_i and A_i which entails the duplication of the text of their formal arguments. In the following we shall use the syntax:

> **do**
>> **rp** $x_1,...,x_n$
>> **if** *"text of the condition"*
>> **by** *"text of the action"*
> **od**

When the Gamma program manipulates several multiset arguments, each consumed element (and each produced element) is explicitly attached to a particular multiset [4,6]. Let us now illustrate the programming style of the language with a few examples. The following program returns the set of prime numbers smaller than N.

prime_numbers(N) = P $(\{2, ..., N\})$ *where*
> $P(M)$ =
>> **do**
>>> **rp** x, y
>>> **if** *multiple(x, y)*
>>> **by** y
>> **od**

The program proceeds by removing from the set $\{2, ..., N\}$ elements that are multiples of an other element in the set.

We consider now the sorting problem: the goal is to organize the elements of an array in increasing order. We use a multiset of pairs *(index,value)* and the program exchanges ill-ordered values until all values are well-ordered.

```
sort(Array) =
                do
                    rp (i,v), (j,w)
                    if (i > j) and (v < w)
                    by (i,w), (j,v)
                od
```

The majority element of a multiset M is an element occurring more than $card(M)/2$ times in the multiset. We propose a solution to the problem of finding the majority element, assuming that such an element exists:

```
maj_elem(M) = m where {m} = P₂(P₁(M))  where
        P₁(M) =
                do
                    rp x, y
                    if  x ≠ y
                    by  ∅
                od
        P₂(M) =
                do
                    rp x, y
                    if  True
                    by  x
                od
```

The interested reader may find in [3] a longer series of examples (string processing problems, graph problems, geometric problems, ...) illustrating the Gamma style of programming. It should be clear that GAMMA is not a programming language in the usual sense of the term. GAMMA programs are executable but any straightforward implementation would be extremely inefficient. We see GAMMA as a convenient intermediate language between specifications and programs: it is possible to express in GAMMA the *idea* of an algorithm without any detail about the execution order or the memory management. For example, you can tell in GAMMA that your strategy to sort a sequence is to exchange values, that you want to find the convex hull by removing the points inside a triangle, and so forth. Further program derivation may specialize these abstract programs by choosing a particular data representation and a particular execution order [5].

GAMMA is currently used in the context of systematic program construction [2,5,6]: GAMMA programs are first derived from a specification in first order logic [2]; then a second step is performed to obtain traditional programs (for sequential or parallel machines) from this GAMMA program [5]. Using an intermediate language like GAMMA makes the derivation easier because it allows a nice separation of concerns: the first step (the derivation of the GAMMA program) is related to the logic of the algorithm, whereas the second step expresses lower level choices such as data representation or execution order.

Another remarkable benefit of using GAMMA in the derivation is that GAMMA programs do not have any sequential implementation bias. In fact it is often the case that problems which are usually considered as inherently sequential turn out to have a parallel solution in GAMMA. As a consequence, GAMMA can be implemented very naturally on parallel machines; the interested reader may refer to [1,4] for the description of parallel implementations of GAMMA.

References

[1] Banâtre, J.-P., Coutant, A., and Le Métayer, D. A Parallel Machine for Multiset Transformation and its Programming Style. Future Generation Computer Systems. 4 (1988) 133-144.

[2] Banâtre, J.-P., and Le Métayer D. The GAMMA model and its discipline of programming. Science of Computer Programming 15 (1990) 55-77.

[3] Banâtre, J.-P., and Le Métayer D. Programming by multiset transformation. Comm. of the ACM, to appear.

[4] Creveuil C., Implementation of GAMMA on the Connection Machine. proc. of the Workshop on Research Directions in High-level Parallel Programming Languages, this volume.

[5] Creveuil C., Techniques d'analyse et de mise en œuvre de programmes Gamma. Thèse de $3^{\text{ème}}$ cycle, Université de Rennes 1, December 1991.

[6] Mussat L., Parallel programming with bags. proc. of the Workshop on Research Directions in High-level Parallel Programming Languages, this volume.

Parallel Programming with Bags

Louis Mussat

IRISA – Campus de Beaulieu, 35042 Rennes Cedex, France

Abstract

We show the relevance of a high level computational model for the development of correct parallel programs. To this end we derive four programs solving classical problems; some of which generally considered as "inherently sequential". The paper is only concerned with correctness and does not address implementation issues.

Introduction

The systematic construction of programs is not an easy task. It's even more difficult when intended for parallel machines; but it is also more crucial because it is very difficult to master parallel programming without method.

Hence the necessity of a computational model allowing to describe algorithms with as few sequentiality constraints as possible. Such a model, called GAMMA, has been proposed in [Banâtre and Le Métayer 1990]. The purpose of this paper is to show its relevance for the derivation of parallel programs.

We proceed in the following way: first, we give the specification of a general class of problem. Next a GAMMA program meeting this specification is constructed using standard techniques—split of the specification into a variant and an invariant part. Then we show that apparently unrelated problems taken from various application fields turn out to be instances of our general specification. As a consequence, GAMMA programs can be derived to solve them in a straightforward way.

The paper is organized as follows. Section 1 gives a short presentation of the GAMMA model. Section 2 introduces some definitions and notations. Section 3 presents the specification of the general problem and the derivation of the corresponding GAMMA program. Section 4 makes use of the abstract derivation to find a parallel solution to four classical problems: the knapsack, the shortest paths, the maximal segment sum and the longest upsequence problems.

1 The GAMMA Model

The main idea underlying this computational model is the description of computations as successive transformations of finite bags. That is, the repetition of the following step, called a *replacement*: elements satisfying a given condition are replaced by zero or more transformed elements. These replacement steps are performed until no combination of elements can satisfy the condition.

So a GAMMA program is a set of *reaction pairs*, whose components are a *condition* (i.e. a predicate characterizing elements to transform) and an *action* (i.e. a function yielding new elements).

There is a restriction upon conditions and actions. They must be *local*, in the sense that they must only involve the seized elements. This locality allows transformations of disjoint subparts of the bags to be executed in parallel. For the sake of conciseness we do not dwell on the GAMMA model here. The interested reader can find more information in [Banâtre and Le Métayer 1990].

For example, a very simple GAMMA program computing the biggest set S included in a bag B is (written in a guarded commands like syntax):

$$S := B;$$
do
$$\exists x \in S, \exists y \in S - \{x\}, \; x = y \longrightarrow S := S - \{x\}$$
od

In the next section we introduce some definitions and notations for bag manipulation, as well as a simpler syntax for GAMMA programs.

2 Notations

2.1 Sets

We denote by **N** the set of natural numbers and by **Z** the set of integers. An ordered set $(C, \prec)$ is said to be discrete if every ascending and upper-bounded chain in C is finite.

2.2 Functions

The set of functions from A to B is denoted $(A \to B)$. Function application is denoted by an infix dot. We use currying; so a function of $(A \times B \to C)$ is also a function of $(A \to (B \to C))$.

2.3 Bags

Loosely speaking, a bag is a set which can contain more than one occurrence of each element. Actually, a function mapping elements to natural numbers fully defines a bag, and conversely. Here we consider only finite bags, hence the

Definition. Let S be a set, a bag B on S is a function of $(S \to \mathbf{N})$ with finite support. We note $S^\star$ the set of all the finite bags on S.

From now on a set is seen as a special bag mapping elements to 0 or 1. This forces us to extend the classical operations on sets to handle bags as well, without changing their meaning when only sets are involved. We do that below, and also introduce new operations.

Let A and B be bags on a set S; we define the following predicates and functions:

membership	:	$\forall x \in S,\ x \in B \iff B.x > 0$
inclusion	:	$A \subseteq B \iff \forall x \in S,\ A.x \leq B.x$
union	:	$\forall x \in S,\ (A \cup B).x = \max.(A.x, B.x)$
intersection	:	$\forall x \in S,\ (A \cap B).x = \min.(A.x, B.x)$
sum	:	$\forall x \in S,\ (A + B).x = A.x + B.x$
difference	:	$\forall x \in S,\ (A - B).x = \max.(0, A.x - B.x)$
cardinal	:	$\#.B = \sum_{x \in S} B.x$

with max and min the maximum and minimum functions on natural numbers.

We also need to apply a function on each element of a bag, an operation called

element-wise application : $\mathrm{map}.f.B = \sum_{x \in S} (B.x * \{f.x\})$

(where the external product $k * B$ is simply $\sum_{i=1}^{k} B$).

This operation is particularly useful with the projections 1, 2 and 3 mapping a tuple on its (respectively) first, second and third component.

2.4 GAMMA Programs

The syntax used to write the simple example given in Sect. 1 is slightly awkward. We introduce now a simpler syntax to describe GAMMA programs.

The guarded command

$$\exists \{x_1, \ldots, x_i\} \subseteq A,\ C.(x_1, \ldots, x_i)$$
$$\longrightarrow A := A - \{x_1, \ldots, x_i\};\ B := B + \{y_1, \ldots, y_j\}$$

is written

$$\mathbf{rp}\ x_1, \ldots, x_i : A$$
$$\mathbf{if}\ \ C.(x_1, \ldots, x_i)$$
$$\mathbf{by}\ y_1, \ldots, y_j : B$$

(**rp** is read "replace")

This triple is called a γ-command. Bags A and B may be the same, if elements are to be picked from and put back into the same bag. On the other hand, one can use more bags by simply adding lists of elements with their source (in the **rp** part) or destination (in the **by** part). By enclosing a set of γ-commands in a **do-od** pair, one obtain a GAMMA program.

According to this new syntax, the example of Sect. 1 is written:

$$S := B;$$
$$\mathbf{do}$$
$$\quad \mathbf{rp}\ x, y : S$$
$$\quad \mathbf{if}\ \ x = y$$
$$\quad \mathbf{by}\ y : S$$
$$\mathbf{od}$$

3 A Program Scheme

The problem we consider is the following. We are given a set S and a function F on S^*, and are requested to evaluate the greatest value that F can take on a particular subset of S^*, characterized by a predicate T. We assume that this greatest value exists. This is a common situation, as will be shown in Sect. 4.

Formally, the problem is to compute

$$\omega = \text{lub}.\{F.B \mid B \in S^* \wedge T.B\}$$

with the assumptions:

(H_0) S and C are sets

(H_1) F is a function of $(S^* \to C)$

(H_2) T is a predicate on S^*

(H_3) $(C, \prec)$ is discrete, with minimal element $\perp$

(H_4)   lub is the least upper bound function on $(C, \prec)$

In order to solve this problem, we need additional hypotheses (H_i) as well as properties (P_i) on F and T, carefully chosen not to be too restrictive. They are introduced when necessary.

3.1 A Recursive Specification

The first step is the search for a recursive definition of ω. A good starting point towards this goal is to express the problem as a composition of simpler ones.

So we make the following new hypotheses:

(H_5) A is a set

(H_6) sT is a predicate on $A \times S^*$

and suppose that sT is related to T by the property:

(P_0) $\forall B \in S^*, \; T.B \iff \exists x \in A, \; sT.x.B$

This allows us to calculate for each x of A the greatest value of F on bags satisfying $sT.x$, and thereafter to compute ω by picking the greatest of these values. Hence we define

$$\Omega = \{(x,m) \mid x \in A \wedge m = \text{lub}.\{F.B \mid B \in S^* \wedge sT.x.B\}\}$$

and we have

$$\omega = \text{lub}.\{m \mid (x,m) \in \Omega\}$$

Now we are left with the computation of Ω. Let's try to find a recursive definition of this set. For this purpose its elements must be interrelated, so we suppose that

(H_7) V is a predicate on $A \times S \times A$

satisfying the properties

(P_1) $\forall \{x,y\} \subseteq A, \forall p \in S, \forall B \in S^*, \; V.x.p.y \wedge sT.y.B \Rightarrow sT.x.(B + \{p\})$

(P$_2$) $\forall x \in A, \forall B \in S^*,\ \#.B > 1 \wedge sT.x.B$

$$\Rightarrow \exists y \in A - \{x\}, \exists p \in B,\ V.x.p.y \wedge sT.y.(B - \{p\})$$

In the sequel V is called the *neighborhood* relation; a *neighbor* of x is an element y of $A - \{x\}$ for which holds $\exists p \in S,\ V.x.p.y$.
Together with the fact that

$$B \in S^* \wedge \#.B \leq 1 \iff B = \emptyset \vee \exists p \in S,\ B = \{p\}$$

these two properties gives the equality (E$_1$)

$$\begin{aligned}
&\{F.B \mid B \in S^* \wedge sT.x.B\} \\
={} &\{F.B \mid sT.x.\emptyset \wedge B = \emptyset\} \\
&+ \{F.B \mid p \in S \wedge sT.x.\{p\} \wedge B = \{p\}\} \\
&+ \{F.(B + \{p\}) \mid p \in S \wedge y \in A - \{x\} \wedge V.x.p.y \wedge B \in S^* \wedge sT.y.B\}
\end{aligned}$$

Bearing in mind that we are looking for a recursive definition of Ω, we focus on the last subset above. First of all, we need $F.(B + \{p\})$ to be computable when $F.B$ is known. So we assume that F is defined as follows.
Let

(H$_8$) $\odot$ be an associative and commutative operator on C, with a unit 1

(H$_9$) f be a function from S to C

then $F.B$ is the reduction with $\odot$ of the bag map.$f.B$, i.e.

(P$_3$) $F.B = \displaystyle\bigodot_{p \in B} f.p$

where the reduction of a bag with $\odot$ is defined by

$$\bigodot_{c \in \{c_1, \ldots, c_n\}} c = c_1 \odot \cdots \odot c_n$$

Please note that 3 indeed defines a function F, by virtues of (H$_8$). Also, note that $F.\emptyset = 1$.
Replacing F by its definition in the right hand side of (E$_1$) gives the equality (E$_2$):

$$\begin{aligned}
&\{F.B \mid B \in S^* \wedge sT.x.B\} \\
={} &\{\ell \mid sT.x.\emptyset \wedge \ell = 1\} \\
&+ \{\ell \mid p \in S \wedge sT.x.\{p\} \wedge \ell = f.p\} \\
&+ \{\ell \odot f.p \mid p \in S \wedge y \in A - \{x\} \wedge V.x.p.y \\
&\qquad\qquad\qquad \wedge B \in S^* \wedge sT.y.B \wedge \ell = F.B\}
\end{aligned}$$

Now, the definition of Ω involves lub; so we would like to express the greatest value of $F.(B + \{p\})$ in terms of the greatest value of $F.B$. Because $F.(B + \{p\}) = F.B \odot f.p$, this requires the following monotonicity property of $\odot$:

(P$_4$) $\forall \{a, b, c\} \in C^*,\ a \prec b \Rightarrow a \odot c \prec b \odot c$

Because $\prec$ is total, this is sufficient to ensure that

$$\forall c \in C, \forall M \in C^*, \ \mathsf{lub}.\{a \odot c \mid a \in M\} = \mathsf{lub}.\{a \mid a \in M\} \odot c$$

from which follows for all x of A:

$$\mathsf{lub}.\{\ell \odot f.p \mid p \in S \wedge y \in A - \{x\} \wedge V.x.p.y \\ \wedge B \in S^* \wedge sT.y.B \wedge \ell = F.B\} \\ = \mathsf{lub}.\{\ell \odot f.p \mid p \in S \wedge y \in A - \{x\} \wedge V.x.p.y \\ \wedge \ell = \mathsf{lub}.\{F.B \mid B \in S^* \wedge sT.y.B\}\}$$

But

$$y \in A - \{x\} \wedge \ell = \mathsf{lub}.\{F.B \mid B \in S^* \wedge sT.y.B\}$$

is equivalent by definition of Ω to

$$y \in A - \{x\} \wedge (y, \ell) \in \Omega$$

Applying lub to both sides of (E_2) and using the above equivalence leads, finally, to a recursive definition of Ω:

$$\Omega = \{(x, m) \mid x \in A \wedge m = \mathsf{lub}.L_x\}$$

where

$$L_x = \ \{\ell \mid sT.x.\emptyset \wedge \ell = \mathbf{1}\} \\ + \{\ell \mid p \in S \wedge sT.x.\{p\} \wedge \ell = f.p\} \\ + \{\ell \odot f.p \mid p \in S \wedge y \in A - \{x\} \wedge V.x.p.y \wedge (y, \ell) \in \Omega\}$$

This ends the first step of the derivation. Now we have to build a GAMMA program computing Ω and ω. This is the purpose of the next section.

3.2 The Program

First of all we rewrite the definition of Ω as a conjunction of formulae. We begin with the equivalence

$$\Omega = \{(x, m) \mid x \in A \wedge m = \mathsf{lub}.L_x\} \\ \iff (\mathsf{map}.1.\Omega = A) \wedge (\forall (x, m) \in \Omega, \ m = \mathsf{lub}.L_x)$$

Then we observe that for any bag $M \in C^*$

$$m = \mathsf{lub}.M \iff (\forall n \in M, \ n \preccurlyeq m) \wedge (m = \bot \vee m \in M)$$

Because

$$n \in L_x \iff (sT.x.\emptyset \wedge n = \mathbf{1}) \\ \vee (\exists p \in S, \ sT.x.\{p\} \wedge n = f.p) \\ \vee (\exists (y, \ell) \in \Omega - \{(x, m)\}, \exists p \in S, \ V.x.p.y \wedge n = \ell \odot f.p)$$

the set Ω is fully defined by the conjunction of the following formulae:

(O_0) $\quad \mathsf{map}.1.\Omega = A$

(O_1) $\quad \forall (x, m) \in \Omega, \ sT.x.\emptyset \Rightarrow m \not\prec \mathbf{1}$

(O_2) $\quad \forall (x, m) \in \Omega, \forall p \in S, \ sT.x.\{p\} \Rightarrow m \not\prec f.p$

$(O_3)\quad \forall\{(x,m),(y,\ell)\} \subseteq \Omega, \forall p \in S,\ V.x.p.y \Rightarrow m \not\preccurlyeq \ell \odot f.p$

$$
\begin{aligned}
(O_4)\quad \forall(x,m) \in \Omega,\ m = \bot \\
&\vee (sT.x.\emptyset \wedge m = \mathbb{1}) \\
&\vee (\exists p \in S,\ sT.x.\{p\} \wedge m = f.p) \\
&\vee (\exists(y,\ell) \in \Omega - \{(x,m)\}, \exists p \in S,\ V.x.p.y \wedge m = \ell \odot f.p)
\end{aligned}
$$

Letting $o = \{\omega\}$ and remembering that

$$\omega = \mathsf{lub}.\{m \mid (x,m) \in \Omega\}$$

we see that o is fully defined by the conjunction of

$(O_5)\quad \forall(x,m) \in \Omega, \forall \ell \in o,\ m \preccurlyeq \ell$

$(O_6)\quad o = \{\bot\} \vee \exists(x,m) \in \Omega,\ o = \{m\}$

We now have to find a variant and an invariant for the program. Obvious candidates for the variant part are (O_1), (O_2), (O_3) and (O_5), because their negations are existential formulae, suitable to form the guards of γ-commands. (O_4) and (O_6) are too strong to be invariant; so they must be weakened. With

$(O_7)\quad \mathsf{map.1}.\Omega + \tilde{A} = A$

$(O_8)\quad \tilde{A} = \emptyset$

$$
\begin{aligned}
(O_9)\quad \forall(x,m) \in \Omega,\ m = \bot \\
&\vee (sT.x.\emptyset \wedge m = \mathbb{1}) \\
&\vee (\exists p \in S,\ sT.x.\{p\} \wedge m = f.p) \\
&\vee (\exists(y,\ell) \in \Omega - \{(x,m)\}, \exists p \in S,\ V.x.p.y \wedge m \preccurlyeq \ell \odot f.p)
\end{aligned}
$$

we have

$$(O_7) \wedge (O_8) \iff (O_0)$$

and

$$(O_3) \wedge (O_9) \iff (O_4)$$

By choosing the following invariant $\mathcal{I}$ and variant $\mathcal{V}$:

$$
\begin{aligned}
\mathcal{I} &\equiv (O_6) \wedge (O_7) \wedge (O_9) \\
\mathcal{V} &\equiv (O_1) \wedge (O_2) \wedge (O_3) \wedge (O_5) \wedge (O_8)
\end{aligned}
$$

one can easily derive the following generic program:

$$\tilde{A} := A;$$
$$\Omega := \emptyset;$$
$$o := \{\perp\};$$

do

    rp $x : \tilde{A}$
    by $(x, \perp) : \Omega$

    rp $(x, m) : \Omega$
    if $(sT.x.\emptyset) \wedge (m \prec \mathbf{1})$
    by $(x, \mathbf{1}) : \Omega$

    rp $(x, m) : \Omega, \ p : S$
    if $(sT.x.\{p\}) \wedge (m \prec f.p)$
    by $(x, f.p) : \Omega, \ p : S$

    rp $(x, m), (y, \ell) : \Omega, \ p : S$
    if $(V.x.p.y) \wedge (m \prec \ell \odot f.p)$
    by $(x, \ell \odot f.p), (y, \ell) : \Omega, \ p : S$

    rp $\ell : o, (x, m) : \Omega$
    if $(\ell \prec m)$
    by $m : o, (x, m) : \Omega$

od;

$$\omega := \mathsf{oneof}.o$$

the termination of which is established in the next section.

3.3 Termination

We first remark that

- Every execution of the first γ-command decreases the cardinal of $\tilde{A}$.
- Every execution of the three middle γ-commands increases the value of the second component of an element of Ω.
- Every execution of the last γ-command increases the value contained in o.

Obviously, the first γ-command can't execute indefinitely. For the next three, we see that

$$\forall (x, m) \in \Omega, \ m = \perp \vee \exists B \in S^\star, T.B \wedge m = F.B$$

is an invariant. So, by definition of ω,

$$\forall (x, m) \in \Omega, \ m \preccurlyeq \omega$$

is also an invariant. Hence, $(C, \prec)$ being discrete, the three middle γ-commands can't execute indefinitely. It follows that the last γ-command cannot either.

A more formal rendering of this proof can be made using the orderings on bags defined in [Dershowitz and Manna 1979].

4 Applications

In this section we address

1. the knapsack problem [Sedgewick 1988, p. 586];
2. the shortest paths problem [Dijkstra and Feijen 1988, p. 107];
3. the maximal segment sum problem [Bentley 1984];
4. the longest upsequence problem [Gries 1981, p. 259].

4.1 The Knapsack Problem

We consider an unlimited number of items, characterized by a size and a value, and a knapsack of capacity K. An item *type* is a (size, value) pair; the set of the item types is denoted I. A bag on I is called a load.

We define the size (resp. value) of a load B as the sum of its items sizes (resp. values), i.e.

$$\text{size}.B = \sum_{i \in B} 1.i \qquad \text{value}.B = \sum_{i \in B} 2.i$$

A knapsack may contain a load if its size do not exceed the capacity K of the knapsack.

The problem is to find the maximal value of a load the knapsack may contain. For such a maximum to exist we assume that item sizes are strictly positive natural numbers. Formally, we have to compute:

$$v = \max.\{\text{value}.B \mid B \in I^* \wedge \text{size}.B \le K\}$$

where max is the maximum function on natural numbers.

Which hypotheses made in Sect. 3 are fulfilled here? We have:

(H_0) I and $\mathbf{N}$ are sets

(H_1)   value is a function of $(I^* \to \mathbf{N})$

(H_2) $(\text{size}.B \le K)$ is a predicate on I^*

(H_3) $(\mathbf{N}, <)$ is discrete, with minimal element 0

(H_4)   max is the least upper bound function on $(\mathbf{N}, <)$

and

(H_8) $+$ is an associative and commutative operator on $\mathbf{N}$, with unit 0

(H_9)   2 is a function from I to $\mathbf{N}$

with

(P_3) $\text{value}.B = \sum_{i \in B} 2.i$

(P_4) $\forall \{a, b, c\} \in \mathbf{N}^*,\ a < b \Rightarrow a + c < b + c$

We must find a set and a predicate for which holds (H_5), (H_6) and (P_0). Making the obvious remark that a load of size less than K has a size between 0 and K induce us to consider the set $\mathbf{N}_K = \{0, 1, \ldots, K\}$ and the predicate sizeq defined by

$$\text{sizeq}.x.B \equiv \text{size}.B = x$$

Obviously, $\mathbf{N}_K$ and sizeq satisfy the hypotheses

(H₅) $\mathbf{N}_K$ is a set

(H₆) sizeq is a predicate on $\mathbf{N}_K \times I^*$

and the property

(P₀) $\forall B \in I^*$, $\mathrm{size}.B \leq K \iff \exists x \in \mathbf{N}_K$, $\mathrm{sizeq}.x.B$

Now we have to find a predicate enjoying (H₇), (P₁) and (P₂). Focusing on the relations between two loads B and $(B + \{i\})$ let us notice that

$$\mathrm{sizeq}.y.B \Rightarrow \mathrm{sizeq}.(y + 1.i).(B + \{i\})$$

i.e.

$$x = y + 1.i \land \mathrm{sizeq}.y.B \Rightarrow \mathrm{sizeq}.x.(B + \{i\})$$

This strongly suggests to adopt as the neighborhood relation the predicate

$$\mathrm{diff}.x.i.y \equiv (x = y + 1.i)$$

This is a good choice because

(H₇) diff is a predicate on $\mathbf{N}_K \times I \times \mathbf{N}_K$

and

(P₁) $\forall \{x, y\} \subseteq \mathbf{N}_K, \forall i \in I, \forall B \in I^*$, $\mathrm{diff}.x.i.y \land \mathrm{sizeq}.y.B \Rightarrow \mathrm{sizeq}.x.(B + \{i\})$

(P₂) $\forall x \in \mathbf{N}_K, \forall B \in I^*$, $\#.B > 1 \land \mathrm{sizeq}.x.B$
$$\Rightarrow \exists y \in \mathbf{N}_K - \{x\}, \exists i \in B, \ \mathrm{diff}.x.i.y \land \mathrm{sizeq}.y.(B - \{i\})$$

Everything is in place for applying the results of Sect. 3. Because of the equivalences

$$\mathrm{sizeq}.x.\emptyset \iff x = 0$$
$$\mathrm{sizeq}.x.\{i\} \iff x = 1.i$$

we obtain the following program:

```
Nₖ := {0, 1, ..., K};
Ω := ∅;
o := {0};
do
    rp x : Nₖ
    by (x, 0) : Ω

    rp (x, m) : Ω
    if (x = 0) ∧ (m < 0)
    by (x, 0) : Ω

    rp (x, m) : Ω, i : I
    if (x = 1.i) ∧ (m < 2.i)
    by (x, 2.i) : Ω, i : I

    rp (x, m), (y, ℓ) : Ω, i : I
    if (x = y + 1.i) ∧ (m < ℓ + 2.i)
    by (x, ℓ + 2.i), (y, ℓ) : Ω, i : I

    rp ℓ : o, (x, m) : Ω
    if (ℓ < m)
    by m : o, (x, m) : Ω
od;
v := oneof.o
```

4.2 The Shortest Paths

A weighted directed graph is given by a set V of vertices and a set E of edges with associated cost.

Writing as a triple (f, t, c) an edge going from f to t with cost c, a path between two vertices a and b is a bag P on E satisfying the recursive property

$$\text{path}.a.b.P \equiv \quad a = b \wedge P = \emptyset$$
$$\vee \; \exists (f, t, c) \in P, \; b = t \wedge \text{path}.a.f.(P - \{(f, t, c)\})$$

The length of a path is defined as the sum of the costs of its edges, i.e.

$$\text{length}.P = \sum_{e \in P} 3.e$$

Let r be a vertex, called the root; the problem is to give for each vertex x of V the minimum length of the paths between r and x. For such a minimum to exist we assume that there is no cycle with negative length in the graph.

So we have to compute the set

$$\Lambda = \{(x, m) \mid x \in V \wedge m = \min.\{\text{length}.P \mid P \in E^\star \wedge \text{path}.r.x.P\}\}$$

This equation is similar to the definition of Ω in Sect. 3. Here we don't have to compute an ω; so we don't have to fulfill (H_2) and (P_0) which relates ω to Ω.

With the definition

$$\text{rel}.x.e.y \equiv (y = 1.e) \wedge (x = 2.e)$$

the following assumptions holds:

(H_0) E and $\mathbf{Z}$ are sets

(H_1) length is a function of $(E^\star \to \mathbf{Z})$

(H_3) $(\mathbf{Z}, >)$ is discrete, with minimal element ∞

(H_4) min is the least upper bound function on $(\mathbf{Z}, >)$

(H_5) V is a set

(H_6) path.r is a predicate on $V \times E^\star$

(H_7) rel is a predicate on $V \times E \times V$

(H_8) $+$ is an associative and commutative operator on $\mathbf{Z}$, with unit 0

(H_9) 3 is a function from E to $\mathbf{Z}$

as well as the properties:

(P_1) $\forall \{x, y\} \subseteq V, \forall e \in E, \forall P \in E^\star, \; \text{rel}.x.e.y \wedge \text{path}.r.y.P \Rightarrow \text{path}.r.x.(P + \{e\})$

(P_2) $\forall x \in V, \forall P \in E^\star, \; \#.P > 1 \wedge \text{path}.r.x.P$
$$\Rightarrow \exists y \in V - \{x\}, \exists e \in P, \; \text{rel}.x.e.y \wedge \text{path}.r.y.(P - \{e\})$$

(P_3) $\text{length}.P = \sum_{e \in P} 3.e$

(P_4) $\forall \{a, b, c\} \in \mathbf{Z}^\star, \; a < b \Rightarrow a + c < b + c$

So with

$$\text{path}.r.x.\emptyset \iff x = r$$
$$\text{path}.r.x.\{e\} \iff (r = 1.e) \land (x = 2.e)$$

we obtain the following GAMMA program:

$$\tilde{V} := V;$$
$$\Omega := \emptyset;$$
do
    rp $x : \tilde{V}$
    by $(x, \infty) : \Omega$

    rp $(x, m) : \Omega$
    if $(x = r) \land (m > 0)$
    by $(x, 0) : \Omega$

    rp $(x, m) : \Omega,\ e : E$
    if $(r = 1.e) \land (x = 2.e) \land (m > 3.e)$
    by $(x, 3.e) : \Omega,\ e : E$

    rp $(x, m), (y, \ell) : \Omega,\ e : E$
    if $(y = 1.e) \land (x = 2.e) \land (m > \ell + 3.e)$
    by $(x, \ell + 3.e), (y, \ell) : \Omega,\ e : E$
od;
$$\Lambda := \Omega$$

4.3 The Longest Upsequence

We consider a sequence of numbers, coded as a set S of pairs, with (v, i) in S if and only if v occur at position i in the sequence. With this representation, S is a sequence if and only if

$$\text{map}.2.S = \{1, 2, \ldots, \#.S\}$$

A subsequence of S is defined as a subset of S; an upsequence U of S is a subsequence of S with the following property:

$$\text{up}.U \equiv \forall \{x, y\} \subseteq U,\ 1.x < 1.y \Rightarrow 2.x < 2.y$$

The length of a (sub)sequence is the cardinal of its representation.

The problem is to compute the length of the longest upsequence of S. Formally :

$$\lambda = \max.\{\#.U \mid U \subseteq S \land \text{up}.U\}$$

With the following definitions:

$$\text{one}.x = 1$$
$$\text{set}.U \equiv \forall \{x, y\} \subseteq U,\ x \neq y$$
$$\text{begin}.x.U \equiv x \in U \land \forall y \in U,\ 2.x \leq 2.y$$
$$\text{before}.x.y \equiv (1.x \leq 1.y) \land (2.x < 2.y)$$
$$T.U \equiv \text{set}.U \land \text{up}.U$$
$$sT.x.U \equiv T.U \land (U = \emptyset \lor \text{begin}.x.U)$$
$$V.x.s.y \equiv (x = s) \land \text{before}.x.y$$

we see that

(H_0) S and $\mathbf{N}$ are sets
(H_1) $\#$ is a function of $(S^\star \to \mathbf{N})$
(H_2) T is a predicate on $S^\star$
(H_3) $(\mathbf{N}, <)$ is discrete, with minimal element 0
(H_4) max is the least upper bound function on $(\mathbf{N}, <)$
(H_5) S is a set
(H_6) sT is a predicate on $S \times S^\star$
(H_7) V is a predicate on $S \times S \times S$
(H_8) $+$ is an associative and commutative operator on $\mathbf{N}$, with unit 0
(H_9) one is a function from S to $\mathbf{N}$

and

(P_0) $\forall U \in S^\star,\; T.U \iff \exists x \in S,\; sT.x.U$
(P_1) $\forall \{x, y\} \subseteq S, \forall s \in S, \forall U \in S^\star,\; V.x.s.y \wedge sT.y.U \Rightarrow sT.x.(U + \{s\})$
(P_2) $\forall x \in S, \forall U \in S^\star,\; \#.U > 1 \wedge sT.x.U$
$$\Rightarrow \exists y \in S - \{x\}, \exists s \in U,\; V.x.s.y \wedge sT.y.(U - \{s\})$$
(P_3) $\#.U = \displaystyle\sum_{x \in U} \text{one}.x$
(P_4) $\forall \{a, b, c\} \in \mathbf{N}^\star,\; a < b \Rightarrow a + c < b + c$

so because
$$sT.x.\emptyset \iff \text{true}$$
$$sT.x.\{s\} \iff x = s$$

a GAMMA program to compute λ is:

```
S̃ := S;
Ω := ∅;
o := {0};
do
    rp x : S̃
    by (x, 0) : Ω

    rp (x, m) : Ω
    if (m < 0)
    by (x, 0) : Ω

    rp (x, m) : Ω, s : S
    if (x = s) ∧ (m < 1)
    by (x, 1) : Ω, s : S

    rp (x, m), (y, ℓ) : Ω, s : S
    if (x = s) ∧ (1.x ≤ 1.y) ∧ (2.x < 2.y) ∧ (m < ℓ + 1)
    by (x, ℓ + 1), (y, ℓ) : Ω, s : S

    rp ℓ : o, (x, m) : Ω
    if (ℓ < m)
    by m : o, (x, m) : Ω
od;
λ := oneof.o
```

4.4 The Maximal Segment Sum

We consider again a sequence of numbers, that is a set S of (value, index) pairs. A segment of S is a subset G of S with only consecutive elements, i.e. satisfying the predicate

$$\text{seg}.G \equiv (G = \emptyset) \vee (\exists x \in G, \forall y \in G, \, 2.x \leq 2.y < 2.x + \#.G)$$

The sum of a segment is the sum of its values:

$$\text{sum}.G = \sum_{x \in G} 1.x$$

The problem is to compute the maximal sum of the segments of S. Formally:

$$\sigma = \max.\{\text{sum}.G \mid G \subseteq S \wedge \text{seg}.G\}$$

Introducing the following definitions:

$$\text{set}.G \equiv \forall \{x, y\} \subseteq G, \, x \neq y$$
$$\text{begin}.x.G \equiv x \in G \wedge \forall y \in G, \, 2.x \leq 2.y$$
$$\text{left}.x.y \equiv (2.x + 1 = 2.y)$$
$$T.G \equiv \text{set}.G \wedge \text{seg}.G$$
$$sT.x.G \equiv T.G \wedge (G = \emptyset \vee \text{begin}.x.G)$$
$$V.x.s.y \equiv (x = s) \wedge \text{left}.x.y$$

we see that

(H$_0$) S and $\mathbf{N}$ are sets

(H$_1$)   sum is a function of $(S^* \to \mathbf{N})$

(H$_2$) T is a predicate on S^*

(H$_3$) $(\mathbf{N}, <)$ is discrete, with minimal element 0

(H$_4$)   max is the least upper bound function on $(\mathbf{N}, <)$

(H$_5$) S is a set

(H$_6$) sT is a predicate on $S \times S^*$

(H$_7$) V is a predicate on $S \times S \times S$

(H$_8$) $+$ is an associative and commutative operator on $\mathbf{N}$, with unit 0

(H$_9$)   1 is a function from S to $\mathbf{N}$

and

(P$_0$) $\forall G \in S^*, \, T.G \iff \exists x \in S, \, sT.x.G$

(P$_1$) $\forall \{x, y\} \subseteq S, \forall s \in S, \forall G \in S^*, \, V.x.s.y \wedge sT.y.G \Rightarrow sT.x.(G + \{s\})$

(P$_2$) $\forall x \in S, \forall G \in S^*, \, \#.G > 1 \wedge sT.x.G$

$$\Rightarrow \exists y \in S - \{x\}, \exists s \in G, \, V.x.s.y \wedge sT.y.(G - \{s\})$$

(P$_3$) $\text{sum}.G = \sum_{x \in G} 1.x$

(P$_4$) $\forall \{a, b, c\} \in \mathbf{N}^*, \, a < b \Rightarrow a + c < b + c$

so because

$$sT.x.\emptyset \iff \text{true}$$
$$sT.x.\{s\} \iff x = s$$

a GAMMA program to compute σ is:

$$\tilde{S} := S;$$
$$\Omega := \emptyset;$$
$$o := \{0\};$$

do

    rp $x : \tilde{S}$
    by $(x, 0) : \Omega$

    rp $(x, m) : \Omega$
    if $(m < 0)$
    by $(x, 0) : \Omega$

    rp $(x, m) : \Omega, \ s : S$
    if $(x = s) \wedge (m < 1.s)$
    by $(x, 1.s) : \Omega, \ s : S$

    rp $(x, m), (y, \ell) : \Omega, \ s : S$
    if $(x = s) \wedge (2.x + 1 = 2.y) \wedge (m < \ell + 1.s)$
    by $(x, \ell + 1.s), (y, \ell) : \Omega, \ s : S$

    rp $\ell : o, (x, m) : \Omega$
    if $(\ell < m)$
    by $m : o, (x, m) : \Omega$

od;
$$\sigma := \text{oneof}.o$$

Conclusion

The programs we have derived do not exhibit explicit parallelism but they can be executed on parallel architectures in a very natural way. [Creveuil 1990] and [Banâtre et al. 1988] describes parallel implementations of GAMMA on synchronous and asynchronous machines. These implementations rely on the property that each reaction can be carried out independently of the others. We believe that the use of a high-level formalism like GAMMA makes the construction of programs for parallel architectures easier for two reasons:

- Programs do not involve low-level operational details, so their derivation from high-level specifications is less difficult.
- Systematic derivation often yields programs with a high degree of potential parallelism that would not have been discovered using a more constrained language. For example, the longest upsequence problem, which is generally considered as inherently sequential turns out to have a parallel solution in GAMMA (Sect. 4.3).

In this respect our approach resembles the UNITY method. Both advocate the separation of program derivation in two steps: first a correct program is built from a specification, then it is implemented on a particular parallel target architecture.

On the other hand, a major difference between GAMMA and UNITY is that the latter is based on the array data structure. We believe that bags are better suited to the formal development of algorithms for the following reasons:

- There is no notion of location in bags; relationships between elements cannot rely on their respective position. This makes problems such as the shortest paths easier to specify, and easier to solve.
- Bags are dynamic data structures, making natural the treatment of dynamically varying size problems.
- Using bags reveals strong similarities between problems usually presented as different, as shown in this paper. After having solved a particular problem, one can often generalize its solution to a class of problems; then a new problem can be solved by a mere instantiation.

References

[Banâtre et al. 1988] Banâtre, J.-P., Coutant, A., and Le Métayer, D.: A Parallel Machine for Multiset Transformation and its Programming Style. *Future Generation Computer Systems*, 4:133–144, 1988.

[Banâtre and Le Métayer 1990] Banâtre, J.-P. and Le Métayer, D.: The GAMMA Model and its Discipline of Programming. *Science of Computer Programming*, 15(1):55–77, November 1990.

[Bentley 1984] Bentley, J.: Algorithm Design Techniques. *Communications of the ACM*, 27(9):865–871, September 1984.

[Creveuil 1990] Creveuil, C.: Implementation of GAMMA on the Connection Machine. In *proc. of the Workshop on Research Directions in High-level Parallel Programming Languages*, this volume.

[Dershowitz and Manna 1979] Dershowitz, N., Manna, Z.: Proving Termination with Multiset Orderings. *Communications of the ACM*, 22(8):465–476, August 1979.

[Dijkstra and Feijen 1988] Dijkstra, E.W., Feijen, W.H.J.: *A Method of Programming*. Addison-Wesley, 1988.

[Gries 1981] Gries, D.: *The Science of Programming*. Springer-Verlag, 1981.

[Sedgewick 1988] Sedgewick, R.: *Algorithms*. Addison Wesley, second edition, 1988.

This article was processed using the LaTeX macro package with LMAMULT style

Implementation of Gamma on the Connection Machine

Christian Creveuil

IRISA – Campus de Beaulieu, 35042 Rennes Cedex – France

1 Introduction

A large number of application fields such as image processing or artificial intelligence, require more and more computational power. To meet these requirements, new machines featuring a significant number of processors have been designed. A typical example is the Connection Machine [9]. It is a massively parallel computer, with 64K processing elements. Each individual processor is not very powerful, but they can collectively handle many problems efficiently. The philosophy of this machine is to assign one processor to each data element, and to perform all operations on data in a parallel and synchronous way. This kind of parallelism is known as *data parallelism* [10], in opposition to *control parallelism* that is achieved through multiple threads of control, operating independently.

These new architectures raise interesting programming problems. In the case of control parallelism, the main difficulty is to manage and to synchronize the different threads of control; it is far more difficult to design correct concurrent programs, than correct sequential programs. On the other hand, data parallel languages are often classical sequential languages, extended with special parallel instructions to operate on multiple data at once. So, programmers still have to explicitly specify the instructions to execute in parallel.

Our view is that very high level languages, which make parallelism implicit, should be used to specify massively parallel applications. We propose in this paper a model, called GAMMA [1], which is based on the chemical reaction metaphor: the execution of a GAMMA program can be seen as a succession of reactions which consume data elements, according to a specific reaction condition, and produce new ones. The computation ends when no more elements can react. Since all reactions operate on disjoint elements, they can take place simultaneously, and GAMMA programs can be naturally executed in a data parallel way. In the following, we present a synchronous execution model of GAMMA programs, and its implementation on the Connection Machine.

Section 2 provides an introduction to the GAMMA formalism and some examples of GAMMA programs. We describe the execution model in Sect. 3, and Sect. 4 presents briefly the Connection Machine, and experimental results of the implementation.

2 The GAMMA Formalism

The basic data-structure in GAMMA is the multiset, which is the same as a set, except that it may contain multiple occurrences of the same element. Such a data structure is especially interesting in the context of parallel programming, because there is no ordering constraint, or hierarchy, between its components. This is to be contrasted with recursively defined data structures such as lists, which impose an ordering on the examination of the elements. As we shall see on the examples, GAMMA programs can attain a high level of implicit parallelism. A second advantage of the multiset is that it is a dynamic data structure, making the expression of dynamically varying size problems easier.

The control structure associated with multisets reflects the lack of hierarchy in the data structure, and entails some kind of chaotic model of execution. The execution of a GAMMA program may be compared to a succession of chemical reactions: each reaction consumes some elements $\{x_1, \ldots, x_n\}$ satisfying a specific *reaction condition* $R(x_1, \ldots, x_n)$ and produces new elements as a result of an *action* $A(x_1, \ldots, x_n)$. The computation ends when no more elements satisfy the reaction condition. Formally, the execution of a GAMMA program operating on a multiset M can be expressed in the following way, in a guarded command language:

$$\textbf{do } (\exists \{x_1, \ldots, x_n\} \subseteq M \text{ such that } R(x_1, \ldots, x_n)) \rightarrow$$
$$\textbf{let } \{x_1, \ldots, x_n\} \subseteq M \text{ such that } R(x_1, \ldots, x_n) \textbf{ in}$$
$$M := (M - \{x_1, \ldots, x_n\}) + A(x_1, \ldots, x_n)$$
$$\textbf{od}$$

The sum and difference of multisets can be defined in term of the number of occurrences of the elements in the multisets:

- *sum*: the number of occurrences of an element in $M_1 + M_2$ is the sum of its numbers of occurrences in M_1 and M_2;
- *difference*: the number of occurrences of an element in $M_1 - M_2$ is the difference of its numbers of occurrences in M_1 and M_2 if the difference is greater than or equal to zero, otherwise it is zero.

The syntax of a simple GAMMA program is the following:

$$\textbf{do}$$
$$\textbf{rp } x_1, \ldots, x_n : M$$
$$\textbf{if } \textit{"text of the condition"}$$
$$\textbf{by } \textit{"text of the action"} : M$$
$$\textbf{od}$$

where **rp** stands for "replace". The notations "$: M$" in the **rp** and in the **by** statements, mean respectively that elements $\{x_1, \ldots, x_n\}$ are removed from M and the elements of the action are produced in M. This definition can be generalized in a straightforward way to several multisets (as we shall see on the third example below), and to multiple pairs (R, A). Let us point out two important properties of GAMMA:

- non-determinism: if the reaction condition holds for several tuples of elements at the same time, the choice made among them is non-deterministic;

– locality: reaction condition and action can be applied to a tuple of elements independently of the rest of the multiset. It follows that several reactions occurring on disjoint elements can take place simultaneously. This is the reason why GAMMA programs often exhibit a high level of potential parallelism.

Examples of GAMMA Programs

Let us now take some examples illustrating the GAMMA programming style. The interested reader may find more details in [2].

Example 1. The following program computes the sum of the elements of its argument multiset:

$sigma(M) =$
   do
      rp $x, y : M$
      by $x + y : M$
   od

The absence of **if** statement denotes the fact that the reaction condition is always true. It should be noticed that no constraint is imposed on the order in which additions are performed. No other language, to our knowledge, would lead to such a concise and unconstrained solution.

Example 2. Let us take the example of the maximum segment sum problem: the input is a sequence of N real numbers and the output is the maximum sum of any segment of the input (the sum of a segment $(x_i, \ldots, x_{i+k})$ is defined as $\sum_{j=i}^{i+k} x_j$). The sequence is represented by a multiset M of couples (i, v), where i denotes the index and v the value. A first GAMMA program computes the multiset of elements (i, v, s), where s is the maximum sum found in any segment that ends at index i; initially, s is set to v. The program is the following:

$all\_maximum\_sums(M) =$
   do
      rp $(i_1, v_1, s_1), (i_2, v_2, s_2) : M$
      if $(i_2 = i_1 + 1) \wedge (s_2 < s_1 + v_2)$
      by $(i_1, v_1, s_1), (i_2, v_2, s_1 + v_2) : M$
   od

Then a second program selects the maximum over all the s fields:

$maximum\_sum(M) =$
   do
      rp $(i_1, v_1, s_1), (i_2, v_2, s_2) : M$
      if $s_1 \geq s_2$
      by $(i_1, v_1, s_1) : M$
   od

The final program is the following:

$maximum\_segment\_sum(M) = s$ **where**
   $\{(i, v, s)\} = maximum\_sum(all\_maximum\_sums(M))$.

Example 3. Let us now consider the knapsack problem [15]. We are given a knapsack of capacity K, and n types of items characterized by a size s_i and a positive value v_i. The problem is to maximize the sum of the values $(\sum v_i)$ of all the items that can be put into the knapsack, without exceeding its capacity $(\sum s_i \leq K)$. We assume that there is an unbounded number of items of each type.

The idea of our solution relies on the dynamic programming paradigm: the maximal sum for all knapsack capacities from 0 up to K is evaluated. Items types are represented by a multiset I of pairs $(size, value)$. We want to calculate the following multiset:

$$C = \{(i, max_i) \mid 0 \leq i \leq K \wedge max_i \text{ is the maximum sum for a knapsack of capacity } i\}.$$

A possible GAMMA program for computing C is the following:

```
all_capacities (C, I) = C' where (C', I') = P(C, I) where
    P(C, I) =
        do
            rp (i, max_i), (j, max_j) : C, (s, v) : I
            if (i ≥ j + s) ∧ (max_i < max_j + v)
            by (i, max_j + v), (j, max_j) : C, (s, v) : I
        od
```

The execution of $all\_capacities\,(\{(0,0),\ldots,(K,0)\}, I)$ yields the expected result. The max_i values are progressively increased in the following way: considering an item (s, v) and two knapsacks of capacity i and j, if the sum of v and the current maximum sum max_j that is achieved with the knapsack of capacity j, is greater than max_i ($max_i < max_j + v$), then max_i is assigned the value $max_j + v$. Of course, for this transformation to be correct, the capacity of the knapsack of size i must not be exceeded ($i \geq j + s$).

A second program selects in C the sum corresponding to the capacity K:

```
select (K, C) =
    do
        rm (i, max_i) : C
        if i ≠ K
    od
```

The notation **rm** (remove) is used when there is not any element to produce.

The final program is the following:

```
knapsack (K, I) = max where
    {(i, max)} = select (K, all_capacities ({(0, 0), ..., (K, 0)}, I)).
```

3 The GAMMA Machine

We now describe a SIMD implementation of the GAMMA model. For the sake of briefness, we consider only binary reaction conditions, and actions producing exactly two elements. Extensions are discussed at the end of the section.

The evaluation of a GAMMA program involves two kinds of tasks:

1. the search for elements satisfying the reaction condition,
2. the application of the action to these elements.

Action application is clearly a local operation: it can be carried out independently of the rest of the multiset. So the main problem is to design a SIMD algorithm to examine all pairs of elements.

3.1 Sketch of the Method

In the remainder of this section we assume that there are as many processors as elements in the multiset. The algorithm examining all pairs of elements is derived from the odd-even transposition sort [11] [14]. Let $x_1, \cdots, x_n$ be the elements of the multiset, where element x_k is stored in the kth processor. The algorithm can be described as follows:

- at odd-numbered steps, elements x_k and x_{k+1}, where k is odd, are examined; exchange of data is then performed for each pair.
- at even-numbered steps, elements x_k and x_{k+1}, where k is even, are examined and again exchange of data takes place.

An example with n equals to 6 is given below.

$$
\begin{array}{llll}
\text{step 1} & x_1 \leftrightarrow x_2 & x_3 \leftrightarrow x_4 & x_5 \leftrightarrow x_6 \\
\text{step 2} & x_2 \quad x_1 \leftrightarrow x_4 & x_3 \leftrightarrow x_6 & x_5 \\
\text{step 3} & x_2 \leftrightarrow x_4 & x_1 \leftrightarrow x_6 & x_3 \leftrightarrow x_5 \\
\text{step 4} & x_4 \quad x_2 \leftrightarrow x_6 & x_1 \leftrightarrow x_5 & x_3 \\
\text{step 5} & x_4 \leftrightarrow x_6 & x_2 \leftrightarrow x_5 & x_1 \leftrightarrow x_3 \\
\text{step 6} & x_6 \quad x_4 \leftrightarrow x_5 & x_2 \leftrightarrow x_3 & x_1 \\
& x_6 \quad x_5 \quad x_4 & x_3 \quad x_2 & x_1
\end{array}
$$

Thus, it takes n steps to perform all the examinations. When two elements x_k and x_{k+1} are examined, reaction conditions $R(x_k, x_{k+1})$ and $R(x_{k+1}, x_k)$ are applied; if one of the conditions holds, the action is applied and two new elements are created.

The last problem to be solved is termination detection. Since it takes n steps to perform all pairs, termination is effective after n successive steps without reaction.

3.2 The Algorithm

We describe the algorithm using a straightforward sequential description language where parallelism is introduced through the following construct:

for all $k \in \{1, \cdots, n\}$ in parallel do S od

which causes processors $P_k, 1 \leq k \leq n$ to execute S in a parallel and synchronous way. We use the following variables:

- i: step number
- j: number of steps without reaction,
- n: number of elements in the multiset,
- k: processor index, $1 \leq k \leq n$,
- $x[k]$: value of the kth processor,

– *reaction*[*k*]: boolean value denoting that a reaction occurred between $x[k]$ and $x[k+1]$.

The algorithm is given below. Each processor P_k only communicate with processor P_{k+1} to access $x[k+1]$ and to perform exchange of $x[k]$ and $x[k+1]$.

```
i := 1; j := 0;
while (j < n)
do
    for all k ∈ {1, ···, n} in parallel
    do
        reaction[k] := false;
        if (k < n ∧ (k + i) mod 2 = 0) then
            if R(x[k], x[k+1]) then
                {x[k], x[k+1]} := A(x[k], x[k+1]); reaction[k] := true
            else
                if R(x[k+1], x[k]) then
                    {x[k], x[k+1]} := A(x[k+1], x[k]); reaction[k] := true
                fi
            fi
            x[k], x[k+1] := x[k+1], x[k]
        fi
    od
    if (⋁ₖ reaction[k]) then j := 0 else j := j + 1 fi
    i := i + 1
od
```

3.3 Extensions

The first extension concerns the number of elements produced by the action. In the basic scheme, we have assumed that the action produces exactly two elements. When the action produces less than two elements, the total number of values decreases, and the number of processors must decrease as well. In order to preserve the locality and regularity of the algorithm , a possible solution is to apply a parallel data compaction algorithm: at each step, the m remaining values are moved simultaneously to the first m processors, and the total number of values is set to m. Let us assume that:

– when a reaction occurs, a *void* value is assigned to one of the two processors if the action produces only one element, and a *void* value is assigned to each of the two processors if the action does not produce any element;
– two special operations, **count** and **enumerate**, are available; **count** determines the number of selected processors, and **enumerate** assigns a distinct number to each selected processor (from 1 up to **count**).

Thus, data compaction takes place in the following way:

    for all $k \in \{1, ···, n\}$ **in parallel do**
        if $x[k] \neq void$ **then**   (1)

$$dest[k] := \textbf{enumerate}; \qquad (2)$$
$$x[dest[k]] := x[k]; \qquad (3)$$
$$n := \textbf{count} \qquad (4)$$

    fi
od

(1) selects processors P_k whose local value x_k is not *void*.

(2) is a synchronous assignment.

(3) moves in a synchronous way values x_k to processors P_{dest_k}.

(4) assigns the value **count** (number of processors selected by (1)) to n.

If the action produces more than two elements, then the total number of values may increase; we apply a similar strategy to move the m additional values to the processors $P_{n+1}, \ldots, P_{n+m}$.

Finally, a more difficult extension concerns N-ary reaction conditions, since we have to examine all subsets of N elements. A straightforward solution is to examine all pairs of one element and one subset of size $N - 1$; so, assigning a subset of elements to each processor, we can reduce the general case to the binary case, and use the same technique as above.

4 Implementation on the Connection Machine

We first describe the architecture of the Connection Machine; then we present experimental results of our implementation on this machine.

4.1 The Architecture of the Connection Machine

The Connection Machine is a fine grained, highly parallel computer, including a parallel processing unit of one to four modules of 16K processors. Each processor has 32Kbytes of memory and a 1 bit-wide ALU. The programming philosophy of the Connection Machine is to assign one processor to each data element, and to perform all operations on data in parallel. If the number of data elements exceeds the number of available physical processors, the system provides a virtual processor mechanism facility: each physical processor can simulate several virtual processors. This mechanism is fully transparent to the user.

The parallel processing unit is connected to one to four front-end computers. Programs running on the Connection Machine are developed and executed on the front-ends. They perform computation in a usual serial way, but can also issue special parallel instructions to the processors of the parallel processing unit. These processors execute commands in SIMD fashion: there is a single instruction stream coming from the front-end which operates on multiple data item simultaneously. Instructions can be executed conditionally according to a state bit; processors whose state bit is unset must wait, while the others are active.

The processors of the parallel processing unit are interconnected according to a boolean 12-cube topology, in the maximal configuration. Each node of the cube consists of 16 fully connected processors. This interconnection network supports three main interprocessor communication mechanisms:

- the most general mechanism is the *router*, which allows any processor to communicate with any other, using the hypercube topology. Messages have to travel from one node to another, until they reach the node containing the destination processor.
- the second mechanism is a faster, but more structured communication mechanism, called the *NEWS grid*. It is a n-dimensional grid which provides a direct way to perform nearest-neighbours communications. Since all processors communicate in the same direction, no collision can occur.
- the third mechanism, called *scanning*, combines communication and computation, for instance finding all the partial sums of all the elements on a particular dimension of the n-grid.

Finally, let us mention data communication mechanisms between the front-end and the processors:

- *broadcasting*: a single value is sent to all processors at once;
- *global scanning*: an associative operator (logical or, and, sum, product, maximum, ...) is applied to one value over all active processors, and the result is returned to the front-end;
- the *scalar memory bus*: the front-end can read or write a value at once in any processor memory.

4.2 Experimental Results

The basic algorithm (binary reaction conditions), extended to actions producing any number of elements, has been implemented in StarLisp, on a 16K processors Connection Machine (StarLisp is a parallel extension of Common Lisp). Thanks to the regularity and locality of computation, the NEWS grid mechanism has been used to support inter-processor communication: the processors are connected according to a one-dimensional grid, and each processor P_k only communicate with processor P_{k+1}.

Figure 1 shows experimental results on two examples: we obtain a logarithmic time algorithm for *sigma*, and a linear time algorithm in the case of *prime_numbers*. The reaction condition of the *sigma* program is always true, and a single element is produced; therefore, the number of elements is reduced by half at each computation step, and it takes $\mathcal{O}(\log n)$ steps to find the result. The *prime-numbers* program removes one element from the multiset at each reaction, and it takes $\mathcal{O}(n)$ steps to eliminate all the multiples.

5 Conclusion

In this paper we have tried to show the relevance of GAMMA to build programs suitable for execution on highly parallel architectures, like the Connection Machine. Parallelism in GAMMA programs can be exploited in a data parallel way, according to a synchronous execution model that is derived from the odd-even transposition sort. Let us point out, however, that this implementation only applies when multiset elements are atomic (integers, reals, tuples, ...): since the Connection Machine processors can only manage static data structures, multiset elements cannot be multisets. A possible solution would be to assign a set of processors to each multiset.

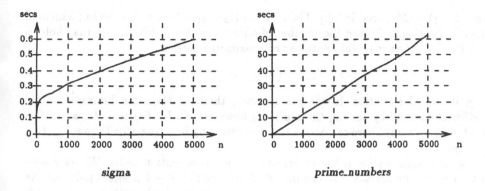

Fig. 1. Results obtained for the *sigma* and *prime_numbers* programs; n represents the number of elements in the multiset.

5.1 Current works

The absolute performances of the parallel implementation described above are not so impressive, because this implementation is based on a rather naïve computation scheme. Optimization methods have been designed for the implementation of GAMMA programs, especially in a sequential context [7]. Let us take the example of the *all_maximum_sums* program. A naïve sequential implementation of this program might lead to an $\mathcal{O}(N^3)$ time complexity algorithm: there are $\mathcal{O}(N^2)$ possible pairs $((i_1, v_1, s_1), (i_2, v_2, s_2))$ and it may be necessary to generate $\mathcal{O}(N)$ times these $\mathcal{O}(N^2)$ pairs to reach the final state. The order in which elements are processed is critical, the worst case occurring when elements are processed in decreasing order of the indexes. This result may be compared to the $\mathcal{O}(N)$ time complexity of a classical sequential algorithm solving the same problem. So an efficient implementation of GAMMA programs requires two types of optimizations:

1. avoiding the systematic examination of all the tuples,
2. finding an efficient execution order.

Let us consider only binary reaction conditions (the results presented below can be generalized to n-ary reaction conditions). To avoid the systematic examination of all the pairs (x, y), the idea is to isolate for each value x a small set $C(x)$ of values y such that $R(x, y)$ may hold. To this end, we try to detect in the reaction condition useful relations between x and y. By useful relations, we mean relations that can be efficiently implemented, ie that allow efficient access to values y from values x. Such relations are for instance *equality* relations

$$C(x) = \{y \mid i.y = f(x)\}$$

where $i.y$ is the projection of y on its ith field. A possible implementation of these relations is hashing: values y can be accessed from x using a hash table. However, there are more efficient implementations; for instance, in the *all_maximum_sums* program, the interesting relation is the *equality* relation ($i_2 = i_1 + 1$). Since field i represents an *index*, and the number of elements in the multiset is static, M can be represented by an array T with element (i, v, s) of M stored in $T[i]$. The relation $(i_2 = i_1 + 1)$ can then be implemented by direct addressing in T, and the number of pairs (x, y) for which $R(x, y)$ may hold is reduced to $N - 1$. Other useful relations are *proximity* relations

$$C(x) = \{y \mid f_1(x) \preceq i.y \preceq f_2(x)\}$$

where $\preceq$ is an order relation. In the general case, these relations can be implemented in an efficient manner by sorting the multiset; however, if i is of type *index* and M is represented by an array T, we can access to the y values by iterating over T from $T[f_1(x)]$ to $T[f_2(x)]$.

The second optimization is the choice of an efficient execution order. We have seen above that it may be necessary to examine $\mathcal{O}(N)$ times the $N - 1$ possible pairs for the *all_maximum_sums* program, depending on the order in which elements are processed. That leads to an $\mathcal{O}(N^2)$ time complexity algorithm, which is still worse than the $\mathcal{O}(N)$ time complexity of the classical algorithm solving this problem. So, the challenge is to define an ordering on the elements, such that termination is reached after only one examination of the possible pairs. The solution on the *all_maximum_sums* program is to process the elements in the increasing order of the indexes. By processing an element x, we mean testing the reaction between x and the elements of $C(x)$. We have formally characterized those orderings with a property involving the reaction condition and the action [7]. Considering a GAMMA program and an ordering, we are able to derive an efficient evaluation order for the program if the property is satisfied. There are simple heuristics for choosing the ordering; one of them is to choose a relation that already appears in the reaction condition, or the reflexive and transitive closure of a relation that appears in the reaction condition. It is the case on the *all_maximum_sums* program, where the execution order is implied by the relation $(i_2 = i_1 + 1)$. Let us also mention that, thanks to its high level nature, GAMMA can be implemented on various architectures; an asynchronous and a shared memory execution models have been defined, and implemented on an Intel iPSC [6] and Encore Multimax [12]. We plan to extend the optimisations to the parallel context in the future.

The GAMMA formalism is also used in the context of program derivation [3] [13]: GAMMA programs can be derived from a specification in first order logic. The derivation is based on the notions of variant and invariant properties. So we can see GAMMA as an intermediate language in a derivation process: the first step is the derivation of a GAMMA program from a specification, and the second step is its translation into an efficient program on a specific architecture.

5.2 Related works

Several formalisms bearing some similarities to GAMMA have been proposed recently. In [5], Chandy and Misra describe a language, called UNITY, and its associated proof system. A UNITY program is essentially a declaration of variables and a set of multiple assignment statements. Program execution consists in selecting non-deterministically some assignment statement, executing it and repeating forever. The main objective of UNITY is the systematic development of programs which can be implemented on different architectures. Program development is carried out in two basics steps: first a correct program is derived from specification, then this program is adapted to the target architecture; this adaptation is achieved by successive transformations of the original program in order to make control explicit. The major differences between GAMMA and UNITY may be summarized as follows:

- UNITY is based on a static data structure, the array, which makes less natural the treatment of dynamically varying size problems.
- the notion of locality is not emphasized as it is in GAMMA. Computations which may be carried out in parallel are determined in a special design phase, which aimed at mapping the UNITY program onto a particular target machine. This phase is carried out as rigorously as possible, but still remains informal.

Let us also mention the Linda approach [4] [8]. Linda contains a few simple commands operating on a tuple space. Adding these tuple space commands to an existing base language produces a parallel programming dialect. Linda's model is based on generative communications. If two processors need to communicate, the producer adds a tuple to a particular domain, and the consumer may read this information from the tuple space. Data and program objects are represented in a uniform way as passive or active tuples. Of course, several processes may be active on the same tuple space, thus allowing parallel tuple processing. Linda is a very simple communication model that can be easily included into existing programming languages. As such, Linda is not a computational model. However, as the same way as the GAMMA model, it shows clearly how advanced data structuring facilities, such as tuple spaces or multisets, may greatly simplify the programming task.

References

[1] Banâtre, J.-P., Le Métayer, D.: A New Computational Model and its Discipline of Programming. INRIA Research Report 566 (1986).
[2] Banâtre, J.-P., Le Métayer, D.: Programming by Multiset Transformation. INRIA Research Report 1205 (1990), to appear in Communications of the ACM.
[3] Banâtre, J.-P., Le Métayer, D.: The GAMMA Model and its Discipline of Programming. Science of Computer Programming 15:1 (1990) 55–79.
[4] Carriero, N., Gelernter, D.: Linda in Context. Communications of the ACM 32:4 (1989) 444–458.
[5] Chandy, K. M., Misra, J.: Parallel Program Design: A Foundation. Addison-Wesley (1988).
[6] Creveuil, C.: Mise en œuvre distribuée de GAMMA sur iPSC. Rapport de DEA, Université de Rennes 1 (1987).
[7] Creveuil, C.: Techniques d'analyses et de mise en œuvre des programmes GAMMA. Thèse de 3ème cycle, Université de Rennes 1 (1991).
[8] Gelernter,D.: Generative Communication in Linda. ACM Transactions on Programming Languages and Systems 7:1 (1985) 80–112.
[9] Hillis, W. D.: The Connection Machine. MIT Press. Cambridge, Mass. (1985).
[10] Hillis, W. D., Steele, G.L.: Data Parallel Algorithms. Communications of the ACM 29:12 (1986) 1170–1183.
[11] Knuth, D.E.: The Art of Computer Programming. Volume 3. Addison Wesley (1972).
[12] Mahéo, Y.: Parallel Implementation of GAMMA on a Shared Memory Architecture. Rapport de DEA, Université de Rennes 1 (1990).

[13] Mussat, L.: Parallel Programming with Bags. Proceedings of the Workshop on Research Directions in High-level Parallel Programming Languages, this volume.

[14] Shih, Z.-C., Chen, G.-H., Lee, R.C.T: Systolic Algorithms to Examine All Pairs of Elements. Communications of the ACM 30:2 (1987) 161–167.

[15] Sedgewick, R.: Algorithms. Addison Wesley (1988) 596–598.

This article was processed using the LaTeX macro package with LMAMULT style

PARALLEL PROGRAMMING WITH PURE FUNCTIONAL LANGUAGES

Rachel Harrison
Department of Electronics and Computer Science
University of Southampton, U.K.

Abstract

The use of pure functional languages is often quoted as facilitating the production of parallel algorithms. In this paper we examine the claim that programs written in pure functional languages can be easily transformed into programs which are suitable for implementation on a parallel machine. In particular, we investigate the transformation of a program to a form which is suitable for implementation on a pipelined process network, and then annotate the resulting network using a declarative language called Caliban.

The case study which is used for this investigation is an abstract programming model which was designed by Banâtre and Le Métayer, chosen as it is a non-trivial application which is not obviously well-suited to implementation in a functional language, and which is itself established as a model for concurrency.

Program transformation is used to improve the efficiency of the implementation of the model for execution on a loosely-coupled multiprocessor. The parallel execution of the resulting algorithm is simulated in order to obtain estimates of performance measurements, and to gauge the effect of changing the granularity of the process network.

Although we find that it is difficult to exploit pipeline parallelism effectively using the transformation techniques investigated here, we see that there is a direct correspondence between programs written in functional languages and distributed process networks, and that this can easily be harnessed by using Caliban. This correspondence, together with the referential transparency of programs written in pure functional languages, indicates that further research into the exploitation of parallelism using these languages is called for.

1. Introduction

In this paper we describe the derivation of a parallel version of an algorithm by transformation from a sequential algorithm written in Miranda[†], a pure functional language with non-strict semantics, and examine the efficiency of the resulting algorithm. This approach gives us the opportunity to test the methodology of Caliban [Kelly 89], a declarative language designed to describe process networks. We intend to use Caliban to annotate the parallel algorithm to indicate which processes need to communicate with each other. We will also be able to investigate the correctness of some of the assumptions behind the design of Caliban.

There are two sorts of parallelism which we could try to harness using the process networks that Caliban was intended for. *Horizontal* parallelism (or *divide and conquer* parallelism) occurs when 2 or more of the arguments of a function are evaluated in parallel. *Vertical* parallelism (or *pipelining*) occurs when a parameter is evaluated in parallel with the function's application to which it is passed. We will attempt to harness pipeline parallelism because the resulting process network will be static, which means that it is easier to analyse and to implement. Also, we desire a general-purpose parallel algorithm: we do not wish to be tied to a particular gamma function or to a particular machine architecture. Finally, we expect static algorithms running on static architectures to be more efficient than dynamic algorithms running on dynamic architectures [Sharp 90]. Caliban's design arose directly from the investigation of the transformation of an algorithm for ray-tracing into an algorithm suitable for implementation on a cyclic, pipelined processor network, and thus we might expect Caliban to be well-suited to this form of transformation.

The methodology of Caliban can be seen as both the transformation of a sequential algorithm into a form suitable for implementation on a parallel architecture and also the subsequent annotation of the parallel algorithm. Thus, for our case study, the Gamma Model [Banâtre 86], we start by transforming the sequential implementation (using the techniques of [Darlington 82] and [Kelly 89]) so that there is only one selection construct, and this is at the top level. We remove the recursive calls by transforming the algorithm to use iteration instead. It is then necessary to transform the resulting iterative algorithm to a cyclic process network. Finally, we separate the operations into processes by distributing the map function throughout the process network. When the annotations are added, the body of the Miranda script remains the same, but a moreover clause is added to indicate which processes are connected by arcs in the process network and so must be placed on processing elements (i.e. processors) which can communicate.

---

† Miranda[TM] is a trademark of Research Software Ltd.

2. The Case Study

The Gamma Model was designed as a multiset transformer: the computation proceeds by the application of a reaction function which tests a number of elements of the multiset for a possible reaction, and an action function which acts on the sets of items which can react to produce new items which are inserted in the multiset. The computation only terminates when no more items can react.

3. Transformation for pipeline parallelism

We now describe how to transform a sequential implementation of the Gamma Model [Harrison 91] into a version which can easily be mapped onto a network of processors. In the algorithm in Figure 1 the parameter n is an integer denoting the arity of the reaction and action functions, which are denoted by r and a respectively. The multiset is represented by the list xs.

```
gamma n r a [] = []                                      || Version 1
gamma n r a xs = xs, ~reacted
             = gamma n r a newset, otherwise
             where
             (newset,reacted) = gamma' (perm n xs)
                             where
                             gamma' [] = (xs,False)
                             gamma' (h:t) = ((a h) ++ (xs--h),True), r h
                                         = gamma' t, otherwise
```

Figure 1

We start by unfolding gamma' by mapping the reaction function over the list of permuted subsets, extracting the first subset to react:

```
gamma n r a [] = []
gamma n r a xs = xs, ~reacted
             = gamma n r a newset, otherwise
             where
             (newset, reacted) = ((a f)++(xs -- f),True),  (foldr (V) False (map r p))
                             = (xs, False), otherwise
                             where
                             p = perm n xs
                             f = select (map r p) p
```

Figure 2

where:

```
select:: [bool] → [*] → *

select [] [] = []
select (False:rest) (y:ys) = select rest ys
select (True:rest) (y:ys) = y
```

The function select takes a list of booleans and a list of items and returns the first item which occurs simultaneously with the value True.

Notice that the expression foldr (V) False does not require its argument to be completely evaluated before a result can be returned.

The variable f represents the data which will flow between a number of processors in the network. We abstract it from the expression (a f) ++(xs -- f) by using two combinators, c1 and c2. We also inline the code for the variable p, giving:

```
gamma n r a [] = []
gamma n r a xs = xs, ~reacted
                    = gamma n r a newset, otherwise
                      where
                      (newset, reacted) =  (c1 (++) (a) ((--) xs)  f,True),
                                                         (foldr (V) False (map r (perm n  xs )))
                            = (xs, False), otherwise
                              where
                              f = c2 select (map r) (perm n  xs)
```

Figure 3

where

```
c1 f g h x = f (g x) (h x)
c2 f g  x = f (g x)  x
```

In the sequential implementation of the algorithm the evaluation of reacted takes place before that of newset. For the parallel version we would like to be able to fire the evaluation of newset and of reacted concurrently, in the hope of joining together the two process networks for reacted and newset. One way that this can be done is by removing the otherwise case from the evaluation of newset and reacted and allowing the computation of newset to take place on every iteration, including the last:

```
gamma n r a [] = []
gamma n r a xs = xs, ~reacted
                    = gamma n r a newset, otherwise
                      where
                      (newset, reacted) =
                              ((c1 (++)(a)((--) xs) )f, (foldr (V) False (map r (perm n  xs ))))
                              where
                              f = c2 select (map r) (perm n  xs)
```

Figure 4

Notice that we now only have one selection process which can change the flow of control, and that this is at the top level. Also, it is only necessary to generate the entire list of permuted subsets on the final iteration.

4. Data driven or demand driven ?

The sequential algorithm relies on the normal order semantics of Miranda to ensure that parameters are only evaluated if and when they are needed. For example, laziness ensures that only the head of (perm n xs) is generated initially, and each successive subset is only generated if the preceding one has been tested and found unable to react.

But if the pipeline is data driven, with subsets being generated as fast as they can be tested for reaction, we may well generate too many permutations. We could try to avoid this by delaying the generation of the second permuted subset until it was known whether or not the first subset could react. This ensures that the process is demand driven but returns us to a sequential implementation: items are generated and tested one at a time.

We conclude that in order to exploit pipeline parallelism we need the process network to be data driven. This means that we will need to be able to buffer the data which arrives at each processor: we assume that this is catered for by the implementation of Caliban.

5. Transformation to cyclic network

The sequential gamma function operates by first testing the permutations of the input set for reaction. If a reaction is possible then a new set is created, and the permutations from this new set are tested, and so on. This technique is inherently sequential, as is the algorithm above which was derived from it: a set is always produced and then tested. This leads to synchronization problems and a loss of potential parallelism. In order to address this problem we now consider the transformation of gamma from a recursive algorithm to a cyclic process network.

Instead of testing on each iteration, we would like to generate a sequence of successive approximations which will iterate towards a steady state. This will remove the dependency between generation and testing, so that a stream of successive values is generated and also tested, hopefully leading to pipeline parallelism. We proceed by transforming the recursive gamma function into an iterative one with two loops, one which generates the sequence of new sets, and the other which tests the sets as they are produced. In doing so we will produce a cyclic process network which will make any potential parallelism more apparent.

To transform gamma from a recursive algorithm to a cyclic process network we follow the transformation methodology developed by Darlington et al. ([Darlington 82], [Kelly 89]). From the algorithm in figure 4, we replace the instances of newset and reacted by their definitions:

```
gamma n r a [] = []
gamma n r a xs = xs, ~ (foldr (V) False (map r (perm n  xs )))
               = gamma n r a ((c1 (++)(a)((--) xs) )f), otherwise
                   where
                     f = c2 (select)(map r)(perm n xs)
```

Figure 5

The function terminates when a multiset is found which satisfies the boolean expression:

~ (foldr (V) False (map r (perm n xs)))

We can transform the termination condition to use the function select to return the first set which satisfies this expression, as we now describe.

Let the list of sets which are produced be denoted by xss. If we define a predicate function done as follows:

```
done 0 = False
done i = ~(foldr (V) False (map r (perm n (xss!i))))
```

then all we need do is to map this function over the infinite list of integers, and use select to find the first set for which done is true:

select (map done ([0..])) xss

If we also define a function till which has two parameters (a predicate function which indexes into a list and the list itself) then we can write the above more succinctly as:

till done xss

where

till pred xss = select (map pred ([0..])) xss

This transforms the predicate part of the gamma function to:

```
till done xss
where
done 0 = False
done i = ~(foldr (V) False (map r (perm n (xss!i))))
```

To generate the list of sets, xss, we apply the same iterative methodology of mapping a function over the infinite list of integers. The first set to be generated will be the original input set. Each successive set is generated from the previous one by removing the reacting subset and adding the result of applying the action function to it. This gives us the generating function, next:

```
next 0 = xs
next i =  (a f)  ++ ((xss!(i-1)) -- f)
```

So we have

```
xss = map next [0..]
```

We encapsulate this by using a function generate:

```
generate f = map f [0..]
```

Putting these two parts together gives us an iterative version of the gamma function:

```
gamma n r a [] = []
gamma n r a xs = till done xss
              where
              done 0 = False
              done i = ~(foldr (V) False (map r (perm n (xss!i))))
              xss = generate next
                  where
                  next i = xs, i = 0
                  next i = (a f) ++ ((xss!(i-1)) -- f), otherwise
                          where
                          f = c2 select (map r)(perm n (xss!(i-1)))
```

We now want to transform the above version into a version which can be represented by a cyclic process network. We start with the definition of xss, unfolding generate:

```
xss = generate next
    = map next [0..]
    = (next 0):(map next [1..])
    = xs:(map next [1..])
```

Now, we must simplify map next [1..]:

```
next 0 = xs
next i =  (a f)++ ((xss!(i-1)) -- f)
         where
         f = c2 select (map r)(perm n (xss!(i-1)))
```

Considering the case for i > 0,

```
next i = trans (xss!(i-1))
         where
         trans p =  (a f)++(p -- f)
```

∴   next i = (trans. (xss!))(i-1)
            where
            trans p = (a f)++(p -- f)

∴   next i = ((trans. (xss!)).(-1)) i
        where
        trans p = (a f)++(p -- f)

which gives:
        xss = xs:(map next [1..])
            = xs:(map ((trans. (xss!)).(-1)) [1..]

Now   map (f.g) = (map f). (map g)

∴ xss = xs:(((map trans). (map (xss!)).(map (-1))) [1..]

Also

(map (-1)) [1..] = [0..]

∴   xss = xs:(map trans). (map (xss!)) [0..]
         = xs:((map trans (map (xss!) [0..])

but (map (xss!) [0..]) = xss

∴   xss = xs:(map trans xss)
            where
            trans p = (p -- f) ++ (a f)

We use the same technique to transform the predicate part of the iterative algorithm, till done xss, which gives:

```
till done xss = select (map test xss) xss
                where
                test x = ~(foldr (V) False (map r (perm n x )))
```

The complete algorithm is given below:

```
gamma n r a [] = []
gamma n r a xs = select (map test xss) xss
                where
                xss = xs:(map trans xss)
                    where
                    trans x = (a f)++(x -- f)
                            where
                            f = c2 select (map r)(perm n x)
                    test x = ~(foldr (V) False (map r (perm n x)))
```

We can transform this algorithm to increase parallelism by distributing the map function throughout :

```
gamma n r a [] = []
gamma n r a xs = select (maptest  xss) xss
                where
                xss = (xs:(maptrans xss))
                     where
                     maptrans xss = map2 (++) (map app xss)(map (sub) xss)
                                     where
                                     sub x= x--(c2 select (map r)(perm n x))
                                     app x = a(c2  select (map r)(perm n x))
                         maptest = ((((map (~)).(map (foldr (V) False))).(map(map r))).(map(perm n)))
```

Figure 6

The function map2 is defined in the standard Miranda environment as follows:

```
map2 :: (*  →  ** →  *** ) → [*] → [**] → [***]
map2 f x y = [ f a b | (a,b) <-  zip2 x  y ]
zip2 :: [*] → [**] → [(*,**)]
zip2 (a:x) (b:y) = (a,b):zip2 x  y
zip2 x  y = []
```

5.1 Annotation using Caliban

We now annotate the above process network, using moreover clauses to indicate which processes are connected by arcs in the process network. A brief introduction to Caliban [Kelly 89] is given below.

The Caliban assertion (arc ds cs) indicates that the expressions named ds and cs are independent processes, and advises that each could be allocated to separate processors. The notation Ôf represents the (unique) name for the expression f e (for some e) which appears once in the body being annotated. The fan operator is used to annotate a process network consisting of a number of processors which are all connected to one particular processor. The compiler must use the simplification rules of Caliban to move all the annotations to the outermost lexical level, and to unfold the expressions involving the network-forming operator fan.

A diagram of the annotated process network corresponding to the algorithm in Figure 6 is given below.

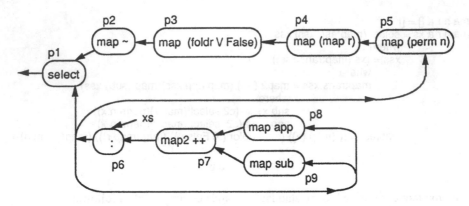

Figure 7

The process network shown above is described by the annotated algorithm in Figure 8.

```
gamma n r a [] =.[]
gamma n r a xs = p1 ((p2.p3.p4.p5) xss) xss
                where
                p1 = select
                p2 = map ~
                p3 = map (foldr V False)
                p4 = map (map r)
                p5 = map (perm n)
                moreover
                (arc ◊p1 ◊p2) ∧ (arc ◊p2 ◊p3) ∧ (arc ◊p3 ◊p4) ∧ (arc ◊p4 ◊p5) ∧
                ∧ (arc ◊p1 interface)
                xss = (p6  xs)(p7 (p8 xss)(p9 xss))
                        where
                        p6 = cons
                        p7 =  map2 (++)
                        p8 = map app
                        p9 = map sub
                            where
                            sub x= x--(c2 select (map r)(perm n x))
                            app x = a(c2  select (map r)(perm n x))
                        moreover
                        (arc ◊p6 ◊p7) ∧ (arc ◊p7 ◊p8) ∧ (fan  ◊◊p7 [◊p8, ◊p9]) ∧
                        (arc ◊p5 ◊p6) ∧ (fan  ◊◊p6 [◊p8, ◊p9])  ∧ (arc ◊p6 ◊p1)
```

Figure 8

6. Further Simplification

The process network clearly shows some potential for horizontal parallelism in the computation of app and sub. (There is also the potential for vertical parallelism if the network is data driven, as we are dealing with an input set of values rather than a single value: this will be discussed later). If we expand the expressions map app (by distributing map throughout and unfolding c2) and map sub then we see that the computations of map (perm n), map (map r) and map2 select are repeated. Whether this is practical or not depends on the number of processors we have available, the communication cost and the number of items in the input set. An alternative process network is shown below:

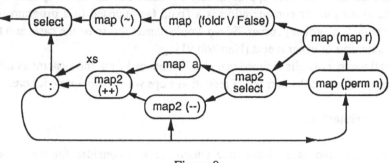

Figure 9

Re-defining maptest and maptrans produces an algorithm which reflects this, as shown in Figure 10:

```
gamma n r a [] = []                                                    || Version 2
gamma n r a xs = select (maptest zs) xss
            where
            zs = (map (map r).(map (perm n))) xss
            xss = xs:(maptrans(map2 select zs(map (perm n) xss)))
                  where
                  maptrans ys = map2 (++) (map2 (--) xss ys)(map a ys)
            maptest = (map (~)).(map (foldr (V) False))
```

Figure 10

We would like to know whether we can guarantee a speed-up on a multiprocessor architecture, when compared to the original sequential Gamma Model executing on a von Neumann architecture. The next section addresses this question.

7. Analysis

We will consider the efficiency of the sequential version of the gamma function which was given in figure 1 (Version 1) and of the algorithm given in figure 10 (Version 2), which simulates a cyclic process network.

7.1 Performance measurements

The total number of reduction steps needed to evaluate an expression can be assumed to be proportional to the total execution time needed to reduce the expression to normal form, if each reduction requires approximately the same amount of computation [Hartel 88]. As the system under consideration is a fixed (as opposed to a program derived) combinator reduction system [Turner 79] we would expect this to be the case, and this was verified by a number of experiments [Harrison 91].

The total number of cells claimed can also be obtained from the system: as this figure is directly proportional to the number of reduction steps we will not quote it here.

7.2 Machine architecture

The architecture of the parallel machine which we will consider for our experiment consists of a network of identical processing elements, each with its own local memory. We assume a static architecture, so that we do not need to be concerned with load balancing. Initially we assume that we have one process per processor. We will also ignore communication costs, allocation costs and transportation costs in our initial estimates.

7.3 Annotation

The annotation of Version 2, using Caliban, is shown below:

```
gamma n r a [] = []
gamma n r a xs = p9 (p8.p7 zs) xss
                where
                p9 = select
                p8 = map ~
                p7 = map (foldr V False)
                zs = (p2.p1) xss
                    where
                    p1 = map (perm n)
                    p2 = map (map r)
                xss = (p10 xs (maptrans (p3 zs(p1 xss))))·
                    where
                    p10 = cons
                    p3 = map2 select
                    maptrans ys = p6 (p5 ys) (p4 xss ys)
                              where
                              p4 = map2 (--)
                              p5 = map a
                              p6 =  map2 (++)
                moreover
                (arc ◊p1 ◊p2) ∧ (arc ◊p2 ◊p3) ∧ (arc ◊p3 ◊p4) ∧ (arc ◊p3 ◊p5) ∧ (arc ◊p5 ◊p6)
                ∧ (arc ◊p4 ◊p6) ∧ (arc ◊p6 ◊p10) ∧ (arc ◊p9 interface) ∧ (arc ◊p2 ◊p7) ∧
                (arc ◊p7 ◊p8) ∧ (arc ◊p8 ◊p9) ∧ (arc ◊p10 ◊p1) ∧ (arc ◊p10 ◊p9) ∧ (arc ◊p1 ◊p3)
```

Figure 11

7.4 Performance analysis

We assume that the network is data driven: as soon as an item is generated, it is transported to the next process or processes which require it. This implies that the communication costs incurred will be larger than those incurred if the whole of the list were transported at once, but such behaviour is necessary in order to achieve pipeline parallelism (as mentioned earlier). This in turn implies that appropriate cons's must be head strict, i.e. when a list is being considered as a stream (a number of cons cells) it is constructed using a version of cons which first evaluates the head. The implementation of this is the responsibility of the Caliban system [Kelly 90].

Consider the following pipeline of communicating processes:

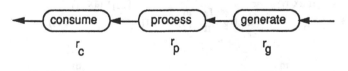

Figure 12

where the names r_g, r_p and r_c denote the total number of reductions that the generate, process and consume processes need (respectively) to reduce their input to normal form.

Assume that the consume process needs to inspect the entire list to produce its output (as is the case for our benchmark). Then, assuming that the cost in time is proportional to the number of reductions, we have:

$$\text{average cost} = \max\left(\frac{r_c}{n} + \frac{r_p}{n} + r_g, \frac{r_c}{n} + r_p + \frac{r_g}{n}, r_c + \frac{r_p}{n} + \frac{r_g}{n}\right)$$

$$= \frac{r_c}{n} + \frac{r_p}{n} + \frac{r_g}{n} + \max\left(r_g - \frac{r_g}{n}, r_p - \frac{r_p}{n}, r_c - \frac{r_c}{n}\right) \tag{1}$$

where n is the number of items in the input list, and max returns the largest of its arguments.

Now consider a network of processes in which horizontal parallelism is possible, for example:

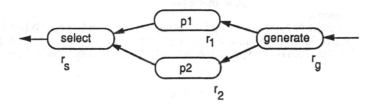

Figure 13

Now, generalising the above network to m processes, p_i, where each process p_i has a reduction cost of r_i:

$$\text{average cost} = \frac{r_g}{n} + \max\left(r_g - \frac{r_g}{n} + \frac{(\overset{m}{_{i=1}}\max r_i)}{n}, \overset{m}{_{i=1}}\max r_i\right) + r_s \tag{2}$$

assuming that $\forall i$, the process p_i must terminate before select can start.

Otherwise, we have:

$$\text{ave. cost} = \frac{r_g}{n} + \frac{(\overset{m}{_{i=1}}\max r_i)}{n} + \max\left(r_g - \frac{r_g}{n}, \overset{m}{_{i=1}}\max r_i - \frac{(\overset{m}{_{i=1}}\max r_i)}{n}, r_s\right) \tag{3}$$

$$= \max\left(r_g + \frac{(\overset{m}{_{i=1}}\max r_i)}{n}, \overset{m}{_{i=1}}\max r_i + \frac{r_g}{n}, r_s + \frac{r_g}{n} + \frac{(\overset{m}{_{i=1}}\max r_i)}{n}\right)$$

Note that this is an approximation: it assumes that the item being chosen by select is not (on average) the last item to be processed, and consequently that select will terminate before the other processes do. If this were not the case, the term $\frac{r_s}{n}$ should be added to the first two terms of the above formula.

7.5 Results

The parallel evaluation of the expression:

gamma 2 divides remove [2,3,4,5,6,7,8,9,10]

where divides [a,b] = b mod a = 0
remove [a,b] = a

was simulated using the distribution of processes described by the Caliban annotation in Figure 11. The expression generates prime numbers. The graph of the reduction numbers for each of the ten processors for the six passes that were needed is given in Figure 14:

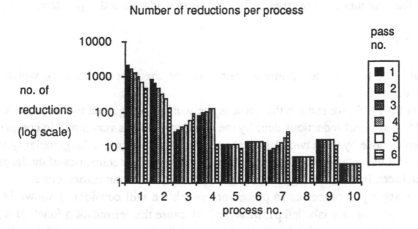

Figure 14

7.6 Cost for a parallel machine

The cost for the simulated parallel machine was calculated using the techniques presented in section 7.4. After some simplification, we have:

$$\text{average cost} = \sum_{i=1}^{5} \left(\frac{r1_i}{n_i} + \frac{r2_i}{n_i}\right) +$$

$$\max\left(\sum_{i=1}^{5} \left(\max\left(r1_i - \frac{r1_i}{n_i}, r2_i - \frac{r2_i}{n_i}, r3_i\right) + \max\left(r4_i, r5_i\right) + \frac{r6_i}{m_i} + \frac{r10_i}{m_i}\right),\right.$$

$$\sum_{i=1}^{5} (\max(r1_i - \frac{r1_i}{n_i} + \frac{r7_i}{n_i}, r2_i - \frac{r2_i}{n_i} + \frac{r7_i}{n_i}, r7_i) + r8_i + r9_i)) +$$

$$\frac{r1_6}{n_6} + \frac{r2_6}{n_6} + (\max(r1_6 - \frac{r1_6}{n_6} + \frac{r7_6}{n_6}, r2_6 - \frac{r2_6}{n_6} + \frac{r7_6}{n_6}, r7_6) + r8_6 + r9_6)$$

where r_{ji} represents the number of reductions needed by process p_j to reduce its expression to normal form on the ith iteration, $n_i = (10-i)P2$ and $m_i = (10-(i+1))$. Substituting in the figures, we find that the average cost is 8476 reductions, which is 187% more reductions than the 2952 reductions needed by the original sequential version.

Comparing the code in Figure 1 with that in Figure 10 gives us the reason for this result. The former utilizes non-strict semantics to ensure that permutations of the multiset are not produced unless they are definitely needed, whereas the latter algorithm generates and tests all possible permutations on each pass, which introduces a considerable and unacceptable computational overhead. The next section addresses this problem.

7.7 Granularity

We would like to find the optimum grain size for the process network which will minimise the speed-down.

From the graph, we can see that most of the work is being done by the processes p1 and p2; the number of reductions done by the other processes is very small in comparison to the number done by these two. A logical step would be to increase the granularity of the program. This has two beneficial effects: we can utilise the lazy semantics of the language to prevent excessive work being done, and we also reduce communication costs.

The mapping of processes to processors which we will consider is shown below, where the processors are labelled p1, p2 and p3. Because the permutation function is now on the same processor as the functions that use it (both in p1 and in p2) it will only generate the number of permuted subsets that are needed, which reduces the amount of work done considerably until the final pass is reached and all the permutations must be produced.

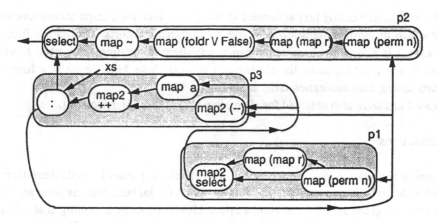

Figure 15

The algorithm which reflects this mapping can be obtained from that given in Figure 13, by changing the definition of maptest and maptrans:

```
gamma n r a [] = []
gamma n r a xs = select (maptest xss) xss
                where
                xss = xs:(maptrans zs)
                     where
                     maptrans ys = map2 (++) (map2 (--) xss ys)(map a ys)
                     zs = c2 (map2 select) (map (map r)) (map (perm n) xss)
                maptest = (map (~)).(map (foldr (V) False)).(map (map r)).(map (perm n))
```

Figure 16

where   c2 f g x = f (g x) x

If we name the processes and incorporate the Caliban annotations, we obtain the algorithm below:

```
gamma n r a [] = []
gamma n r a xs = p2 xss
                where
                p2 = select (maptest xss)
                xss = p3 p1
                     where
                     p1 = c2 (map2 select) (map (map r)) (map (perm n) xss)
                     p3 ys = xs:(map2 (++)(map2 (--) xss ys)(map a ys))
                maptest = (map (~)).(map (foldr (V) False)).(map (map r)).(map (perm n))
                moreover
                (arc ◊p1 ◊p3) ∧ (arc ◊p3 ◊p2) ∧ (arc ◊p2 interface)
```

Figure 17

When the parallel evaluation of this algorithm is simulated we obtain a 29% speed-up over the sequential version.

As well as harnessing lazy semantics in order to reduce the computational overhead, we have also minimized transportation and communication costs. The output from the processor p1 is a single subset which can react; there is no longer the need to either generate or transport the entire list of permuted subsets. Also, because we now have only three processors, communication costs are reduced.

Speed-ups were also obtained for alternative sets of data [Harrison 91].

7.8 Conclusions

The analysis above shows that finding an efficient parallel implementation by transformation of a lazy, sequential algorithm is not a trivial task, and involves searching for an optimal grain size for the computation. However, even assuming that we have achieved an improvement of 29%, this figure was arrived at without taking into account the cost of mapping processes to processors, communication costs, transportation costs and allocation costs.

The above exercise also shows that laziness is inherently sequential: as soon as we attempt to transform a lazy sequential algorithm to an algorithm which can be mapped onto a process network we risk losing the laziness which made the sequential version efficient. Compile time analysis could be used in order to determine those functions which can safely be reduced in parallel.

7.9 Related work

The granularity problem associated with producing parallel programs has been addressed by a number of people ([Hudak 85], [Goldberg 88], [Mohr 90]).

The point that non-strict semantics hinder parallel evaluation has been made by others; for example, in [Burn 90], where the assumption is made that implicit parallelism will be harnessed efficiently by the compiler, it is stated that "lazy evaluation ... is unsuitable for a parallel implementation". The suggested solution is to use evaluation transformers [Burn 87].

8. Alternative approaches

8.1 Alternative methods for parallelism

A naïve analysis of the Gamma Model indicates that the reaction function can be performed on all the subsets concurrently. But in general the action function can only be performed concurrently on those subsets which are disjoint, to prevent undesirable side-effects.

For a multiprocessor architecture we could postulate the following procedure:

Test all subsets concurrently
perform the action on sets which can react and are disjoint
repeat

For dyadic action and reaction functions it would certainly be possible to introduce divide and conquer parallelism by recursively splitting the input list in half. But the question then arises as to how to shuffle the resulting items so as to ensure that all possible subsets have been tried, and how to detect termination. Points such as these led us to conclude that although the tests for reaction can all be done simultaneously it would still be necessary to permute the items, and as there is no simple way to divide the list of permutations into disjoint subgroups the action functions could not be executed concurrently.

It is straightforward to annotate an algorithm using Caliban to indicate that divide-and-conquer parallelism is intended. Consider the general expression of a divide-and-conquer algorithm [Kelly 89]:

```
div_and_conq (simply_sol, combine, decompose, trivial) problem
            = solve problem
        where
        solve problem = simply_sol problem, trivial problem
                      = combine subsols, otherwise
                    where
                    subsols = map solve subprobs
                        where
                        subprobs=decompose problem
                        moreover
                        fan arc interface subsols
```

This annotation indicates that a tree of processes should be spawned, as we would expect. However, the use of moreover in this case is difficult to implement, as it cannot be resolved until run-time (because it is only then that the number of subsolutions is determined and we can unfold the call to decompose).

Notice that specialised gamma functions, such as those which take monadic reaction and action functions, have more potential for parallelism, as there is no longer any need to permute items. Here we could certainly use divide and conquer parallelism, splitting the list until we have singletons.

Similarly, we can use divide and conquer parallelism with specialised gamma functions which take a dyadic action function and a reaction function which allows all items to react, because it is not necessary to produce a list of permuted subsets.

If we do take a more specialised approach, we may find that we could produce very efficient machines for evaluating particular gamma functions by exploiting data parallelism.

8.2 Alternative methods of annotation

Numerous methods of annotation have been suggested in the literature, as have annotational languages. For example, the sandwich function [Hartel 88] the combinators PAR and SYNCH [Hughes 83] and the languages ParAlfl [Hudak 85, Hudak 86], CFP [Eekelen 89], PFL [Holmström 83] and Crystal [Chen 86]. However, Caliban has the advantage of being both declarative and sufficiently abstract for clear and concise annotations.

9. Conclusions

The estimated speed-up of nearly 30%, obtained for the large grain parallel gamma function in section 7.8 with three processors, is disappointing, and we must conclude that we have not managed to harness pipeline parallelism in an efficient manner. The amount of transformation which had to be done in order to obtain the cyclic network was not insignificant. However, this burden could be relieved by automation. Once the cyclic process network had been obtained, it was relatively trivial to use Caliban to annotate the network to show how it could be mapped on to a loosely-coupled multiprocessor. It also proved very simple to change the algorithm to reflect alternative grain sizes, and to provide the corresponding annotations to reflect the changes.

There are three reasons for the failure we experienced:

• the first parallel version required functions to be strict, and this change from non-strict semantics necessitated additional computation.

• in order to exploit pipeline parallelism, it was necessary to considerably increase the amount of computation involved (compare figures 1 and 17).

• each processor is dependent on at least one other for input: this could introduce delays. If we assume that the machine has a very high inter-process communication bandwidth, then neighbouring processors would be able to access each other's memories almost as fast as their own, and this problem may be reduced.

We must ask what conclusions we can draw about Caliban's utility from this investigation. Consider first the following assumption [Kelly 87]: "Good (parallel) programs comprise (of) collections of processes and data structures whose communications interdependencies form a relatively low-connectivity network". As the parallel gamma function cannot be described as a good parallel program, our experimental evidence does not support this claim. Another assumption states that "a (functional) program denotes a distributed network of processes ... this alternative reading of the program text ... does promise much improved performance, whilst keeping pragmatic concerns within the language's expressive grasp, with the attendant benefits of the functional approach". Certainly, we can agree that it is possible to see the correspondence between a functional program and a process network, (also noted by [Henderson 80, Sheeran 84, Patel 85, Schlag 87]) but unfortunately, the hoped-for performance improvement was not in evidence. Nor can we provide any evidence for the statement that "The pipelining transformation is of some independent interest, being applicable to quite a broad class of interesting problems". However, we would agree that Caliban succeeds in one of its objectives, in that it does enable a wide variety of parallel algorithms to be expressed, and also that it does seem well-suited to programming networks of processors, such as transputer networks [INMOS 87], [Pountain 87].

Further investigation into Caliban's applicability will be necessary, and will be much facilitated by a working implementation. Clearly, the Gamma Model was designed to exploit data parallelism, whereas Caliban was designed as a method of annotating process networks: these facts help to explain our inability to effectively harness any potential parallelism in this case.

References

[Banâtre 86] J.-P. Banâtre, D. Le Métayer, A new computational model and its discipline of programming, *INRIA Research Report,* 566, 1986.

[Burn 87] G.L. Burn, Evaluation transformers - A model for the parallel evaluation of functional languages (extended abstract), in G. Kahn, (editor), Proceedings of the Functional Programming Languages and Computer Architecture Conference, Springer-Verlag, pp. 446-470, September 1987.

[Burn 90] G.L. Burn, Implementing Lazy Functional Languages on Parallel Architectures, in P.C. Treleaven, (editor), *Parallel Computers Object-Oriented, Functional, Logic,* John Wiley & Sons Ltd., 1990, pp. 101-134.

[Chen 86] M.C. Chen, A parallel language and its compilation to multiprocessor architectures or VLSI. In *Conference Record of the 13th Annual ACM Symposium on Principles of Programming Languages,* January 1986.

[Darlington 82]
J. Darlington, Program Transformation, in J. Darlington, P. Henderson, D.A. Turner, (editors), *Functional Programming and its Applications: An Advanced Course,* Cambridge University Press, 1982.

[Eekelen 89] M.C.J.D. van Eekelen, M.J. Plasmeijer, J.E.W. Smetsers, Communicating Functional Processes, *Technical Report no. 89-3,* University of Nijmegen, Department of Informatics, March 1989.

[Goldberg 88]
B. Goldberg, Buckwheat: Graph Reduction on a Shared-Memory Multiprocessor, In *ACM Conference on Lisp and Functional Programming,* 1988.

[Harrison 91] R. Harrison, *Pure Functional Languages and Parallelism,* University of Southampton, PhD thesis, 1991.

[Hartel 88]   P. H. Hartel, *Performance Analysis of Storage Management in Combinator Graph Reduction*, Dept. of Comp. Sys, University of Amsterdam, PhD Thesis, 1988.

[Henderson 80]
P. Henderson, *Functional Programming Application and Implementation*, Prentice-Hall International, 1980.

[Holmström 83]
S. Holmström, PFL: A Functional Language for Parallel Programming, and its Implementation, *Report No.7, Programming Methodology Group*, University of Gothenburgh, 1983.

[Hudak 85]   P. Hudak, B. Goldberg, Serial Combinators: 'Optimal' Grains of Parallelism, in *Functional Programming Languages and Computer Architectures*, Springer-Verlag, LNCS 201, pp. 382-388, 1985.

[Hudak 86]   P. Hudak, Para-functional Programming: A Paradigm for Programming Multiprocessor Systems, *Conference Record of the 13th Annual ACM Symposium on Principles of Programming Languages*, pp. 243-254, 1986.

[Hughes 83] R.J.M. Hughes, *The Design and Implementation of Programming Languages*, thesis submitted for the degree of Doctor of Philosophy, University of Oxford, 1983.

[INMOS 87]   INMOS Ltd, *IMS T800 Transputer*, INMOS, Bristol, Feb. 1987.

[Kelly   87] P.H.J. Kelly, *Functional Programming for Loosely-Coupled Multiprocessors*, Westfield College, University of London, PhD Thesis, 1987.

[Kelly   89] P.H.J. Kelly, *Functional Programming for Loosely-Coupled Multiprocessors*, The MIT Press, 1989.

[Kelly 90]   P.H.J. Kelly, *The Implementation of Caliban*, Private communication, 1990.

[Mohr 90]   E. Mohr, D.A. Kranz, R.H. Halstead, Jr., Lazy Task Creation: A Technique for Increasing the Granularity of Parallel Programs, in *ACM Conference on Lisp and Functional Programming*, pp. 185-197, 1990.

[Patel 85]   D. Patel, M. Schlag, M. Ercegovac, vFP: An Environment for the Multi-level Specification, Analysis and Synthesis of Hardware Algorithms, in *Functional Programming Languages and Computer Architectures*, Nancy, France, LNCS 201, pp. 238-255, 1985.

[Pountain 87] D. Pountain, D. May, *A tutorial introduction to OCCAM programming*, INMOS Ltd., Bristol, 72 OCC 046 00, March 1987.

[Schlag 87] M. Schlag, The Planar Topology of Programs, in *Functional Programming Languages and Computer Architectures*, Portland, Oregon, LNCS 274, 1987.

[Sharp 90]   D.W.N. Sharp, *Functional Language Program Transformation for Parallel Computer Architectures*, Department of Computing, Imperial College of Science, Technology and Medicine, University of London, PhD Thesis, 1990.

[Sheeran 84] M. Sheeran, µFP: a language for VLSI design, in *Proceedings ACM Conference on Lisp and Functional Programming*, pp. 104-112, 1984.

[Turner 79] D.A. Turner, A new implementation technique for applicative languages, *Software Practice and Experience*, 9 (1), pp. 31-49, 1979.

Parallel Programming in Maude*

José Meseguer and Timothy Winkler

SRI International, Menlo Park, CA 94025, and
Center for the Study of Language and Information,
Stanford University, Stanford, CA 94305

1 Introduction

Declarative programming greatly facilitates the conceptual aspects of the programming task. In this approach, programming the solution to such a problem becomes a matter of formally axiomatizing the problem in an adequate logic. In this way, the essential aspects of the problem can be captured and expressed in the program, which becomes easier to understand than programs written in conventional languages. This freedom from the idiosyncratic choices of low level representation and control forced upon a programmer by conventional languages brings also with it a freedom from sequentialization and this opens up new possibilities for parallelism. Besides, since rigorous reasoning about concurrent programs can be more difficult than reasoning about sequential ones, the need for approaches amenable to formal methods is even greater than usual in a parallel context, and this makes declarative approaches particularly attractive.

However, in spite of the benefits offered by declarative programming, this approach has so far been confined to functional programming, where the underlying logic is equational logic—in first order or higher order versions depending on the language—or to relational programming based on Horn logic. In both the functional and relational cases the logic describes static, Platonic, structures such as functions and relations on sets. This makes such approaches nice but limited, especially when the problems that have to be resolved have a dynamic character. Applications of this kind include operating systems, simulations, information systems, communications software, and robotics. Certainly, attempts to deal with such issues in a functional or relational context have been made—for example, the functional treatment of input-output issues with streams, or the entire subfield of concurrent logic programming attest to this fact—but it seems fair to say that, up to now, they have for the most part been somewhat inconclusive because they have either involved baroque and complicated solutions, or have compromised the original connections with logic in the search for operational flexibility.

It seems to us that these difficulties are intrinsic not to the *idea* of declarative programming, but to the standard logics on which the functional and relational approaches

* Supported by Office of Naval Research Contracts N00014-90-C-0086 and N00014-88-C-0618, and by the R&D Association for Future Electron Devices as a part of the R&D of Basic Technology for Future Industries sponsored by NEDO (New Energy and Industrial Technology Development Organization).

have been based, because such logics were originally designed as tools in the foundations of mathematics, and do not have adequate conceptual resources to deal with action and change. The long-standing embarrassment of the so-called "frame problem" is a good case in point. This suggests approaching the problem of finding adequate declarative languages for concurrent programming primarily as a problem of *logic design*, i.e., of finding new logics—perhaps quite different from the standard ones—that are a good match for the task. The language design space can in this view be understood as a space of "general logics" in the sense made formally precise in [39].

Maude is based on a simple logic of action called *rewriting logic* in the sense that Maude programs are rewriting logic theories, and concurrent computation in Maude exactly corresponds to deduction in rewriting logic. The main goal of the Maude language is to extend declarative programming beyond its present static realizations to naturally cover many dynamic and concurrent applications that at present are considered beyond the scope of declarative programming. In particular, Maude aims at bringing concurrent programming and object-oriented programming within the fold of declarative programming, and also at unifying those paradigms with the functional programming paradigm.

Deduction in rewriting logic corresponds to concurrent rewriting and provides a very general and flexible model of concurrent computation that contains as special cases many well-known models of parallel computation. We briefly discuss several of these specializations in Section 2.6; a fuller account is given in [43]. In the context of the Mont Saint-Michel workshop, where one of the aims was to better understand the relationships between different parallel programming languages and their corresponding models of computation, this had the conceptually pleasant result of providing a unifying formal framework in which several of the parallel languages that were presented, including Unity [13], Gamma [9], the Chemical Abstract Machine [11], and certain functional programming languages, could be compared and could be placed in context.

Because of the generality, abstractness and simplicity of its concurrent rewriting model, we view Maude as a *machine-independent parallel language*. The requirements that machine-independence makes on a parallel language can be nicely conveyed by means of an illuminating metaphor due to Charles Seitz [48]:

> "You get an essentially correct picture of the relationship between programs and machines if you think of concurrent programs as analogous to granular materials that can be poured into vessels of different shapes and sizes. The large sequential programs we have been writing for years are monolithic and will not pour at all. The moderately partitioned concurrent programs that we write for the medium-grain hypercube multicomputers are like gravel—gravel pours, but with some difficulty. The finest grain size we can achieve today in writing programs resembles a fine sand that pours like a liquid. The point of this analogy is that as a computing problem is expressed in terms of smaller execution units, it becomes feasible to run it on a wider variety of machines."

The declarative nature of Maude is an important advantage in this regard, because a Maude module is an *unordered set* of logical statements called rewrite rules, which constitute the module's basic execution units. Such rules are simple local actions that can be executed in constant time *any time*—with no sequencing requirements—and *anywhere*—perhaps in very many different pieces of the data at once. In fact, parallelism in a Maude program is entirely *implicit* and agrees with J. Misra's dictum[2] that "the best way of doing parallel programming is to forget about parallelism."

Rewriting logic provides a framework not only for programming, but also for specification, and Maude, as well as its functional sublanguage OBJ3 [23, 22], is in this sense a *wide spectrum language* which integrates specifications and program modules within a formal framework. In Maude nonexecutable specifications are called *theories*, and their axioms are used to impose formal requirements on program modules and on the interfaces of parameterized modules. Rewriting logic—in the full generality of its precise definition which allows rewriting modulo an arbitrary set of structural axioms—is quite adequate for specification purposes but is too general for programming purposes. Therefore, program modules should belong to an adequate subset of the logic for which efficient implementations are possible.

In keeping with the wide spectrum nature of the language, this linguistic separation can be attained by distinguishing three levels: a nonexecutable specification level for which no restrictions—except for being somehow expressible in a finite amount of text—are imposed, a more restricted executable specification and rapid prototyping level, called Maude, where a certain degree of inefficiency can be tolerated in exchange for greater expressiveness, and a programming level, called Simple Maude, determined by a smaller subset of rewriting logic for which efficient implementations can be provided. We discuss these levels in Section 3, as well as our ideas for implementing Simple Maude in a very wide variety of parallel architectures. We also discuss the issue of *multilingual extensions*—that would permit reuse and parallelization of code written in conventional languages by integrating it within Maude—and, more generally, the possibility of using Maude to integrate open heterogeneous systems.

Maude's three types of modules—functional, system, and object-oriented—are introduced with examples in Section 2. This section also discusses rewriting logic and the concurrent rewriting model of computation. A communication protocol example illustrating basic features of the language is discussed in Section 4. The model theory of rewriting logic and its use for giving a mathematical, initial model, semantics to Maude's modules is discussed in Section 5. The paper concludes with some remarks about future developments.

Acknowledgements

We express our thanks to Prof. Joseph Goguen for our long term collaboration on the OBJ and FOOPS languages [23, 22, 25], concurrent rewriting [24] and its implementation on the RRM architecture [26, 5], all of which have directly influenced this work. The first author thanks Prof. Ugo Montanari—for joint work on the semantics of Petri nets [44, 45]—and Dr. Narciso Martí-Oliet—for joint work on the semantics of linear logic and its relationship to Petri nets [36, 37]; both collaborations have also been a source of inspiration for the ideas presented here. In addition, Dr. Narciso Martí-Oliet provided many helpful comments and suggestions for improving the exposition. Our joint work with Mr. Patrick Lincoln on program transformations for object-oriented modules and on language implementation techniques for the Rewrite Rule Machine has also influenced several passages in Section 3. Finally, we also thank all our fellow members of the OBJ and

---

[2] As remembered by the authors after a seminar talk at SRI International in 1990, with no attempt to be literally exact.

RRM teams, past and present, and in particular Dr. Hitoshi Aida, Dr. Claude Kirchner and Dr. Sany Leinwand.

2 Maude and Concurrent Rewriting

Concurrent rewriting is motivated with examples of *functional* and *system* modules in Maude. The system module examples show that the traditional interpretation of rewrite rules as equations must be abandoned and that a new logic and model theory are needed. Rewriting logic provides the answer; in it, concurrent computation by rewriting coincides with logical deduction. Maude's *object-oriented* modules are also introduced. Although they are entirely reducible to system modules, they are very well suited for a wide variety of applications, deserve a syntax of their own, and are based on a logical theory of concurrent objects that has a nice expression in terms of rewriting logic.

2.1 Functional Modules

The idea of concurrent rewriting is very simple. It is the idea of *equational simplification* that we are all familiar with from our secondary school days, *plus* the obvious remark that we can do many of those simplifications independently, i.e., in *parallel*. Consider for example the following Maude functional modules written in a notation entirely similar to that of OBJ3 [23, 22]:

```
fmod NAT is                          fmod NAT-REVERSE is
  sort Nat .                           protecting NAT .
  op 0 : -> Nat .                      sort Tree .
  op s_ : Nat -> Nat .                 subsorts Nat < Tree .
  op _+_ : Nat Nat -> Nat [comm] .     op _^_ : Tree Tree -> Tree .
  vars N M : Nat .                     op rev : Tree -> Tree .
  eq N + 0 = N .                       var N : Nat .
  eq (s N) + (s M) = s s (N + M) .     vars T T' : Tree .
endfm                                  eq rev(N) = N .
                                       eq rev(T ^ T') =
                                             rev(T') ^ rev(T) .
                                     endfm
```

The first module defines the natural numbers in Peano notation, and the second defines a function to reverse a binary tree whose leaves are natural numbers. Each module begins with the keyword fmod followed by the module's name, and ends with the keyword endfm. A module contains sort and subsort declarations introduced by the keywords sort and subsorts stating the different sorts of data manipulated by the module and how those sorts are related. As in OBJ3, Maude's type structure is *order-sorted* [27]; therefore, it is possible to declare one sort as a *subsort* of another; for example, the declaration Nat < Tree states that every natural number is a tree consisting of a single node. It is also possible to *overload* function symbols for operations that are defined at several levels of a sort hierarchy and agree on their results when restricted to common subsorts; for example, an addition operation _+_ may be defined for sorts Nat, Int, and Rat of natural, integer, and rational numbers with

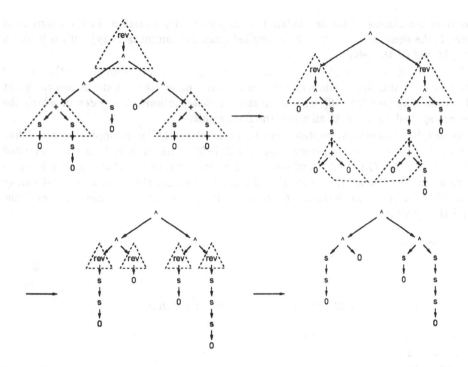

Fig. 1. Concurrent rewriting of a tree of numbers.

Nat < Int < Rat .

Each of the functions provided by the module, as well as the sorts of their arguments and the sort of their result, is introduced using the keyword op. The syntax is user-definable, and permits specifying function symbols in "prefix," (in the NAT example the function s_), "infix" (_+_) or any "mixfix" combination as well as standard parenthesized notation (rev). Variables to be used for defining equations are declared with their corresponding sorts, and then equations are given; such equations provide the actual "code" of the module. The statement **protecting NAT** imports NAT as a *submodule* of NAT-REVERSE and asserts that the natural numbers are not modified in the sense that no new data of sort Nat is added, and different numbers are not identified by the new equations declared in NAT-REVERSE.

To compute with such modules, one performs equational simplification by using the equations from left to right until no more simplifications are possible. Note that this can be done *concurrently*, i.e., applying several equations at once, as in the example of Figure 1, in which the places where the equations have been matched at each step are marked. Notice that the function symbol _+_ was declared to be commutative by the attribute[3] [comm]. This not only asserts that the equation N + M = M + N is satisfied in the intended semantics, but it also means that when doing simplification we are allowed to apply the rules for addition not just to *terms*—in a purely syntactic way—but

---

[3] In Maude, as in OBJ3, it is possible to declare several attributes of this kind for an operator, including also associativity and identity, and then do rewriting modulo such properties.

to *equivalence classes* of terms *modulo* the commutativity equation. In the example of Figure 1, the equation `N + 0 = N` is applied (modulo commutativity) with `0` both on the right *and* on the left.

A particularly appealing feature of this style of concurrent programming is the *implicit* nature of the parallelism. Since in the two modules above the equations are confluent and terminating (see [32, 18] for a definition of these notions) the *order* in which the rules are applied does not at all affect the final result.

As in OBJ3, functional modules can be *parameterized*. For example, we can define a parameterized module by generalizing the `NAT-REVERSE` module to a parameterized `REVERSE[X :: TRIV]` module in which the set of data that can be stored in tree leaves is a parameter. In parameterized modules, the properties that the parameter must satisfy are specified by one or more *parameter theories*. In this case, the parameter theory is the trivial theory `TRIV`

```
fth TRIV is
  sort Elt .
endft
```

which only requires a set `Elt` of elements. We can then define

```
fmod REVERSE[X :: TRIV] is
  sort Tree .
  subsorts Elt < Tree .
  op _^_ : Tree Tree -> Tree .
  op rev : Tree -> Tree .
  var E : Elt .
  vars T T' : Tree .
  eq rev(E) = E .
  eq rev(T ^ T') = rev(T') ^ rev(T) .
endfm
```

Such a parameterized module can then be instantiated by providing an interpretation—called a *view*—for the parameter sort `Elt` in a given module. For example, if we interpret `Elt` as the sort `Nat` in the `NAT` module, then we obtain an instantiation equivalent to the module `NAT-REVERSE` in our first example. The syntax for this instantiation is

```
make NAT-REVERSE is REVERSE[NAT] endmk .
```

As in OBJ3, the denotational semantics of functional modules is given by the *initial algebra*[4] associated to the syntax and equations in the module [29, 27], i.e., associated to the *equational theory* that the module represents. Up to now, most work on term rewriting has dealt with that case. However, the true possibilities of the concurrent rewriting model are by no means·restricted to this case; we consider below a very important class of Maude modules, called *system modules*, that cannot be dealt with within the initial algebra framework.

---

[4] For example, the initial algebra of the `NAT` module is of course the natural numbers with successor and addition.

2.2 System Modules

Maude system modules perform concurrent rewriting computations in exactly the same way as functional modules; however, their behavior is not functional. Consider the module show below, **NAT-CHOICE**, which adds a nondeterministic choice operator to the natural numbers.

```
mod NAT-CHOICE is
   extending NAT .
   op _?_ : Nat Nat -> Nat .
   vars N M : Nat .
   rl N ? M => N .
   rl N ? M => M .
endm
```

The intuitive *operational behavior* of this module is quite clear. Natural number addition remains unchanged and is computed using the two rules in the **NAT** module. Notice that any occurrence of the choice operator in an expression can be eliminated by choosing either of the arguments. In the end, we can reduce any ground expression to a natural number in Peano notation. The *mathematical semantics* of the module is much less clear. If we adopt any semantics in which the models are algebras satisfying the rules as equations—in particular an initial algebra semantics—it follows by the rules of equational deduction with the two equations in **NAT-CHOICE** that

$$N = M$$

i.e., everything collapses to one point. Therefore, the declaration **extending NAT**, whose meaning is that two distinct natural numbers in the submodule **NAT** are not identified by the new equations introduced in the supermodule **NAT-CHOICE**, is violated in the worse possible way by this semantics; yet, the operational behavior in fact respects such a declaration. To indicate that this is not the semantics intended, system modules are distinguished from functional modules by means of the keyword **mod** (instead of the previous **fmod**). Similarly, a new keyword **rl** is used for rewrite rules—instead of the usual **eq** before each equation—and the equal sign is replaced by the new sign "**=>**" to suggest that **rl** declarations must be understood as "rules" and not as equations in the usual sense. At the operational level the equations introduced by the keyword **eq** in a functional module are also implemented as rewrite rules; the difference however lies in the *mathematical semantics* given to the module, which for modules like the one above should *not* be the initial algebra semantics. We need a logic and a model theory that are the perfect match for this problem. For this solution to be in harmony with the old one, the new logic and the new model theory should *generalize* the old ones.

System modules can also be parameterized. For example, we could have defined a parameterized module with a nondeterministic choice operator

```
mod CHOICE[X :: TRIV] is
   op _?_ : Elt Elt -> Elt .
   vars A B : Elt .
   rl A ? B => A .
   rl A ? B => B .
endm
```

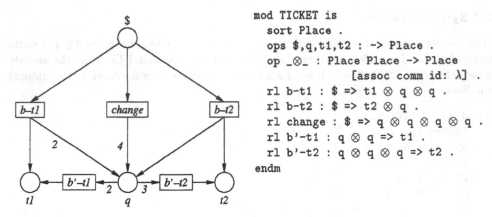

```
mod TICKET is
   sort Place .
   ops $,q,t1,t2 : -> Place .
   op _⊗_ : Place Place -> Place
                      [assoc comm id: λ] .
   rl b-t1 : $ => t1 ⊗ q ⊗ q .
   rl b-t2 : $ => t2 ⊗ q .
   rl change : $ => q ⊗ q ⊗ q ⊗ q .
   rl b'-t1 : q ⊗ q => t1 .
   rl b'-t2 : q ⊗ q ⊗ q => t2 .
endm
```

Fig. 2. A Petri net and its code in Maude.

and could have obtained a module equivalent to NAT-CHOICE by means of the module expression

make NAT-CHOICE is CHOICE[NAT] endmk .

Another interesting example of a system module that illustrates both Maude's expressiveness and the generality of the concurrent rewriting model is the Petri net in Figure 2, which represents a machine to buy subway tickets. With a dollar we can buy a ticket $t1$ by pushing the button $b-t1$ and get two quarters back; if we push $b-t2$ instead, we get a longer distance ticket $t2$ and one quarter back. Similar buttons allow purchasing the tickets with quarters. Finally, with one dollar we can get four quarters by pushing *change*. The corresponding system module, TICKET, is given in the same figure. Note that the rules in this module are *labelled* by the name of the transition which they represent. A key point about this module is that the operator ⊗—corresponding to *multiset union*—has been declared *associative*, *commutative*, and having an *identity* element λ. Therefore, concurrent rewriting in this module is performed *modulo* the associativity, commutativity and identity axioms for ⊗. Therefore, we can disregard parentheses and the order of the arguments. We call such a rewriting *ACI-rewriting*. In this example, *ACI*-rewriting captures exactly the concurrent computations of the Petri net. Suppose, for example, that we begin in a state with four quarters and two dollars. Then, by first concurrently pushing the buttons $b'-t1$ and $b-t2$, and then concurrently pushing the buttons $b'-t2$ and $b-t2$ we end up with a ticket for the shorter distance, three tickets for the longer distance and a quarter, as shown in the two steps of concurrent *ACI*-rewriting below:

$$q⊗q⊗q⊗q⊗\$⊗\$ \longrightarrow q⊗q⊗t1⊗t2⊗q⊗\$ \longrightarrow t2⊗t1⊗t2⊗t2⊗q.$$

As in the NAT-CHOICE example, this example also shows that initial algebra semantics is entirely inadequate to handle system modules with a nonfunctional behavior. In this case, interpreting the rules as equations would force the nonsensical identification of the three states above. System modules denote *concurrent systems*, not algebras, and rewriting logic is a logic that expresses directly the concurrent computations of such systems.

2.3 Rewriting Logic

Rewriting logic is defined, and concurrent rewriting is formalized as deduction in such a logic.

Basic Universal Algebra. For the sake of simplifying the exposition, we treat the *unsorted* case; the many-sorted and order-sorted cases can be given a similar treatment. Therefore, a set Σ of function symbols is a ranked alphabet $\Sigma = \{\Sigma_n \mid n \in \mathbb{N}\}$. A Σ-algebra is then a set A together with an assignment of a function $f_A : A^n \longrightarrow A$ for each $f \in \Sigma_n$ with $n \in \mathbb{N}$. We denote by T_Σ the Σ-algebra of ground Σ-terms, and by $T_\Sigma(X)$ the Σ-algebra of Σ-terms with variables in a set X. Similarly, given a set E of Σ-equations, $T_{\Sigma,E}$ denotes the Σ-algebra of equivalence classes of ground Σ-terms modulo the equations E (i.e., modulo provable equality using the equations E); in the same way, $T_{\Sigma,E}(X)$ denotes the Σ-algebra of equivalence classes of Σ-terms with variables in X modulo the equations E. Let $t =_E t'$ denote the congruence modulo E of two terms t, t', and let $[t]_E$ or just $[t]$ denote the E-equivalence class of t.

Given a term $t \in T_\Sigma(\{x_1, \ldots, x_n\})$, and terms $u_1, \ldots, u_n$, $t(u_1/x_1, \ldots, u_n/x_n)$ denotes the term obtained from t by *simultaneously substituting* u_i for x_i, $i = 1, \ldots, n$. To simplify notation, we denote a sequence of objects $a_1, \ldots, a_n$ by $\bar{a}$, or, to emphasize the length of the sequence, by $\bar{a}^n$. With this notation, $t(u_1/x_1, \ldots, u_n/x_n)$ is abbreviated to $t(\bar{u}/\bar{x})$.

The Rules of Rewriting Logic. We are now ready to introduce the new logic that we are seeking, which we call *rewriting logic*. A *signature* in this logic is a pair (Σ, E) with Σ a ranked alphabet of function symbols and E a set of Σ-equations. Rewriting will operate on equivalence classes of terms modulo a given set of equations E. In this way, we free rewriting from the syntactic constraints of a term representation and gain a much greater flexibility in deciding what counts as a *data structure*; for example, string rewriting is obtained by imposing an associativity axiom, and multiset rewriting by imposing associativity and commutativity. Of course, standard term rewriting is obtained as the particular case in which the set E of equations is empty. The idea of rewriting in equivalence classes is well known (see, e.g., [32, 18]).

Given a signature (Σ, E), *sentences* of the logic are sequents of the form $[t]_E \longrightarrow [t']_E$ with t, t' Σ-terms, where t and t' may possibly involve some variables from the countably infinite set $X = \{x_1, \ldots, x_n, \ldots\}$. A *theory* in this logic, called a rewrite theory, is a slight generalization of the usual notion of theory—which is typically defined as a pair consisting of a signature and a set of sentences for it—in that, in addition, we allow rules to be labelled. This is very natural for many applications, and customary for automata—viewed as labelled transition systems—and for Petri nets, which are both particular instances of our definition.

Definition 1. A *(labelled)* rewrite theory[5] $\mathcal{R}$ is a 4-tuple $\mathcal{R} = (\Sigma, E, L, R)$ where Σ is a ranked alphabet of function symbols, E is a set of Σ-equations, L is a set called the

---

[5] We consciously depart from the standard terminology, that would call $\mathcal{R}$ a *rewrite system*. The reason for this departure is very specific. We want to keep the term "rewrite system" for the *models* of such a theory, which will be defined in Section 5 and which really are systems with a dynamic behavior. Strictly speaking, $\mathcal{R}$ is not a system; it is only a static, linguistic, *presentation* of a class of systems—including the initial and free systems that most directly embody our dynamic intuitions about rewriting.

set of *labels*, and R is a set of pairs $R \subseteq L \times (T_{\Sigma,E}(X)^2)$ whose first component is a label and whose second component is a pair of E-equivalence classes of terms, with $X = \{x_1, \ldots, x_n, \ldots\}$ a countably infinite set of variables. Elements of R are called *rewrite rules*[6]. We understand a rule $(r, ([t], [t']))$ as a labelled sequent and use for it the notation $r : [t] \longrightarrow [t']$. To indicate that $\{x_1, \ldots, x_n\}$ is the set of variables occurring in either t or t', we write[7] $r : [t(x_1, \ldots, x_n)] \longrightarrow [t'(x_1, \ldots, x_n)]$, or in abbreviated notation $r : [t(\overline{x}^n)] \longrightarrow [t'(\overline{x}^n)]$. $\square$

Given a rewrite theory $\mathcal{R}$, we say that $\mathcal{R}$ *entails* a sequent $[t] \longrightarrow [t']$ and write $\mathcal{R} \vdash [t] \longrightarrow [t']$ if and only if $[t] \longrightarrow [t']$ can be obtained by finite application of the following *rules of deduction*:

1. **Reflexivity.** For each $[t] \in T_{\Sigma,E}(X)$,

$$\overline{[t] \longrightarrow [t]}$$

2. **Congruence.** For each $f \in \Sigma_n$, $n \in \mathbb{N}$,

$$\frac{[t_1] \longrightarrow [t_1'] \quad \ldots \quad [t_n] \longrightarrow [t_n']}{[f(t_1, \ldots, t_n)] \longrightarrow [f(t_1', \ldots, t_n')]}$$

3. **Replacement.** For each rewrite rule $r : [t(x_1, \ldots, x_n)] \longrightarrow [t'(x_1, \ldots, x_n)]$ in R,

$$\frac{[w_1] \longrightarrow [w_1'] \quad \ldots \quad [w_n] \longrightarrow [w_n']}{[t(\overline{w}/\overline{x})] \longrightarrow [t'(\overline{w'}/\overline{x})]}$$

4. **Transitivity.**

$$\frac{[t_1] \longrightarrow [t_2] \quad [t_2] \longrightarrow [t_3]}{[t_1] \longrightarrow [t_3]}$$

Equational logic (modulo a set of axioms E) is obtained from rewriting logic by adding the following rule:

5. **Symmetry.**

$$\frac{[t_1] \longrightarrow [t_2]}{[t_2] \longrightarrow [t_1]} \quad .$$

With this new rule, sequents derivable in equational logic are *bidirectional*; therefore, in this case we can adopt the notation $[t] \leftrightarrow [t']$ throughout and call such bidirectional sequents *equations*.

In rewriting logic a sequent $[t] \longrightarrow [t']$ should not be read as "$[t]$ *equals* $[t']$," but as "$[t]$ *becomes* $[t']$." Therefore, rewriting logic is a logic of *becoming* or *change*, not a logic of

---

[6] To simplify the exposition the rules of the logic are given for the case of *unconditional* rewrite rules. However, all the ideas and results presented here have been extended to conditional rules in [43] with very general rules of the form

$$r : [t] \longrightarrow [t'] \ \textit{if} \ [u_1] \longrightarrow [v_1] \wedge \ldots \wedge [u_k] \longrightarrow [v_k].$$

This of course increases considerably the expressive power of rewrite theories, as illustrated by several of the examples of Maude modules presented in this paper.

[7] Note that, in general, the set $\{x_1, \ldots, x_n\}$ will depend on the representatives t and t' chosen; therefore, we allow any possible such qualification with explicit variables.

equality in a static Platonic sense. Adding the symmetry rule is a *very strong* restriction, namely assuming that *all change is reversible*, thus bringing us into a timeless Platonic realm in which "before" and "after" have been identified. A related observation is that [t] should not be understood as a *term* in the usual first-order logic sense, but as a *proposition*—built up using the *logical connectives* in Σ—that asserts being in a certain *state* having a certain *structure*. The rules of rewriting logic are therefore rules to reason about *change in a concurrent system*. They allow us to draw valid conclusions about the evolution of the system from certain basic types of change known to be possible thanks to the rules R.

Concurrent Rewriting as Deduction. A nice consequence of having defined rewriting logic is that concurrent rewriting, rather than emerging as an operational notion, actually *coincides* with deduction in such a logic.

Definition 2. Given a rewrite theory $\mathcal{R} = (\Sigma, E, L, R)$, a (Σ, E)-sequent $[t] \longrightarrow [t']$ is called:

– a 0-*step concurrent $\mathcal{R}$-rewrite* iff it can be derived from $\mathcal{R}$ by finite application of the rules 1 and 2 of rewriting deduction (in which case $[t]$ and $[t]'$ necessarily coincide);
– a *one-step concurrent $\mathcal{R}$-rewrite* iff it can be derived from $\mathcal{R}$ by finite application of the rules 1-3, with at least one application of rule 3; if rule 3 is applied exactly once, we then say that the sequent is a one-step *sequential $\mathcal{R}$-rewrite*;
– a *concurrent $\mathcal{R}$-rewrite* (or just a *rewrite*) iff it can be derived from $\mathcal{R}$ by finite application of the rules 1-4.

We call the rewrite theory $\mathcal{R}$ *sequential* if all one-step $\mathcal{R}$-rewrites are necessarily sequential. A sequential rewrite theory $\mathcal{R}$ is in addition called *deterministic* if for each $[t]$ there is at most one one-step (necessarily sequential) rewrite $[t] \longrightarrow [t']$. □

The usual notions of confluence, termination, normal form, etc., as well as the well known Church-Rosser property of confluent rules remain unchanged when considered from the perspective of concurrent rewriting [43]. Indeed, concurrent rewriting is a more convenient way of considering such notions than the traditional way using sequential rewriting.

2.4 Object-Oriented Modules

This section introduces Maude's object-oriented modules and presents the logical theory of concurrent objects on which they are based. This theory expresses concurrent object-oriented computation in terms of concurrent *ACI*-rewriting. We discuss the most basic ideas about objects and the evolution of an object-oriented system by concurrent rewriting of its configuration, which is made up of a collection of objects and messages; the reader is referred to [40] for a more detailed account. In addition, we also discuss how this theory provides an abstract semantics for Actors [3] which appear as a special case. In spite of previous formalization efforts [2, 15], actors have not, in our opinion, received a treatment at an abstract enough level. The many details involved in the usual descriptions can become a real obstacle for gaining a clear mathematical understanding of actors.

An *object* can be represented as a term

$$\langle O : C \mid a_1 : v_1, \ldots, a_n : v_n \rangle$$

where O is the object's name, belonging to a set OId of *object identifiers*, C is its class, the a_i's are the names of the object's *attributes*, and the v_i's are their corresponding *values*, which typically are required to be in a sort appropriate for their corresponding attribute. The *configuration* is the distributed state of the concurrent object-oriented system and is represented as a multiset of objects and messages according to the following syntax:

```
subsorts Object Msg < Configuration .
op __ : Configuration Configuration -> Configuration
                              [assoc comm id: ∅] .
```

where the operator __ is associative and commutative with identity $\emptyset$ and plays a role entirely similar to that played by the operator $\otimes$ for Petri nets. The system evolves by concurrent rewriting (modulo *ACI*) of the configuration by means of rewrite rules specific to each particular system, whose lefthand and righthand sides may in general involve patterns for several objects and messages.

Intuitively, we can think of messages as "travelling" to come into contact with the objects to which they are sent and then causing "communication events" by application of rewrite rules. In the model, this travelling is accounted for in a very abstract way by the *ACI* axioms. This abstract level supports both synchronous and asynchronous communication and provides great freedom and flexibility to consider a variety of alternative implementations at lower levels. Such abstraction from implementation details makes possible high level reasoning about concurrent object-oriented programs and their semantics without having to go down into the specific details of how communication is actually implemented.

In Maude, concurrent object-oriented systems can be defined by means of *object-oriented modules*—introduced by the keyword omod—using a syntax more convenient than that of system modules because it assumes acquaintance with basic entities such as objects, messages and configurations, and supports linguistic distinctions appropriate for the object-oriented case. For example, the ACCOUNT object-oriented module below specifies the concurrent behavior of objects in a very simple class Accnt of bank accounts, each having a bal(ance) attribute, which may receive messages for crediting or debiting the account, or for transferring funds between two accounts. We assume that a functional module INT for integers with a subsort relation Nat < Int and an ordering predicate _>=_ is available.

```
omod ACCOUNT is
  protecting INT .
  class Accnt .
  att bal : Accnt -> Nat .
  msgs credit,debit : OId Nat -> Msg .
  msg transfer_from_to_ : Nat OId OId -> Msg .
  vars A B : OId .
  vars M N N' : Nat .
  rl credit(A,M) < A : Accnt | bal: N > => < A : Accnt | bal: N + M > .
```

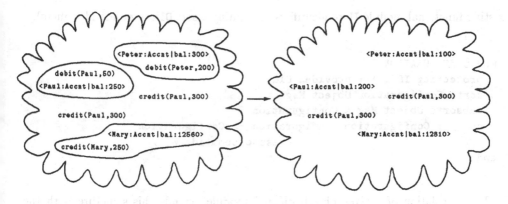

Fig. 3. Concurrent rewriting of bank accounts.

```
rl debit(A,M) < A : Accnt | bal: N > => < A : Accnt | bal: N - M >
   if N >= M .
rl transfer M from A to B
     < A : Accnt | bal: N > < B : Accnt | bal: N' > =>
     < A : Accnt | bal: N - M > < B : Accnt | bal: N' + M >
     if N >= M .
endom
```

In this example, the only attribute of an account—introduced by the keyword att— is its **bal**(ance), which is declared to be a value in **Nat**. The three kinds of messages involving accounts are **credit**, **debit**, and **transfer** messages, whose user definable syntax is introduced by the keyword **msg**. The rewrite rules specify in a declarative way the behavior associated to the credit, debit, and transfer messages. The commutative monoid structure of the configuration provides the top level distributed structure of the system and allows concurrent application of the rules. For example, Figure 3 provides a snapshot in the evolution by concurrent rewriting of a simple configuration of bank accounts. To simplify the picture, the arithmetic operations required to update balances have already been performed. However, the reader should bear in mind that the values in the attributes of an object can also be computed by means of rewrite rules, and this adds yet another important level of concurrency to a concurrent object-oriented system—which might be called *intra-object concurrency*. Intra-object concurrency seems to be absent from the standard models and languages for concurrent object-oriented programming, where only *inter-object concurrency* is considered.

Reduction to System Modules. Although Maude's object-oriented modules provide a convenient syntax for programming object-oriented systems, their semantics can be *entirely reduced* to that of system modules, i.e., we can regard the additional syntax as syntactic sugar and nothing else. In fact, each object-oriented module can be translated into a corresponding system module whose semantics *is* by definition that of the original object-oriented module. The most basic structure shared by all object-oriented modules is made explicit by the **CONFIGURATION** system module below (we assume an already existing functional module ID of identifiers containing a sort OId of object identifiers).

```
mod CONFIGURATION is
  protecting ID . *** provides OId
  sorts Configuration Object Msg .
  subsorts Object Msg < Configuration .
  op __ : Configuration Configuration -> Configuration
                          [assoc comm id: 0] .
endm
```

The translation of a given object-oriented module extends this structure with the classes, messages and rules introduced by the module. For example, the following system module ACCOUNT# is the translation of the ACCOUNT module above.

```
mod ACCOUNT# is
  extending CONFIGURATION .
  protecting INT .
  sort Accnt .
  subsorts Accnt < Object .
  ops credit,debit : OId Nat -> Msg .
  op transfer_from_to_ : Nat OId OId -> Msg .
  op bal._replyto_ : OId OId -> Msg .
  op to_bal._is_ : OId OId Nat -> Msg .
  op <_: Accnt | bal:_> : OId Nat -> Accnt .
  vars A B : OId .
  vars M N N' : Nat .
  rl credit(A,M) < A : Accnt | bal: N > => < A : Accnt | bal: N + M > .
  rl debit(A,M) < A : Accnt | bal: N > => < A : Accnt | bal: N - M >
       if N >= M .
  rl transfer M from A to B
       < A : Accnt | bal: N > < B : Accnt | bal: N' > =>
       < A : Accnt | bal: N - M > < B : Accnt | bal: N' + M >
       if N >= M .
  rl (bal. A replyto B) < A : Accnt | bal: N > =>
       < A : Accnt | bal: N > (to B bal. A is N) .
endm
```

Note the introduction of operators bal._replyto_ and to_bal._is_ corresponding to messages by which an object can request the balance of a given account and receive a reply from the account as specified by the last rewrite rule. This capability is built in for object-oriented modules—unless an attribute has been declared hidden—and therefore was not mentioned in the original ACCOUNT module. Although the translation above is correct, we are simplifying the picture somewhat. As we shall discuss later, for purposes of inheritance a somewhat more sophisticated translation is preferable.

General Form of the Rules. In Maude, the general form required of rewrite rules used to specify the behavior of an object-oriented system is as follows:

$$(\dagger) \quad M_1 \ldots M_n \, \langle O_1 : C_1 \,|\, attrs_1 \rangle \ldots \langle O_m : C_m \,|\, attrs_m \rangle$$
$$\longrightarrow \langle O_{i_1} : C'_{i_1} \,|\, attrs'_{i_1} \rangle \ldots \langle O_{i_k} : C'_{i_k} \,|\, attrs'_{i_k} \rangle$$
$$\langle Q_1 : D_1 \,|\, attrs''_1 \rangle \ldots \langle Q_p : D_p \,|\, attrs''_p \rangle$$
$$M'_1 \ldots M'_q$$
$$\textit{if } C$$

where the Ms are message expressions, $i_1, \ldots, i_k$ are different numbers among the original $1, \ldots, m$, and C is the rule's condition. A rule of this kind expresses a *communication event* in which n messages and m distinct objects participate. The *outcome* of such an event is as follows:

- the messages $M_1, \ldots, M_n$ disappear;
- the *state* and possibly even the *class* of the objects $O_{i_1}, \ldots, O_{i_k}$ may change;
- all other objects O_j vanish;
- new objects $Q_1, \ldots, Q_p$ are created;
- new messages $M'_1, \ldots, M'_q$ are sent.

There are also some additional requirements to ensure the proper behavior of the rules ($\dagger$) that are discussed in [40]. Notice that, since some of the attributes of an object—as well as the parameters of messages—can contain object names, very complex and dynamically changing patterns of communication can be achieved by rules of this kind.

We call a communication event (and therefore its corresponding rule) *asynchronous* if only one object appears in the lefthand side. Otherwise, the communication is called *synchronous* and the objects appearing in the lefthand side are said to *synchronize* in the event. For example, the rules for crediting and debiting accounts describe asynchronous communication events, whereas the rule for transferring funds between two accounts forces them to synchronize.

We refer the reader to [40] for a more complete treatment of object-oriented concurrency in Maude, and for more examples. In particular, an important topic treated there is the *creation* and *deletion* of objects, which can also be treated by concurrent *ACI*-rewriting in a variety of ways and without any problems. Object creation is typically initiated by means of a "new" message of the form

$$new(C \,|\, attrs)$$

which specifies the new object's class and initialization values for its attributes, and has the effect of creating a new object with those properties and with a fresh new name.

Inheritance. Class inheritance is directly supported by Maude's order-sorted type structure. A subclass declaration $C < C'$ in an object-oriented module omod $\mathcal{O}$ endom is interpreted as a subsort declaration $C < C'$ in its system module translation mod $\mathcal{O}\#$ endm. The effect in the signature of $\mathcal{O}\#$ is that the attributes of all the superclasses as well as the newly defined attributes of a subclass appear in the syntax definition of the constructor operator for objects in the subclass. Rules are also inherited; at the level of the translation $\mathcal{O}\#$ this is accomplished by performing a slightly more sophisticated translation of the rules than that performed for the ACCOUNT module. First of all, it is convenient to use an *ACI* representation of an object's set of attribute-value pairs, so that the commas separating them are understood as a binary *ACI* operator. To simplify notation let $\overline{a:v}$ denote the attribute-value pairs $a_1 : v_1, \ldots, a_n : v_n$. Secondly, we can introduce a convention by which only some of the attributes of an object have to be mentioned explicitly. Namely we allow the attributes appearing in the pattern for an object O in the lefthand and righthand sides of rules to be any two arbitrary subsets of the attributes of the object. We can picture this as follows

$$\ldots \langle O : C \mid \overline{al : vl}, \overline{ab : vb} \rangle \ldots \longrightarrow \ldots \langle O : C \mid \overline{ab : vb'}, \overline{ar : vr} \rangle \ldots$$

where $\overline{al}$ are the attributes only appearing on the *left*, $\overline{ab}$ are the attributes appearing on *both* sides, and $\overline{ar}$ are the attributes appearing only on the *right*. What this abbreviates is a rule of the form

$$\ldots \langle O : C \mid \overline{al : vl}, \overline{ab : vb}, \overline{ar : x}, attrs \rangle \ldots \longrightarrow \ldots \langle O : C \mid \overline{al : vl}, \overline{ab : vb'}, \overline{ar : vr}, attrs \rangle \ldots$$

where $\overline{x}$ are new "don't care" variables and *attrs* matches the remaining attribute-value pairs. The attributes mentioned only on the left are preserved unchanged, the original values of attributes mentioned only on the right don't matter, and all attributes not explicitly mentioned are left unchanged. Thirdly, by introducing a sort ClId for class identifiers and using a variable for the class identifier C appearing in an object, it is possible to turn rules associated with a class C into more general rules that check whether the class identifier C' of the matched object is smaller than C in the subclass ordering. In this way, the rules can be used as given not only for the original class in which they were defined, but also for any subclasses of it that could be introduced later.

Actors. Actors [3, 2] provide a flexible and attractive style of concurrent object-oriented programming. However, their mathematical structure, although already described and studied by previous researchers [15, 2], has remained somewhat hard to understand and, as a consequence, the use of formal methods to reason about actor systems has remained limited. The present logical theory of concurrent objects sheds new light on the mathematical structure of actors and provides a new formal basis for the study of this important and interesting approach.

Specifically, the general logical theory of concurrent objects presented in this paper yields directly as a special case an entirely declarative approach to the theory and programming practice of actors. The specialization of our model to that of actors can be obtained by first clarifying terminological issues and then studying their definition by Agha and Hewitt [3].

Actor theory has a terminology of its own which, to make things clearer, we will attempt to relate to the more standard terminology employed in object-oriented programming. To the best of our understanding, the table in Figure 4 provides a basic terminological correspondence of this kind.

The essential idea about actors is clearly summarized in the words of Agha and Hewitt [3] as follows:

"An actor is a computational agent which carries out its actions in response to processing a communication. The actions it may perform are:

Actors	OOP
Script	Class declaration
Actor	Object
Actor Machine	Object State
Task	Message
Acquaintances	Attributes

Fig. 4. A dictionary for Actors.

- Send communications to itself or to other actors.
- Create more actors.
- Specify the *replacement behavior*."

The "replacement behavior" is yet another term to describe the new "actor machine" produced after processing the communication, i.e., the new state of the actor.

We can now put all this information together and simply conclude that a logical axiomatization in rewriting logic of an actor system—which is of course at the same time an *executable* specification of such a system in Maude—exactly corresponds to the special case of a concurrent object-oriented system in our sense whose rewrite rules instead of being of the general form (†) are of the special asynchronous and unconditional form

$$M \langle O : C \mid attrs \rangle$$
$$\longrightarrow \langle O : C' \mid attrs' \rangle$$
$$\langle Q_1 : D_1 \mid attrs_1'' \rangle \ldots \langle Q_p : D_p \mid attrs_p'' \rangle$$
$$M_1' \ldots M_q'$$

Therefore, the present theory is considerably *more general* than that of actors. In comparison with existing accounts about actors [3, 2] it seems also fair to say that our theory is *more abstract* so that some of those accounts can now be regarded as *high level architectural descriptions* of particular ways in which the abstract model can be implemented. In particular, the all-important *mail system* used in those accounts to buffer communication is the implementation counterpart of what in our model is abstractly achieved by the *ACI* axioms. Another nice feature of our approach is that it gives a *truly concurrent* formulation—in terms of concurrent *ACI*-rewriting—of actor computations, which seems most natural given their character. By contrast, Agha [2] presents an interleaving model of sequentialized transitions. Agha is keenly aware of the inadequacy of reducing the essence of true concurrency to nondeterminism and therefore states (pg. 82) that the correspondence between his interleaving model and the truly concurrent computation of actors is "*representationalistic, not metaphysical*." Finally, it is important to point out that, in our account, the way in which an object changes its state as a consequence of receiving a message may involve many concurrent rewritings of its attributes, i.e., objects exhibit intra-object concurrency; by contrast, typical actor languages treat change of object state as a sequential computation.

There is one additional aspect important for actor systems and in general for concurrent systems, namely *fairness*. For actors, this takes the form of requiring *guarantee of mail delivery*. In the concurrent rewriting model it is possible to state precisely a variety

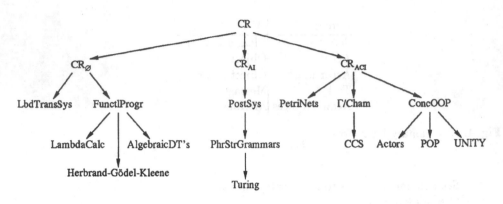

Fig. 5. Unification of Concurrency Models.

of fairness conditions and, in particular, the guarantee of mail delivery for the special case of actors. Details will appear elsewhere.

2.5 Modularity and Parameterization

In Maude a module can have *submodules*. Functional modules can only have functional submodules, system modules can have both functional and system submodules[8]. For example, NAT was declared a submodule of NAT-CHOICE. The meaning of submodule relations in which the submodule and the supermodule are both of the same kind is the obvious one, i.e., we augment the signature, equations, labels, and rules of the submodule by adding to them the corresponding ones in the supermodule; we then give semantics to the module so obtained according to its kind, i.e., functional or system (the mathematical semantics of Maude modules is discussed in Section 5). The semantics of a system module having a functional submodule is somewhat more delicate; this case is treated in [41].

As in OBJ3, Maude also has *theories* to specify semantic requirements for interfaces and to make high level assertions about modules; they can be functional, system, or object-oriented; the examples in this section have only used functional theories; a longer example in Section 4 also uses an object-oriented theory. Also as in OBJ, Maude has *parameterized modules*—again of the three kinds—and *views* that are theory interpretations relating theories to modules or to other theories. Details regarding the semantics of all these aspects of the language will appear elsewhere[9].

2.6 Generality of the Concurrent Rewriting Model

Concurrent rewriting is a very general model of concurrency from which many other models—besides those discussed in this paper—can be obtained by specialization. Space limitations preclude a detailed discussion, for which we refer the reader to [43, 41].

---

[8] Object-oriented modules can have submodules of the three kinds, but after reducing object-oriented modules to system modules no new issues appear for them.

[9] Some basic results about views and parameterization for system modules have already been given in [42].

However, we can summarize such specializations using Figure 5, where CR stands for concurrent rewriting, the arrows indicate specializations, and the subscripts $\emptyset$, AI, and ACI stand for syntactic rewriting, rewriting modulo associativity and identity, and ACI-rewriting respectively. Within syntactic rewriting we have labelled transitions systems, which are used in interleaving approaches to concurrency; functional programming (in particular Maude's functional modules) corresponds to the case of confluent[10] rules, and includes the λ-calculus (see Section 3.1) and the Herbrand-Gödel-Kleene theory of recursive functions. Rewriting modulo AI yields Post systems and related grammar formalisms, including Turing machines. Besides the general treatment by ACI-rewriting of concurrent object-oriented programming that contains Actors as a special case [3], rewriting modulo ACI includes Petri nets [47], the Gamma language of Banâtre and Le Mètayer [9], and Berry and Boudol's *chemical abstract machine* [11] (which itself specializes to CCS [46]), as well as Unity's model of computation [13]; another special case is Engelfriet et al.'s POPs and POTs higher level Petri nets for actors [20, 19].

3 Maude as a Machine-Independent Language

Although concurrent rewriting is a general and flexible model of concurrency and can certainly be used to reason formally about concurrent systems at a high level of abstraction, it would not be reasonable to implement this model for programming purposes in its fullest gènerality. This is due to the fact that, in its most general form, rewriting can take place *modulo* an arbitrary equational theory E which could be undecidable. Of course, a minimum practical requirement for E is the existence of an algorithm for finding all the matches modulo E for a given rule and term; however, for some axioms E this process, even if it is available, can be quite inefficient, so that its implementation should be considered a theorem proving matter, or at best something to be supported by an implementation for uses such as rapid prototyping and execution of specifications, but probably should not be made part of a programming language implementation. A good example is general AC-rewriting, which can be quite costly for complicated left-hand side patterns; this can be acceptable for rapid prototyping purposes—in fact, the OBJ3 interpreter [23, 22] supports this as well as rewriting modulo other similar sets of axioms E—but seems to us impractical for programming purposes even if a parallel implementation is considered[11].

In this regard, it is useful to adopt a *transformational* point of view. For specification purposes we can allow the full generality of the concurrent rewriting model, whereas for programming purposes we should study subcases that can be efficiently implemented; executable specifications hold a middle ground in which we can be considerably more tolerant of inefficiencies in exchange for a greater expressiveness. The idea is then to develop program transformation techniques that are semantics-preserving and move us from specifications to programs, and from less efficient programs—perhaps just executable specifications—to more efficient ones. This transformational approach fits in very nicely with the design of Maude which, as with OBJ3 in the functional case, can be regarded

---

[10] Although not reflected in the picture, rules confluent *modulo* equations E are also functional.

[11] Of course, even in a case like this there can be different opinions. Banâtre, Coutant, and Le Mètayer have in fact considered parallel machine implementations of AC-rewriting for their Gamma language [8].

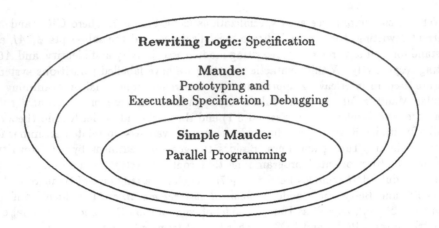

Fig. 6. Maude and Simple Maude as subsets of Rewriting Logic.

as a wide spectrum language that integrates both specification and computation. Indeed, Maude *theories* (cf. Section 2.5), whether functional, system, or object-oriented, are used for specification purposes and therefore need not be executable[12]. Regarding Maude modules, a distinction should be made between use for rapid prototyping and executable specification, and use for programming, with more stringent restrictions imposed in the latter case.

Regarding language design and language implementations, this suggests considering two subsets of rewriting logic. The first subset gives rise to Maude—in the sense that Maude modules are rewriting logic theories in that subset—and can be supported by an interpreter implementation adequate for rapid prototyping, debugging, and executable specification. The second, smaller subset gives rise to Simple Maude, a sublanguage meant to be used for programming purposes for which a wide variety of machine implementations could be developed. A number of program transformation techniques can then support passage from general rewrite theories to Maude modules and from them to modules in Simple Maude. Figure 6 summarizes the three levels involved.

A matter like this, where decisions about what to implement or not to implement due to efficiency reasons must be made, is, and should be regarded as, an *open-ended* process; basically because new implementation ideas and new linguistic conventions will be found as more experience is gained that will enlarge the subset of the logic supported by an implementation. Therefore, our remarks in this section should be understood as our present thinking on the matter, with no pretensions to settle all the issues once and for all. However, our approach to the design of Maude and Simple Maude can be described in broad outlines with sufficient precision for the purposes at hand, including implementation issues.

Regarding Maude and its implementation as an interpreter, we plan to support rewrit-

---

[12] In fact, for the sake of greater expressiveness they may even be theories in logics different from rewriting or equational logic; details will appear elsewhere.

ing modulo all the axioms supported by OBJ3, where a binary operator can be declared to be associative and/or commutative and/or having a neutral element, and rewriting modulo a combination of those axioms is supported by the implementation. In particular, all the examples in Section 2 are legal Maude modules. The Maude interpreter will support rapid prototyping and debugging of system designs and specifications that, if desired, could also be used to derive an efficient system by applying to them a series of semantics-preserving transformations and refinement steps bringing the entire program within the Simple Maude sublanguage; some program transformations can be automated so that a user can write certain types of programs in a more abstract way in Maude and could leave the task of transforming them into Simple Maude programs to a compiler.

Simple Maude represents our present design decisions about the subset of rewriting logic that could be implemented efficiently in a wide variety of machine architectures. In fact, we regard Simple Maude as a *machine-independent parallel programming language*. Admittedly, the existence of such an animal is seriously doubted by some people, who consider machine-independent parallel languages a chimera. However, we believe that the generality and abstractness of the concurrent rewriting model can—when adequately restricted to allow efficient implementations—provide a truly machine-independent parallel language which could be executed with reasonable efficiency on many parallel architectures; Section 3.2 discusses our present ideas about such implementations. Since, at present, writing parallel programs often requires a good acquaintance with the idiosyncrasies of a particular parallel machine, and porting programs developed for one parallel machine to another type of machine is in general a difficult and time-consuming task, there are of course obvious and important benefits to be gained from having a machine-independent parallel language. As we discuss later in this section, Simple Maude can also support multilingual extensions, allowing the parallelization of code written in conventional languages. More generally, Maude's concurrent rewriting model could serve as the glue for putting together open heterogeneous systems encompassing many different machines and special I/O devices. Finally, the simple mathematical semantics of Maude should also allow the use of this semantic framework as a basis for programming tools with very broad applicability, e.g., program analysis, program optimization, and verification tools.

3.1 Simple Maude

This section discusses the language conventions for functional, system and object-oriented modules in Simple Maude.

Rewriting Modulo Church-Rosser and Terminating Equations. As work on compilation techniques for functional languages has amply demonstrated, syntactic rewriting, i.e., rewriting modulo an empty set of structural axioms, can be implemented efficiently on sequential machines; our experience leads us to believe that this can be done even more efficiently on parallel machines (more on this later). Therefore, functional or system modules with an empty set E of structural axioms are the easiest to implement and belong to Simple Maude. A closely related class of modules also allowed in Simple Maude is that of functional or system modules having an associated rewrite theory $\mathcal{R} = (\Sigma, E, L, R)$ such that the set E of structural axioms is Church-Rosser and terminating and has the additional property that, for the rewrite theory $\mathcal{R}' = (\Sigma, \emptyset, L, R)$, whenever we have

$\mathcal{R}' \vdash t \longrightarrow t'$ we also have $\mathcal{R}' \vdash can_E(t) \longrightarrow can_E(t')$, where $can_E(t)$ denotes the canonical form to which the term t is reduced by the equations E used as rewrite rules. Under such circumstances we can implement rewriting modulo E by syntactic rewriting with the rewrite theory $\mathcal{R}'' = (\Sigma, \emptyset, L, R \cup E)$ provided that we restrict our attention to sequents of the form $can_E(t) \longrightarrow can_E(t')$ which faithfully represent $\mathcal{R}$-rewritings in E-equivalence classes. For modules of this kind the structural axioms $u = v$ in E are introduced by the syntax

```
ax u = v .
```

A functional module defined by a rewrite theory $\mathcal{R}$ of this kind has the same initial algebra as the functional module defined by the associated rewrite theory $\mathcal{R}''$. However, the semantics of both modules as defined in Section 5 is different. For system modules of this kind, the semantics associated with $\mathcal{R}$ and with the rewrite theory $\mathcal{R}''$ that simulates it are even more different. Even for functional modules, the possibility of allowing a distinction between rules and structural axioms in this way is quite convenient and meaningful. For example, we can in this way avoid all the fuss with variables and substitution in the standard lambda calculus notation by defining a functional module **LAMBDA** corresponding to the $\lambda\sigma$-calculus of Abadi, Cardelli, Curien, and Lévy [1] in which we interpret their *Beta* rule as the only rule, and their set σ of Church-Rosser and terminating equations for explicit substitution as the set E of structural axioms. The point is that σ-equivalence classes are isomorphic to standard lambda expressions (modulo α conversion), and rewritings in σ-equivalence classes corresponds to β-reductions.

There are of course a variety of strategies by which we can interleave E-rewriting and R-rewriting in the implementation of modules of this kind, and some strategies can be more efficient than others. It could also be possible to generalize the class of modules that can be implemented by syntactic rewriting by giving weaker conditions on the relationship between R and E that are still correct assuming a particular strategy for interleaving R- and E-rewritings.

Object-Oriented Modules. In Maude, the essence of concurrent object-oriented computation is captured by concurrent ACI-rewriting using rules of the general form (†) described in Section 2.4. In a sequential interpreter this can be *simulated* by performing ACI-rewriting using an ACI-matching algorithm. However, in a parallel implementation ACI-rewriting should be realized exclusively by means of *communication*.

The problem is that realizing general AC- or ACI-rewriting in this way can require unacceptable amounts of communication and therefore can be very inefficient, even for rules of the form (†) introduced in object-oriented modules that make a somewhat limited use of ACI-rewriting because no variables are ever used to match multisets. For this reason, our approach is to only allow in Simple Maude object-oriented modules conditional rules of the form

$$
\begin{aligned}
(\ddagger) \quad & M \; \langle O : C \mid attrs \rangle \\
& \longrightarrow \langle O : C' \mid attrs' \rangle \\
& \quad \langle Q_1 : D_1 \mid attrs_1'' \rangle \ldots \langle Q_p : D_p \mid attrs_p'' \rangle \\
& \quad M_1' \ldots M_q' \\
& \quad if \; C
\end{aligned}
$$

involving only one object and one message in their lefthand side, as well as "active object" conditional rules of the form

$$(\S) \quad \langle O : C \mid attrs \rangle$$
$$\longrightarrow \langle O : C' \mid attrs' \rangle$$
$$\langle Q_1 : D_1 \mid attrs_1'' \rangle \ldots \langle Q_p : D_p \mid attrs_p'' \rangle$$
$$M_1' \ldots M_q'$$
$$if \ C$$

Specifically, the lefthand sides in rules of the form (‡) should fit the general pattern

$$M(O) \ \langle O : C \mid attrs \rangle$$

where O could be a variable, a constant, or more generally—in case object identifiers are endowed with additional structure—a term. Under such circumstances, an efficient way of realizing AC-rewriting by communication is available to us for rules of the form (‡), namely we can associate object identifiers with specific addresses in the machine where the object is located and send messages addressed to the object to the corresponding address. For example, a rule to credit money to an account can be implemented this way by routing the credit message to the location of its addressee so that when both come into contact the rewrite rule for crediting the account can be applied. Rules of the form (§) are even simpler to implement, since their matching does not require any communication by messages; however, both types of rules assume the existence of a basic mechanism for sending the messages generated in the righthand side to their appropriate destination.

How should the gap between the more general rules (†) allowed in Maude modules and the more restricted rules (‡) and (§) permitted in Simple Maude modules be mediated? Our approach to this problem—in forthcoming joint work with Patrick Lincoln—has been to develop program transformation techniques that, under appropriate fairness assumptions, guarantee that rewriting with rules of the form (†) can be simulated by rewriting using rules of the form (‡) and (§). The basic idea is that a (†) rule in general requires the synchronization of several objects—what in some contexts is called a *multiparty interaction*—but this synchronization can be achieved in an asynchronous way by an appropriate sending of messages using rules of the form (‡). Transformations of this kind can be automated and relegated to a compiler, so that a user could write object-oriented modules in Maude and not have to worry about the corresponding expression of his program in Simple Maude. However, Simple Maude is already quite expressive—in particular, more expressive than Actors—and many programs will fall naturally within this class without any need for further transformations.

As Maude, Simple Maude will also have basic support for object creation and deletion and for broadcasting; some initial ideas on these matters are discussed in [40], and further elaborations will appear elsewhere.

System Modules. The strategy followed for Simple Maude's object-oriented modules can be generalized to system modules[13] so that they can also perform concurrent AC-rewriting by asynchronous message-passing communication. A reasonable way to achieve

---

[13] As discussed before, we also allow Simple Maude system modules where the structural axioms E are given by Church-Rosser and terminating equations.

this generalization is to consider system modules that contain the CONFIGURATION module introduced in Section 2.4 as a submodule, but that need not adhere to the linguistic conventions of object-oriented modules. Recall that the relevant sorts in CONFIGURATION are Object, Msg, OId, and Configuration, and the key operation is the *ACI* union __ of configurations.

The only occurrence of the operator __ that is allowed in lefthand sides of rules should be in rules of the form

$$t(I)\, t'(I) \longrightarrow t''$$

where $t(I)$ has sort Msg, $t'(I)$ has sort Object, I is a variable, a constant, or more generally a term of sort OId, and is the leftmost-outermost term of sort OId in both $t(I)$ and $t'(I)$. The term t'' could involve none, one, or several occurrences of the __ operator.

Regarding the actual implementation of rules like the one above by communication, the following could be done:

1. A ground term $t'(I)$ of sort Object with I its leftmost-outermost subterm of sort OId should have a fixed address in the machine, and the identifier I should be treated as a name for that address[14].
2. Any ground term $t(I)$ of sort Msg with I its leftmost-outermost subterm of sort OId should be sent to the address named by the identifier I, so that when $t(I)$ and the term named by I come into contact, matching of the appropriate rewrite rules can be attempted.

Of course, for this scheme to be viable, it must be required that—having specified a subset of terms allowed as *initial states*—the rules in the system module never lead to a configuration in which two objects share a leftmost-outermost identifier, i.e., no identifier should simultaneously name more than one object.

3.2 Sequential, SIMD, MIMD, and MIMD/SIMD Implementations

Simple Maude can be implemented on a wide variety of parallel architectures. The diagram in Figure 7 shows the relationship among some general classes that we have considered. There are two orthogonal choices giving rise to four classes of machines: the processing nodes can be either a single sequential processor or a SIMD array of processors, and there can be either just a single processing node or a network of them. The arrows in the diamond denote specializations from a more general and concurrent architecture to degenerate special cases, with the sequential case at the bottom. The arrows pointing to the left correspond to specializing a network of processing nodes to the degenerate case with only one processing node; the arrows pointing to the right correspond to specializing a SIMD array to the degenerate case of a single processor.

The sequential case corresponds to a single conventional sequential processor. In this case, at most one rule is applied to a single place in the data at a time. The SIMD (single instruction stream, multiple data) case corresponds to the Connection Machine (CM-2), DAP, and MasPar architectures (all of these are discussed in [50]). From the point of view

---

[14] We could instead have explicit operators name : Object -> OId, and addressee : Msg -> OId, and require that these be explicitly defined for all system entities; this would be a better abstract description, but for the sake of conciseness we will use the conventions described above.

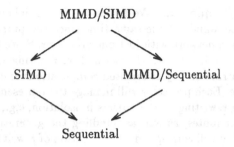

Fig. 7. Specialization relationships among parallel architectures.

of rewriting, this corresponds to applying rewrite rules one at a time, possibly to many places in the data. The MIMD/Sequential (multiple instruction stream, multiple data) case corresponds to the Intel iPSC [50], NCUBE [50], Touchstone Delta [30], Mosaic [48], J-machine [17], etc. These machines are networks of conventional sequential processors; we consider shared memory machines such as Alliant or Sequent [50] to also fit in this category. In terms of rewriting, this is the case of many different rewrite rules being applied at many different places at once, but only one rule is applied at one place in each processor. The MIMD/SIMD case corresponds to the Rewrite Rule Machine (RRM) [28, 6, 5, 4], in which the processing nodes are two-dimensional SIMD arrays realized on a chip and the higher level structure is a network operating in MIMD mode. This also corresponds to applying many rules to many different places in the data, but here a single rule may be applied at many places simultaneously within a single processing node. This approach exploits VLSI technology by providing extremely fine-grain parallelism (we plan to have hundreds of simple processors on a chip).

Simple Maude has been chosen so that concurrent rewriting with rules in this sublanguage should be relatively easy to implement in any of the four classes of machines discussed above. We first make two observations of a more general nature and then discuss more particular implementation issues for each of the four classes of machines. The observations are:

1. For all the various implementations it is necessary to have a mechanism for addressing the various objects of the system. We will not describe in detail how this is implemented (the specific choice of implementation will probably be affected by the underlying hardware), but will simply assume that given an address of an object, it is straightforward to route messages to the processor associated with that object.
2. For syntactic rewriting ($E = \emptyset$) or for rewriting modulo Church-Rosser and terminating equations, the two MIMD classes—MIMD/Sequential and MIMD/SIMD— require some mechanisms for load balancing and for rewriting instances of the lefthand side of a rule that overlap two or more processing nodes. Mechanisms of this kind are for instance discussed in [4]. Even though a SIMD machine is regarded in the above classification as a single processing node, similar issues arise inside such a node in the interaction between processors. For the sequential case the problem of lefthandside instances overlapping several processing nodes does not arise.

Sequential and MIMD/Sequential. We discuss the sequential and MIMD/Sequential implementations of Simple Maude at the same time since the purely sequential case is just the degenerate case of a network with just one processor. Since the case of syntactic rewriting and of rewriting modulo Church-Rosser and terminating equations has already been discussed, we concentrate on object-oriented computations and their generalization to the system module case. Each processor will manage the representation of some number of objects, performing rewriting on the objects in isolation, e.g., rewriting functional subterms of the object attributes, as well as handling the generation and reception of messages. Message handling will correspond to application of rewrite rules to the system configuration. The basic treatment of messages is to forward them to other processors if they are addressed to remote objects, or to associate them with their target in the current processor. When a message arrives, it is easy to identify the relevant rewrite rules. In the typical case, as soon as the message is available, a rule can be applied (and possibly new messages will be generated). The implementation ideas for this case generalize ideas used in more conventional message passing systems; however, certain anomalies encountered in such systems such as the so-called "inheritance anomaly" [38] can be overcome by the greater flexibility of the concurrent rewriting model. In the case of a single processor, messages never need to be forwarded to another processor. We believe that the case of shared memory multiprocessors is very similar to the single processor case.

SIMD. In the case of SIMD machines, we expect that the individual processing nodes will represent parts of objects or more generally parts of terms, and that the global execution will proceed in a rule-by-rule fashion. The code to find matches for a rule and to perform replacements will be repeatedly broadcast to all elements of the SIMD array. In order to avoid wasted effort, it is important to use some sort of global feedback on pattern matching, to control the broadcast of the code for a rule (or for a related collection of rules). An attempt to apply a rule may fail, and the overall correctness of the system should depend only on an assumption of fair rule application. In addition to broadcasting code for rewrite rules, it will be necessary to execute SIMD code for supporting processes such as message passing and garbage collection. An example of implementation work along these lines is [31]. We have developed compilation techniques for compiling rewrite rules onto the SIMD single-chip processor of the RRM, which also corresponds to this case [5].

MIMD/SIMD. The MIMD/SIMD case corresponds to the RRM [28]. In this case, local execution is carried out by extremely fine-grain SIMD execution, and on a larger scale, execution is coordinated in a MIMD message-passing fashion. The implementation techniques within a single SIMD processing node correspond to those for the SIMD case [5]. The handling of interactions between the processing nodes is primarily by asynchronous message passing, which has no critical timing requirements. It is possible that a large computation is carried out purely in the functional sublanguage where the message passing will be implicit. For this case, the basic operations on functional terms are a remote read and a remote allocation [4].

3.3 Multilingual Extensions

Advances in programming practice are not simply a matter of technical breakthroughs. Very large amounts of money and effort may have been invested in developing applications in conventional sequential code making it impractical in the short run to reprogram such applications from scratch. Also, the difficulties involved in easing the transition to a new language for programmers should not be underestimated. For all these reasons, finding a flexible transition path from conventional programming to advanced techniques in parallel programming is a pressing and important practical problem. Thanks to its flexible model of computation, Maude can be used in conjunction with conventional code—which can in this way be parallelized—to solve this problem. What we need is to add appropriate multilingual extensions to the language. We briefly sketch how this can be done and discuss related work. Our ideas are still preliminary; more work is obviously needed to develop them more fully.

We have the goal of allowing the integration within Maude of modules written in conventional languages such as C and Fortran; this will support reuse and parallelization of code originally developed for sequential machines. The way in which this can be accomplished generalizes a facility already available in Maude's functional sublanguage (OBJ) for defining *built-in sorts* and *built-in rules* [23, 22]. This facility has provided valuable experience with multilingual support, in this case for OBJ and Lisp, and can be generalized to a facility for defining *built-in modules* in Maude. Such built-in modules have abstract interfaces that allow them to be integrated with other Maude modules and to be executed concurrently with other computations. Internally, however, they are treated as "black boxes." In particular, Maude's model of computation provides a simple way of gluing a parallel program together out of sequential pieces of code written in conventional languages. Built-in modules may provide either a functional datatype, or an object-oriented class. In the first case, the treatment will be extremely similar to that provided in OBJ. In the second case, the abstract interface will be provided by the specification of the messages that act upon the new class of objects.

The use of built-in definitions of objects will also allow the incorporation of I/O devices, and special purpose hardware devices into Maude programs in a clean and natural way. One difference from OBJ is that it will always be possible to provide completely abstract specifications of these objects, whereas in OBJ, system and object-oriented phenomena could only be partially treated.

Related efforts in multilingual support for parallel programming include: the *Linda* language developed by D. Gelernter and his collaborators at Yale [12], the *Strand* language designed by I. Foster and S. Taylor [21], the *Program Composition Notation* (PCN) designed by K. M. Chandy and S. Taylor at Caltech [14], and the *GLU* language developed by R. Jagannathan and A. Faustini at SRI International [33].

Linda provides a "tuple space" solution to the parallelization of conventional code and has received relatively wide acceptance; its main use seems to be in coarse grain parallelism.

Strand is a language in the tradition of concurrent logic programming, but it has the important additional advantage of being multilingual and therefore allowing parallelization of conventional code by means of the synchronization mechanism provided by Strand's logical variables. Strand seems quite appealing as a way to achieve coarse grain parallelism for conventional code.

PCN combines ideas from Strand and from the Unity language [13]. As with Strand, it is multilingual and can be used for coarse grain parallelization of pieces of sequential code. Due to the cost of its synchronization mechanism through logical variables, it seems to be most effective when the bulk of the computation is performed by the embedded sequential code.

GLU uses a dataflow model of parallel computation to put together heterogeneous systems and to coordinate the computations of their coarse-grain components.

Maude shares with Linda, Strand, PCN, and GLU the goal of supporting reuse of code written in different sequential languages. The main difference between Maude and those languages seems to be the greater abstractness, simplicity and generality of its concurrent rewriting model of computation that in our view make Maude a good candidate for a machine-independent parallel language not only in the area of coarse grain MIMD computation emphasized by most of those languages, but also for fine grain SIMD computation and even for implementations combining SIMD and MIMD computing. Other advantages of Maude are its high level declarative style, and its solid mathematical foundation that supports the application of formal methods. Finally, Maude also provides advanced programming-in-the-large reusability techniques such as parameterized programming and module inheritance that can substantially advance the state of the art in parallel programming methodology.

3.4 Open Heterogeneous Systems

Future computing environments will be heterogeneous, involving many different machine architectures, and evolving, with components being attached and removed over time. It has long been recognized that message passing models provide one of the best ways to integrate distributed heterogeneous systems; this is the basis of remote procedure call implementations, and services such as NFS (Sun's Network File System). Designs based on message passing also make it relatively easy to add or remove resources, and to deal with variations in the size of parallel architectures (the number of processing nodes). The advantage of the concurrent rewriting model is that it integrates message passing within a simple and mathematically precise abstract model of computation and can therefore be used as both a framework and a language for the integration of heterogeneous systems.

In addition, this model can provide multilingual support in the context of systems that are heterogeneous in language as well as in hardware. In order to incorporate something (whether it be a special purpose processor, I/O device, or a program written in C) into the abstract model, it is just necessary to treat it as a black box and to specify its interface to the system, i.e., the message protocol that is used for interacting with it.

Besides wishing to investigate further the advantages of Maude and its concurrent rewriting model for the integration of heterogeneous systems, we would like to explore the information hiding capabilities of this model for the application of formal methods. For example, a large component of a system could be specified as a simple black box component, with simple assertions about the messages that are produced by the component based on those received, e.g., specifying security properties. This would allow reasoning about a large system at a low level of complexity, but in a way that is completely accurate.

4 A Communication Protocol Example

If a communication mechanism does not provide reliable, in-order delivery of messages, it may be necessary to generate this service using the given unreliable basis. The following Maude example shows how this might be done. Since unreliable communication is a more serious issue across different machines, this example illustrates the application of Maude to heterogeneous open systems. This was derived from the alternating bit protocol as presented in Lam and Shankar [34], although, since we do not assume in-order delivery, we cannot use the alternating bit protocol. The same kind of example is discussed in a somewhat different way in Chandy and Misra [13]. The following definition creates a generic, fault-tolerant connection between a specific sender and receiver pair. Notice that—thanks to the abstractness of the concurrent rewriting model and to the parameterization mechanisms of the language—the module is very general in several respects:

- it makes very few assumptions about the communication between sender and receiver;
- the parameter ELT can be instantiated to any type of data to be sent;
- the parameters S and R can be instantiated to any two previously defined classes of objects.

The requirement that the parameters S and R have to satisfy is expressed by the object-oriented theory CLASS below, whose Cl sort can be instantiated to any class of an object-oriented module. To disambiguate the use of the parameter sort Cl in S and R, we use the notation Cl.S and Cl.R.

```
oth CLASS is
  class Cl .
endoth

omod PROTOCOL[ELT :: TRIV, S :: CLASS, R :: CLASS] is
  protecting LIST[ELT] .
  protecting NAT .

  subsorts Elt < Contents .
  op empty : -> Contents .
  msg to:_(_,_) : OId Elt Nat -> Msg . *** data to receiver
  msg to:_ack_ : OId Nat -> Msg . *** acknowledgement to sender

  class Sender .
  subclass Sender < Cl.S .
  att rec : Sender -> OId . *** the receiver
  att sendq : Sender -> List . *** outgoing queue
  att sendbuff : Sender -> Contents . *** empty or current data
  att sendcnt : Sender -> Nat . *** sender sequence number

  vars S R : OId .
  var N : Nat .
  var E : Elt .
```

```
    var L : List .
    var C : Contents .

    rl produce :
        < S : Sender | rec: R, sendq: E . L,
          sendbuff: empty, sendcnt: N > =>
        < S : Sender | rec: R, sendq: L, sendbuff: E, sendcnt: N + 1 > .

    rl send :
        < S : Sender | rec: R, sendq: L, sendbuff: E, sendcnt: N > =>
        < S : Sender | rec: R, sendq: L, sendbuff: E, sendcnt: N >
        (to: R (E,N)) .

    rl rec-ack :
        < S : Sender | rec: R, sendq: L, sendbuff: C, sendcnt: N >
        (to: S ack M) =>
        < S : Sender | rec: R, sendq: L,
                       sendbuff: (if N == M then empty else C fi),
                       sendcnt: N > .

    class Receiver .
    subclass Receiver < Cl.R .
    att sender : Receiver -> OId . *** the sender
    att recq : Receiver -> List . *** incoming queue
    att reccnt : Receiver -> Nat . *** receiver sequence number

    rl receive :
        < R : Receiver | sender: S, recq: L, reccnt: M > (to: R (E,N)) =>
        (if N == M + 1 then
           < R : Receiver | sender: S, recq: L . E, reccnt: M + 1 >
         else
           < R : Receiver | sender: S, recq: L, reccnt: M >
         fi)
        (to: S ack N)
endom
```

Under reasonable fairness assumptions, these definitions will generate a reliable, in-order communication mechanism from an unreliable one. The message counts are used to ignore all out-of-sequence messages. The fairness assumption will ensure that the send action and corresponding receive actions will be repeated until a rec-ack can be performed; thus each produce necessarily leads to a corresponding rec-ack. Note that the send operation is enabled until the corresponding rec-ack occurs.

We can explicitly model the fault modes of the communication channel as in the following definition:

```
omod PROTOCOL-IN-FAULTY-ENV[ELT :: TRIV, S :: CLASS, R :: CLASS] is
    extending PROTOCOL[ELT,S,R] .
```

```
    var M : Msg .

    rl duplicate :
      M => M M .

    class Destroyer .
    attrs sender rec : Destroyer -> OId .
    attr cnt : Destroyer -> Nat .

    var N : Nat .
    var E : Elt .
    vars S R D : OId .

    rl destroy1 :
        < D : Destroyer | sender: S, rec: R, cnt : N > (to: R (E,N)) =>
        < D : Destroyer | sender: S, rec: R, cnt : N > .

    rl destroy2 :
        < D : Destroyer | sender: S, rec: R, cnt : N > (to: S ack N) =>
        < D : Destroyer | sender: S, rec: R, cnt : N > .

    rl limited-injury :
        < D : Destroyer | sender: S, receiver: R, cnt : N > =>
        < D : Destroyer | sender: S, receiver: R, cnt : N + 1 > .
  endom
```

Messages may be duplicated or destroyed. The `limited-injury` rule, under an assumption of fair application of the total set of rules, will ensure that messages are not always destroyed. The new system, with the `Destroyer`, will also satisfy the same correctness condition.

5 Semantics

In this section we discuss models for rewriting logic and explain how such models are used to give semantics to modules in Maude. We will focus on the basic ideas and intuitions and leave out some of the details, which can be found in [41, 42].

We first sketch the construction of initial and free models for a rewrite theory $\mathcal{R} = (\Sigma, E, L, R)$. Such models capture nicely the intuitive idea of a "rewrite system" in the sense that they are systems whose states are E-equivalence classes of terms, and whose transitions are concurrent rewritings using the rules in R. Such systems have a natural *category* structure [35], with states as objects, transitions as morphisms, and sequential composition as morphism composition, and in them behavior exactly corresponds to deduction.

Given a rewrite theory $\mathcal{R} = (\Sigma, E, L, R)$, the model that we are seeking is a category $\mathcal{T}_\mathcal{R}(X)$ whose objects are equivalence classes of terms $[t] \in T_{\Sigma, E}(X)$ and whose morphisms are equivalence classes of "proof terms" representing proofs in rewriting deduction, i.e., concurrent $\mathcal{R}$-rewrites. The rules for generating such proof terms, with the specification of their respective domain and codomain, are given below; they just "decorate" with proof terms the rules 1-4 of rewriting logic. Note that in the rest of this paper we always use "diagrammatic" notation for morphism composition, i.e., $\alpha; \beta$ always means the composition of α *followed by* β.

1. **Identities.** For each $[t] \in T_{\Sigma,E}(X)$,

$$\overline{[t] : [t] \longrightarrow [t]}$$

2. **Σ-structure.** For each $f \in \Sigma_n$, $n \in \mathbb{N}$,

$$\frac{\alpha_1 : [t_1] \longrightarrow [t'_1] \quad \dots \quad \alpha_n : [t_n] \longrightarrow [t'_n]}{f(\alpha_1, \dots, \alpha_n) : [f(t_1, \dots, t_n)] \longrightarrow [f(t'_1, \dots, t'_n)]}$$

3. **Replacement.** For each rewrite rule $r : [t(\overline{x}^n)] \longrightarrow [t'(\overline{x}^n)]$ in R,

$$\frac{\alpha_1 : [w_1] \longrightarrow [w'_1] \quad \dots \quad \alpha_n : [w_n] \longrightarrow [w'_n]}{r(\alpha_1, \dots, \alpha_n) : [t(\overline{w}/\overline{x})] \longrightarrow [t'(\overline{w'}/\overline{x})]}$$

4. **Composition.**

$$\frac{\alpha : [t_1] \longrightarrow [t_2] \quad \beta : [t_2] \longrightarrow [t_3]}{\alpha; \beta : [t_1] \longrightarrow [t_3]}$$

Convention and Warning. In the case when the same label r appears in two different rules of R, the "proof terms" $r(\overline{\alpha})$ can sometimes be *ambiguous*. We will always assume that such ambiguity problems *have been resolved* by disambiguating the label r in the proof terms $r(\overline{\alpha})$ if necessary. With this understanding, we adopt the simpler notation $r(\overline{\alpha})$ to ease the exposition.

Each of the above rules of generation defines a different operation taking certain proof terms as arguments and returning a resulting proof term. In other words, proof terms form an algebraic structure $\mathcal{P}_{\mathcal{R}}(X)$ consisting of a graph with nodes $T_{\Sigma,E}(X)$ and with identity arrows and with operations f (for each $f \in \Sigma$), r (for each rewrite rule), and $\_;\_$ (for composing arrows). Our desired model $T_{\mathcal{R}}(X)$ is the quotient of $\mathcal{P}_{\mathcal{R}}(X)$ modulo the following equations[15]:

1. **Category.**
   (a) *Associativity.* For all α, β, γ

$$(\alpha; \beta); \gamma = \alpha; (\beta; \gamma)$$

   (b) *Identities.* For each $\alpha : [t] \longrightarrow [t']$

$$\alpha; [t'] = \alpha \quad and \quad [t]; \alpha = \alpha$$

2. **Functoriality of the Σ-algebraic structure.** For each $f \in \Sigma_n$, $n \in \mathbb{N}$,
   (a) *Preservation of composition.* For all $\alpha_1, \dots, \alpha_n, \beta_1, \dots, \beta_n$,

$$f(\alpha_1; \beta_1, \dots, \alpha_n; \beta_n) = f(\alpha_1, \dots, \alpha_n); f(\beta_1, \dots, \beta_n)$$

---

[15] In the expressions appearing in the equations, when compositions of morphisms are involved, we always implicitly assume that the corresponding domains and codomains match.

(b) *Preservation of identities.*

$$f([t_1], \ldots, [t_n]) = [f(t_1, \ldots, t_n)]$$

3. **Axioms in** E. For $t(x_1, \ldots, x_n) = t'(x_1, \ldots, x_n)$ an axiom in E, for all $\alpha_1, \ldots, \alpha_n$,

$$t(\alpha_1, \ldots, \alpha_n) = t'(\alpha_1, \ldots, \alpha_n)$$

4. **Exchange.** For each $r : [t(x_1, \ldots, x_n)] \longrightarrow [t'(x_1, \ldots, x_n)]$ in R,

$$\frac{\alpha_1 : [w_1] \longrightarrow [w_1'] \quad \ldots \quad \alpha_n : [w_n] \longrightarrow [w_n']}{r(\overline{\alpha}) = r(\overline{[w]}); t'(\overline{\alpha}) = t(\overline{\alpha}); r(\overline{[w']})}$$

Note that the set X of variables is actually a parameter of these constructions, and we need not assume X to be fixed and countable. In particular, for $X = \emptyset$, we adopt the notation $\mathcal{T}_\mathcal{R}$. The equations in 1 make $\mathcal{T}_\mathcal{R}(X)$ a category, the equations in 2 make each $f \in \Sigma$ a functor, and 3 forces the axioms E. The exchange law states that any rewriting of the form $r(\overline{\alpha})$—which represents the *simultaneous* rewriting of the term at the top using rule r *and* "below," i.e., in the subterms matched by the rule—is equivalent to the sequential composition $r(\overline{[w]}); t'(\overline{\alpha})$ corresponding to first rewriting on top with r and then below on the matched subterms. The exchange law also states that rewriting at the top by means of rule r and rewriting "below" are processes that are independent of each other and therefore can be done in any order. Therefore, $r(\overline{\alpha})$ is also equivalent to the sequential composition $t(\overline{\alpha}); r(\overline{[w']})$. Since $[t(x_1, \ldots, x_n)]$ and $[t'(x_1, \ldots, x_n)]$ can be regarded as functors $\mathcal{T}_\mathcal{R}(X)^n \longrightarrow \mathcal{T}_\mathcal{R}(X)$, the exchange law just asserts that r is a *natural transformation* [35], i.e.,

Lemma 3. For each $r : [t(x_1, \ldots, x_n)] \longrightarrow [t'(x_1, \ldots, x_n)]$ in R, the family of morphisms

$$\{r(\overline{[w]}) : [t(\overline{w}/\overline{x})] \longrightarrow [t'(\overline{w}/\overline{x})] \mid \overline{[w]} \in T_{\Sigma, E}(X)^n\}$$

is a natural transformation $r : [t(x_1, \ldots, x_n)] \Longrightarrow [t'(x_1, \ldots, x_n)]$ between the functors

$$[t(x_1, \ldots, x_n)], [t'(x_1, \ldots, x_n)] : \mathcal{T}_\mathcal{R}(X)^n \longrightarrow \mathcal{T}_\mathcal{R}(X).$$

$\square$

What the exchange law provides in general is a way of *abstracting* a rewriting computation by considering immaterial the order in which rewrites are performed "above" and "below" in the term; further abstraction among proof terms is obtained from the functoriality equations. The equations 1-4 provide in a sense the *most abstract* "true concurrency" view of the computations of the rewrite theory $\mathcal{R}$ that can reasonably be given. In particular, we can prove that all proof terms have an equivalent expression as a composition of one-step rewrites:

Lemma 4. For each $[\alpha] : [t] \longrightarrow [t']$ in $\mathcal{T}_\mathcal{R}(X)$, either $[t] = [t']$ and $[\alpha] = [[t]]$, or there is an $n \in \mathbb{N}$ and a chain of morphisms $[\alpha_i]$, $0 \leq i \leq n$ whose terms α_i describe one-step (concurrent) rewrites

$$[t] \xrightarrow{\alpha_0} [t_1] \xrightarrow{\alpha_1} \quad \ldots \quad \xrightarrow{\alpha_{n-1}} [t_n] \xrightarrow{\alpha_n} [t']$$

such that $[\alpha] = [\alpha_0; \ldots; \alpha_n]$. In addition, we can always choose all the α_i corresponding to sequential rewrites, i.e., we can decompose $[\alpha]$ into an interleaving sequence. $\square$

The category $\mathcal{T}_{\mathcal{R}}(X)$ is just one among many *models* that can be assigned to the rewriting theory $\mathcal{R}$. The general notion of model, called an $\mathcal{R}$-system, is defined as follows:

Definition 5. Given a rewrite theory $\mathcal{R} = (\Sigma, E, L, R)$, an $\mathcal{R}$-*system* $\mathcal{S}$ is a category $\mathcal{S}$ together with:

- a (Σ, E)-algebra structure given by a family of functors

$$\{f_{\mathcal{S}} : \mathcal{S}^n \longrightarrow \mathcal{S} \mid f \in \Sigma_n, n \in \mathbb{N}\}$$

  satisfying the equations E, i.e., for any $t(x_1, \ldots, x_n) = t'(x_1, \ldots, x_n)$ in E we have an identity of functors $t_{\mathcal{S}} = t'_{\mathcal{S}}$, where the functor $t_{\mathcal{S}}$ is defined inductively from the functors $f_{\mathcal{S}}$ in the obvious way.
- for each rewrite rule $r : [t(\overline{x})] \longrightarrow [t'(\overline{x})]$ in R a natural transformation $r_{\mathcal{S}} : t_{\mathcal{S}} \Longrightarrow t'_{\mathcal{S}}$.

An $\mathcal{R}$-*homomorphism* $F : \mathcal{S} \longrightarrow \mathcal{S}'$ between two $\mathcal{R}$-systems is then a functor $F : \mathcal{S} \longrightarrow \mathcal{S}'$ such that it is a Σ-algebra homomorphism—i.e., $f_{\mathcal{S}} * F = F^n * f_{\mathcal{S}'}$, for each f in Σ_n, $n \in \mathbb{N}$—and such that "F preserves R," i.e., for each rewrite rule $r : [t(\overline{x})] \longrightarrow [t'(\overline{x})]$ in R we have the identity of natural transformations $r_{\mathcal{S}} * F = F^n * r_{\mathcal{S}'}$, where n is the number of variables appearing in the rule. This defines a category $\mathcal{R}\text{-}Sys$ in the obvious way. $\square$

What the above definition captures formally is the idea that the models of a rewrite theory *are systems*. By a "system" we of course mean a machine-like entity that can be in a variety of *states*, and that can change its state by performing certain *transitions*. Such transitions are of course transitive, and it is natural and convenient to view states as "idle" transitions that do not change the state. In other words, a system can be naturally regarded as a *category*, whose objects are the states of the system and whose morphisms are the system's transitions.

For *sequential* systems such as labelled transition systems this is in a sense the end of the story; such systems exhibit *nondeterminism*, but do not have the required algebraic structure in their states and transitions to exhibit true concurrency (see [41, 42]). Indeed, what makes a system *concurrent* is precisely the existence of an additional *algebraic structure*. Ugo Montanari and the first author first observed this fact for the particular case of Petri nets for which the algebraic structure is precisely that of a commutative monoid [45, 44]; this has been illustrated by the TICKET example in Section 2.2 where the commutative monoid operation $\otimes$ made possible the concurrent firing of several transitions. However, this observation holds in full generality for *any algebraic structure whatever*. What the algebraic structure captures is twofold. Firstly, *the states themselves are distributed according to such a structure*; for Petri nets the distribution takes the form of a *multiset* that we can visualize with tokens and places; for a functional program involving just syntactic rewriting, the distribution takes the form of a *labelled tree structure* which can be spatially distributed in such a way that many transitions (i.e., rewrites) can happen concurrently in a way analogous to the concurrent firing of transitions in a Petri net; a concurrent object-oriented system as specified by a Maude module combines in a sense aspects of the functional and Petri net examples, because its configuration evolves by multiset ACI-rewriting but, underneath such transitions for objects and messages, arbitrarily complex concurrent computations of a functional nature can take place in order to update the values of object attributes as specified by appropriate functional submodules. Secondly, *concurrent transitions are themselves distributed according*

$$
\begin{array}{rcl}
System & \longleftrightarrow & Category \\
State & \longleftrightarrow & Object \\
Transition & \longleftrightarrow & Morphism \\
Procedure & \longleftrightarrow & Natural\ Transformation \\
Distributed\ Structure & \longleftrightarrow & Algebraic\ Structure
\end{array}
$$

Fig. 8. The mathematical structure of concurrent systems.

to the same algebraic structure; this is what the notion of $\mathcal{R}$-system captures, and is for example manifested in the concurrent firing of Petri nets, the evolution of concurrent object-oriented systems and, more generally, in any type of concurrent rewriting.

The expressive power of rewrite theories to specify concurrent transition systems[16] is greatly increased by the possibility of having not only transitions, but also *parameterized transitions*, i.e., *procedures*. This is what rewrite rules—with variables—provide. The family of states to which the procedure applies is given by those states where a component of the (distributed) state is a substitution instance of the lefthand side of the rule in question. The rewrite rule is then a *procedure*[17] which transforms the state *locally*, by replacing such a substitution instance by the corresponding substitution instance of the righthand side. The fact that this can take place concurrently with other transitions "below" is precisely what the concept of a *natural transformation* formalizes. The table of Figure 8 summarizes our present discussion.

A detailed proof of the following theorem on the existence of initial and free $\mathcal{R}$-systems for the more general case of conditional rewrite theories is given in [43], where the soundness and completeness of rewriting logic for $\mathcal{R}$-system models is also proved. Below, for $\mathcal{C}$ a category, $Obj(\mathcal{C})$ denotes the set of its objects.

Theorem 6. $\mathcal{T}_{\mathcal{R}}$ is an initial object in the category $\underline{\mathcal{R}\text{-}Sys}$. More generally, $\mathcal{T}_{\mathcal{R}}(X)$ has the following universal property: Given an $\mathcal{R}$-system $\mathcal{S}$, each function $F : X \longrightarrow Obj(\mathcal{S})$ extends uniquely to an $\mathcal{R}$-homomorphism $F^{\natural} : \mathcal{T}_{\mathcal{R}}(X) \longrightarrow \mathcal{S}$. $\square$

5.1 Preorder, Poset, and Algebra Models

Since $\mathcal{R}$-systems are an "essentially algebraic" concept[18], we can consider classes Θ of $\mathcal{R}$-systems defined by the satisfaction of additional equations. Such classes give rise to full subcategory inclusions $\Theta \hookrightarrow \mathcal{R}\text{-}Sys$, and by general universal algebra results about essentially algebraic theories (see, e.g., [10]) such inclusions are *reflective* [35], i.e., for each $\mathcal{R}$-system $\mathcal{S}$ there is an $\mathcal{R}$-system $R_{\Theta}(\mathcal{S}) \in \Theta$ and an $\mathcal{R}$-homomorphism $\rho_{\Theta}(\mathcal{S}) :$ $\mathcal{S} \longrightarrow R_{\Theta}(\mathcal{S})$ such that for any $\mathcal{R}$-homomorphism $F : \mathcal{S} \longrightarrow \mathcal{D}$ with $\mathcal{D} \in \Theta$ there is a unique $\mathcal{R}$-homomorphism $F^{\diamond} : R_{\Theta}(\mathcal{S}) \longrightarrow \mathcal{D}$ such that $F = \rho_{\Theta}(\mathcal{S}); F^{\diamond}$. The assignment $\mathcal{S} \longmapsto R_{\Theta}(\mathcal{S})$ extends to a functor $\underline{\mathcal{R}\text{-}Sys} \longrightarrow \Theta$, called the *reflection functor*.

---

[16] Such expressive power is further increased by allowing *conditional* rewrite rules, a more general case to which all that is said in this paper has been extended in [43].

[17] Its *actual parameters* are precisely given by a substitution.

[18] In the precise sense of being specifiable by an "essentially algebraic theory" or a "sketch" [10]; see [43].

Therefore, we can consider subcategories of $\mathcal{R}$-Sys that are defined by certain equations and be guaranteed that they have initial and free objects, that they are closed by subobjects and products, etc. Consider for example the following equations:

$$\forall f, g \in Arrows,\ f = g \ \text{ if } \ \partial_0(f) = \partial_0(g) \wedge \partial_1(f) = \partial_1(g)$$
$$\forall f, g \in Arrows,\ f = g \ \text{ if } \ \partial_0(f) = \partial_1(g) \wedge \partial_1(f) = \partial_0(g)$$
$$\forall f \in Arrows,\ \partial_0(f) = \partial_1(f).$$

where $\partial_0(f)$ and $\partial_1(f)$ denote the source and target of an arrow f respectively. The first equation forces a category to be a preorder, the addition of the second requires this preorder to be a poset, and the three equations together force the poset to be *discrete*, i.e., just a set. By imposing the first one, the first two, or all three, we get full subcategories

$$\mathcal{R}\text{-}Alg \subseteq \mathcal{R}\text{-}Pos \subseteq \mathcal{R}\text{-}Preord \subseteq \mathcal{R}\text{-}Sys.$$

A routine inspection of $\mathcal{R}$-$Preord$ for $\mathcal{R} = (\Sigma, E, L, R)$ reveals that its objects are pre-ordered Σ-algebras $(A, \leq)$ (i.e., preordered sets with a Σ-algebra structure such that all the operations in Σ are monotonic) that satisfy the equations E and such that for each rewrite rule $r : [t(\overline{x})] \longrightarrow [t'(\overline{x})]$ in R and for each $\overline{a} \in A^n$ we have, $t_A(\overline{a}) \geq t'_A(\overline{a})$. The poset case is entirely analogous, except that the relation $\leq$ is a partial order instead of being a preorder. Finally, $\mathcal{R}$-Alg is the category of ordinary Σ-algebras that satisfy the equations $E \cup unlabel(R)$, where the *unlabel* function removes the labels from the rules and turns the sequent signs " $\longrightarrow$ " into equality signs.

The reflection functor associated with the inclusion $\mathcal{R}$-$Preord \subseteq \mathcal{R}$-$Sys$, sends $\mathcal{T}_{\mathcal{R}}(X)$ to the familiar $\mathcal{R}$-*rewriting relation*[19] $\to_{\mathcal{R}(X)}$ on E-equivalence classes of terms with variables in X. Similarly, the reflection associated to the inclusion $\mathcal{R}$-$Pos \subseteq \mathcal{R}$-$Sys$ maps $\mathcal{T}_{\mathcal{R}}(X)$ to the partial order $\geq_{\mathcal{R}(X)}$ obtained from the preorder $\to_{\mathcal{R}(X)}$ by identifying any two $[t], [t']$ such that $[t] \to_{\mathcal{R}(X)}[t']$ and $[t'] \to_{\mathcal{R}(X)}[t]$. Finally, the reflection functor into $\mathcal{R}$-Alg maps $\mathcal{T}_{\mathcal{R}}(X)$ to $T_{\mathcal{R}}(X)$, the free Σ-algebra on X satisfying the equations $E \cup unlabel(R)$; therefore, the classical *initial algebra semantics* of (functional) equational specifications reappears here associated with a very special class of models which—when viewed as systems—have only trivial identity transitions.

5.2 The Semantics of Maude

This paper has shown that, by generalizing the logic and the model theory of equational logic to those of rewriting logic, a much broader field of applications for rewrite rule programming is possible—based on the idea of programming *concurrent systems* rather than *algebras*, and including, in particular, concurrent object-oriented programming. The same high standards of mathematical rigor enjoyed by equational logic can be maintained in giving semantics to a language like Maude in the broader context of rewriting logic. We present below a specific proposal for such a semantics having the advantages of keeping functional modules as a sublanguage with a more specialized semantics. Another appealing characteristic of the proposed semantics is that the operational and mathematical semantics of modules are related in a particularly nice way. As already mentioned, all

---

[19] It is perhaps more suggestive to call $\to_{\mathcal{R}(X)}$ the *reachability relation* of the system $\mathcal{T}_{\mathcal{R}}(X)$.

the ideas and results in this paper extend without problem[20] to the *order-sorted* case; the unsorted case has only been used for the sake of a simpler exposition. Therefore, all that is said below is understood in the context of order-sorted rewriting logic.

We have already seen that object-oriented modules can be reduced to equivalent system modules having the same behavior but giving a more explicit description of the type structure. Therefore, of the three kinds of modules existing in Maude, namely functional, system and object-oriented, we need only provide a semantics for functional and system modules; they are respectively of the form fmod $\mathcal{R}$ endfm, and mod $\mathcal{R}'$ endm, for $\mathcal{R}$ and $\mathcal{R}'$ rewriting theories[21]. Their semantics is given in terms of an *initial machine* linking the module's operational semantics with its denotational semantics. The general notion of a machine is as follows.

Definition 7. For $\mathcal{R}$ a rewrite theory and $\Theta \hookrightarrow \mathcal{R}\text{-}Sys$ a reflective full subcategory, an $\mathcal{R}$-*machine over* Θ is an $\mathcal{R}$-homomorphism $[\![\_]\!] : \mathcal{S} \longrightarrow \mathcal{M}$, called the machine's *abstraction map*, with $\mathcal{S}$ an $\mathcal{R}$-system and $\mathcal{M} \in \Theta$. Given $\mathcal{R}$-machines over Θ, $[\![\_]\!] : \mathcal{S} \longrightarrow \mathcal{M}$ and $[\![\_]\!]' : \mathcal{S}' \longrightarrow \mathcal{M}'$, an $\mathcal{R}$-machine *homomorphism* is a pair of $\mathcal{R}$-homomorphisms (F, G), $F : \mathcal{S} \longrightarrow \mathcal{S}'$, $G : \mathcal{M} \longrightarrow \mathcal{M}'$, such that $[\![\_]\!]; G = F; [\![\_]\!]'$. This defines a category $\mathcal{R}\text{-}Mach/\Theta$; it is easy to check that the initial object in this category is the unique $\mathcal{R}$-homomorphism $\mathcal{T}_\mathcal{R} \longrightarrow R_\Theta(\mathcal{T}_\mathcal{R})$. $\square$

The intuitive idea behind a machine $[\![\_]\!] : \mathcal{S} \longrightarrow \mathcal{M}$ is that we can use a *system* $\mathcal{S}$ to *compute* a result relevant for a *model* $\mathcal{M}$ of interest in a class Θ of models. What we do is to perform a certain computation in $\mathcal{S}$, and then output the result by means of the abstraction map $[\![\_]\!]$. A very good example is an *arithmetic machine* with $\mathcal{S} = \mathcal{T}_{\text{NAT}}$, for NAT the rewriting theory of the Peano natural numbers corresponding to the module NAT[22] in Section 2, with $\mathcal{M} = \mathbb{N}$, and with $[\![\_]\!]$ the unique homomorphism from the initial NAT-system $\mathcal{T}_{\text{NAT}}$; i.e., this is the initial machine in NAT-*Mach*/NAT-*Alg*. To compute the result of an arithmetic expression t, we perform a terminating rewriting and output the corresponding number, which is an element of $\mathbb{N}$.

Each choice of a reflective full subcategory Θ as a category of models yields a different semantics. As already implicit in the arithmetic machine example, the *semantics of a functional module*[23] fmod $\mathcal{R}$ endfm is the initial machine in $\mathcal{R}\text{-}Mach/\mathcal{R}\text{-}Alg$. For the *semantics of a system module* mod $\mathcal{R}$ endm not having any functional submodules. We propose the initial machine in $\mathcal{R}\text{-}Mach/\mathcal{R}\text{-}Preord$, but other choices are also possible. On the one hand, we could choose to be as concrete as possible and take $\Theta = \mathcal{R}\text{-}Sys$ in which case the abstraction map is the identity homomorphism for $\mathcal{T}_\mathcal{R}$. On the other hand, we could instead be even more abstract, and choose $\Theta = \mathcal{R}\text{-}Pos$; however, this would have the unfortunate effect of collapsing all the states of a cyclic rewriting, which seems undesirable for many "reactive" systems. If the machine $\mathcal{T}_\mathcal{R} \longrightarrow \mathcal{M}$ is the semantics of a functional or system module with rewrite theory $\mathcal{R}$, then we call $\mathcal{T}_\mathcal{R}$ the module's

---

[20] Exercising of course the well known precaution of making explicit the universal quantification of rules.

[21] This is somewhat inaccurate in the case of system modules having functional submodules, which is treated in [41], because we have to "remember" that the submodule in question is functional.

[22] In this case E is the commutativity attribute, and R consists of the two rules for addition.

[23] For this semantics to behave well, the rules R in the functional module $\mathcal{R}$ should be *confluent* modulo E.

operational semantics, and $\mathcal{M}$ its *denotational semantics*. Therefore, the operational and denotational semantics of a module can be extracted from its initial machine semantics by projecting to the domain or codomain of the abstraction map. Note that this makes Maude a *logic programming language* in the general axiomatic sense of [39].

6 Concluding Remarks

Within the space constraints of this paper it is impossible to do justice to the wealth of related literature on concurrent object-oriented programming, term rewriting, abstract data types, concurrency theory, Petri nets, linear and equational logic, ordered, continuous and nondeterministic algebras, etc. A lengthier report [43] contains 123 such references.

The present paper is a report of work in progress. Although the logical foundations of Maude are well established, much remains to be done to move the ideas forward in several directions, including the following:

- More experience should be gained with examples to advance the language design and to further explore the capabilities of the language. In particular, Maude's object-oriented aspects should be further developed. This will also help in sharpening and expanding the boundaries of Maude and Simple Maude.
- Specification and verification aspects need to be studied. The logics of specification should not be limited to equational and rewriting logic. Rewriting logic should be embedded within a richer logic to be used for specification purposes. This will increase the expressiveness of Maude's functional, system and object-oriented theories.
- The study of parameterization and modularity issues, already initiated in [42] and [41] respectively, should be advanced.
- The work on program transformations to derive more efficient and more easily implementable modules from less efficient ones or even from specifications should be continued and advanced. More generally, the design of machine-independent program analysis and program optimization tools based on the concurrent rewriting model should be explored.
- Implementation and compilation techniques for various classes of parallel architectures should be studied in more detail, trying to achieve the greatest possible degree of portability and genericity across different machine implementations. A Maude interpreter should be developed, as well as a portable parallel implementation of Simple Maude.
- Multilingual extensions and uses of Maude in the context of open heterogeneous systems need to be studied in greater detail.
- Maude's multiparadigm capabilities should be further extended. In particular, the inclusion of Horn clause logic programming could be based on a map of logics (in the sense of [39]) between Horn logic and rewriting logic. This approach should be compared in detail with work on concurrent logic programming [49] and with other recent proposals to provide a semantic basis for concurrent Horn clause programming such as those of Corradini and Montanari [16], and Andreoli and Pareschi's work on linear logic programming [7].

References

1. M. Abadi, L. Cardelli, P.-L. Curien, and J.-J. Lévy. Explicit Substitution. In *Proc. POPL'90*, pages 31–46. ACM, 1990.
2. G. Agha. *Actors*. MIT Press, 1986.
3. G. Agha and C. Hewitt. Concurrent programming using actors. In A. Yonezawa and M. Tokoro, editors, *Object-Oriented Concurrent Programming*. MIT Press, 1988.
4. H. Aida, J. Goguen, S. Leinwand, P. Lincoln, J. Meseguer, B. Taheri, and T. Winkler. Simulation and performance estimation for the rewrite rule machine. Submitted for publication, 1991.
5. Hitoshi Aida, Joseph Goguen, and José Meseguer. Compiling concurrent rewriting onto the rewrite rule machine. In S. Kaplan and M. Okada, editors, *Conditional and Typed Rewriting Systems, Montreal, Canada, June 1990*, pages 320–332. Springer LNCS 516, 1991.
6. Hitoshi Aida, Sany Leinwand, and José Meseguer. Architectural design of the rewrite rule machine ensemble. To appear in J. Delgado-Frias and W.R. More, editors, *Proc. Workshop on VLSI for Artificial Intelligence and Neural Networks*, Oxford, September 1990; also, Tech. Report SRI-CSL-90-17, December 1990.
7. Jean-Marc Andreoli and Remo Pareschi. LO and behold! Concurrent structured processes. In *ECOOP-OOPSLA'90 Conference on Object-Oriented Programming, Ottawa, Canada, October 1990*, pages 44–56. ACM, 1990.
8. J.-P. Banâtre, A. Coutant, and D. Le Mètayer. Parallel machines for multiset transformation and their programming style. *Informationstechnik it*, 30(2):99–109, 1988.
9. J.-P. Banâtre and D. Le Mètayer. The Gamma model and its discipline of programming. *Science of Computer Programming*, 15:55–77, 1990.
10. M. Barr and C. Wells. *Toposes, Triples and Theories*. Springer-Verlag, 1985.
11. Gérard Berry and Gérard Boudol. The Chemical Abstract Machine. In *Proc. POPL'90*, pages 81–94. ACM, 1990.
12. N. Carriero and D. Gelernter. Linda in context. *Communications of the Association for Computing Machinery*, 32:444–458, April 1989.
13. K. Mani Chandy and Jayadev Misra. *Parallel Program Design: A Foundation*. Addison-Wesley, 1988.
14. K. Mani Chandy and Stephen Taylor. *An Introduction to Parallel Programming*. Addison-Wesley, 1991.
15. Will Clinger. Foundations of actor semantics. Technical report AI-TR-633, Massachusetts Institute of Technology, Artificial Intelligence Laboratory, 1981.
16. Andrea Corradini and Ugo Montanari. An algebraic semantics of logic programs as structured transition systems. In S. Debray and M. Hermenegildo, editors, *North American Conference on Logic Programming*, pages 788–812. MIT Press, 1990.
17. William Dally. Network and processor architecture for message-driven computers. In R. Suaya and G. Birtwistle, editors, *VLSI and Parallel Computation*, pages 140–222. Morgan Kaufmann, 1990.
18. N. Dershowitz and J.-P. Jouannaud. Rewrite systems. In J. van Leeuwen, editor, *Handbook of Theoretical Computer Science, Vol. B*, pages 243–320. North-Holland, 1990.
19. J. Engelfriet, G. Leih, and G. Rozenberg. Parallel object-based systems and Petri nets, I and II. Technical Report 90-04,90-05, Dept. of Computer Science, University of Leiden, February 1990.
20. J. Engelfriet, G. Leih, and G. Rozenberg. Net-based description of parallel object-based systems, or POTs and POPs. In J. W. de Bakker, W. P. de Roever, and G. Rozenberg, editors, *Foundations of Object-Oriented Languages, Noordwijkerhout, The Netherlands, May/June 1990*, pages 229–273. Springer LNCS 489, 1991.
21. Ian Foster and Stephen Taylor. *Strand: new concepts in parallel programming*. Prentice Hall, 1990.

22. J.A. Goguen, T. Winkler, J. Meseguer, K. Futatsugi, and J.-P. Jouannaud. Introducing OBJ. Technical report, Computer Science Lab, SRI International, 1991. To appear in J.A. Goguen, D. Coleman and R. Gallimore, editors, *Applications of Algebraic Specification Using OBJ*, Cambridge University Press.

23. Joseph Goguen, Claude Kirchner, Hélène Kirchner, Aristide Mégrelis, José Meseguer, and Timothy Winkler. An introduction to OBJ3. In Jean-Pierre Jouannaud and Stephane Kaplan, editors, *Proceedings, Conference on Conditional Term Rewriting, Orsay, France, July 8-10, 1987*, pages 258–263. Springer LNCS 308, 1988.

24. Joseph Goguen, Claude Kirchner, and José Meseguer. Concurrent term rewriting as a model of computation. In R. Keller and J. Fasel, editors, *Proc. Workshop on Graph Reduction, Santa Fe, New Mexico*, pages 53–93. Springer LNCS 279, 1987.

25. Joseph Goguen and José Meseguer. Unifying functional, object-oriented and relational programming with logical semantics. In Bruce Shriver and Peter Wegner, editors, *Research Directions in Object-Oriented Programming*, pages 417–477. MIT Press, 1987. Preliminary version in *SIGPLAN Notices*, Volume 21, Number 10, pages 153-162, October 1986; also, Technical Report CSLI-87-93, Center for the Study of Language and Information, Stanford University, March 1987.

26. Joseph Goguen and José Meseguer. Software for the rewrite rule machine. In *Proceedings of the International Conference on Fifth Generation Computer Systems, Tokyo, Japan*, pages 628–637. ICOT, 1988.

27. Joseph Goguen and José Meseguer. Order-sorted algebra I: Equational deduction for multiple inheritance, overloading, exceptions and partial operations. Technical Report SRI-CSL-89-10, SRI International, Computer Science Lab, July 1989. Given as lecture at Seminar on Types, Carnegie-Mellon University, June 1983. Submitted for publication.

28. Joseph Goguen, José Meseguer, Sany Leinwand, Timothy Winkler, and Hitoshi Aida. The rewrite rule machine. Technical Report SRI-CSL-89-6, SRI International, Computer Science Lab, March 1989.

29. Joseph Goguen, James Thatcher, Eric Wagner, and Jesse Wright. Initial algebra semantics and continuous algebras. *Journal of the Association for Computing Machinery*, 24(1):68–95, January 1977.

30. *HOT Chips II*. IEEE, 1990. Record of Symposium held at Santa Clara University August 20–21, 1990.

31. Paul Hudak and Eric Mohr. Graphinators and the duality of SIMD and MIMD. In *ACM Symposium on Lisp and Functional Programming*, pages 224–234. ACM, 1988.

32. Gerard Huet. Confluent reductions: Abstract properties and applications to term rewriting systems. *Journal of the Association for Computing Machinery*, 27:797–821, 1980. Preliminary version in *18th Symposium on Mathematical Foundations of Computer Science*, 1977.

33. R. Jagannathan and A.A. Faustini. The GLU programming language. Technical Report SRI-CSL-90-11, SRI International, Computer Science Laboratory, November 1990.

34. Simon S. Lam and A. Udaya Shankar. A relational notation for state transition systems. *IEEE Transactions on Software Engineering*, SE-16(7):755–775, July 1990.

35. Saunders MacLane. *Categories for the working mathematician*. Springer-Verlag, 1971.

36. Narciso Martí-Oliet and José Meseguer. From Petri nets to linear logic. In D.H. Pitt et al., editor, *Category Theory and Computer Science*, pages 313–340. Springer LNCS 389, 1989. Final version in *Mathematical Structures in Computer Science*, 1:69-101, 1991.

37. Narciso Martí-Oliet and José Meseguer. An algebraic axiomatization of linear logic models. In G.M. Reed, A.W. Roscoe, and R. Wachter, editors, *Topology and Category Theory in Computer Science*, pages 335–355. Oxford University Press, 1991. Also Technical Report SRI-CSL-89-11, SRI International, Computer Science Lab, December 1989.

38. Satoshi Matsuoka, Ken Wakita, and Akinori Yonezawa. Inheritance anomaly in object-oriented concurrent programming languages. Dept. of Information Science, University of Tokyo, January 1991.

39. José Meseguer. General logics. In H.-D. Ebbinghaus et al., editor, *Logic Colloquium '87*, pages 275–329. North-Holland, 1989.

40. José Meseguer. A logical theory of concurrent objects. In *ECOOP-OOPSLA '90 Conference on Object-Oriented Programming, Ottawa, Canada, October 1990*, pages 101–115. ACM, 1990.

41. José Meseguer. Rewriting as a unified model of concurrency. In *Proceedings of the Concur '90 Conference, Amsterdam, August 1990*, pages 384–400. Springer LNCS 458, 1990.

42. José Meseguer. Rewriting as a unified model of concurrency. Technical Report SRI-CSL-90-02, SRI International, Computer Science Laboratory, February 1990. Revised June 1990.

43. José Meseguer. Conditional rewriting logic as a unified model of concurrency. Technical Report SRI-CSL-91-05, SRI International, Computer Science Laboratory, February 1991. To appear in *Theoretical Computer Science*, 94, 1992.

44. José Meseguer and Ugo Montanari. Petri nets are monoids: A new algebraic foundation for net theory. In *Proc. LICS'88*, pages 155–164. IEEE, 1988.

45. José Meseguer and Ugo Montanari. Petri nets are monoids. *Information and Computation*, 88:105–155, 1990. Appeared as SRI Tech Report SRI-CSL-88-3, January 1988.

46. Robin Milner. *Communication and Concurrency*. Prentice Hall, 1989.

47. Wolfgang Reisig. *Petri Nets*. Springer-Verlag, 1985.

48. Charles L. Seitz. Concurrent architectures. In R. Suaya and G. Birtwistle, editors, *VLSI and Parallel Computation*, pages 1–84. Morgan Kaufmann, 1990.

49. E. Shapiro. The family of concurrent logic programming languages. *ACM Computing Surveys*, 21:413–510, 1989.

50. Arthur Trew and Greg Wilson, editors. *Past, Present, Parallel: A Survey of Parallel Computing at the Beginning of the 1990s*. Springer-Verlag, 1991.

Part 4: Parallel Program Design

Parallel Program Design

Jean-Pierre Banâtre

Irisa, Campus de Beaulieu, 35042 Rennes Cedex, France

It is often advocated that parallel programming is more difficult than sequential programming. Some design methodologies for sequential programs have been proposed but similar methods do not exist for parallel program design. Papers presented in this session report experiences in parallel program design which show that robust and reliable parallel programming is feasible if an appropriate discipline is obeyed.

The first two papers deal with the systematic design of systolic algorithms. These algorithms represent a basic paradigm for programming massively parallel architectures with an underlying communication model based on systolic arrays. The regularity of systolic arrays makes it possible to derive algorithms from very high level specifications such as recurrent equations.

In their paper, Hervé Le Verge and Patrice Quinton describe ALPHA, a functional language (and its associated derivation method) based on recurrence equations. The specifications of the problem to be solved are expressed in ALPHA and after some transformation steps a systolic algorithm, also described in ALPHA, is produced. The method is applied to palindrome recognition.

Another method is proposed by Michael Barnett and Christian Lengauer. Their transformation technique takes as input a systolizable source program and the abstract description of a systolic array and it returns a program which emulates this systolic array. The method is applied to the linear phase filter.

The paper by Henrik Hulgaard, Per H. Christensen, and Jørgen Staunstrup introduces a technique for automatic synthesis of delay insensitive circuits from high level programs written in a language called "synchronized transitions". Application specific circuits are described as synchronized transitions, formally verified and automatically translated into asynchronous circuits. Formal verifications are used in particular to check that the initial specification can be implemented as a delay insensitive circuit.

H Peter Hofstee, Johan J. Lukkien and Jan L.A. van de Snepscheut take a sequential program as starting point and transform it into a distributed algorithm. The method is applied to the implementation of a task pool. The produced algorithm takes care of the distribution of the tasks over processors and ensures load balancing. The transformation is guided by a careful distribution of data over processes.

Michel Sintzoff shows that dynamical systems can be studied in the framework of the theory of non-deterministic programs. Fixpoints and termination are the natural counterparts in the theory of programs of two fundamental concepts of dynamical systems: equilibrium and stability. The approach is illustrated with the analysis of a collection of classical examples.

Daniel Herman and Laurent Trilling introduce a new control structure, called Distributed Procedure Call, for the description of parallel algorithms. This control structure is used to develop a distributed sort program.

This section gives the impression that substantial progress has been made in the design of parallel programs. Some common techniques are emerging and should be consolidated by further research.

The palindrome systolic array revisited[*]

Hervé Le Verge and Patrice Quinton

IRISA-CNRS, Campus de Beaulieu, 35042 Rennes Cedex, France
e-mail : quinton@irisa.fr

1 Introduction

As density of integrated circuit increases, parallel arrays – i.e. systolic arrays[Kun82], wavefront arrays[KAGR82], regular iterative arrays[Rao85], to name a few types of such architectures – become one of the favorite architectural style of special-purpose system designers. The reasons are well known. Parallel arrays have high performances and are modular, and these properties make them well suited for implementing systems commonly found in many application areas. On the other hand, the main concern of system designers is to produce as quickly as possible a special-purpose system – i.e. a combination of hardware and software – without default. Parallel regular arrays are complex algorithms, thus difficult to master. This often leads to errors in the design process.

The purpose of this article is to present a language, ALPHA, and its use for the synthesis of regular arrays. To this end, we consider the famous example of the palindrome recognizer, which has served as a support for the illustration of various design methodologies. This algorithm is considered by Cole[Col69], who describes a systolic array. Leiserson and Saxe[LS81] consider this example to illustrate their Systolic Conversion Theorem. More recently, Van de Snepscheut and Swenker[dSS89] also investigate the derivation of parallel algorithms for the palindrome recognition, by means of stepwise refinement method.

In Sect. 2, we first summarize the characteristics of the ALPHA language. Then, Sect. 3 explains in detail the synthesis of a real-time palindrome recognizer, thus illustrating the potential of ALPHA.

2 The ALPHA language

The principles of ALPHA have been presented in detail elsewhere[DVQS91, DGL*91, LMQ91]. The purpose of this section is just to introduce the non familiar reader with the notations and main ideas of the language.

The ALPHA language is based on the recurrence equation formalism. It is therefore an *equational language*, whose constructs are well-suited to the expression of regular

---

[*] This work was partially funded by the French Coordinated Research Program C^3 and by the Esprit BRA project NANA.

algorithms. The ALPHA language can also be used to describe *synchronous systems,* and therefore, provides a natural framework for the transformation of *algorithm specifications* into *architectures.* Interactive transformations of ALPHA programs can be done using the ALPHA DU CENTAUR environment, implemented with the language design system CENTAUR[BCD*87]. ALPHA DU CENTAUR includes a library of mathematical routines that are used to search efficient transformations of programs.

2.1 The basics

An ALPHA program is a collection of single assignment equations. ALPHA follows the classical principles of a *structured, strongly typed functional language.*

To explain the language, let us consider the ALPHA program, also called a *system of equations,* presented in Fig. 1 which represents an iterative version of the calculation

```
system example ( X : {i|1 ≤ i ≤ 3} of integer )
returns ( s : integer );
var
sum : {i|0 ≤ i ≤ 3} of integer ;
let
sum = case
      {i|i = 0} : 0.(i →);
      {i|1 ≤ i ≤ 3} : X + sum.(i → i − 1);
      esac;
s    = sum.(→ 3);
tel ;
```

Fig. 1. Example of ALPHA program

$s = \sum_{i=1}^{3} X_i$. This program takes an input variable X, indexed on the set $\{i|1 \leq i \leq 3\}$ of integer, and returns an integer s. Moreover, there is local variable *sum,* defined on the set $\{i|0 \leq i \leq 3\}$. Between the keywords **let** and **tel**, we find the definition of *sum* and *s*. Each definition provides a synonymy between a variable and an ALPHA expression. ALPHA variables and expressions are in fact functions from an index domain of $\mathbf{Z}^n$ – the *spatial domain* of the variable or the expression– to a set of values of a given type (boolean, integer, real, in the current version.) Spatial domains of ALPHA variables are restricted to integral points of convex polyhedral domains (see [Sch86] for notions on convex polyhedra).

2.2 Motionless and spatial operators

ALPHA expressions are obtained by combining variables (or recursively, expressions) together with two sorts of operators : *motionless operators* and *spatial operators.*

Motionless operators are the generalization of classical operators to ALPHA expressions. Operators defined in such a way are usual unary and binary operators on basic types, and the conditional operator **if..then..else**. As an example, given one-dimensional variables X and Y, the expression $X + Y$ represents a function defined on the intersection of the domains of X and Y, and whose value at index i is $X_i + Y_i$.

Spatial operators are the only operators which operate explicitly on spatial domains. The *dependence operator* combines *dependence functions* and expressions. Dependence functions are affine mapping between spatial domains, and are denoted $(i, j, \ldots \rightarrow f(i, j, ..))$ where f is an affine mapping. Given an expression E and a dependence function dep, $E.dep$ denotes the composition of functions E and dep. As an example, the expression $sum.(i \rightarrow i - 1)$ denotes the expression whose i-th element is sum_{i-1}. Note that constants are defined on $\mathbf{Z}^0$, and $(\rightarrow i)$ denotes the mapping from $\mathbf{Z}^0$ to $\mathbf{Z}$: the definition $s = sum.(\rightarrow 3)$ in Fig. 1 says that s is sum_3 (the value of sum at index 3.) The *restriction* operator restricts the domain of an expression, by means of linear constraints. In Fig. 1, the expression $\{i | 1 \leq i \leq 3\} : X + sum.(i \rightarrow i - 1)$ restricts the domain of $X + sum.(i \rightarrow i - 1)$ to the segment $[1, 3]$. The **case** operator combines expressions defined on disjoint domains into a new expression, as the variable sum of program shown in Fig. 1.

The spatial operators allow recurrence equations to be expressed. In Fig. 1, the value of the variable sum is the sequence of partial sums of the elements of X and is defined by means of a **case**, whose first branch specifies the initialization part and the second one the recurrence itself.

2.3 Basic transformations

As any functional language, ALPHA follows the substitution principle : any variable can be substituted by its definition, without changing the meaning of the program. Substituting sum in the definition of s in program of Fig. 1, gives the program shown in Fig. 2. One

```
system example (  X : {i|1 ≤ i ≤ 3} of integer )
returns (  s : integer );
var
sum : {i|0 ≤ i ≤ 3} of integer ;
let
sum = case
        {i|i = 0} : 0.(i →);
        {i|i > 0} : X + sum.(i → i − 1);
        esac;
s    = ( case
        {i|i = 0} : 0.(i →);
        {i|i > 0} : X + sum.(i → i − 1);
        esac).(→ 3);
tel ;
```

Fig. 2. Program 1 after substituting sum by its definition

can show that any ALPHA expression can be rewritten in an equivalent expression, called its *normal form*, whose structure is composed of a unique **case**, and all dependencies are directly associated with variables and constants. This normal form is also called *Case-Restriction-Dependence* form. The normalization process often simplifies an expression, and can be used, together with the substitution, to do a symbolic simulation of an ALPHA program. For example, the definition of s in program (2) becomes after normalization :

$$s = X.(\rightarrow 3) + sum.(\rightarrow 2);$$

and by repeating this process :

$$s = X.(\rightarrow 3) + (X.(\rightarrow 2) + (X.(\rightarrow 1) + 0.(\rightarrow)));$$

which is just the definition of s.

A *change of basis* can be applied to the index space of any local variable, using a straightforward syntactic transformation of the equations [LMQ90]: in order to apply the change of basis defined by a unimodular dependence function *dep* to a variable X, one needs to replace the definition domain of X by its image by *dep*, to replace right-hand side occurrences of X by $X.dep$, and finally to replace the equation $X = exp$ by $X = exp.dep^{-1}$. The case when *dep* is not unimodular can be dealt with by first embedding the variable X in a higher dimensional index space. The change of basis transformation is the core of *space-time reindexing*, as will be shown below.

3 Synthesis of a real-time palindrome recognizer

The goal of the following ALPHA exercise is to show how the classical systolic palindrome array described in [Col69] can be synthesized from "as high-level a specification as possible". After describing this initial specification, we outline each one of the transformations needed to reach an ALPHA program "reasonably close" to the hardware description of the solution. All transformations, but a few ones that we will mention, were performed using ALPHA DU CENTAUR, that is to say, fully automatically. However, the choice of the transformations to be applied and the order of their applications was manual. We should emphasize that the goal was *not* to find out a new palindrome recognizer, but rather to prove by construction the correctness of an implementation of the classical solution.

3.1 The problem and its initial specification

Let $a = a_0.....a_{n-1}$ be a string of n characters. It is said to be a *palindrome* if, for all i, $0 \leq i \leq n - 1$, a_i is equal to a_{n-i-1}. The problem we want to solve is to find out a *real-time palindrome recognizer*, that is to say, a device which reads a_i in increasing order of i, and answers immediately after reading a_{n-1} whether $a_0....a_{n-1}$ is a palindrome or not. From this informal description of the algorithm, we get the first ALPHA program of Fig. 3. The program takes the string a as input, and returns a boolean function *pal*, defined as

$$pal_n = \bigwedge_{0 \leq i < (n-1)/2} (a_i = a_{n-i-1}). \tag{1}$$

Without loss of generality, the actual program presents the derivation of a *bounded* palindrome array, able only to handle strings of at most 8 symbols. The definition of *pal* uses the reduction operator **red** od ALPHA, whose precise description and operation are beyond the scope of this paper[Lev91].

```
system palindrome ( a : {i|7 ≥ i ≥ 0} of integer )
returns ( pal : {n|n ≥ 1} of integer );

let
pal = red( ∧ , (i, n → n) , {i, n|8 ≥ n ≥ 2i + 2} : a.(i, n → i) = a. (i, n → −i + n − 1) );
tel ;
```

Fig. 3. Initial specification of the palindrome algorithm

3.2 Serialization of the reduction operator

Figure 4 shows the program, after replacing the reduction operator by a recurrence. To do so, we need to introduce a new variable, p, defined over a domain of dimension 2. This variable is defined by a recurrence, initialized with the null element of $\wedge$, i.e., **true**. The recurrence is done by decreasing value of the index i in the reduction of equation (1). The result pal of the program is now defined by $pal_n = p_{0,n}$.

```
system palindrome ( a : {i|i ≥ 0; 7 ≥ i} of integer )
returns ( pal : {n|n ≥ 1} of integer );
var
p : {i, n|i ≥ 0; 8 ≥ n; n ≥ 2i + 2} ,
    {i, n|i ≥ 1; 2i + 1 ≥ n; n ≥ 2i; 8 ≥ n} of boolean ;
let
pal = {i|8 ≥ i; i ≥ 2} : p.(i → 0, i);
p   = case
      {i, n|i ≥ 1; 2i + 1 ≥ n; n ≥ 2i; 8 ≥ n} : true.(i, n →);
      {i, n|i ≥ 0; 8 ≥ n; n ≥ 2i + 2} : p.(i, n → i + 1, n) ∧
      a.(i, n → i) = a. (i, n → −i + n − 1);
      esac;
tel ;
```

Fig. 4. Version after serialization of $\bigwedge$

3.3 Uniformization

The next transformation, referred to as *uniformization, pipelining*, or *localization* in the literature, is rather complex. The definition of p in the program of Fig. 4 contains two instances of the variable a which are not two-dimensional. The uniformization transformation aims to replace these instances by new variables $A1$ and $A2$, which are defined by induction on the domain of the variable p, in such a way that the arguments of the equation be defined on the same domain, thus leading to *uniform recurrence equations*[KMW67]. The interested reader will find in [QD89] details on this transformation.

```
system palindrome ( a : {i|i ≥ 0; 7 ≥ i} of integer )
returns ( pal : {n|n ≥ 1} of integer );
var
A2 : {i, n|i ≥ 0; 8 ≥ n; n ≥ 2i + 1} of integer;
A1 : {i, n|i ≥ 0; 8 ≥ n; n ≥ 2i + 2} of integer;
p  : {i, n|i ≥ 0; 8 ≥ n; n ≥ 2i + 2} ,
     {i, n|n ≥ 2i; i ≥ 1; 8 ≥ n; 2i + 1 ≥ n} of boolean ;
let
pal = {i|8 ≥ i; i ≥ 2} : p.(i → 0, i);
p  = case
         {i, n|n ≥ 2i; i ≥ 1; 8 ≥ n; 2i + 1 ≥ n} : true.(i, n →);
         {i, n|i ≥ 0; 8 ≥ n; n ≥ 2i + 2} : p.(i, n → i + 1, n) ∧ A1 = A2;
         esac;
A1 = case
         {i, n|i ≥ 0; 3 ≥ i; n = 2i + 2} : a.(i, n → i);
         {i, n|i ≥ 0; 8 ≥ n; n ≥ 2i + 3} : A1.(i, n → i, n − 1);
         esac;
A2 = case
         {i, n|i = 0; 8 ≥ n; n ≥ 1} : a.(i, n → −i + n − 1);
         {i, n|8 ≥ n; i ≥ 1; n ≥ 2i + 1} : A2.(i, n → i − 1, n − 1);
         esac;
tel ;
```

Fig. 5. Version after uniformization

3.4 Connecting $A1$ and $A2$

The uniformization of the occurrences of a in the definition of p done in Sect. 3.3, has
the effect of introducing two different flows of a data: one for the variable $A1$, and one
for $A2$. This situation, although perfectly correct, is undesirable from the point of view
of the architecture design, as it will result in two flows of data carrying the same values.
To avoid this problem, one can "connect" these flows, by noticing that the initial values
of $A1$, defined in the branch

$$\{i, n|i ≥ 0; 3 ≥ i; n = 2i + 2\} : a.(i, n → i);$$

of the case expression, are in fact equal to $A2.(i, n → i, n−1)$. The result is shown in Fig.
6. This rather heuristic transformation cannot be done automatically. However, one can

```
A1 = case
         {i, n|i ≥ 0; 3 ≥ i; n = 2i + 2} : A2.(i, n → i, n − 1);
         {i, n|i ≥ 0; 8 ≥ n; n ≥ 2i + 3} : A1.(i, n → i, n − 1);
         esac;
```

Fig. 6. Connection $A1$ and $A2$

prove that the resulting program is equivalent by repeated substitution and normalization
of $A2$ in the new equation.

3.5 Initialization of p

A similar transformation has to be applied to the initialization part of the equation which defines p. The idea behind this transformation is, by anticipating the final shape of the architecture, to avoid broadcasting an initialization control signal to all the cells of the architecture. To this end, the initialization part of the definition of p is split in two sub-equations, each one defined on one segment domain (see Fig. 7). Then, uniformization is applied on each new equation.

```
p = case
      {i, n|7 ≥ 2i; i ≥ 1; 2i + 1 = n} : true.(i, n →);
      {i, n|i ≥ 1; 4 ≥ i; n = 2i} : true.(i, n →);
      {i, n|i ≥ 0; 8 ≥ n; n ≥ 2i + 2} : p.(i, n → i + 1, n) ∧ A1 = A2;
    esac;
```

Fig. 7. Splitting the initialization part of the definition of p

```
system palindrome ( a : {i|i ≥ 0; 7 ≥ i} of integer )
returns ( pal : {n|n ≥ 1} of integer );
var
init2 :   {i, n|i ≥ 1; 4 ≥ i; n = 2i} of boolean;
init1 :   {i, n|7 ≥ 2i; i ≥ 1; 2i + 1 = n} of boolean;
      ...
let
p     =   case
            {i, n|7 ≥ 2i; i ≥ 1; 2i + 1 = n} : init1;
            {i, n|i ≥ 1; 4 ≥ i; n = 2i} : init2;
            {i, n|i ≥ 0; 8 ≥ n; n ≥ 2i + 2} : p.(i, n → i + 1, n) ∧ A1 = A2;
          esac;
      ...
init1 =   case
            {i, n|3 = n; 1 = i} : true.(i, n →);
            {i, n|7 ≥ 2i; i ≥ 2; 2i + 1 = n} : init1.(i, n → i − 1, n − 2);
          esac;
init2 =   case
            {i, n|2 = n; 1 = i} : true.(i, n →);
            {i, n|i ≥ 2; 4 ≥ i; n = 2i} : init2.(i, n → i − 1, n − 2);
          esac;
tel ;
```

Fig. 8. Uniformization of initialization signals

3.6 Embedding and change of basis

The last transformation of the program is known in the literature as *space-time reindexing*. It corresponds to finding a time axis and a processor axis in the index space, in such a way that the resulting system of equations represent the operation of a synchronous architecture. Techniques to do this are well-known (see [Mol82], among many others). In the present case, the time component, i.e, the time at which calculation (i, n) is done, is $t(i, n) = 2n - i$, and the space component, i.e. the number of the processor calculating (i, n) is simply i. In term of ALPHA program transformation, space-time reindexing amounts to operate a change of basis, as described in Subsect. 2.3. However, a careful analysis of the dependencies reveals that the period of the cells of the desired architecture is 2, i.e., each cell operates only every other tick of the clock. As a consequence, one cannot use directly a *unimodular* change of basis. To circumvent this problem, one uses the following trick : first, local variables are *embedded* in a three-dimensional space, simply by adding a new index (k for example), arbitrarily set to 0. The effect of this embedding is illustrated in Fig. 9 for variable *A2*. Then, one performs a unimodular change

---

```
system palindrome ( a : {i|i ≥ 0; 7 ≥ i} of integer )
returns ( pal : {n|n ≥ 1} of integer );
var
    ...
A2 :     {i, n, k|i ≥ 0; 8 ≥ n; n ≥ 2i + 1; k = 0} of integer;
    ...
let
    ...
A2 =    case
        {i, n, k|i = 0; 8 ≥ n; n ≥ 1; k = 0} : a. (i, n, k → −i + n − 1);
        {i, n, k|8 ≥ n; i ≥ 1; n ≥ 2i + 1; k = 0} : A2.(i, n, k → i − 1, n − 1, 0);
        esac;
    ...
tel ;
```

Fig. 9. After embedding

of basis, chosen in such a way that its *projection* on the first two indexes correspond to the desired, non unimodular, space-time transformation. In our example, the change of basis we are looking for is $(t, p, k) = (2n - i + k, i, n + k)$. The same change of basis is performed on all variables, except *init1* and *init2* which are additionally translated by $(t, p, k) = (-3, -1, 0)$ in such a way that the initialization signal enter cell number 0 of the array. The result is shown in Fig. 10. It can readily be interpreted as the systolic architecture depicted in Fig. 11. The array has *period* 2, and uses $n/2$ cells. Notice that the initialization of the cells is *fully systolic*, as the operation of the array makes no assumption on the initial state of the registers of the cells: all data and control signals enter the array in cell 0, and results are obtained in real-time in cell 0 as well.

```
system palindrome ( a : {i|i ≥ 0; 7 ≥ i} of integer )
returns ( pal : {n|n ≥ 1} of integer );
var
init2 : {t, p, k|8 ≥ k; 2p + 2 = k; k ≥ 2; 2t + 6 = 3k} of boolean;
init1 : {t, p, k|19 ≥ 2t; 3p + 2 = t; t ≥ 2; 2t + 5 = 3k} of boolean;
A2   : {t, p, k|8 ≥ k; 2t ≥ 3k + 1; 2k = t + p; 2k ≥ t} of integer;
A1   : {t, p, k|p ≥ 0; t ≥ 3p + 4; 16 ≥ t + p; 2k = t + p} of integer;
p    : {t, p, k|2k ≥ t + 1; 2t ≥ 3k; 2k = t + p; 3k + 1 ≥ 2t; 8 ≥ k} ,
       {t, p, k|p ≥ 0; t ≥ 3p + 4; 16 ≥ t + p; 2k = t + p} of boolean ;
let
pal  = {i|8 ≥ i; i ≥ 2} : p.(i → 2i, 0, i);
p    = case
       {t, p, k|25 ≥ 2t; t = 3p + 2; t ≥ 5; 2t = 3k + 1} : init1.(t, p, k → t − 3, p − 1, k);
       {t, p, k|t ≥ 3; 3p = t; 12 ≥ t; 3k = 2t} : init2.(t, p, k → t − 3, p − 1, k);
       {t, p, k|p ≥ 0; t ≥ 3p + 4; 16 ≥ t + p; 2k = t + p} :
               p.(t, p, k → t − 1, p + 1, k) ∧ A1 = A2;
       esac;
A1   = case
       {t, p, k|13 ≥ t; 3p + 4 = t; t ≥ 4; 2t = 3k + 2} : A2.(t, p, k → t − 2, p, t + p − k − 1);
       {t, p, k|p ≥ 0; t ≥ 3p + 6; 16 ≥ t + p; 2k = t + p} : A1.(t, p, k → t − 2, p, k − 1);
       esac;
A2   = case
       {t, p, k|t ≥ 2; p = 0; 16 ≥ t; 2k = t} : a.(t, p, k → t − k − 1);
       {t, p, k|p ≥ 1; t ≥ 3p + 2; 16 ≥ t + p; t + p = 2k} : A2.(t, p, k → t − 1, p − 1, k − 1);
       esac;
init1 = case
       {t, p, k|3 = k; p = 0; 2 = t} : true.(t, p, k →);
       {t, p, k|t ≥ 5; 3p + 2 = t; 19 ≥ 2t; 3k = 2t + 5} :
               init1.(t, p, k → t − 3, p − 1, t + p − k + 2);
       esac;
init2 = case
       {t, p, k|t = 0; p = 0; 2 = k} : true.(t, p, k →);
       {t, p, k|9 ≥ t; t = 3p; t ≥ 3; 2t + 6 = 3k} : init2.(t, p, k → t − 3, p − 1, t + p − k + 2);
       esac;
tel ;
```

Fig. 10. The final ALPHA program

4 Conclusion

We have described the ALPHA language, and illustrated its use for the derivation of a palindrome real-time recognizer. The ALPHA DU CENTAUR environment includes a translator to the input language of a standard cell VLSI generator, which accepts as input a subset of ALPHA very similar to the final version of the palindrome. Its use for the automatic synthesis of a systolic correlator is reported in [DGL*91]. Our experience with ALPHA has shown us that it is a very concise means of describing regular algorithms, and of deriving correct parallel arrays for these algorithms. In particular, the possibility of expressing all steps of the algorithm transformations using a unique language is very convenient.

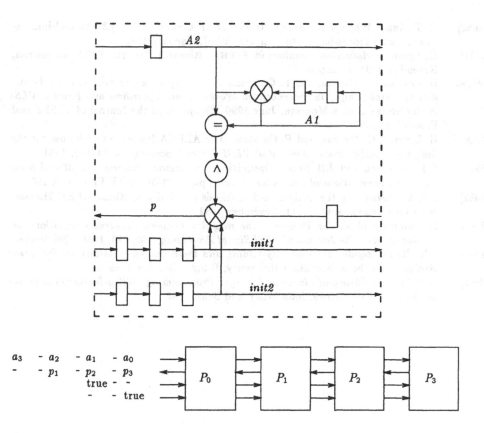

Fig. 11. Cell structure and architecture

References

[BCD*87] P. Borras, D. Clément, Th. Despeyroux, J. Incerpi, G. Kahn, B. Lang, and V. Pascual. *CENTAUR: the System.* Technical Report 777, INRIA, 1987.

[Col69] S.N. Cole. Real-time computation by n-dimensional iterative arrays of finite-state machines. *IEEE Tr. on Computer*, 18(4):349–365, 1969.

[DGL*91] C. Dezan, E. Gautrin, H. Leverge, P. Quinton, and Y. Saouter. Synthesis of systolic arrays by equation transformations. In *ASAP'91*, IEEE, Barcelona, Spain, September 1991.

[dSS89] J.L.A. Van de Snepscheut and J.B. Swenker. On the design of some systolic algorithms. *JACM*, 36:826–840, 1989.

[DVQS91] C. Dezan, H. Le Verge, P. Quinton, and Y. Saouter. The ALPHA DU CENTAUR environment. In P. Quinton and Y. Robert, editors, *International Workshop Algorithms and Parallel VLSI Architectures II*, North-Holland, Bonas, France, June 1991.

[KAGR82] S.Y. Kung, K.S. Arun, R.J. Gal-Ezer, and D.V.B. Rao. Wavefront array processor: language, architecture, and applications. *IEEE Trans. on Computers*, C-31(11):1054–1066, Nov 1982.

[KMW67] R.M. Karp, R.E. Miller, and S. Winograd. The organization of computations for uniform recurrence equations. *Journal of the Association for Computing Machinery*, 14(3):563–590, July 1967.

[Kun82]   H. T. Kung. Why systolic architectures? *IEEE Computer*, 15(1):37–46 multiprocessors, parallel processing, systolic arrays, VLSI,, January 1982.

[Lev91]   H. Leverge. *Reduction operators in* ALPHA. Research Report, IRISA, adressirisa, November 1991. to appear.

[LMQ90]   H. Leverge, C. Mauras, and P. Quinton. A language-oriented approach to the design of systolic chips. In *International Workshop on Algorithms and Parallel VLSI Architectures*, Pont-à-Mousson, June 1990. To appear in the Journal of VLSI Signal Processing, 1991.

[LMQ91]   H. Leverge, C. Mauras, and P. Quinton. The ALPHA language and its use for the design of systolic arrays. *Journal of VLSI Signal Processing*, 3:173–182, 1991.

[LS81]   C.E. Leiserson and J.B. Saxe. Optimizing synchronous systems. In *22th Annual Symp. on Foundations of Computer Science*, pages 23–36, IEEE Press, Oct 1981.

[Mol82]   D.I. Moldovan. On the analysis and synthesis of VLSI algorithms. *IEEE Transactions on Computers*, C-31(11), November 1982.

[QD89]   P. Quinton and V. Van Dongen. The mapping of linear recurrence equations on regular arrays. *The Journal of VLSI Signal Processing*, 1:95–113, 1989. Quinton89c.

[Rao85]   S.K. Rao. *Regular Iterative Algorithms and their Implementations on Processor Arrays*. PhD thesis, Standford University, U.S.A., October 1985.

[Sch86]   A. Schrijver. *Theory of Linear and Integer Programming. Wiley-Interscience series in Discrete Mathematics*, John Wiley and Sons, 1986.

This article was processed using the LaTeX macro package with LMAMULT style

The Synthesis of Systolic Programs

Michael Barnett[1] *and Christian Lengauer*[2]

[1] Department of Computer Sciences, The University of Texas at Austin, Austin, Texas 78712–1188, USA, e-mail: mbarnett@cs.utexas.edu
[2] Department of Computer Science, University of Edinburgh, Edinburgh EH9 3JZ, Scotland, UK, e-mail: lengauer@dcs.ed.ac.uk

1 Introduction

This workshop contains essentially three different approaches to the implementation of high-level parallel programming languages; each has its merits and short-comings:

- One performs a naive mechanical compilation and tolerates a possibly many-fold overhead in execution. This approach makes sense in prototype implementations of very abstract languages like GAMMA [BCM88, BM90] and Unity [CM88]. Languages at that high a level of abstraction are principally useful for the specification and semantic analysis of parallelism. The rationale of a naive parallel implementation is that the correctness and simplicity of the high-level program is much more important than the efficiency of its implementation; it may also be hoped that the computational overhead will mostly be spent in excessive parallelism rather than in added execution time (e.g., in GAMMA). The limitations of today's parallel architectures can be serious to prohibitive, but it is expected that future architectures will remedy this situation.
- One performs a manual down-coding of the high-level program onto an available parallel architecture, making problem-dependent adjustments and optimizations as necessary. This approach has been demonstrated, for example, by Bragodia [Bra91] and van de Snepscheut [HLvdS91]. It opens the way to high-quality implementations of programs in a large variety of problem domains. It has been reported that a manual down-coding – even from the level of Unity to assembly language – need not necessarily be a problem for very good programmers [Piz91].
- One develops a mechanical compilation scheme that yields implementations suitable for contemporary parallel architectures. The price one pays is that the problem domain to which this compilation scheme applies is comparatively restricted and that knowledge of the problem domain is necessary for efficient parallelism. The gain is that the programmer is protected from delving into the lower levels of abstraction that the high-level language is trying to hide. This is our approach. Our problem domain is systolic arrays [KL80] and our compilation scheme makes use of the geometric theory of systolic design [KMW67].

In [BL91], we report on a compilation method that takes a systolizable source program and the abstract description of a systolic array for this program (which can be derived by other techniques [HL87, Qui84, RK88]) and returns a distributed program that emulates the systolic array. Here, we apply this method to the linear phase filter [Kun88]. We choose this example for two reasons: (1) it served recently to demonstrate another systolization method, ALPHA [LMQ90], which has also been presented at this workshop [LQ91], and (2) it leads to some small extensions of our method as originally proposed [BL91].

2 Notation

The application of a function f to an argument x is denoted by $f.x$. Function application is left-associative and has higher binding power than any other operator. We will occasionally use the lambda notation for functions. The set of points that a linear function f maps to zero will be called the *null space* of f and denoted null.f. Other properties of linear functions that we use include their dimensionality and rank.

We identify n-tuples with points (or vectors) in n-space; primarily we are concerned with points whose coordinates are all integer. $x.i$ denotes the i-th coordinate of point x. When a tuple is not to be identified with a point, it is written with surrounding angled brackets rather than parentheses.

Integers are denoted by the letters i through n, and points by the letters w through z. Thus, $m * n$ is the product of two scalar quantities, while $m * x$ is the multiplication of a point by a scalar; it represents the componentwise multiplication by m. The symbol / is used for division; it may appear in two different contexts. m/n denotes the ordinary division of two numbers. x/m represents the division of each component of x by the number m, i.e., $(1/m) * x$. We denote the integer m such that $m * y$ equals x by $x//y$. It is only well-defined if x is a multiple of y.

Quantification over a dummy variable, x, is written ($\mathbf{Q}\ x : R.x : P.x$), following [DS90]. $\mathbf{Q}$ is the quantifier, R is a function of x representing the range, and P is a term that depends on x. The symbol $\mathbf{A}$ is used for universal quantification, $\mathbf{E}$ for existential quantification. (set $x : R.x : P.x$) is equivalent to the more traditional $\{P.x \mid R.x\}$.

Our derivations are in the equational proof format of Dijkstra [DS90]. Curly brackets enclose supporting comments of an equation.

$\mathbb{N}$, $\mathbb{Z}$, and $\mathbb{Q}$ represent the set of natural numbers, the set of integers, and the set of rational numbers respectively. The sign function has the definition:

$$
\begin{aligned}
\text{sgn}.m \ = \ &\textbf{if } m < 0 \to -1 \\
&[]\ m = 0 \to \ \ 0 \\
&[]\ m > 0 \to +1 \\
&\textbf{fi}
\end{aligned}
$$

3 The Source Format

To be systolizable, a program must conform to a specific syntactic format. The restrictions of this format cater to a geometric theory that is the basis for the derivation and simplification of the distributed target program. In this section, we state these requirements and some basic concepts of the theory. The next section applies the method in the construction of the linear filter program. Newcomers to systolic design may want to consult a recent survey on the subject [LX91a].

Our scheme expects two pieces of information: a sequential program for the problem and the abstract description of a compatible systolic array.

3.1 The Program

The source program must meet enough restrictions to correspond to a systolic array. Basically, it must consist of a number of perfectly nested loops, and its array variables must be accessed in certain regular, simple ways, essentially, corresponding to uniform recurrences [KMW67]. There are some additional restrictions that will be removed in later work. More precisely:

$$\textbf{for } x_0 = lb_0 \leftarrow st_0 \rightarrow rb_0$$
$$\textbf{for } x_1 = lb_1 \leftarrow st_1 \rightarrow rb_1$$
$$\ddots$$
$$\textbf{for } x_{r-1} = lb_{r-1} \leftarrow st_{r-1} \rightarrow rb_{r-1}$$
$$(x_0, x_1, \ldots, x_{r-1})$$

We call the space $\mathcal{I}$ of iterations, or *basic statements*, defined by the loops the program's *index space*; $\mathcal{I} \subset \mathbb{Z}^r$. Let the range of i be $0 \le i < r$. The bounds lb_i (left bound) and rb_i (right bound) are linear expressions in a set of variables called the *problem size*; they must satisfy $(\textbf{A } i : 0 \le i < r : lb_i \le rb_i)$. The steps st_i are either -1 or $+1$; different step widths can be coded into the arguments of the basic statement. Interpreted as a sequential program, if the step is positive, the loop is executed from the left bound to the right bound; if the step is negative, it is executed from the right bound to the left bound. An instantiation of the basic statement with values for the loop indices, each within its bounds, is also called a basic statement when no confusion should arise. If the difference is important, we refer to the former as an *instance* of the basic statement.

The following definitions are for imperative source programs, but the method can be rephrased for functional source programs.

An *indexed variable* is a function from a finite subset of $\mathbb{Z}^{r-1}$ to a set of elements; $r-1$ is the *dimension* of the indexed variable. The domain of the function is not any arbitrary subset of $\mathbb{Z}^{r-1}$; in each dimension, it is a non-empty sequence of consecutive integers. That is, the index space of the variable is a convex polytope. The elements of the range are called the *elements* of the indexed variable. If there are multiple references to the same indexed variable in a program, certain criteria must be met [BD88].

A *stream* is specified by a pair: the name of an indexed variable and an index vector. An *index vector* is an $(r-1)$-tuple; each component is a linear expression of the loop indices (but with no constants in the expression). It is represented by a linear function called the *index map*. For instance, if the indexed variable A is written in a source program (with three loops whose indices are i, j, and k) as $A[i+k, j-k]$ then the index map is the function $(\lambda (i,j,k).(i+k, j-k))$. The index map has dimension $(r-1) \times r$ and must have rank $r-1$. A stream specifies the set of elements of the indexed variable that are accessed by the points in the index space (formally, it is the image of the index space under the index map). $\mathcal{S}$ denotes the set of streams of the program.

3.2 The Systolic Array

A systolic array is completely defined by two distribution functions: **step** and **place**. An additional useful function that is defined in terms of **step** and **place** is **flow**. We restrict ourselves to linear systolic arrays; that is, we assume **place** and **step** to be linear functions.

step : $\mathcal{I} \longrightarrow \mathbf{Z}$ specifies the temporal distribution; elements mapped to the same step number are performed in parallel. step defines a partial order that respects the data dependences in the source program.

place : $\mathcal{I} \longrightarrow \mathbf{Z}^{r-1}$ specifies the spatial distribution. The range of place, called the *computation space*, has one dimension less than the number of nested loops.

flow : $\mathcal{S} \longrightarrow \mathbb{Q}^{r-1}$ specifies the direction and distance that data elements traverse at each step.

Automatic systolic design systems exist that derive a time-minimal step and check a proposed place for consistency with step.

At present, our compilation scheme is restricted to systolic arrays with neighbouring connections only; place must be chosen accordingly. We do permit fractional flows: a stream element may take several steps to reach a neighbouring process; the respective communication channel must have buffers to hold these elements on their journey. A systolic array has only neighbouring connections when stream elements do not skip over any processors. To specify the restriction we define a predicate nb on points in $\mathbf{Z}^n$:

$$nb.x = (\mathbf{A}\, i : 0 \leq i < n : |x.i| \leq 1)$$

and then require that:

$$(\mathbf{A}\, s : s \in \mathcal{S} : (\mathbf{E}\, n : n > 0 : nb.(n * \text{flow}.s))) \tag{1}$$

For simplicity, we require that neighbouring points in the computation space are not more than one unit apart (in any dimension). This means that the only coefficients in place are -1, 0, and $+1$. Other coefficients are used to scale the array; this is immaterial for the generation of distributed programs but may be useful in certain applications.

4 The Linear Phase Filter

This section covers the example of the linear phase filter. We proceed as follows:

Sect. 4.1. We start with the problem specification.

Sect. 4.2. We provide an imperative source program that is a straight-forward refinement of the specification.

Sect. 4.3. The format of the source program violates certain requirements. We state these and hint how extensions of the compilation scheme can deal with them.

Sect. 4.4. We provide the second part of the source, the place function, and specify the resulting systolic array. Systolic design methods derive the step function automatically.

Sect. 4.5. We derive the size and shape of the process space.

Sect. 4.6. We derive the elements of the process space, i.e., the sequence of computations that cells execute.

Sect. 4.7. We derive the layout of the i/o processes.

Sect. 4.8. We derive the sequence of stream elements that i/o processes inject to or extract from the array.

Sect. 4.9. We derive the number of stream elements that cells must propagate before or after the computation; this is necessary for stream elements whose first or last use is not at the border of the array.

Sect. 4.10. We determine where additional cells are necessary to buffer elements of slow moving streams.

Sect. 4.11. We combine our results and state the complete distributed program.

4.1 The Specification

The linear phase filter is used for signal processing; it is a digital filter that introduces a time delay whose length corresponds to the slope of the signal.

The linear phase filter is a convolution [Qui84] whose coefficients form a palindrome. The following is a specification of the linear phase filter of order 3 [Kun88]:

$$(\mathbf{A}\ i : 6 \leq i : y_i = (\mathbf{sum}\ j : 1 \leq j \leq 3 : a_j * (x_{i-j+1} + x_{i+j-6})))$$

The values a_1, a_2, a_3 and (set $i : 1 \leq i : x_i$) are given.

4.2 The Source Program

The following program represents an imperative refinement of the specification. It assumes that each element of array y has an initial value of 0.

$$
\begin{aligned}
&\textbf{int}\ a[1..3],\ x[1..\infty],\ y[6..\infty] \\
&\textbf{for}\ i = 6 \leftarrow 1 \rightarrow \infty \\
&\quad \textbf{for}\ j = 1 \leftarrow 1 \rightarrow 3 \\
&\quad\quad (i, j)
\end{aligned}
$$

The basic statement is refined to:

$$(i, j) :: \quad y[i] := y[i] + a[j] * (x[i-j+1] + x[i+j-6])$$

4.3 Violations of the Required Source Format

This source program violates three restrictions of our method, as reported in [BL91]; we propose extensions for each of them, but do not prove their correctness here.

First, the loop bounds are required to be linear expressions in a set of variables called the problem size. This makes the index space a rectangular polytope. Yet, the first loop in the program specifies an infinite right bound, yielding a polyhedron (an unbounded polytope). We may allow infinity in the source provided that, later on, we are not required to implement something impossible, such as a computation at infinity. In Sect. 4.6 we show that it is possible to maintain this condition in the linear phase filter.

Our method works by the symbolic manipulation of linear equations. During the symbolic simplification, an infinite loop bound is treated like any other program variable; we denote it by *infty*. If the infinite loop bound remains after simplification, we instantiate it with the value ∞ and apply the arithmetic rules for infinity, e.g., $\infty \pm \text{const} = \infty$.

Second, we restrict ourselves to indexed variables with a finite domain; in the linear phase filter, both x and y have an infinite domain. Our method may be extended to allow such variables, again, as long as we do not specify anything impossible. We are aware that the target language may not allow such variables, but assume for now that it does.

Third, each index vector must correspond to a linear function; i.e., there may not be additive constants in any component. Both occurrences of indexed variable x in the linear phase filter have constants in the index vector.

We extend our concept of a stream, s, to a triple: $s = \langle v, M_s, \mathit{off}_s \rangle$, where v is an indexed variable, M_s an index map and off_s a constant vector in $\mathbf{Z}^{r-1}$ called the *offset*. Given a point x in the index space of the program, the element of v that the stream accesses is $M_s.x + \mathit{off}_s$.

4.4 The Systolic Array

We emulate the following array, which can be derived from the given program for the linear phase filter [LMQ90]:

$$\text{step}.(i,j) = 2*i+j$$
$$\text{place}.(i,j) = j$$

The computation space is one-dimensional. Its points have one integer coordinate; we name it p. For brevity, we shall refer to stream $y[i]$ as y, $a[j]$ as a, $x[i-j+1]$ as $x1$, and $x[i+j-6]$ as $x2$. The index maps of streams y, a, $x1$, and $x2$ are $M_y = (\lambda\,(i,j).i)$, $M_a = (\lambda\,(i,j).j)$, $M_{x1} = (\lambda\,(i,j).i-j)$, and $M_{x2} = (\lambda\,(i,j).i+j)$. The offsets are 0, 0, 1, and -6, respectively.

Let M_s be the index map of stream s, and let w be an element of the null space of M_s. The flow of stream s is [BL91]:

$$\text{flow}.s = \text{place}.w/\text{step}.w$$

We pick: $(0,1) \in \text{null}.M_y$, $(1,0) \in \text{null}.M_a$, $(1,1) \in \text{null}.M_{x1}$, and $(1,-1) \in \text{null}.M_{x2}$. (Null spaces contain more than one element. Any element may be used.) Then, the flows of the streams are: flow.$y = 1$, flow.$a = 0$, flow.$x1 = 1/3$, and flow.$x2 = -1$. We load the stationary stream a into the array before the first computation and recover it afterwards. The user must specify the direction in which the data transfers take place with a *loading & recovery vector*. It is used in the definition of the i/o processes in place of the zero flow. Let the loading & recovery vector for a be 1.

Fig. 1 depicts the systolic array at the first step. The dark array cell is active.

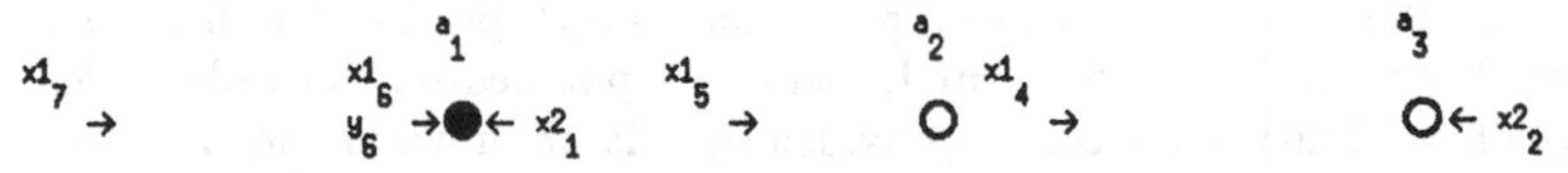

Fig. 1. The systolic array for the linear phase filter.

4.5 The Computation Processes – Layout

At present, our method creates a rectangular process layout [BL91]; we call it the *process space* and denote it by $\mathcal{P}$. The process space is the rectangular closure of the computation space (Sect. 4.4); the computation space may be any convex polytope. For the linear phase filter (in fact, for any one-dimensional systolic array), the computation space is rectangular, and the process and the computation space coincide.

The process space is described by the *process space basis*, a set of two points: $\{minP, maxP\}$. The general method for their derivation is to create a set of points, one for each component in the range of place:

$$(\text{set } k : 0 \leq k < r-1 : x_k) \tag{2}$$

Each point, x_k, is in $\mathbf{Z}^r$: coefficient c_i of loop index x_i in component k in the definition of place determines component i of x_k. For $minP$:

$$
\begin{aligned}
x_k.i = \ &\textbf{if } \text{sgn}.c_i > 0 \rightarrow lb_i \\
&[] \ \text{sgn}.c_i = 0 \rightarrow 0 \\
&[] \ \text{sgn}.c_i < 0 \rightarrow rb_i \\
&\textbf{fi}
\end{aligned}
\tag{3}
$$

For $maxP$, lb_i and rb_i are interchanged in the definition. Point x_k determines component k of $minP$ ($maxP$); it is component k of the result of applying place to x_k:

$$(\textbf{A } k : 0 \leq k < r-1 : minP.k = \text{place}.x_k.k)$$

(This is evaluated symbolically when the loop bounds are not integer constants.) Of course, when $x_k = x_{k'}$, only one evaluation is necessary.

In the linear phase filter, the range of place has only one component; so only one point, x_0, needs to be derived. The coefficient of i is 0, that of j is 1; from Equ. (3), $x_0.0 = 0$, while $x_0.1$ is the left (right) bound of the second loop:

$$minP = \text{place}.(0, lb_1) = \text{place}.(0, 1) = 1$$
$$maxP = \text{place}.(0, rb_1) = \text{place}.(0, 3) = 3$$

4.6 The Computation Processes – Basic Statements

Each computation process is a loop. Sequences of computations, as they occur in systolic programs, are more conveniently represented by repeaters than by for-loops. A *repeater* is a triple, ⟨first, last, inc⟩: first is the first element of the sequence, last the last element and inc the increment by which successive elements are derived (it is also called the *iteration vector* [RK88]). In a computation repeater, first and last are instances of the basic statement – in the case of the linear phase filter, (i, j).

inc:

Let w be an arbitrary element of the null space of place, and

$$k = (\text{gcd } i : 0 \leq i < r : w.i)$$

The definition of inc is [BL91]:

$$\text{inc} = \text{sgn}.(\text{step}.w) * w/k$$

The sign ensures that the partial order prescribed by step is adhered to. Pick $(5, 0) \in$ null.place; then $k = 5$ and inc $= (1, 0)$.

first and last:

We are dealing with a *simple* place function [LBH91]: one in which each component of the range is a distinct loop index. This corresponds to a projection of the index space along one of its axes and makes the derivation of first and last particularly easy. Let $j.i$ be the component in the range of place that contains the loop index x_i: one loop index does not appear in the range; for that value of i, $j.i$ is undefined. For simple place functions, first is defined as follows [BL91]:

$$
\begin{array}{l}
(\text{A } y : y \in \mathcal{P} : \\
\quad (\text{A } i : 0 \le i < r : \text{first}.y.i \;=\; \textbf{if } \text{sgn}.(\text{inc}.i) > 0 \;\;\rightarrow\;\; lb_i \\
\qquad\qquad\qquad\qquad\qquad\qquad [] \;\; \text{sgn}.(\text{inc}.i) = 0 \;\;\rightarrow\;\; y.(j.i) \\
\qquad\qquad\qquad\qquad\qquad\qquad [] \;\; \text{sgn}.(\text{inc}.i) < 0 \;\;\rightarrow\;\; rb_i \\
\qquad\qquad\qquad\qquad\qquad \textbf{fi }))
\end{array}
$$

In last, lb_i and rb_i are interchanged. The non-zero component of inc is inc.0; since it is positive, $\text{first}.y.0 = lb_0 = 6$ and $\text{last}.y.0 = rb_0 = \infty$. The other components of first and last are the corresponding coordinates of the process space – in this case, p. That is, $\text{first}.p = (6, p)$ and $\text{last}.p = (\infty, p)$.

As mentioned in Sect. 4.3, we must take care not to specify something unimplementable. Infinity in a component of first or place is not permitted. Infinity in a component of last indicates non-termination of (part of) the distributed program. In this case, the communications specified to succeed the computations will never happen and can be ignored. If non-termination is specified but not really intended, as in converging computations, more complex schemes are necessary. Sometimes, infinity can be eliminated in the compilation process (Sect. 4.9).

4.7 The I/O Processes – Layout

We leave the i/o code somewhat abstract; presently, we implement an i/o process for each point on the boundary of the process space.

For each stream s and each non-zero component k of flow.s, the set of i/o processes is defined as follows:

$$
\mathcal{IO}_s.k = (\text{set } w : w \in \mathcal{P} \,\wedge\, (w.k = \min\mathcal{P}.k \,\vee\, w.k = \max\mathcal{P}.k) : w)
$$

Since the process space of the linear phase filter is one-dimensional, there is only one set of i/o processes per stream. Each stream has one i/o process at $\min\mathcal{P}$ and one at $\max\mathcal{P}$. For all streams but $x2$, the input process is located at coordinate 1, and the output process at coordinate 3. For $x2$, the locations are reversed.

4.8 The I/O Processes – Communication

An i/o process is also a repeater; it represents a sequence of stream elements to be communicated. That is, first and last of an i/o repeater are index vectors of stream elements.

Streams are defined on indexed variables, but not all elements of the variable need to be part of the stream. Which elements are depends on the stream's index map and offset, as well as on the program's index space. For a definition of the i/o processes, we must characterize the elements of the variable's index space that are part of the stream. We call this the *access space*, A_s; for stream $s = \langle v, M_s, off_s \rangle$:

$$A_s = (\text{set } x : x \in \mathcal{I} : M_s.x + off_s)$$

Just as for the process space, the rectangular closure of the access space is represented by a basis that consists of a minimal and a maximal point; we call them $min A_s$ and $max A_s$. They are derived using a set of points, just as in Equ. (2); each point is defined as in Equ. (3). $min A_s$ is defined just as $min \mathcal{P}$, $max A_s$ just as $max \mathcal{P}$.

In analogy with the derivation of the process space basis, component k of $min A_s$ ($max A_s$) is derived from x_k:

$$(\text{A } k : 0 \leq k < r - 1 : min A_s.k = (M_s.x_k + off_s).k) \tag{4}$$

For one-dimensional indexed variables, the rectangular closure is equal to the access space. Consider, for example, $x1$. Because the range of M_{x1} has only one component, only one point is needed. For $min A_{x1}$, following Equ. (3), the point is (lb_0, rb_1), the coefficient of i is positive, and that of j is negative. The point (rb_0, lb_1) is used for $max A_{x1}$. Then, according to Equ. (4):

$$min A_{x1} = M_{x1}.(lb_0, rb_1) + off_{x1} = M_{x1}.(6, 3) + 1 = 4$$

$$\begin{aligned} max A_{x1} &= M_{x1}.(rb_0, lb_1) + off_{x1} = M_{x1}.(infty, 1) + 1 \\ &= infty - 1 + 1 = infty = \infty \end{aligned}$$

Because of our restriction to nearest-neighbour communication, the increment between successive elements of a stream along a communication channel is calculated by applying the index map of each stream to the increment between successive computations; the offsets do not matter:

$$inc_s = M_s.inc$$

The provided loading & recovery vector (Sect. 4.4) is used as inc_a. All one-dimensional streams are simple streams. *Simple* streams have exactly one non-zero component in inc_s. Each i such that $inc_s.i = 0$ identifies the component in the range of place that matches component i in the stream's index map. For each such i, let $j.i$ be the number of that component in the range of place. Again, simplicity leads to a particularly easy derivation, this time of $first_s$ and $last_s$:

$$\begin{aligned} &(\text{A } y : y \in \mathcal{P} : \\ &\quad (\text{A } i : 0 \leq i < r - 1 : first_s.y.i = \text{ if } sgn.(inc_s.i) > 0 \rightarrow \quad min A_s.i \\ &\qquad\qquad\qquad \text{[] } sgn.(inc_s.i) = 0 \rightarrow y.(j.i) + off_s.i \\ &\qquad\qquad\qquad \text{[] } sgn.(inc_s.i) < 0 \rightarrow \quad max A_s.i \\ &\qquad\qquad \text{fi })) \end{aligned}$$

In the derivation of $last_s$, $min A_s$ and $max A_s$ are interchanged. Because the streams are one-dimensional, $first_s$ and $last_s$ only have one component each. Omitting the derivations, the final results for all streams are shown in Tab. 1.

Table 1. Streams: access space and i/o repeaters.

s	M_s	off_s	$minA_s$	$maxA_s$	$first_s$	$last_s$	inc_s
y	$(\lambda(i,j).i)$	0	6	∞	6	∞	1
a	$(\lambda(i,j).j)$	0	1	3	1	3	1
$x1$	$(\lambda(i,j).i-j)$	1	4	∞	4	∞	1
$x2$	$(\lambda(i,j).i+j)$	-6	1	∞	1	∞	1

4.9 The Computation Processes – Data Propagation

Before the computation, each process propagates a number of stream elements until its first stream element arrives. After the process has finished its computation, it propagates a number of stream elements from other processes. The former is called *soaking*, the latter *draining*. In each case, the number may be zero. A non-zero number indicates that the first or last use of a stream is inside the array, not at the border.

For stationary streams, the convention is that, on loading, the process stores the first element that it receives into a local variable and propagates the rest. On recovery, the process propagates all elements from other processes and then ejects its local element. The number of elements to be propagated on soaking and on recovery is defined by the same formula. Similarly, the number of elements to be propagated on draining and on loading is defined by the same formula. For process p and stream s:

$$soak_s.p = ((M_s.(\text{first}.p) + off_s) - \text{first}_s.p)//inc_s \qquad (5)$$

$$drain_s.p = (\text{last}_s.p - (M_s.(\text{last}.p) + off_s))//inc_s \qquad (6)$$

We derive soaking and draining code for the three moving streams and loading and recovery code for the stationary stream. Since inc_s is in $\mathbb{Z}$ in the linear phase filter, integer division replaces "$//$". The offset of streams y and a is 0. Note the treatment of infinity (variable *infty*).

Stream y:

$soak_y.p$
$=$ { Equ. (6) }
$(M_y.(\text{first}.p) - \text{first}_y.p)/inc_y$
$=$ { preceding derivations }
$(M_y.(6,p) - 6)/1$
$=$ { simplification }
0

$drain_y.p$
$=$ { Equ. (6) }
$(\text{last}_y.p - M_y.(\text{last}.p))/inc_y$
$=$ { preceding derivations }
$(infty - M_y.(infty, p))/1$
$=$ { simplification }
$infty - infty$
$=$ { simplification }
0

Stream a:

recovery code for a
$=$ { recovery = soaking }
$soak_a.p$
$=$ { Equ. (6) }
$(M_a.(\text{first}.p) - \text{first}_a.p)/\text{inc}_a$
$=$ { previous derivations }
$(M_a.(6,p) - 1)/1$
$=$ { simplification }
$p-1$

loading code for a
$=$ { loading = draining }
$drain_a.p$
$=$ { Equ. (6) }
$(\text{last}_a.p - M_a.(\text{last}.p))/\text{inc}_a$
$=$ { previous derivations }
$(3 - M_a.(infty,p))/1$
$=$ { simplification }
$3-p$

Stream $x1$:

$soak_{x1}.p$
$=$ { Equ. (6) }
$((M_{x1}.(\text{first}.p)+off_{x1})$
$\quad - \text{first}_{x1}.p)/\text{inc}_{x1}$
$=$ { preceding derivations }
$((M_{x1}.(6,p))+1)-4)/1$
$=$ { simplification }
$(6-p+1)-4$
$=$ { simplification }
$3-p$

$drain_{x1}.p$
$=$ { Equ. (6) }
$(\text{last}_{x1}.p -$
$\quad (M_{x1}.(\text{last}.p)+off_{x1}))/\text{inc}_{x1}$
$=$ { preceding derivations }
$(infty - (M_{x1}.(infty,p)+1))/1$
$=$ { simplification }
$(infty - (infty-p+1))$
$=$ { simplification }
$p-1$

Stream $x2$:

$soak_{x2}.p$
$=$ { Equ. (6) }
$((M_{x2}.(\text{first}.p)+off_{x2})$
$\quad - \text{first}_{x2}.p)/\text{inc}_{x2}$
$=$ { preceding derivations }
$((M_{x2}.(6,p))+-6)-1)/1$
$=$ { simplification }
$(6+p-6)-1$
$=$ { simplification }
$p-1$

$drain_{x2}.p$
$=$ { Equ. (6) }
$(\text{last}_{x2}.p -$
$\quad (M_{x2}.(\text{last}.p)+off_{x2}))/\text{inc}_{x2}$
$=$ { preceding derivations }
$(infty - (M_{x2}.(infty,p)-6))/1$
$=$ { simplification }
$(infty - (infty+p-6))$
$=$ { simplification }
$-p+6$

4.10 The Buffer Processes

For a stream s, let d be the witness for the existentially quantified variable in Equ. (1). We denote the number of buffers between neighbouring processes by $buff_s$:

$$buff_s = d - 1$$

For all streams s other than $x1$, $buff_s = 0$. For $x1$, the witness is 3, so $buff_{x1} = 2$; we create a set of pairs of single-element buffer processes. For the sake of regularity, we insert buffers between the input process for stream $x1$ and the first computation process (at coordinate 1). Each buffer process uses the i/o repeaters as the bounds for a loop, the body consisting of a matching receive and send.

4.11 The Final Program

The distributed program is written in a language-independent notation, which can be directly translated to any particular distributed programming language with asynchronous parallelism and synchronous communication.

The construct **parfor** denotes the parallel composition of a set of indexed processes; **par** denotes the parallel composition of arbitrary processes. Sequential composition is indicated by vertical alignment (as in occam [INM84, INM88]). Each stream s has its own set of channels. Channels are distributed shared data structures indexed as arrays: for process y, channel $s\_chan[y]$ connects to process $y - \text{flow}.s$, channel $s\_chan[y + \text{flow}.s]$ connects to process $y + \text{flow}.s$. The notation **pass** s_chan, n stands for the program:

> **for** $counter = 1 \leftarrow 1 \rightarrow n$ **do**
> **receive** foo **from** $s\_chan[y]$
> **send** foo **from** $s\_chan[y + \text{flow}.s]$

The scope of the variables $counter$ and foo are local to the program. The notation **load** s, s_chan, n stands for the program:

> **receive** s **from** $s\_chan[y]$
> **pass** s_chan, n

The notation **recover** s, s_chan, n stands for the program:

> **pass** s_chan, n
> **send** s **to** $s\_chan[y + \text{flow}.s]$

The basic statement of the distributed program is:

> $(i, j) ::$ **par**
> **receive** y **from** $y\_chan[p]$
> **receive** $x1$ **from** $x1\_buff[p, 2]$
> **receive** $x2$ **from** $x2\_chan[p]$
> $y := y + a * (x1 + x2)$
> **par**
> **send** y **to** $y\_chan[p+1]$
> **send** $x1$ **to** $x1\_chan.[p+1]$
> **send** $x2$ **to** $x2\_chan.[p-1]$

The distributed program for the linear phase filter is displayed in Tab. 2.

Table 2. The distributed program for the linear phase filter.

```
chan y_chan[1..4], a_chan[1..4], x1_chan[1..4], x2_chan[0..3]
chan x1_buff[1..3, 1..2]
par
  /********** Input Processes **********/
  send y ⟨6, ∞, 1⟩ to y_chan[1]
  send a ⟨1, 3, 1⟩ to a_chan[1]
  send x1 ⟨4, ∞, 1⟩ to x1_chan[1]
  send x2 ⟨1, ∞, 1⟩ to x2_chan[3]
  /********** Buffer Processes **********/
  parfor p = 1 ← 1 → 3
    parfor foo = 1 ← 1 → 2
      for bar = 0 ← 1 → n
        int baz
        if foo = 1 → receive baz from x1_chan[p]
        [] foo = 2 → receive baz from x1_buff[p, foo−1]
        fi
        send baz to x1_buff[p, foo]
  /********** Computation Processes **********/
  parfor p = 1 ← 1 → 3
    int y, a, x1, x2
    load a , a_chan , p−1
    pass x1_chan , 3−p
    pass x2_chan , p−1
    ⟨(6,p), (∞,p), (1,0)⟩
    pass x1_chan , p−1
    pass x2_chan , −p+6
    recover a , a_chan , 3−p
  /********** Output Processes **********/
  receive y ⟨6, ∞, 1⟩ from y_chan[4]
  receive a ⟨1, 3, 1⟩ from a_chan[4]
  receive x1 ⟨4, ∞, 1⟩ from x1_chan[4]
  receive x2 ⟨1, ∞, 1⟩ from x2_chan[0]
```

5 Conclusions

Our systolizing compilation scheme works also in more general situations. The most significant generalization is the use of a multi-dimensional or non-simple place function [BL91]. Essentially, the method can emulate a (significant) subset of systolic arrays that are specified by linear distribution functions (**step** and **place**). We are presently working on relaxing the remaining restrictions. One important step is to admit any convex polytope, not just rectangular polytopes. Together with the treatment of infinity described here, an extension to non-rectangular polytopes will admit also pointed cones (i.e., source programs in which each loop has at most one infinite bound).

We have an implementation of our scheme. At present, the output is in the form of repeaters; a further translation into distributed languages like occam or distributed C can be easily envisaged.

Our work differs from the representation of systolic programs in ALPHA [LQ91] and Unity [CM88] in style. Their representation of synchronous systolic programs is based on space-time recurrence equations that are prescribed by the distribution functions [Che86]. Of ALPHA and Unity, ALPHA is more suitable for a systolizing compilation. It expects the source program in the form of recurrence equations (restricted functional programs). We use an imperative source program. The equivalence of the two forms is stated in [BD88], and our scheme can be redefined for recurrence equations. The main difference is not in the source but in the focus, method and target. We manipulate the source representation in a geometric model and translate the resulting elements into a language-independent distributed programming notation for direct further translation into a low-level target language with asynchronous parallelism. This makes our target suitable for programmable distributed processor networks. It also saves us from having to require the unimodularity of the index transformation [LQ91]. ALPHA preserves the synchrony of the systolic array and, therefore, requires unimodularity. It uses a common notation for the description of the original program, the transformations used to derive the final program, and the final program itself. So does Unity.

Both Unity and GAMMA do not facilitate the specification of sequencing. Their non-deterministic nature is a new and interesting high-level programming paradigm, but it makes them, at present, less suitable for systolic design. Present systolic design methods require the specification of enough sequencing to obtain a dependence graph [RK88]. Different choices of sequencing can lead to systolic arrays of greatly varying quality and no generally applicable mechanical ways of choosing are known [HL87, LX91b, Raj90].

The earliest systematic attempt at a software realization of systolic arrays known to us is SDEF [EC87]. SDEF is a programming system that takes recurrence equations and a systolic array and fills in a distributed program skeleton. It expects constant loop bounds, i.e., its systolic programs are not parameterized in the problem size. Others working on systolizing compilation include Ribas [Rib90], and Ramanujam and Sadayappan [RS89]. Ribas generates distributed programs for a specific architecture: the processor array Warp [AAG+87]. He arrives at more concrete and efficient code than ours, but his method handles a smaller class of systolic arrays; its source restrictions are more severe, as are those of Ramanujam and Sadayappan.

Our systolic programs are still abstract and are, in several aspects, not optimal for the current generation of commercial programmable processor networks. Systolic programs tend to contain a fine grain of parallelism that requires as much communication as computation. The difference in the cost of communication compared to computation (in current machines, approximately an order of magnitude in favour of computation) make a coarser grain of parallelism desirable. Our experience is that structural modifications of the ideal distributed program can be cumbersome at the level of distributed code [LS90]. Extended design methods exist for the projection [LK88, XL91] and partitioning [BDD90, MF86] of systolic arrays. Our compilation scheme needs to be adapted to apply to arrays modified in this way. Ribas [Rib90] demonstrates for projections and Ramanujam and Sadayappan [RS89] for partitioning how this might be done, at the price of restricting the source format further. Optimizations that address specific properties of machine instructions (e.g., the parallelism of computation and communication in transputers [GK90]) can be performed in the translation to a specific target language.

Recently, there has been significant progress in the development of distributed computer architectures that support systolic computations. The T9000 transputer with its C104 VLSI routing chip [INM91] provides better performance in communication, and new finer-grain networks like the Mosaic of CalTech [Sei90] or the Rewrite Rule Machine (RRM) of SRI [ALM90] also provide a larger number of processors. The Rewrite Rule Machine may be particularly suitable for systolic computations; recurrence equations can be viewed as rewrite rules, and initial experiments with hand-coded systolic programs have been extremely encouraging [Mes91]. Programmable networks for bit-level algorithms are already being marketed, e.g., the Altera [Alt90], the Xilinx [Xil91], and the CAL [GK89, KG90].

6 Acknowledgements

The second author thanks Patrice Quinton for supporting a visit of IRISA before the workshop and for useful discussions during that visit. Thanks to José Meseguer for a draft reading and comments. Financial support was received from the Lockheed Missiles and Space Corporation, grant no. 26-7603-35, and the Science and Engineering Research Council, grant no. GR/G55457.

References

[AAG+87] M. Annaratone, E. Arnould, T. Gross, H. T. Kung, M. Lam, O. Menzilcioglu, and J. A. Webb. The Warp computer: Architecture, implementation, and performance. *IEEE Trans. on Computers*, C-36(12):1523–1538, Dec. 1987.

[ALM90] H. Aida, S. Leinwand, and J. Meseguer. Architectural design of the rewrite rule ensemble. In J. Delgado-Frias and W. R. Moore, editors, *Proc. Int. Workshop on VLSI for Artificial Intelligence and Neural Networks*, 1990. Also: Technical Report SRI-CSL-90-17, SRI International, Dec. 1990.

[Alt90] Altera Corporation. *Data Book*. Altera Corporation, 1990.

[BCM88] J.-P. Banâtre, A. Coutant, and D. Le Métayer. A parallel machine for multiset transformation and its programming style. *Future Generation Computer Systems*, 4(2):133–144, Sept. 1988.

[BD88] J. Bu and E. F. Deprettere. Converting sequential iterative algorithms to recurrent equations for automatic design of systolic arrays. In *Proc. IEEE Int. Conf. on Acoustics, Speech and Signal Processing (ICASSP 88), Vol. IV: VLSI; Spectral Estimation*, pages 2025–2028. IEEE Press, 1988.

[BDD90] J. Bu, E. F. Deprettere, and P. Dewilde. A design methodology for fixed-size systolic arrays. In S. Y. Kung and E. E. Swartzlander, editors, *Application Specific Array Processors*, pages 591–602. IEEE Computer Society Press, 1990.

[BL91] M. Barnett and C. Lengauer. A systolizing compilation scheme. Technical Report ECS-LFCS-91-134, Department of Computer Science, University of Edinburgh, Jan. 1991. Abstract: *Proc. 1991 Int. Conf. on Parallel Processing, Vol. II*, Pennsylvania State University Press, 1991, 305–306.

[BM90] J.-P. Banâtre and D. Le Métayer. The GAMMA model and its discipline of programming. *Science of Computer Programming*, 15(1):55–77, Nov. 1990.

[Bra91] R. Bragodia. UNITY to UC: Case studies in parallel program construction. In this proceedings, 1991.

[Che86]   M. C. Chen. A design methodology for synthesizing parallel algorithms and architectures. *J. Parallel and Distributed Computing*, 3(4):461–491, 1986.

[CM88]   K. M. Chandy and J. Misra. *Parallel Program Design*. Addison-Wesley, 1988.

[DS90]   E. W. Dijkstra and C. S. Scholten. *Predicate Calculus and Program Semantics.* Texts and Monographs in Computer Science. Springer-Verlag, 1990.

[EC87]   B. R. Engstrom and P. R. Cappello. The SDEF systolic programming system. In S. K. Tewksbury B. W. Dickinson and S. C. Schwartz, editors, *Concurrent Computations*, chapter 15. Plenum Press, 1987.

[GK89]   J. P. Gray and T. A. Kean. Configurable hardware: A new paradigm for computation. In C. L. Seitz, editor, *Advanced Research in VLSI*. MIT Press, 1989.

[GK90]   I. Graham and T. King. *The Transputer Handbook*. Prentice-Hall, 1990.

[HL87]   C.-H. Huang and C. Lengauer. The derivation of systolic implementations of programs. *Acta Informatica*, 24(6):595–632, Nov. 1987.

[HLvdS91] H. P. Hofstee, J. J. Lukkien, and J. L. van de Snepscheut. A distributed implementation of a task pool. In this proceedings, 1991.

[INM84]   INMOS Ltd. occam *Programming Manual*. Series in Computer Science. Prentice-Hall Int., 1984.

[INM88]   INMOS Ltd. occam 2 *Reference Manual*. Series in Computer Science. Prentice-Hall Int., 1988.

[INM91]   INMOS Ltd. *The T9000 transputer ● Products Overview ● Manual*. SGS-Thompson Microelectronics Group, first edition, 1991.

[KG90]   T. A. Kean and J. P. Gray. Configurable hardware: Two case studies of micro-grain computation. *J. VLSI Signal Processing*, 2(1):9–16, Sept. 1990.

[KL80]   H. T. Kung and C. E. Leiserson. Algorithms for VLSI processor arrays. In C. Mead and L. Conway, editors, *Introduction to VLSI Systems*, chapter 8.3. Addison-Wesley, 1980.

[KMW67]   R. M. Karp, R. E. Miller, and S. Winograd. The organization of computations for uniform recurrence equations. *J. ACM*, 14(3):563–590, July 1967.

[Kun88]   S.-Y. Kung. *VLSI Processor Arrays*. Prentice-Hall Int., 1988.

[LBH91]   C. Lengauer, M. Barnett, and D. G. Hudson. Towards systolizing compilation. *Distributed Computing*, 5(1):7–24, 1991.

[LK88]   P. Lee and Z. Kedem. Synthesizing linear-array algorithms from nested for loop algorithms. *IEEE Trans. on Computers*, C-37(12):1578–1598, Dec. 1988.

[LMQ90]   H. Leverge, C. Mauras, and P. Quinton. A language-oriented approach to the design of systolic chips. In E. F. Deprettere and A.-J. van der Veen, editors, *International Workshop on Algorithms and Parallel VLSI Architectures, Vol. A: Tutorials*, pages 309–327. Elsevier (North-Holland), 1990. To appear in *J. VLSI Signal Processing*.

[LQ91]   H. Leverge and P. Quinton. Derivation of parallel algorithms with the ALPHA language. In this proceedings, 1991.

[LS90]   C. Lengauer and J. W. Sanders. The projection of systolic programs. *Formal Aspects of Computing*, 2:273–293, 1990.

[LX91a]   C. Lengauer and J. Xue. Recent developments in systolic design. Technical Report ECS-LFCS-91-176, Department of Computer Science, University of Edinburgh, Sept. 1991.

[LX91b]   C. Lengauer and J. Xue. A systolic array for pyramidal algorithms. *J. VLSI Signal Processing*, 3(3):239–259, 1991.

[Mes91]   J. Meseguer. Personal communication, Aug. 1991.

[MF86]   D. I. Moldovan and J. A. B. Fortes. Partitioning and mapping algorithms into fixed-size systolic arrays. *IEEE Trans. on Computers*, C-35(1):1–12, Jan. 1986.

[Piz91]   A. Pizzarello. Industrial experience in the use of UNITY. In this proceedings, 1991.

[Qui84] P. Quinton. Automatic synthesis of systolic arrays from uniform recurrent equations. In *Proc. 11th Ann. Int. Symp. on Computer Architecture*, pages 208–214. IEEE Computer Society Press, 1984.

[Raj90] S. V. Rajopadhye. Algebraic transformations in systolic array synthesis: A case study. In L. J. M. Claesen, editor, *Formal VLSI Specification and Synthesis (VLSI Design Methods-I)*, pages 361–370. North-Holland, 1990.

[Rib90] H. B. Ribas. *Automatic Generation of Systolic Programs from Nested Loops*. PhD thesis, Department of Computer Science, Carnegie-Mellon University, June 1990. Technical Report CMU-CS-90-143.

[RK88]   S. K. Rao and T. Kailath. Regular iterative algorithms and their implementations on processor arrays. *Proc. IEEE*, 76(3):259–282, Mar. 1988.

[RS89]   J. Ramanujam and P. Sadayappan. A methodology for parallelizing programs for multicomputers and complex memory multiprocessors. In *Supercomputing '89*, pages 637–646. ACM Press, 1989.

[Sei90] C. E. Seitz. Multicomputers. In C. A. R. Hoare, editor, *Developments in Concurrency and Communication*, chapter 5, pages 131–200. Addison-Wesley, 1990.

[Xil91] Xilinx, Inc. *The Programmable Gate Array Data Book*. Xilinx, Inc., 1991.

[XL91]   J. Xue and C. Lengauer. On one-dimensional systolic arrays. In *Proc. ACM Int. Workshop on Formal Methods in VLSI Design*. Springer-Verlag, Jan. 1991. To appear.

This article was processed using the LaTeX macro package with LMAMULT style

Synthesizing Delay Insensitive Circuits from Verified Programs

Henrik Hulgaard, Per H. Christensen and Jørgen Staunstrup

Department of Computer Science,
Technical University of Denmark, DK-2800 Lyngby,
Denmark.
E-mail: `jst@id.dth.dk`

1 Introduction

In this paper we present a technique for automatic synthesis of delay insensitive circuits from high level programs written in a language called SYNCHRONIZED TRANSITIONS. This language is intended for both formal verification and synthesis, making it possible to use the *same* description (program) for formal verification, possibly with the assistance of a mechanical theorem prover, and for automated synthesis. As the synthesis is performed without manual intervention, *the fabricated chip corresponds exactly to the description that has been formally verified*. A circuit is described as many small processes, called transitions, executing concurrently. Therefore, each process can be realized as a sub-circuit independently of other processes. The entire chip consists of sub-circuits with the same structure, simplifying both the synthesis and the layout generation.

The majority of digital chips constructed today are synchronous. However, in recent years there has been a revival in research activity in asynchronous circuits. Asynchronous circuits do not have global synchronization signals, which makes them more robust and often faster than synchronous circuits. They are potentially faster, because the speed is determined by the *average* case of factors like temperature, power variation, data dependence, and fabrication parameters. For traditional synchronous designs, the speed is limited by the *worst case* of these factors. Problems with clock skew are avoided and the power consumption is smoother. A subset of asynchronous circuits are *delay insensitive*, i.e. they function correctly disregarding delays in wires and gates.

Our approach to delay insensitivity is briefly explained in Sect. 2. A more thorough explanation can be found in [10]. In Sect. 3 the verification aspect is considered. The synthesis technique is described in Sect. 4, and in Sect. 5 we describe a compiler that implements this technique.

2 Delay Insensitivity

Delay insensitive circuits operate correctly regardless of delays in wires and gates. Such circuits can operate as fast as the technology, implementation, operating conditions, and input data allow. In delay insensitive designs, no global clock is used. Instead, the progress of computation is controlled by the values of state variables. The lack of timing assumptions enables us to give a simple formal characterization of delay insensitivity; accordingly, delay insensitive designs are well suited for formal verification.

We describe the design of a delay insensitive circuit with a program written in SYNCHRONIZED TRANSITIONS. Such programs form the basis for both formal verification and synthesis. This section describes how the high level program may be used to test whether the design allows for realization as a delay insensitive circuit. The language is very restricted; it only includes constructs reflecting the computations of VLSI circuits. As many parts of a VLSI circuit operate simultaneously, a SYNCHRONIZED TRANSITIONS program is highly concurrent. It describes a computation as a set of independent, concurrently executing transitions. A transition consists of a guard (a precondition) and a multiple assignment, e.g.,

$$\ll \text{ready} \rightarrow \text{light, count} := \text{TRUE, limit} \gg$$

When the guard (`ready`) is satisfied, the assignment (`light, count:= TRUE, limit`) is executed. The operands in guards and assignments, e.g., `ready` and `count`, are state variables. A complete presentation of SYNCHRONIZED TRANSITIONS can be found in [10]. A typical program consists of many transitions, and the semantics allows transitions to be executed in any order. This non-determinism appears as an arbitrary delay between satisfying the precondition of a transition and the subsequent assignment, a conservative model of the unknown duration of delays in the circuits which realize the transition. The designer has to ensure that the functionality of the design is unaffected by the execution order.

A transition corresponds to a subcircuit where the expressions are realized using simple gates. The state variables specify wires connecting subcircuits. If, for example, `ready` is used in several transitions, the corresponding subcircuits are connected by wires carrying the value of `ready`.

The changes of a physical signal between logical values may not occur at the same time for all circuit elements. There are many causes for this, for example, the time needed for a change of voltage to be transmitted along a wire, or variations in threshold voltages of transistors. In a synchronous design, the clock period is needs to be long enough to guarantee that all signals have settled before the values stored in latches are updated. A delay insensitive design must function correctly regardless of the magnitude of delays in gates or wires. We have chosen to model this with explicit "wires" where the values at the two ends may differ. Consider, for example, a wire carrying the value of the state variable x. To describe a wire delay on this wire, we introduce a new state variable, x', and a wire transition:

$$\ll x' := x \gg$$

When x is assigned a new value, it may take some time before the wire transition is executed and x' gets the new value of x. Let t be a transition that reads x. To model an arbitrary delay between a change of x and the detection of this change by t, we modify t so that it reads x' instead of x. By introducing a new wire transition and state variable for each transition that reads x, changes of x can arrive in any order. We call the introduction of a wire transition and corresponding modification of transitions reading the "delayed" variable a wire transformation.

Definition 1 Delay Insensitivity. A program is delay insensitive if and only if its computation is unaffected by an arbitrary number of wire transformations.

A more formal definition of delay insensitivity is given in [10], similar definitions can be found in [7, 11]. It is not practical to verify that a program is delay insensitive using this definition of delay insensitivity, since it would require consideration of the entire correctness argument for all possible wire transformations. However, for a restricted set of programs, it can be shown once and for all that they are delay insensitive, thus avoiding explicit constructing the wire transformations, see Sect. 3.2.

Delay insensitivity in practice

In [6], it has been proved that a circuit which is delay insensitive at gate level, can only consist of C-elements, inverters, and wires. As the set of computations that can be performed with these basic elements is limited, useful circuits are in general not entirely delay insensitive.

To be useful in practice, a design technique for delay insensitive circuits must aim for delay insensitivity at higher levels than the gate level. This means that the circuit will have some localized delay assumptions. A program which meets the definition of delay insensitivity given above allows for a circuit realization where arbitrary delays can be tolerated on the wires corresponding to all state variables. However, the realization might have internal signals that are not modeled in the program, these signals cannot be guaranteed to be delay insensitive.

When describing the circuit in SYNCHRONIZED TRANSITIONS the designer may choose the level at which he wants the description to be delay insensitive. By making a very low level (ultimately a gate level) description of the circuit in SYNCHRONIZED TRANSITIONS satisfy the definition, he aims for a circuit which is delay insensitive at this low level. It is outside the scope of this paper to discuss the performance issues involved in choosing the right level of delay insensitivity. In this paper, the term delay insensitive is used with respect to the variables explicitly mentioned in the program text.

3 Formal Verification

The nature of VLSI production makes it impractical to construct circuits experimentally by trial and error. Detailed circuit design and fabrication are time consuming processes where the turn around time is measured in weeks or months. This motivates developing design methods and verification techniques which are applicable in the early phases of the design process. We are currently experimenting with formal methods which enables the designer to conduct rigorous verification of desired properties. The verification can be supported by a mechanical theorem prover. One of the questions addressed in this work is, whether it is possible to use the same circuit description, formulated as a high level program, for both synthesis and formal verification; this has been phrased as the WYVIWYF principle: What You Verify Is What You Fabricate.

In this paper the synthesis aspects are emphasized, but first we sketch our approach to verification. Formal verification could be an economic way of revealing and preventing some types of design errors. It does not cover all types of errors, for example, fabrication faults which by nature must be found by testing the physical VLSI chips. Formal verification must always be based on a formalizable model of the physical circuit; hence, there will be aspects of the chip not covered by formal verification, this could, for example, be the case for power requirements or noise sensitivity. These properties are not covered by the formal models considered here. Our emphasis has been on functional properties of the design and certain timing aspects.

3.1 Using Invariants

As an example, consider the design of a VLSI chip for controlling a traffic light. Assume, that there are two state variables, NorthSouth and EastWest which at all times indicate the colors of the lights in the two directions. An obvious requirement for such a traffic light is:

$$I : \text{NorthSouth} = \text{red} \lor \text{EastWest} = \text{red}$$

That is, in any state at least one of the lights is red. The requirement I is called an invariant and it is formally shown that each transition in the traffic light design maintains the invariant. This is done by showing that the state changes effected by each transition preserves the invariant assuming that it held before the transition was executed. A program consists of a fixed set of transitions, determined by the program text; each of these must be shown to maintain the invariant. We have found that a mechanical theorem prover can facilitate this verification. The Larch theorem prover LP has been integrated in the tools used for VLSI design with SYNCHRONIZED TRANSITIONS [3]. There is a compiler which translates a program with invariants into a list of proof obligations in the format required by LP. Frequently, the theorem prover can automatically verify the invariants. In some cases, some human interaction is needed at crucial steps of the verification. Details of our approach to formal verification and preliminary experience has been reported elsewhere [3].

3.2 Verifying Delay Insensitivity

Not all programs in SYNCHRONIZED TRANSITIONS can be directly realized by delay insensitive circuits, in fact only a very limited set of designs have such realizations. To avoid wasted design effort, our design methods allows checking for delay insensitivity at the source program level, and these checks can be performed early in the design process. If we wanted to use the formal definition of delay insensitivity as a basis for these checks, it would require an argument that considers the infinite set of programs that can be constructed by all possible wire transformations. To simplify this task, we have formulated two implementation conditions that are sufficient to guarantee that a program is delay insensitive. The first condition, *Consumed Values*, requires that the value of a state variable may not change until all transitions that read the variable have used the old value. This guarantees that each value is propagated to all readers before the next value is generated. The second implementation condition, *Correspondence*, is a restriction on successive pairs of states at which a transition can be executed. This restriction ensures that no transition is spuriously activated due to wire delays. Formal definitions of these implementation conditions are given in [10]. Both of these conditions can be formulated as invariants that can be verified using the methods described above.

The program text which is compiled to proof obligations is identical to the program text used by the synthesis tool described in the remainder of this paper. As mentioned above, this is a central tenet of our approach, *the same description is used for both verification and synthesis.* The language SYNCHRONIZED TRANSITIONS reflects this duality; all constructs have been designed with this in mind, they must allow both synthesis of efficient circuits and formal verification at a reasonably abstract level.

4 Synthesis

Synthesis is the transformation of a behavioral description (a program in SYNCHRONIZED TRANSITIONS) to a lower level structural description. Synthesis of a program in SYNCHRONIZED TRANSITIONS can be done one transition at a time. This is in contrast to most other synthesis methods, where the entire description is synthesized as a whole. A program in SYNCHRONIZED TRANSITIONS describes a circuit as a number of concurrent transitions, each of which can be implemented as an independent subcircuit. In each of these, simple gates are used to realize the precondition (boolean function) and expression (assigned value). A circuit that corresponds to the entire program is obtained by connecting the sub-circuits. In this way, the synthesis is localized, and synthesis of complex programs is easily decomposed. This section deals with a technique for synthesizing a single transition. It is based on a design methodology described by Singh [9]. Consider a transition t assigning a single Boolean variable, x:

$$t : \ll f(u_1, u_2, \ldots, u_n) \rightarrow x := g(v_1, v_2, \ldots, v_m) \gg$$

State variables are realized as wires connecting the transitions that use them. For example, if a state variable is written in a transition t^1 and is read by two transitions t^2 and t^3, a wire connects the three transitions t^1, t^2, and t^3.

The circuitry corresponding to f and g is integrated. Consider first a state where x must be changed to 1. The main idea is to use a separate Muller C-element for each of the states, where the output x is assigned the value 1 ($f \wedge g = 1$). These states are called 1-states. If there are N 1-states, the synthesized circuit has N C-elements. The output of each of the N C-elements are connected to an OR-gate (with N inputs), which has x as its output, see Fig. 1. If there is only a single 1-state ($N = 1$), the OR-gate is omitted. There are similarities with a traditional sum of products realization of a Boolean function, here C-elements replace the AND terms.

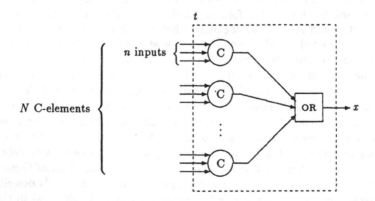

Fig. 1. Structure of a synthesized transition

Each of the N 1-states are considered separately. To each 1-state corresponds exactly one C-element. Each C-element has as many inputs, n, as there are different variables read by the transition. All input variables are connected to every C-element. For each C-element corresponding to a 1-state, logic is added in order to assure that all inputs to the C-element becomes 1 in exactly that 1-state. So far, the states where x is reset to 0 have not been considered. However, the same circuitry can be used to do that if the design meets a simple restriction called The Alternation condition (defined in Subsect. 4.1). The synthesis technique has the advantage of being very simple, and therefore it is acceptable that it only works for a subset of delay insensitive designs. Our experience so far is that this restriction is not a serious practical hindrance. In Sect. 4.5 we sketch a number of designs all meeting the restriction.

This description of the synthesis technique stresses its simplicity. Each transityion is synthesized to a sub-circuit with the structure shown in Fig. 1. The number of C-elements increase exponentially ìn the number of variables in the transition which is synthesized, but is independent on the total number of variables in the program. In practice, transitions tend to be small and simple with only a few variables, resulting in few C-elements per transition. Furthermore, techniques exist to reduce the number of C-elements by merging them, but these techniques have not yet been fully examined.

4.1 The Alternation Condition

When constructing delay insensitive circuits, values must be represented in a way that makes it possible to detect when a variable is assigned a value. This can, for example, be achieved with a dual-rail code. Such variables are in the following called dual variables. The dual-rail code uses three values: True (T), False (F), and Empty (E). A dual variable holding an E-value is called empty, and a dual variable holding either a T- or F-value is called valid. The predicate *valid* denotes whether a variable is valid. A Boolean variable is considered valid if it is 1, and empty if it is 0. If the values of all variables in two states have different valid-value, the two states are called reverse:

Definition 2 Reverse state. A state $R = (r_1, r_2, \ldots, r_n)$ is called a reverse of the state $S = (s_1, s_2, \ldots, s_n)$, written as $rev(R, S)$, if and only if

$$\forall i \in [1; n] : valid(r_i) \neq valid(s_i)$$

For example, the states $S = (T, E, E, 1)$ and $R = (E, F, T, 0)$ are reverse of each other. Other reverse states to S are $R' = (E, F, F, 0)$, $R'' = (E, T, F, 0)$, and $R''' = (E, T, T, 0)$.

Let t be a transition in a program P, and S a state in the state space of P, then S^t denotes the projection of the state space containing only state variables read or written by t.

Definition 3 Alternation condition. The transition t:
$\ll f(\ldots) \rightarrow x := g(\ldots) \gg$, assigning a single variable, fulfills the Alternation condition if and only if

$$\forall S^t, R^t : f(S^t) \wedge rev(S^t, R^t) \Rightarrow f(R^t) \wedge rev(g(S^t), g(R^t))$$

Informally, the Alternation condition requires that: if the precondition is satisfied in a state S^t, it must also be satisfied in every state R^t reverse to S^t, and the values assigned in reverse states, R^t, must be reverse to S^t. Consider the following transition:

$$\ll (\mathbf{pred} = \mathbf{E}) \neq (\mathbf{succ} = \mathbf{E}) \rightarrow \mathbf{out} := \mathbf{pred} \gg$$

The states that fulfill the precondition are (pred, succ) ∈ {(E, T), (E, F), (T, E), (F, E)}. For each of these states, the precondition is also satisfied for all reverse states. For example, the reverse states for the state (pred, succ) = (E, T) are (T, E) and (F, E), which both satisfy the precondition. When the precondition is satisfied in two reverse states, the assigned values are also reverse. Hence, the transition fulfills the Alternation condition.

4.2 Correctness of the Synthesis Technique

Consider again the transition, t,

$$t : \ll f(u_1, u_2, \ldots, u_n) \to x := g(v_1, v_2, \ldots, v_m) \gg$$

which is synthesized into the circuit shown in Fig. 1. Whenever a state is reached, that fulfills the precondition and makes the assigned value 1, all inputs to exactly one of the C-elements are 1, thereby making the output 1. The Alternation condition assures that the output is properly reset; when a reverse state is reached, all inputs to the C-element becomes 0, and the output becomes 0.

It can be proved that when a transition is synthesized in the way described, the realized sub-circuit is functionally equivalent to the transition. By "functionally equivalent" we mean that

- Whenever the transition assigns the value v to a variable x, the output of the realization becomes v.
- Whenever the output of the realization becomes the value v, the transition can assign v to the variable x.

The proof is given in [4, App. B]. Furthermore, it has been proved that neither hazard nor timing problems occur in the circuits generated by the synthesis.

4.3 Delay Assumptions

As mentioned in Sect. 2, any asynchronous circuit will be delay *sensitive* at some level. When a transition is synthesized using the presented method, the assumption is made that the delay of an input forking out to different C-elements is negligible. This is an assumption made by the synthesis method, and it restricts the way the layout of the synthesized circuit can be constructed. It should be stressed again that *all variables explicitly mentioned in the transitions* (the inputs and outputs in Fig. 1) *are delay insensitive*.

4.4 Example: Synthesis of a FIFO Element

In this section a simple example is presented, illustrating the synthesis procedure. It is done in a number of steps. The transformations described in these steps have been implemented in a compiler which is described briefly in Sect. 5.

A FIFO (First In First Out) queue is a data structure which holds a sequence of data. There are two external operations on a FIFO queue: insertion and removal. Data are always removed in the same order as they are inserted. A FIFO queue can be described with the following program:

$$\ldots \; \| \; \ll (q[i]=E) \neq (q[i+2]=E) \; \rightarrow \; q[i+1] := q[i] \gg \; \| \; \ldots$$

q is an array of duals. Here, the i'th stage is shown; the remaining stages are similar. The transition in each stage of the queue depends on the states of the two neighbors. Inputs must alternate between the empty value and valid values. When a new datum is available at the input of the queue ($q[1] \neq E$), it is propagated down the array until it reaches another valid value. When the input has the empty value ($q[1] = E$), this value (E) propagates until it reaches another empty value. In a stable configuration, the stages at the "tail" of the queue all hold the same value, and the stages at the "head" alternate between empty and valid values. To propagate a queue element from $q[i]$ to $q[i+1]$, $q[i]$ and $q[i+2]$ must be different. This ensures that $q[i+1]$ and $q[i+2]$ are different after the transition. Hence, completion of the propagation can be determined. This is essential for the proper operation of a delay insensitive circuit.

It is not difficult to show that this design is delay insensitive according to our definition. In Sect. 4.1 it was shown that it fulfills the Alternation condition (with a different naming of the variables), and thus the synthesis technique can be applied. A dual variable, e.g., $q[i+1]$ is represented with a pair of booleans called $q[i+1].t$ and $q[i+1].f$. The states where the precondition holds are listed in Fig. 2, with the corresponding values being assigned to $q[i+1]$. The pairs of digits in the table represents the ".t" and ".f" value of a dual variable, respectively. Consider $q[i+1].t$ first. There is only one state, where the precondition is satisfied and $q[i+1].t$ is set to 1. Hence, only one C-element is needed. In this state, $q[i]$ is T and $q[i+2]$ is E. The synthesis technique described in Sect. 4 requires all input variables to be connected to each C-element. Different connections are used depending on the type and value of the variable: A Boolean variable is connected directly if the variable is 1 in the considered 1-state, otherwise an inverter is inserted between the variable and the C-element. For a dual variable the ".t"-part of the variable is connected to the C-element if the variable is T in the considered 1-state. Similarly, the ".f"-part of the variable is connected to the C-element if the variable is F in the state. If the variable is E, the ".t"- and ".f"-part of the variable are connected to a NOR-gate, which has its output connected to the C-element.

The circuit for $q[i+1].f$ is synthesized similarly. A C-element and a NOR-gate are used. The realization of the FIFO element is shown in Fig. 2. The q signals are delay insensitive, whereas the internal signals (the outputs of the NOR-gates and the forks at the

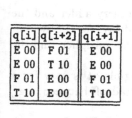

q[i]	q[i+2]	q[i+1]
E 00	F 01	E 00
E 00	T 10	E 00
F 01	E 00	F 01
T 10	E 00	T 10

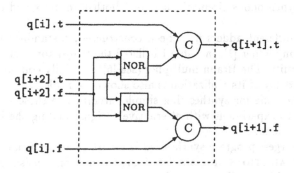

Fig. 2. Realization of a FIFO element

input of the NOR-gates) are not delay insensitive. The method generates two NOR-gates with identical inputs; these can be merged.

From this level of the synthesis, the layout is generated. The layout of the FIFO element shown in Fig. 3 is generated using a commercial layout synthesis tool [2]. This example is very small, but illustrates the steps of synthesis. The entire transformation from the program in SYNCHRONIZED TRANSITIONS to layout is done without manual intervention.

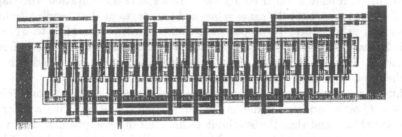

Fig. 3. Layout of FIFO element, generated automatically

4.5 Larger Examples

Many examples have been synthesized and found to function correctly by simulating the generated layout. A few of these are presented in this subsection to illustrate sizes and delays for delay insensitive realizations of well-known circuits. The number of transistors in the realization is used as a measure of the synthesized circuits size. This is an approximation because factors such as regularity and routing complexity have a significant influence on the area of a circuit. The delays are estimated by assigning a C-element 2 units of delay, a NOR/NAND-gate 1.5 units delay and an inverter a single unit delay. Obviously, this is a rough approximation of actual delays, but it serves well to illustrate differences between the circuits. When estimating the performance of a delay insensitive circuit, the average delay is usually the relevant measure. Because of the delay insensitivity, the circuit can execute as fast as current data and operating conditions allow. It is not necessary to accommodate for the worst case combination in every step as it is the case in synchronous circuits. Therefore, both min, max and average delays are given in Table 1.

Two different adders have been constructed; a standard ripple-carry adder and the Brent-Kung adder [1]. In Table 1 is listed the transistor count and delays for the synthesized circuits. The Braun multiplier (see [5]) is a fully combinational multiplier, and the size and delay of its realization is also shown in Table 1.

As the time for synthesizing simple circuits like these is negligible, it is easy for a designer to experiment with alternative designs, finding the best tradeoff between, e.g., speed and area.

The largest program synthesized is a part of an artificial neural net. The SYNCHRONIZED TRANSITIONS program describing the neuron consists of 620 lines. The layout was constructed manually using a full custom design system before the synthesis tool was finished. This chip consists of about 6000 transistors and the core area is 4.4 mm². It

Table 1. Transistor counts and delays for automatically synthesized delay insensitive adders and multipliers.

Design	Transistors	Min delay	Average delay	Max delay
8-bit ripple-carry adder	1524	10	38	66
8-bit Brent-Kung adder	4540	21	30	36
4-bit Braun multiplier	3380	38	39	40

took several man months to do the circuit design, test and layout. The chip has been fabricated and demonstrated to work. The same program has been synthesized automatically, the transistor count is almost the same. The translation of the program to a layout took less than 10 minutes. The synthesized chip was simulated on transistor level, and the results are identical to simulation of the manually designed chip. This example shows that the tools can be used for realistic designs, with a considerable saving in design time.

5 Implementation

The synthesis technique has been implemented as a compiler, transforming a program in SYNCHRONIZED TRANSITIONS to a netlist. A commercial layout generation system [2] is used for transformation of the netlist to a layout. By using a commercial system, we avoided writing routers, compactors, a.o.

The Steps of Synthesis

The synthesis tool accepts a delay insensitive program (fulfilling the Alternation condition), and transforms it to a realization that is functionally equivalent. The result of the synthesis is a new program directly describing the realization. The transitions have no preconditions, which means that the program can be considered a netlist, it is therefore called an ST netlist. This is compiled into a hardware descriptive language, MODEL. The MODEL description can be transformed to a layout by the layout system. Using the syntax of SYNCHRONIZED TRANSITIONS for describing the netlist has the advantage that it can be simulated and formally verified after the synthesis has been performed, using the same methods as for the high level program. This has facilitated our testing of the synthesis technique and tools. When the ST netlist is transformed to MODEL, the simulator in the layout system can simulate the synthesized circuit at transistor level. The steps of synthesis and layout generation are shown in Fig. 4.

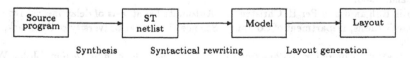

Fig. 4. Transformations from source to layout

6 Related Work

Many of the ideas of asynchronous switching circuits were first developed in the 1950's [8]. In this period, the primary concern was gate delays. With today's VLSI technology, wire delays are also significant. This shift of emphasis is clearly reflected in our definition of delay insensitivity.

At Caltech, Alain Martin and his colleagues have explored another approach to designing delay insensitive circuits which is also based on parallel programming. Their approach is based on a specification in a high level language using message passing, and applying systematic transformations to obtain the final design. Our emphasis has been somewhat different, stressing issues of *verification* and formal models of delay insensitive circuits.

7 Conclusion

We have described the synthesis aspects of a design technique for delay insensitive circuits. The cornerstone of this technique is the language SYNCHRONIZED TRANSITIONS. Programs in this language can be verified formally using tools supporting mechanical verification. In this paper we have described a tool for synthesizing delay insensitive circuits. Hence, we have demonstrated that it is feasible to use the same abstract description for both verification and synthesis.

Acknowledgements

Mark Greenstreet has contributed significantly to the development of SYNCHRONIZED TRANSITIONS and its use for designing delay insensitive circuits. Niels Mellergaard made the first translators on which the synthesis tool is based. Christian D. Nielsen and Mark Greenstreet have given us many valuable comments on earlier versions of this paper. Our work has been supported by the Danish Technical Research Council.

References

1. Richard P. Brent and H. T. Kung. A regular layout for parallel adders. *IEEE Transactions on Computers*, 31(3), 1982.
2. European Silicon Structures Limited. *Solo 1400 Reference Manuals*, January 1990.
3. Stephen J. Garland, John V. Guttag, and Jørgen Staunstrup. Verification of VLSI circuits using LP. In *The Fusion of Hardware Design and Verification*. IFIP WG. 10.2, North Holland, 1988.
4. Henrik Hulgaard and Per H. Christensen. Automated synthesis of delay insensitive circuits. Master's thesis, Department of Computer Science, Technical University of Denmark, August 1990.
5. Kai Hwang. *Computer Arithmetic: Principle, Architecture, and Design*. John Wiley & Sons, 1979.
6. Alain J. Martin. The limitations to delay-insensitivity in asynchronous circuits. Technical report, Department of Computer Science, California Institute of Technology, 1990. Caltech-CS-TR-90-02.

7. Charles E. Molnar, T.P. Fang, and F.U. Rosenberg. Synthesis of delay-insensitive modules. In Henry Fuchs, editor, *1985 Chapel Hill Conference on Very Large Scale Integration*, pages 67–86. Computer Science Press, 1985.

8. David E. Muller and W.S. Bartky. A theory of asynchronous circuits. In *Annals of the Computation Laboratory of Harvard University*, volume 29. Harvard University Press, 1959.

9. Narinder P. Singh. A design methodology for self-timed systems. Master's thesis, Laboratory for Computer Science, MIT, 1981. Technical Report TR-258.

10. Jørgen Staunstrup and Mark R. Greenstreet. Synchronized Transitions. In Jørgen Staunstrup, editor, *Formal Methods for VLSI Design*. North-Holland/Elsevier, 1990.

11. J.T. Udding. *Classification and Composition of Delay-Insensitive Circuits*. PhD thesis, Eindhoven University of Technology, 1984.

A Distributed Implementation of a Task Pool

H. Peter Hofstee, Johan J. Lukkien, Jan L. A. van de Snepscheut
Computer Science
California Institute of Technology
Pasadena, CA 91125

In this paper we present a distributed algorithm to implement a task pool. The algorithm can be used to implement a processor farm, i.e., a collection of processes that consume tasks from the task pool and possibly produce tasks into it. There are no restrictions on which process consumes which task nor on the order in which tasks are processed. The algorithm takes care of the distribution of the tasks over the processes and ensures load balancing. We derive the algorithm by transforming a sequential algorithm into a distributed one. The transformation is guided by the distribution of the data over processes. First we discuss the case of two processes, and then the general case of one or more processes.

Keywords: load balancing, processor farm, distributed computation.

1. Program notation

For the sequential part of the algorithms, we use Edsger W. Dijkstra's guarded command language [1]. For statements $S0$ and $S1$, statement $S0\|S1$ denotes their concurrent execution. The constituents $S0$ and $S1$ are then called processes. The statements may share variables (cf. [5]). We transform our algorithms in such a way, however, that the final code contains no shared variables and all synchronization and communication is performed by message passing. The semantics of the message passing primitives is as described in [4]. The main difference with C.A.R. Hoare's proposal in [2] is in the naming of channels rather than processes. In [3], the same author proposes to name channels instead of processes in communication commands, but differs from our notation by using one name per channel instead of our two: output command $R!E$ in one process is paired with input command $L?v$ in another process by declaring the pair (R, L) to be a channel between the two processes. Each channel is between two processes only. When declaring (R, L) to be a channel, we write the name on which the output actions are performed first and the name on which the input actions are performed last.

For an arbitrary command A, let cA denote the number of completed A actions, i.e., the number of times that command A has been executed since initiation of the program's execution. The *synchronization requirement* (cf. [4]) fulfilled by a channel (R, L) is that

$$\mathbf{c}\,R = \mathbf{c}\,L$$

holds at any point in the computation.

The execution of a command results either in the completion of the action or in its suspension when its completion would violate the synchronization requirement. From suspension until completion an action is *pending* and the process executing the action is delayed. We introduce boolean $\mathbf{q}\,A$ equal to the predicate "an A action is pending". Associated with a channel (R, L) we use $\overline{R} \equiv \mathbf{q}R!$ and $\overline{L} \equiv \mathbf{q}L?$ as defined in [7]. $\overline{L}$, pronounced *probe of L*, evaluates to *true* if an $R!$ action is pending, and to *false* otherwise. The *progress requirement* states that actions are suspended only if their completion would violate the synchronization requirement, i.e., channel (R, L) satisfies

$$\neg\mathbf{q}\,R \ \vee \ \neg\mathbf{q}\,L \quad .$$

The nth R action is said to match the nth L action. The completion of a matching pair of actions is called a *communication*. The *communication requirement* states that execution of matching actions $R!E$ and $L?v$ amounts to the assignment $v := E$. The semantics of the if statement is reinterpreted (cf. [2]). If all guards in an if statement evaluate to *false*, its execution results in suspension of the execution rather than **abort**. When the guards contain no shared variables, an if statement that is suspended remains suspended and therefore this definition is compatible with the original semantics.

2. Statement of the problem

Given is a finite, constant number of processes $C_{(0 \leq i < N)}$ capable of consuming or producing tasks. Associated with each of these processes is a pool process P_i. Each process C_i communicates only with its pool process. The pool processes also communicate with one another. Each pool can hold an unbounded number of tasks. (We will address bounded pool sizes in section 6.) The problem is to construct pool processes in such a way that no process C_i is idle forever if there is enough work to be done.

We do not want to impose restrictions on the processes C_i . Since a process C_i might, once activated, produce another task at any time, we cannot expect the algorithm for the pool to terminate. The requirements for the program can be formulated as follows:

(0). A situation in which a process is idle whereas there are enough tasks in the network to keep all processes busy does not persist.

(1). If the processes C_i do not consume or produce tasks, the number of communications is bounded.

The first requirement guarantees progress, whereas the second requirement guarantees quiescence in the absence of communications between the C_i and P_i .

Coming up with the proper formalization of the first condition is nontrivial. On the one hand the condition should not be overly restrictive, since this will give rise to a large communication overhead. On the other hand several candidates for this condition had to be rejected because they allowed stable states that were undesirable. We finally replaced the first condition with the following:

(0)'. Either communications are pending or $(\forall i :: p_i \leq T) \vee (\forall i :: p_i \geq T)$.

(0)". There is no deadlock.

T is some fixed positive number, the threshold, and p_i denotes the number of elements in pool i. If we assume items are communicated one at a time, the solution seems obvious; select a pair of pools where one has more than T and the other has less than T elements and send an element from the fuller to the emptier pool. Written as a global sequential program, and ignoring the processes C_i and the actual communication of tasks, we obtain the program in Figure 1. The quantified expression ($\| i :: guarded\text{-}command_i$) should be interpreted as one guarded command for every i.

$$\textbf{do } (\| \ i,j :: p_i < T \ \wedge \ p_j > T \rightarrow p_i, p_j := p_i + 1, p_j - 1 \ ) \textbf{ od}$$

–Figure 1–

The negation of the guards is $(\forall i :: p_i \leq T) \vee (\forall i :: p_i \geq T)$. Termination is guaranteed by the bound function $\sum_i |p_i - T|$. This sequential algorithm can be transformed into a distributed algorithm on a fully connected graph. However, since the resulting algorithm would not scale well with the size of the graph, we do not pursue this solution here.

We have tried to solve this problem by an approach similar to that in [6], that is, by examining a linear communication network for the processes P_i and by introducing variables that will approach $(\exists j : 0 \leq j < i : p_j < T)$ etc.. This gives rise to an extremely complicated algorithm if we do not want to make assumptions about the C_i, mainly because any global information is volatile.

3. An asymmetric solution

If the process graph is not fully connected, the problem cannot be solved in a symmetric way on the basis of information about a process and its neighbors only. To see this, consider the following series of values for the pools:

$$p_0 = T - 1 \qquad p_1 = T \qquad p_2 = T + 1$$

A symmetric bound function such as $\sum_i |p_i - T|$ would not be decreased by communicating an item from pool P_2 to pool P_1 or from pool P_1 to pool

P_0. Stated differently, a solution that would do this cannot be expected to satisfy our second condition: we cannot put an upperbound on the number of communications.

The solution is as follows. We break the symmetry by constructing a rooted, directed tree. We define $p\text{-}edge_{ij}$ to be true just when an edge from i to j directed towards the root exists in the tree. We define w_i to be the distance in the tree of node i from the root. We ensure progress by building our solution on the following bound function:

$$\sum_i |p_i - T| \cdot w_i$$

We have now solved the problem of the 'equalities' in our previous example. After assigning weight i to pool P_i we now have, for example, that communicating a task from P_2 to P_1 decreases the bound function, whereas a communication from P_1 to P_0 increases the bound function. The global effect is that 'equalities' will tend to accumulate from the leaves on up. Our solution, written once again as a global sequential program is:

$$\begin{aligned}
&\mathbf{do}\ (\![\,i,j : p\text{-}edge_{ij} : p_i > T\ \ \wedge\ \ p_j \leq T \rightarrow p_i, p_j := p_i - 1, p_j + 1) \\
&\ [\!]\ \ (\![\,i,j : p\text{-}edge_{ij} : p_i < T\ \ \wedge\ \ p_j \geq T \rightarrow p_i, p_j := p_i + 1, p_j - 1) \\
&\mathbf{od}
\end{aligned}$$

–Figure 2–

Upon termination, $p_i > T$ in any node, implies $p_{root} > T$, as can easily be proven by induction on the length of a path along $p\text{-}edges$ from i to the root. Similarly, $p_i < T$ in any node implies $p_{root} < T$. Upon termination we have, therefore $\neg(\exists i, j :: p_i < T\ \wedge\ p_j > T)$ which is equivalent to $(\forall i :: p_i \leq T) \vee (\forall i :: p_i \geq T)$.

4. Program transformation

We now transform the global sequential solution into a local and distributed one. We limit ourselves to two processes for now. Process P_0 is the designated root. The only edge in the tree is from P_1 to P_0. In this case our sequential solution simplifies to Figure 3. It describes the combined effect of P_0 and P_1.

Next, we split it into two processes. We introduce new variables q_i to hold the value of the p_i of the other process. Using channels (OUT_0, IN_1), and (OUT_1, IN_0) to communicate tasks, we obtain the program in Figure 4 in which we have eliminated all shared variables.

$$\textbf{do } p_1 > T \;\; \land \;\; p_0 \leq T \rightarrow p_1, p_0 := p_1 - 1, p_0 + 1$$
$$\;\;\| \;\; p_1 < T \;\; \land \;\; p_0 \geq T \rightarrow p_1, p_0 := p_1 + 1, p_0 - 1$$
$$\textbf{od}$$

–Figure 3–

$\mathbf{P_0} \equiv \quad \{ initialization \; establishes \; q_1 = p_1 \}$
$$\textbf{do } q_1 > T \;\; \land \;\; p_0 \leq T \rightarrow IN_1?task; q_1, p_0 := q_1 - 1, p_0 + 1$$
$$\;\;\| \;\; q_1 < T \;\; \land \;\; p_0 \geq T \rightarrow OUT_1!task; q_1, p_0 := q_1 + 1, p_0 - 1$$
$$\textbf{od}$$

$\mathbf{P_1} \equiv \quad \{ initialization \; establishes \; q_0 = p_0 \}$
$$\textbf{do } p_1 > T \;\; \land \;\; q_0 \leq T \rightarrow OUT_0!task; p_1, q_0 := p_1 - 1, q_0 + 1$$
$$\;\;\| \;\; p_1 < T \;\; \land \;\; q_0 \geq T \rightarrow IN_0?task; p_1, q_0 := p_1 + 1, q_0 - 1$$
$$\textbf{od}$$

–Figure 4–

The invariant $p_0 = q_0 \;\land\; p_1 = q_1$ guarantees that communications are started under the same condition in both processes. Statement $OUT_1!task$ selects an arbitrary task from the part of the pool stored in $\mathbf{P_0}$ and transmits it via channel OUT_1. Since guard $p_0 \geq T$ holds, the local task pool is nonempty. Statement $IN_1?task$ receives a task via channel IN_1 and adds it to the local part of the task pool. We leave the rest of the verification of this program to the reader.

The next transformation includes the processes C_i. We simulate their effect by including the line

$$\overline{P_i} \rightarrow P_i?p_i$$

where the channel $(\ldots, P_i)$ connects each pool process to its computing process. The invariant $p_0 = q_0 \;\land\; p_1 = q_1$ of the previous program can now no longer be maintained without extra communication. To keep this extra communication to a minimum, we keep track of the last communicated values of the p_i in the variables op_i and start a new communication only if a change in p_i affects one of the guards in its neighboring pool process. We cannot predict when another communication may be started by the other process, therefore the communication channels have to be probed. After a communication has started, we must first update the values of the q_i to ensure that communicating a task will indeed result in progress, and to ensure that communications match. This suggests the program shown in Figure 5. To simplify the initialization we start with an empty task pool.

$$\mathbf{P_0} \equiv \; p_0, q_1, op_0 := 0, 0, 0;$$
$$\mathbf{do} \;\; true \to$$
$$\mathbf{if} \; \overline{IN_1} \; \vee$$
$$(q_1 > T \;\; \wedge \;\; p_0 \leq T) \vee (q_1 < T \;\; \wedge \;\; p_0 \geq T) \vee$$
$$(sign(p_0 - T) \neq sign(op_0 - T)) \to$$
$$(OUT_1!p_0 \parallel IN_1?q_1); \; op_0 := p_0;$$
$$\mathbf{do} \; q_1 > T \wedge p_0 \leq T \to$$
$$IN_1?task; q_1, p_0, op_0 := q_1 - 1, p_0 + 1, op_0 + 1$$
$$\| \;\; q_1 < T \wedge p_0 \geq T \to$$
$$OUT_1!task; q_1, p_0, op_0 := q_1 + 1, p_0 - 1, op_0 - 1$$
$$\mathbf{od}$$
$$\| \;\; \overline{P_0} \; \to \; P_0?p_0$$
$$\mathbf{fi}$$
$$\mathbf{od}$$

$$\mathbf{P_1} \equiv \; q_0, p_1, op_1 := 0, 0, 0;$$
$$\mathbf{do} \;\; true \to$$
$$\mathbf{if} \; \overline{IN_0} \; \vee$$
$$(p_1 > T \;\; \wedge \;\; q_0 \leq T) \vee (p_1 < T \;\; \wedge \;\; q_0 \geq T) \vee$$
$$(sign(p_1 - T) \neq sign(op_1 - T)) \to$$
$$(OUT_0!p_1 \parallel IN_0?q_0); \; op_1 := p_1;$$
$$\mathbf{do} \; p_1 > T \wedge q_0 \leq T \to$$
$$OUT_0!task; p_1, q_0, op_1 := p_1 - 1, q_0 + 1, op_1 - 1$$
$$\| \;\; p_1 < T \wedge q_0 \geq T \to$$
$$IN_0?task; p_1, q_0, op_1 := p_1 + 1, q_0 - 1, op_1 + 1$$
$$\mathbf{od}$$
$$\| \;\; \overline{P_1} \; \to \; P_1?p_1$$
$$\mathbf{fi}$$
$$\mathbf{od}$$

–Figure 5–

We prove the generalization of this algorithm to the tree described in section 3. The program can be found in Figure 6. The channels are (OUT_{ij}, IN_{ji}), for which $p\text{-}edge_{ij} \lor p\text{-}edge_{ji}$. For those i and j we have introduced variables op_{ij} to keep track of the value of p_i last communicated from process $\mathbf{P}_i$ to process $\mathbf{P}_j$ and variables q_{ij} to hold the values of the p_j last communicated by process $\mathbf{P}_j$.

$$
\begin{aligned}
\mathbf{P}_i \equiv \quad & p_i := 0; \; (; \, j : p\text{-}edge_{ij} \lor p\text{-}edge_{ji} : q_{ij}, op_{ij} := 0,0); \\
& \mathbf{do} \; true \rightarrow \\
& \quad \mathbf{if} \quad ([\!|\, j : p\text{-}edge_{ji} : \\
& \qquad \overline{IN_{ij}} \; \lor \\
& \qquad (q_{ij} > T \;\land\; p_i \le T) \lor (q_{ij} < T \;\land\; p_i \ge T) \lor \\
& \qquad (sign(p_i - T) \ne sign(op_{ij} - T)) \rightarrow \\
& \qquad\quad (OUT_{ij}!p_i \parallel IN_{ij}?q_{ij}); \; op_{ij} := p_i; \\
& \qquad\quad \mathbf{do} \; q_{ij} > T \land p_i \le T \rightarrow \\
& \qquad\qquad IN_{ij}?task; q_{ij}, p_i, op_{ij} := q_{ij} - 1, p_i + 1, op_{ij} + 1 \\
& \qquad\quad [\!| \;\; q_{ij} < T \land p_i \ge T \rightarrow \\
& \qquad\qquad OUT_{ij}!task; q_{ij}, p_i, op_{ij} := q_{ij} + 1, p_i - 1, op_{ij} - 1 \\
& \qquad\quad \mathbf{od} \\
& \qquad) \\
& \quad [\!| \quad ([\!|\, j : p\text{-}edge_{ij} : \\
& \qquad \overline{IN_{ij}} \; \lor \\
& \qquad (p_i > T \;\land\; q_{ij} \le T) \lor (p_i < T \;\land\; q_{ij} \ge T) \lor \\
& \qquad (sign(p_i - T) \ne sign(op_{ij} - T)) \rightarrow \\
& \qquad\quad (OUT_{ij}!p_i \parallel IN_{ij}?q_{ij}); \; op_{ij} := p_i; \\
& \qquad\quad \mathbf{do} \; p_i > T \land q_{ij} \le T \rightarrow \\
& \qquad\qquad OUT_{ij}!task; p_i, q_{ij}, op_{ij} := p_i - 1, q_{ij} + 1, op_{ij} - 1 \\
& \qquad\quad [\!| \;\; p_i < T \land q_{ij} \ge T \rightarrow \\
& \qquad\qquad IN_{ij}?task; p_i, q_{ij}, op_{ij} := p_i + 1, q_{ij} - 1, op_{ij} + 1 \\
& \qquad\quad \mathbf{od} \\
& \qquad) \\
& \quad [\!| \; \overline{P_i} \;\; \rightarrow \; P_i?p_i \\
& \quad \mathbf{fi} \\
& \mathbf{od}
\end{aligned}
$$

−*Figure 6*−

We need the following invariant: $(\forall i, j :: q_{ij} = op_{ji})$. The invariant holds initially and continues to hold because the statement $(OUT_{ij}!p_i \parallel IN_{ij}?q_{ij}); op_{ij} := p_i$ in process $\mathbf{P}_i$ pairs with statement $(OUT_{ji}!p_j \parallel IN_{ji}?q_{ji}); op_{ji} := p_j$ in process $\mathbf{P}_j$ to yield the assignment $op_{ij}, q_{ji}, op_{ji}, q_{ij} := p_i, p_i, p_j, p_j$ which clearly maintains the invariant. Furthermore assignment $q_{ij}, p_i, op_{ij} := q_{ij} - 1, p_i + 1, op_{ij} + 1$ in the first alternative of the first innermost do construct of process $\mathbf{P}_i$ is guaranteed to match with assignment $p_i, q_{ij}, op_{ij} := p_i - 1, q_{ij} + 1, op_{ij} - 1$ in the second innermost do construct in process $\mathbf{P}_j$ because the preceding statements establish $p_i = q_{ji} \land p_j = q_{ij}$. The other alternative is similar and both pairs maintain the invariant. Finally, statement $P_i?p_i$ does not change q_{ij} or op_{ij}.

We check our three requirements one by one:

(0)'. Either there are communications pending or $(\forall i :: p_i \leq T) \lor (\forall i :: p_i \geq T)$.

We assume all processes have been suspended on the guards in the if statements and that $(\exists i, j :: p_i < T \land p_j > T)$ and derive a contradiction as in section 3. If $p_i < T$ and all guards are false, then $(\forall j : p\text{-}edge_{ij} : q_{ij} < T)$. Unless i is the root, such a j exists. The invariant implies $op_{ji} < T$ for that j and the falsity of the guard $sign(p_j - T) \neq sign(op_{ji} - T)$ implies $p_j < T$. By induction $p_{root} < T$. By symmetry we also have $p_{root} > T$, which establishes the contradiction.

(0)". There is no deadlock.

The graph we have constructed is a tree. Since this is an acyclic structure, and since the algorithm guarantees that two processes cannot deadlock when they are committed to communicating with one another, there is no cycle in the communication dependencies. Therefore there is no deadlock.

(1). If the processes $\mathbf{C}_i$ do not consume or produce tasks, the number of communications is bounded.

A bound function that decreases on every repetition of the outermost do construct (other than communications between a $\mathbf{P}_i$ and a $\mathbf{C}_i$) is

$$\sum_i |p_i - T| \cdot w_i + (\mathbf{N}i, j : p\text{-}edge_{ij} \lor p\text{-}edge_{ji} : p_i \neq q_{ji})$$

The proof is as follows. An execution of the first alternative in process $\mathbf{P}_i$ always matches with the execution of the second alternative in some process $\mathbf{P}_j$ for which $p\text{-}edge_{ji}$. For any such pair the first sum can never increase due to the fact that the first pair of communications establishes $p_i = q_{ji} \land p_j = q_{ij}$. If before the communication either $(sign(p_i - T) \neq sign(op_{ij} - T))$ in $\mathbf{P}_i$ or $(sign(p_j - T) \neq sign(op_{ji} - T))$ in $\mathbf{P}_j$, then the assignments $op_{ij} := p_i$ and $op_{ji} := p_j$ in $\mathbf{P}_i$ and $\mathbf{P}_j$ respectively, in conjunction with the invariant, $op_{ij} = q_{ji} \land op_{ji} = q_{ij}$, imply that the variant function decreases. If $(sign(p_i - T) = sign(op_{ij} - T))$ in $\mathbf{P}_i$ and $(sign(p_j - T) = sign(op_{ji} - T))$ in $\mathbf{P}_j$, but all guards in the innermost do statements evaluate to false, so that the first part of the variant function does not decrease, either q_{ij} in $\mathbf{P}_i$ or q_{ji} in $\mathbf{P}_j$ must have changed in the first pair of communications and the second term in the invariant has decreased.

Note. The algorithm in Figure 6 can be somewhat simplified by omitting $(p_i > T \wedge q_{ij} \leq T) \vee (p_i > T \wedge q_{ij} \geq T)$ from the guard of the second outermost alternative. This can be done because for any pair $\mathbf{P}_i, \mathbf{P}_j$ of processes that may communicate the following holds:

$$(p_i > T \ \wedge \ q_{ij} \leq T) \vee (p_i < T \ \wedge \ q_{ij} \geq T)$$
$$\Rightarrow$$
$$(q_{ji} > T \ \wedge \ p_j \leq T) \vee (q_{ji} < T \ \wedge \ p_j \geq T) \vee$$
$$sign(p_i - T) \neq sign(op_{ij} - T) \vee$$
$$sign(p_j - T) \neq sign(op_{ji} - T)$$

which can be proven by using the invariant $op_{ij} = q_{ji} \ \wedge \ op_{ji} = q_{ij}$.

5. More thresholds

If we want to put stronger bounds on how much the pools can be allowed to differ, we can add more thresholds in a straightforward manner. Condition $(\forall i :: p_i \leq T) \vee (\forall i :: p_i \geq T)$ is replaced by $(\forall k :: (\forall i :: p_i \leq T_k) \vee (\forall i :: p_i \geq T_k))$. The algorithm is given in Figure 7.

The proof that our first two requirements are still being met is nearly identical to the case with one threshold and is left to the reader. However, to guarantee that the number of communications, on the absence of communications with the computing processes, is bounded, we have to insist that the threshold values differ by at least two. A bound function is then given by the following two-tuple, and the ordering is lexicographic ordering.

$$\left(\sum_i p_i^2 + (Ni, j : p\text{-}edge_{ij} \vee p\text{-}edge_{ji} : p_i \neq q_{ji}), \sum_i (MINk :: |p_i - T_k| \cdot w_i) \right)$$

Without proof we state that, as in the previous algorithm, on every communication between two processes $\mathbf{P}_i$ and $\mathbf{P}_j$, either a task is being communicated, or the second term in the first element of the two-tuple decreases. If a task is being communicated, and p_i and p_j differed originally by more than one, the sum over the squares decreases. Without loss of generality we can state $w_i < w_j$, therefore $p\text{-}edge_{ji} = true$. If p_i and p_j originally differed by exactly one, then it follows that originally $p_i = T_k$ for some k and $|p_j - T_k| = 1$ for that k. The communication of the task then reduces the second element of the two-tuple by $w_j - w_i$. The fact that the T_k differ by at least two, is needed here to guarantee that the k's for which the terms in the second element of the two tuple are minimal do not change.

$$P_i \equiv p_i := 0; \ (; \ j : p\text{-}edge_{ij} \lor p\text{-}edge_{ji} : q_{ij}, op_{ij} := 0, 0);$$

$$\textbf{do } true \to$$

$$\textbf{if } (\llbracket j : p\text{-}edge_{ji} :$$

$$\overline{IN_{ij}} \lor$$

$$(\exists k :: (q_{ij} > T_k \ \land \ p_i \leq T_k) \lor (q_{ij} < T_k \ \land \ p_i \geq T_k)) \lor$$

$$(\exists k :: sign(p_i - T_k) \neq sign(op_{ij} - T_k)) \to$$

$$(OUT_{ij}!p_i \parallel IN_{ij}?q_{ij}); \ op_{ij} := p_i;$$

$$\textbf{do } (\exists k :: q_{ij} > T_k \land p_i \leq T_k) \to$$

$$\qquad IN_{ij}?task; q_{ij}, p_i, op_{ij} := q_{ij} - 1, p_i + 1, op_{ij} + 1$$

$$\llbracket \ (\exists k :: q_{ij} < T_k \land p_i \geq T_k) \to$$

$$\qquad OUT_{ij}!task; q_{ij}, p_i, op_{ij} := q_{ij} + 1, p_i - 1, op_{ij} - 1$$

$$\textbf{od}$$

$$)$$

$$\llbracket \ (\llbracket j : p\text{-}edge_{ij} :$$

$$\overline{IN_{ij}} \lor$$

$$(\exists k :: (p_i > T_k \ \land \ q_{ij} \leq T_k) \lor (p_i < T_k \ \land \ q_{ij} \geq T_k)) \lor$$

$$(\exists k :: sign(p_i - T_k) \neq sign(op_{ij} - T_k)) \to$$

$$(OUT_{ij}!p_i \parallel IN_{ij}?q_{ij}); \ op_{ij} := p_i;$$

$$\textbf{do } (\exists k :: p_i > T_k \land q_{ij} \leq T_k) \to$$

$$\qquad OUT_{ij}!task; p_i, q_{ij}, op_{ij} := p_i - 1, q_{ij} + 1, op_{ij} - 1$$

$$\llbracket \ (\exists k :: p_i < T_k \land q_{ij} \geq T_k) \to$$

$$\qquad IN_{ij}?task; p_i, q_{ij}, op_{ij} := p_i + 1, q_{ij} - 1, op_{ij} + 1$$

$$\textbf{od}$$

$$)$$

$$\llbracket \ \overline{P_i} \ \to \ P_i?p_i$$

$$\textbf{fi}$$

$$\textbf{od}$$

–*Figure 7*–

We can greatly reduce the amount of computation needed to evaluate the guards in the algorithm in Figure 7 by maintaining variables tl_i and tg_i such that

$$tl_i \leq p_i \leq tg_i \ \land \ ((\exists k :: tl_i = T_k) \lor tl_i = 0) \ \land$$
$$((\exists k :: tg_i = T_k) \lor tg_i = poolsize) \ \land$$
$$\neg(\exists k :: tl_i < T_k \leq p_i \lor p_i \leq T_k < tg_i)$$

All existential quantifications can then be removed from the guards.

6. Finite pool sizes

If the size of the pools is fixed, it is possible that our algorithm attempts to add a task to a pool that has reached its capacity. Not much can be done about the situation where all pools are full, but it would be problematic if the program would deadlock in a situation where pool space is available in another processor. Since a communication between two pool processes does not increase the size of the largest pool, a problem can only occur in the communications between the C_i and their P_i. If we replace the single channel by two channels, one over which tasks are consumed, and one over which tasks are produced, and replace the guard for P_{prod} by $\overline{P}_{prod} \land p_i < poolsize$ and assume that tasks are produced one at a time, the problem is solved. We can ensure that computation power is used efficiently until all buffers fill up by choosing one of the thresholds to be $poolsize - 1$.

7. Discussion

This paper is an attempt to deal in a systematic way with a problem that in our experience occurs frequently. In the past when solving a distributed programming problem of this type, we would construct the C_i for that particular problem, think of a strategy that would provide a decent load balance, and construct P_i for that specific problem. The present solution seems to be more general.

Acknowledgement

We thank Nan Boden for helpful comments on the manuscript.

References

[1] E.W. Dijkstra, *A Discipline of Programming*, (Prentice Hall, Englewood Cliffs, NJ 1976).

[2] C.A.R. Hoare, Communicating Sequential Processes, *Comm. ACM* (1978) 666-677.

[3] C.A.R. Hoare, *Communicating Sequential Processes*, (Prentice-Hall International Series in Computer Science, 1985)

[4] A.J. Martin, An Axiomatic Definition of Synchronization Primitives, *Acta Informatica* 16, (1981) 219-235.

[5] S. Owicki, D. Gries, An Axiomatic Proof Technique for Parallel programs, *Acta Informatica* 6, (1976) 319-340.

[6] H. P. Hofstee, A. J. Martin, J. L. A. van de Snepscheut, Distributed Sorting, *Science of Computer Programming* 15 (1990) 119-133

[7] A.J. Martin, The Probe: An Addition to Communication Primitives, *Information Processing Letters* 20 (1985) 125-130

INVARIANCE AND CONTRACTION BY INFINITE ITERATIONS OF RELATIONS

Michel Sintzoff

University of Louvain [1]

1 Introduction

This paper results from a study of dynamical systems in the context of the theory of non-deterministic programs, e.g. parallel ones. Indeed, both the theory of programs and that of dynamical systems are based on the fundamental concepts of invariance (viz. fixpoint or equilibrium) and contraction (viz. progress, termination, or stability). It is thus tempting to analyze discrete-time dynamical systems in terms of programs. For instance, the characteristic doubling-map can be expressed as follows :

$$S = \begin{array}{ll} [\, 0 \leqslant x < 1/2 & \rightarrow x := 2x \\ [\!]\, 1/2 \leqslant x \leqslant 1 & \rightarrow x := 2x - 1 \\ ]\ \text{where } x \in Real \end{array}$$

This approach allows to extend known results about deterministic dynamical systems on continuous spaces to non-deterministic systems and to discrete domains. Interesting dynamics such as mixing is caused by a conjunction of invariance and contraction on the past and the future of system behaviours viewed together.

The paper assumes a basic knowledge of the logic of iterative programs (e.g. [Dij]) and of the mathematics of dynamical systems (e.g. [Wgg]).

Exercises are grouped at the end, to show their common structure better.

Conventions:

We often denote function application by a dot, viz. $f.a$ for $f(a)$. Function composition is written from right to left : $(f \circ g)(a) = f(g(a)) = f.g.a$. We use a linear notation for bound variables in quantifier-like operators Ω :

$$\Omega\, i \in A : c(i) : E(i) \quad \text{stands for} \quad \underset{c(i)}{\Omega\, E(i)} \quad \text{where } i \in A$$

For instance, $\Sigma i \in Nat : 1 \leqslant i \leqslant N : i^2$ can be read $\sum_{i=1}^{n} i^2$.

We abbreviate **false** by **f** and **true** by **t**, and identify a predicate on states with the set of states verifying that predicate; we thus speak of, e.g., inclusion between predicates or emptiness of predicates. A state is an element, or point, in the set of states, or state space. Typical state-spaces are Cartesian products of numbers; states then are tuples. We assume each decreasing chain of predicates has a limit.

If Σ is a finite alphabet, then Σ^* (resp. Σ^∞) is the set of finite (resp. infinite) words over Σ, and

---

[1]Unité d'Informatique, pl. Ste-Barbe 2, B-1348 Louvain-la-Neuve, Belgium.

$$\Sigma^\omega = \Sigma^* \cup \Sigma^\infty, \quad \Sigma^* \Sigma^\infty = \Sigma^\infty \Sigma^* = \Sigma^\infty.$$

In proofs, a justification may be written on the line immediately above the formula it justifies.

2 Transition-system programs

These constitute an elementary subset [Snt] of the non-deterministic guarded commands [Dij]; a wider subset was considered in [vLS]. A **transition-system program**, or **program** for short, is a finite set of transition expressions consisting of a boolean expression, or guard, $b_i.x$ and a substitution $x := e_i.x$, where x is the vector of state-variables. Guards may overlap, so that transition programs define relations rather than functions. In a substitution $x := e_i.x$ (a.k.a. assignment), e_i is a tuple of terms expressing a function between state tuples; each map e_i is defined on b_i :

$$\forall x : (b_i.x \Rightarrow \exists v : v = e_i.x) \tag{1}$$

A map e_i may be applied on a state u iff $b_i.u$ is true; it is required maps e_i be invertible. To sum up,

if $\quad S_i = (b_i.x \to x := e_i.x)$, for $i \in \Sigma$ and $\Sigma = \{1, 2, \ldots, N\}$,

then $\quad S = [\![\, [\!] \, i \in \Sigma : S_i]\!]$

$\qquad\qquad = [\, b_1.x \to x := e_1.x \, [\!] \, \ldots \, [\!] \, b_N.x \to x := e_N.x \,]$

A transition-system program represents a non-deterministic choice between deterministic functions, and thus defines a relation between states. If S has the form above, the relation uSv is defined by

$$\begin{aligned} uSv &= \quad \bigvee i \in \Sigma : uS_iv \\ uS_iv &= \quad b_i.u \wedge (v = e_i.u) \end{aligned} \tag{2}$$

To recover a functional, deterministic framework, we use the two predicate transformers S_- et S_+, viz. two functions between sets of states : $S_-.P$ and $S_+.P$ respectively define the **pre-image** and the **post-image** of a predicate P by the relation defined by S. In other words, $S_-.P$ yields the set of states which are related by S to states in P, whereas $S_+.P$ yields the set of states to which states in P are related by S.

For any relation R, we define thus the direct and inverse predicate-transformers R_+ and R_-; they can be called the post- and the pre-former :

$$\begin{aligned} (R_+.P).x &= \quad \exists u : uRx \wedge P.u \\ (R_-.P).x &= \quad \exists v : xRv \wedge P.v \end{aligned}$$

If R' is the inverse of R, then $R'_+ = R_-$.
For a program S, we have

$$(S_+.P).x = \quad \exists u : uSx \wedge P.u$$
$$= \quad \bigvee i \in \Sigma : (S_{i+}.P).x \tag{3}$$
$$(S_-.P).x = \quad \exists v : xSv \wedge P.v$$
$$= \quad \bigvee i \in \Sigma : (S_{i-}.P).x$$

The more restrictive backward transformer $wp.S$ [Dij] yields the weakest precondition

$$(wp.S).P = S_-.P \wedge \neg S_-.\neg P$$

This is the set of states from which P can be reached by the relation S, and from which the relation S may not fail to reach P. The corresponding forward transformer $sp.S$ yields the strongest postcondition

$$(sp.S).P = S_+.P \wedge \neg S_+.\neg P$$

These simple definitions of the more restrictive transformers only hold for single-step transition relations S.

Notations :

$$R_\pm^{n+1} \quad = R_\pm^n \circ R_\pm, \qquad R_\pm^0.P \quad = P$$

$$S_{+,-}.P \quad = S_+.P \wedge S_-.P$$

Thus

$$S_{+,-}.P = \bigvee i, j \in \Sigma : S_{i+}.P \wedge S_{j-}.P$$

The post-pre-former $S_{+,-}$ will play a central rôle.

2.1 Properties of predicate transformers

Strictness :

$$S_\pm.\mathbf{f} = \mathbf{f}$$

Or-distributivity :

$$S_\pm.(P \vee Q) = S_\pm.P \vee S_\pm.Q$$

Monotonicity :

$$S_\pm.P \Rightarrow S_\pm.(P \vee Q) \tag{4}$$

And-distributivity :

If S defines a (deterministic) function, then

$$S_\pm.(P \wedge Q) = S_\pm.P \wedge S_\pm.Q$$

The above, admittedly redundant, properties are verified easily.

And-continuity :

If $P_{n+1} \Rightarrow P_n$ for all n,

$$S_\pm.(\forall n \in Nat : P_n) = (\forall n \in Nat : S_\pm.P_n) \tag{5}$$

Indeed, for all m,

$$
\begin{aligned}
& S_\pm.(\forall n : 1 \leqslant n \leqslant m : P_n) \\
& \{P_{n+1} \Rightarrow P_n, \text{ for each } n\} \\
= \ & S_\pm.P_m \\
& \{S_\pm.P_{n+1} \Rightarrow S_\pm.P_n \text{ by monotonicity (4) of } S_\pm, \text{ for each } n\} \\
= \ & \forall n : 1 \leqslant n \leqslant m : S_\pm.P_n
\end{aligned}
$$

The and-continuity of $S_\pm$ follows for $m \to \infty$. QED

Semi-inversion :

$$P \wedge S_\pm.t \Rightarrow S_\pm.S_\mp.P \tag{6}$$

Indeed, for the case $P \wedge S_+.t$,

$$
\begin{aligned}
& P.x \wedge (S_+.t).x \\
& \{\text{defn (3) of } S_+\} \\
= \ & P.x \wedge \exists u : uSx \wedge t \\
& \{\text{logic}\} \\
= \ & \exists u, v : uSx \wedge P.x \wedge (x = v) \\
& \{\text{substitution rule and logic}\} \\
\Rightarrow \ & \exists u, v : uSx \wedge uSv \wedge P.v \\
& \{\text{logic}\} \\
= \ & \exists u : uSx \wedge (\exists v : uSv \wedge P.v) \\
& \{\text{defn (3) of } S_-\} \\
= \ & \exists u : uSx \wedge (S_-.P).u \\
& \{\text{defn (3) of } S_+\} \\
= \ & (S_+.S_-.P).x
\end{aligned}
$$

When S is deterministic, viz. functional, the implication in the proof and in the thesis can be replaced by an equivalence. The proof of the second case, for $P \wedge S_-.t$, is similar. QED

The rules of semi-inversion hold when the program S reduces to a single transition S_i, which is deterministic :

$$P \wedge S_{i\pm}.t \Leftrightarrow S_{i\pm}.S_{i\mp}.P \tag{7}$$

Iterated transformers :

Two-way iterations of transformers are subsumed under one-way iterations:

$$\forall n \geqslant 1 : \forall i,j \in \Sigma : S_{i-}.S_{-}^n.t \wedge S_{j+}.S_{+}^n.t \Rightarrow S_{j+}.S_{-}^n.t \wedge S_{i-}.S_{+}^n.t \qquad (8)$$

Indeed, for all i,j :

$$S_{i-}.S_{-}^n.t \wedge S_{j+}.S_{+}^n.t$$

$\quad \{S_{i-}$ and S_{j+} are (2) in S_- and $S_+\}$
$\Rightarrow \quad S_{-}^{n+1}.t \wedge S_{+}^{n+1}.t \wedge S_{i-}.S_{-}^n.t \wedge S_{j+}.S_{+}^n.t$

$\quad \{S_{-}^{n+1}.t \Rightarrow S_{-}^{n-1}.t$ by monotonicity (4) of S_-, and similarly for S_+;
$\quad S_{i-}.S_{-}^n.t \Rightarrow S_{i-}.t$ by monotonicity of S_{i-}, and similarly for $S_{j+}\}$
$\Rightarrow \quad S_{-}^{n-1}.t \wedge S_{+}^{n-1}.t \wedge S_{i-}.t \wedge S_{j+}.t$

$\quad \{$semi-inversions (7) for $P = S_{-}^{n-1}.t$ and $P = S_{+}^{n-1}.t\}$
$= \quad S_{j+}.S_{j-}.S_{-}^{n-1}.t \wedge S_{i-}.S_{i+}.S_{+}^{n-1}.t$

$\quad \{S_{i-}$ and S_{j+} are (2) in S_- and $S_+\}$
$\Rightarrow \quad S_{j+}.S_{-}^n.t \wedge S_{i-}.S_{+}^n.t$

2.2 Effective use of transformers

Quantifiers over states should preferably be eliminated when deriving expressions for $S_+.P$ and $S_-.P$. In particular, for S_-,

$\quad (S_-.P).x$
$\quad \{$defns (3) and (2) of S_- and $S_{i-}\}$
$= \quad \bigvee i \in \Sigma : \exists v : b_i.x \wedge (v = e_i.x) \wedge P.v$
$\quad \{(1)$ and substitution rule$\}$
$= \quad \bigvee i \in \Sigma : b_i.x \wedge P.e_i.x$

This well-known elimination can be adapted as follows for S_+; assume we find Q_i's such that $Q_i.e_i.x = b_i.x \wedge P.x$ for each i and all x :

$\quad (S_+.P).x$
$\quad \{$defns (3) and (2) of S_+ and $S_{i+}\}$
$= \quad \bigvee i \in \Sigma : \exists u : b_i.u \wedge (x = e_i.u) \wedge P.u$
$\quad \{$assumption about each Q_i, and substitution rule$\}$
$= \quad \bigvee i \in \Sigma : Q_i.x$

Moreover, it is may be feasible to derive an inverse S' of S : then $S_+ = S'_-$.

3 Invariance

Invariant predicates defined for programs (e.g.[Fld, Dij, vLS]) are in fact positively invariant : they are preserved by direct iterations, towards the future. On the other hand, invariant sets for dynamical systems (e.g.[Dvn, Wgg]) in general must be completely invariant, i.e. positively as well as negatively : they are preserved by direct as well as inverse transitions, and thus define sets of states indefinitely accessible in the future and in the past. This explains why dynamical systems are often required to be invertible state-functions; this technical constraint is superfluous here since the past and future behaviours of programs are respectively characterized by forward and backward set-functions, viz. by the predicate transformers S_+ and S_-. A predicate P is preserved by some direct application of S, in the future, if P implies its pre-image $S_-.P$ by S_-; for the past, we apply S_+ in a similar way. To define negative and positive invariants for programs, we use thus S_+ and S_- respectively.

3.1 Invariant predicates

A predicate J is an **invariant** of a transition program S iff J implies its post-image and its pre-image by S:

$$J \Rightarrow S_+.J \wedge S_-.J$$
$$\text{i.e.} \quad J = J \wedge S_{+,-}.J \tag{9}$$

Each state in J results by S from a past state in J, and it is also related by S to a future state in J : thus J holds in some infinite past and infinite future.

For any program S, the fixpoint equation (9) has a unique maximal solution, which can be computed iteratively and is called **the** invariant of S.

The proof is standard. Consider the predicate transformer F such that

$$F.P = P \wedge S_{+,-}.P$$

The transformer F is and-continuous since it is a conjunction of and-continuous transformers; see (5). Hence, by Tarski's fixpoint theorem [Trk], the equation

$$X = F.X$$

has a unique maximal, i.e. weakest, solution in the lattice of predicates with the order

$$P \leqslant Q \text{ iff } P \Rightarrow Q$$

and with the maximal element **true**. This maximal solution J_{max} is the limit of successive iterations

$$
\begin{aligned}
J^{(0)} &= \textbf{true} \\
J^{(n+1)} &= F.J^{(n)} \\
J_{max} &= \forall n \in Integer : J^{(n)} \\
&= lim\, n : n \to \infty : J^{(n)}
\end{aligned}
\tag{10}
$$

QED

From now on, we assume the invariants are the maximal ones for the given ordering, and we write J for J_{max}.

Also by Tarski's theorem, the maximal solution of

$$J = J \wedge S_{+,-}.J$$
$$\text{viz.} \quad J \Rightarrow S_{+,-}.J$$

is that of

$$J = S_{+,-}.J \tag{11}$$

In [vLS], invariants K are maximal solutions of

$$K \Rightarrow S_-.K \tag{12}$$

and thus are positive invariants only; they may be preserved indefinitely in the future but not in the past : from K one reaches K again by S, but not all states in K can be reached from K. Consider, for instance, the program

$$S = \quad [0 \leqslant x \leqslant 3 \rightarrow x := x - 1$$
$$[\,]-1 \leqslant x \leqslant 1 \rightarrow x := x + 1$$
$$] \text{ where } x \in Integer$$

Its maximal positive invariant is $-1 \leqslant x \leqslant 3$, whereas its maximal (negative and positive) invariant is $0 \leqslant x \leqslant 1$: the future of $-1 \leqslant x \leqslant 3$ is in $-1 \leqslant x \leqslant 3$, but $x = -1 \vee x = 2 \vee x = 3$ cannot be verified infinitely often.

3.2 Invariant-preserving programs

A program S necessarily **preserves** a predicate P iff

$$P \Rightarrow (wp.S).P$$
$$\tag{13}$$
$$\text{viz.} \quad P \Rightarrow S_-.P \wedge \neg S_-.\neg P$$

Thus, from each state in P, at least one transition in S must lead to P again, and no transition applicable from a state in P may fail to lead to P.

Given a transition program S having the invariant J, we can easily refine it into a program T which preserves J. We simply restrict the guards $b_i.x$ in S on the basis of J :

$$\text{if} \quad S = \quad [[\,]i \in \Sigma : b_i.x \rightarrow x := e_i.x]$$

$$\text{then} \quad T = \quad [[\,]i \in \Sigma : p_i.x \rightarrow x := e_i.x]$$

$$\text{where } p_i \wedge J \Rightarrow S_{i-}.J, \quad \text{e.g. } p_i = \neg J \vee S_{i-}.J.$$

Of course, each $p_i \wedge J$ should be maximal : do not take $p_i = $ **false**. Further details and justifications of this transformation follow similar ones in [vLS].

For the little example hereabove (Section 3.1), a corresponding program which preserves the invariant $x = 0 \vee x = 1$ is

$$T = \begin{array}{l} [\, 1 \leqslant x \to x := x - 1 \\ \, [\!] \, x \leqslant 0 \to x := x + 1 \\ \,] \text{ where } x \in Integer \end{array}$$

Henceforth we assume programs preserve their invariants, unless stated otherwise.

3.3 Factorized expression of invariants

Each iterate $J^{(n)}$ in (10) can be decomposed into negative and positive parts :

$$\forall n \geqslant 0 : J^{(n)} = S_+^n.t \land S_-^n.t \tag{14}$$

viz.

$$t \xrightarrow{S_+^n} J^{(n)} \xleftarrow{S_-^{(n)}} t$$

The proof is by induction. The cases $n = 0$ and $n = 1$ hold by definitions of $J^{(0)}$ and $J^{(1)}$. Assume now the property is verified by $J^{(n)}$ for $n \geqslant 1$; then,

$$J^{(n+1)}$$

$\qquad$ {defns (10) and (3) of $J^{(n+1)}$ and $S_\pm$ }

$= \quad \bigvee i, j \in \Sigma : S_{i-}.J^{(n)} \land S_{j+}.J^{(n)}$

$\qquad$ {induction hypothesis; and-distributivity of $S_{i\pm}$}

$= \quad \bigvee i, j \in \Sigma : S_{i-}.S_-^n.t \land S_{i-}.S_+^n.t \land S_{j+}.S_-^n.t \land S_{j+}.S_+^n.t$

$\qquad$ {redundancy (8) of two-way iterations}

$= \quad \bigvee i, j \in \Sigma : S_{i-}.S_-^n.t \land S_{j+}.S_+^n.t$

$\qquad$ {defns (3) of $S_\pm$}

$= \quad S_-.S_-^n.t \land S_+.S_+^n.t$

QED

$\qquad$ Let us then introduce the negative and positive invariants J_- and J_+ as maximal fixpoints of the equations

$$J_\pm = S_\mp.J_\pm \tag{15}$$

These fixpoints can be derived iteratively [Trk]:

$$\begin{array}{ll} J_\pm^{(0)} & = t \\ J_\pm^{(n+1)} & = S_\mp.J_\pm^{(n)} \\ \\ J_\pm & = \forall n : J_\pm^{(n)} \end{array} \tag{16}$$

$\qquad$ The predicate J_- is the set of states resulting from infinite iterations of S; it is invariant under all backward iterations. The predicate J_+ is the set of states beginning infinite, forward iterations of S; it is the same as K in (12). We observe

$$J_{\pm}^{(n)} = S_{\mp}^n.t \tag{17}$$
$$J^{(n)} = J_-^{(n)} \wedge J_+^{(n)}$$
$$J = J_- \wedge J_+$$

viz.

$$t \xrightarrow{S_+^{(n)}} J_-^{(n)} \quad \text{and} \quad J_+^{(n)} \xleftarrow{S_-^{(n)}} t$$

3.4 Traces

We analyze the dynamics of transition-system programs in terms of traces, i.e. sequences of transitions, rather than in terms of orbits, i.e. sequences of states. In the presence of non-determinism, one orbit may be generated by different traces. Moreover, traces may generate sequences of sets of states; this is well in line with our predicate-based, viz. set-based, approach: the predicate transformers S_{i+} and S_{i-} are associated with the basic trace i of length one.

Let $S = [\,[]\,i \in \Sigma : S_i]$ be a program. A **finite (one-way)-trace** is an element of the monoid Σ^*, viz. a finite word over Σ. An **infinite (one-way)-trace** is an element of Σ^∞, viz. an infinite word over Σ. A **(two-way) trace** is a pair (σ, τ) of one-way traces, expressing the past and the future respectively. The transitions close to the present occur at the end of σ and at the beginning of τ.

We parametrize transformers $S_{\tau-}$ and $S_{\sigma+}$ by traces τ and σ : for any $\sigma, \tau \in \Sigma^*, \sigma', \tau' \in \Sigma^\omega$, or $\sigma, \tau \in \Sigma^\omega, \sigma', \tau' \in \Sigma^*$,

$$S_{\sigma\sigma'+} = S_{\sigma'+} \circ S_{\sigma+} \tag{18}$$
$$S_{\tau\tau'-} = S_{\tau-} \circ S_{\tau'-}$$

3.5 Trace-based expressions of invariants

The iterative construction of invariants can be parametrized by traces, instead of iteration ranks as in (10) and (16). Indeed, $S_{i+}.t$ is the set of states coming from some state by S_i, and is thus the set of states with possible past trace i. Similarly, $S_{j-}.t$ is the set of states going to some state by S_j, and is thus the set of states with possible future trace j. In general, $S_{\sigma+}.t$ is the set of states with past trace σ and $S_{\tau-}.t$ is the set of states with future trace τ.

We thus introduce the following definitions, for any $\sigma, \tau \in \Sigma^\omega$,

$$J_{\sigma,\tau} = S_{\sigma+}.t \wedge S_{\tau-}.t \tag{19}$$
$$J_{\sigma,} = S_{\sigma+}.t$$
$$J_{,\tau} = S_{\tau-}.t$$

viz.

$$t \xrightarrow{S_{\sigma+}} J_{\sigma,\tau} \xleftarrow{S_{\tau-}} t$$
$$t \xrightarrow{S_{\sigma+}} J_{\sigma,}$$
$$J_{,\tau} \xleftarrow{S_{\tau-}} t$$
$$J_{\sigma,\tau} = J_{\sigma,} \wedge J_{,\tau}$$

By repeatedly using $J_{\sigma i,} = S_{i+}.J_{\sigma,}$ and $J_{,j\tau} = S_{j-}.J_{,\tau}$ given (19) and (18), the iterates $J^{(n)}$ in (10) may be decomposed w.r.t. traces:

$$J^{(n)} = \quad \bigvee \sigma, \tau \in \Sigma^n \quad : J_{\sigma,\tau} \tag{20}$$
$$J_-^{(n)} = \quad \bigvee \sigma \in \Sigma^n \quad : J_{\sigma,}$$
$$J_+^{(n)} = \quad \bigvee \tau \in \Sigma^n \quad : J_{,\tau}$$

Similarly for the limits :

$$J = \quad \bigvee \sigma, \tau \in \Sigma^\infty \quad : J_{\sigma,\tau} \tag{21}$$
$$J_- = \quad \bigvee \sigma \in \Sigma^\infty \quad : J_{\sigma,}$$
$$J_+ = \quad \bigvee \tau \in \Sigma^\infty \quad : J_{,\tau}$$

Monotonicity of components w.r.t. traces :

For any $\sigma, \tau \in \Sigma^*, \sigma', \tau' \in \Sigma^\omega$, or $\sigma, \tau \in \Sigma^\omega, \sigma', \tau' \in \Sigma^*$,

$$J_{\sigma'\sigma,\tau\tau'} \quad \Rightarrow \quad J_{\sigma,\tau} \tag{22}$$

Indeed,

$$
\begin{aligned}
& J_{\sigma'\sigma,\tau\tau'} \\
& \{\text{defns (19) and (18)}\} \\
= \ & S_{\sigma+}.S_{\sigma'+}.t \wedge S_{\tau-}.S_{\tau'-}.t \\
& \{\text{monotonicity of } S_{\sigma+} \text{ and } S_{\tau-} \text{ given (4) and (18)}\} \\
\Rightarrow \ & S_{\sigma+}.t \wedge S_{\tau-}.t \\
& \{\text{defn (19) }\} \\
= \ & J_{\sigma,\tau}
\end{aligned}
$$

Translations :

For any $\rho \in \Sigma^*$ and $\sigma, \tau \in \Sigma^\omega$,

$$S_{\rho+}.J_{\sigma,\rho\tau} = \quad J_{\sigma\rho,\tau} \tag{23}$$
$$S_{\rho-}.J_{\sigma\rho,\tau} = \quad J_{\sigma,\rho\tau}$$

Indeed, in case $\rho = j$,

$$S_{j+}.J_{\sigma,j\tau}$$

{defns (19) and (18) for $J_{\sigma,j\tau}$; and-distributivity of S_{j+}}

$$= \quad S_{j+}.S_{\sigma+}.t \land S_{j+}.S_{j-}.S_{\tau-}.t$$

{semi-inversion (7) for $P = S_{\tau-}.t$}

$$= \quad S_{j+}.S_{\sigma+}.t \land S_{\tau-}.t \land S_{j+}.t$$

{$S_{j+}.A \Rightarrow S_{j+}.t$, by monotonicity (4) of S_{j+}}

$$= \quad S_{j+}.S_{\sigma+}.t \land S_{\tau-}.t$$

{defns (19) and (18) for $J_{\sigma j,\tau}$}

$$= \quad J_{\sigma j,\tau}$$

The case for a general ρ follows directly. The proof for $S_{\rho-}$ is similar. QED

We can reexpress these translations in terms of a **symbolic-shift map** sh having the inverse hs ; for $i, j \in \Sigma$ and $\sigma, \tau \in \Sigma^\infty$,

$$
\begin{aligned}
sh(\sigma, j\tau) &= (\sigma j, \tau) \\
hs(\sigma i, \tau) &= (\sigma, i\tau) \\
S_{j+}.J_{\sigma,j\tau} &= J_{sh(\sigma,j\tau)} \\
S_{i-}.J_{\sigma i,\tau} &= J_{hs(\sigma i,\tau)}
\end{aligned}
\tag{24}
$$

The effect of $S_{\rho+}$ or $S_{\rho-}$ can be defined similarly using iterates $(sh)^n$ or $(hs)^n$ where n is the length of ρ.

3.6 Fullness of invariants

Some $J_{\sigma,\tau}$ may well turn out to be empty, in which case the trace (σ, τ) cannot be realized. The richness of the dynamics depends on that of the set of allowed traces, viz. of the set of non-empty components $J_{\sigma,\tau}$. We here focus on the maximal case where all traces can be realized.

Let $S = [\![ ]\!]i \in \Sigma : S_i]$ be a program preserving its invariant J. The latter is a **full invariant** iff

$$\forall \sigma, \tau \in \Sigma^\infty : \quad \exists x : J_{\sigma,\tau}.x \tag{25}$$
$$\text{viz.} \quad \forall \sigma, \tau \in \Sigma^\infty : \quad J_{\sigma,\tau} \neq \mathbf{f}$$

Thus no disjunct in the trace-based decomposition (21) of J is empty : for all σ and τ, there exists a state with possible past σ and possible future τ. This corresponds to full shifts in symbolic dynamics. We can thus reuse classical results [Wgg] w.r.t. the symbolic-shift map sh (24).

If the invariant of a program S is full and Σ contains at least two symbols, then the set $\mathfrak{T} = \Sigma^\infty \times \Sigma^\infty$ of its two-way traces has

1. a countable infinity of periodic traces consisting of traces of all periods;
2. an uncountable infinity of non-periodic traces; and
3. a dense trace.

In this case, we say $\mathfrak{T}$ is a **dense multitude** of traces. The hypothesis of fullness could be relaxed by adapting techniques concerning subshifts [Wgg].

A degenerate example of full invariant is

$$
\begin{aligned}
S &= [S_1 : x = 0 \quad \rightarrow x := 3x \\
&\quad [\!]\, S_2 : x = 0 \quad \rightarrow x := x/5 \\
&\quad] \\
J &= (x = 0) \\
J_{\sigma,\tau} &= (x = 0) \\
J_{\sigma,\tau} &\neq \mathbf{f}, \qquad \text{for all } \sigma, \tau \in \Sigma^\infty
\end{aligned}
$$

There are exactly one state, one orbit, but a dense multitude of traces. The existence of a dense multitude of orbits implies the same for traces, but not conversely in general.

If J is a full invariant, then

$$
\forall \sigma, \tau \in \Sigma^* \quad : \quad J \wedge J_{\sigma,\tau} \neq \mathbf{f} \tag{26}
$$

viz. each iterate $J_{\sigma,\tau}$ contains states from J. Indeed, take any $J_{\sigma'\sigma,\tau\tau'}$ with $\sigma', \tau' \in \Sigma^\infty$:

$$
\begin{aligned}
J_{\sigma'\sigma,\tau\tau'} &\Rightarrow J \quad && \{\text{ decomposition (21) of } J\} \\
J_{\sigma'\sigma,\tau\tau'} &\Rightarrow J_{\sigma,\tau} \quad && \{\text{ monotonicity (22) of components w.r.t. traces}\} \\
J_{\sigma'\sigma,\tau\tau'} &\neq \mathbf{f} \quad && \{\text{fullness of } J\}
\end{aligned}
$$

Topological semi-transitivity :

If J is a full invariant, then for all $\sigma_1, \tau_1, \sigma_2, \tau_2 \in \Sigma^*$, there exist states in $J \wedge J_{\sigma_2,\tau_2}$ which come from states in $J \wedge J_{\sigma_1,\tau_1}$ by a finite sequence of transitions:

$$
\forall \sigma_1, \tau_1, \sigma_2, \tau_2 \in \Sigma^* \quad : \quad S_{\tau_1\sigma_2+}.(J \wedge J_{\sigma_1,\tau_1}) \wedge (J \wedge J_{\sigma_2,\tau_2}) \neq \mathbf{f} \tag{27}
$$

Thus, each part $J \wedge J_{\sigma_1,\tau_1}$ contains states which evolve into states belonging to any other part $J \wedge J_{\sigma_2,\tau_2}$. This corresponds to a weak form of **topological transitivity** [Wgg]: it applies only to the components $J \wedge J_{\sigma,\tau}$ of the invariant.

This is proved as follows. For any $\sigma_1, \tau_1, \sigma_2, \tau_2 \in \Sigma^*$, and $\sigma, \tau \in \Sigma^\infty$, take the sets $J_{\sigma\sigma_1,\tau_1\sigma_2\tau_2\tau}$ and $J_{\sigma\sigma_1\tau_1\sigma_2,\tau_2\tau}$:

$$
\begin{aligned}
J_{\sigma\sigma_1,\tau_1\sigma_2\tau_2\tau} &\Rightarrow J \quad && \{\text{ trace-based defn (21) of } J\} \\
&\Rightarrow J_{\sigma_1,\tau_1} \quad && \{\text{ monotonicity (22) of components}\} \\
S_{\tau_1\sigma_2+}.J_{\sigma\sigma_1,\tau_1\sigma_2\tau_2\tau} &= J_{\sigma\sigma_1\tau_1\sigma_2,\tau_2\tau} \quad && \{\text{ past-to-future translation (23)}\} \\
J_{\sigma\sigma_1\tau_1\sigma_2,\tau_2\tau} &\Rightarrow J \quad && \{\ (21)\ \} \\
&\Rightarrow J_{\sigma_2,\tau_2} \quad && \{\ (22)\ \} \\
&\neq \mathbf{f} \quad && \{J \text{ is full}\}
\end{aligned}
$$

This result can also be formulated using pre-images; in any $J \wedge J_{\sigma_1,\tau_1}$ there are states which go to any other $J \wedge J_{\sigma_2,\tau_2}$:

$$\forall \sigma_1,\tau_1,\sigma_2,\tau_2 \in \Sigma^* \quad : \quad (J \wedge J_{\sigma_1,\tau_1}) \wedge S_{\tau_1\sigma_2-}.(J \wedge J_{\sigma_2,\tau_2}) \neq \mathbf{f} \tag{28}$$

viz.

$$J \wedge J_{\sigma_1,\tau_1} \neq \mathbf{f} \xrightleftharpoons[S_{\tau_1\sigma_2-}]{S_{\tau_1\sigma_2+}} J \wedge J_{\sigma_2,\tau_2} \neq \mathbf{f}$$

Eventual maximal fan-out and minimal fan-in :

In case J is full, **each** $J \wedge J_{\sigma,\tau}$ $(\sigma,\tau \in \Sigma^m)$ contains pre-images, by **some** S_-^p, of points taken from **all** $J \wedge J_{\sigma',\tau'}$ $(\sigma',\tau' \in \Sigma^n)$, for any ranks m and n. Thus each $J \wedge J_{\sigma,\tau}$ contains a pre-image, by a finite iteration of S, of a set of points distributed over all the trace-based components of J. More precisely :

Let J be a full invariant, m and n be any integers, and σ,τ be any traces in Σ^m. Then,

$$\exists p \geqslant 0 : \forall \sigma',\tau' \in \Sigma^n \quad : \quad (J \wedge J_{\sigma,\tau}) \wedge S_-^p.(J \wedge J_{\sigma',\tau'}) \neq \mathbf{f} \tag{29}$$

Indeed, choose $p = m + n$; for each $\sigma',\tau' \in \Sigma^n$,

$$(J \wedge J_{\sigma,\tau}) \wedge S_-^p.(J \wedge J_{\sigma',\tau'})$$
$$\{ \text{trace-based decomposition (21) of } S_-^p \text{ with } \tau\sigma' \in \Sigma^p \}$$
$$\Leftarrow \quad (J \wedge J_{\sigma,\tau}) \wedge S_{\tau\sigma'-}.(J \wedge J_{\sigma',\tau'})$$
$$\{ \text{topological semi-transitivity (28)} \}$$
$$\neq \quad \mathbf{f}.$$

QED

If some $J_{\sigma,\tau}$ $(\sigma,\tau \in \Sigma^m)$ is a singleton, and some J_{σ_1,τ_1} and J_{σ_2,τ_2} $(\sigma_1,\tau_1, \sigma_2,\tau_2 \in \Sigma^n)$ are disjoint, then S must be non-deterministic : from the unique state in $J \wedge J_{\sigma,\tau}$, one must reach two distinct states by a finite iteration of S.

A similar reasoning, using (27) instead of (28), shows the dual property of *eventual minimal fan-in* : for any m and n, there are sets of states, distributed over **all** components $J \wedge J_{\sigma',\tau'}$ $(\sigma',\tau' \in \Sigma^m)$, which are mapped by **some** S_+^p into states contained in **any** component $J \wedge J_{\sigma,\tau}$ $(\sigma,\tau \in \Sigma^n)$.

3.7 Sufficient conditions for fullness

To prove the fullness of the invariant of a program, it suffices to find two sets Φ and Ψ of predicates such that:

(i) $\forall A \in \Phi, B \in \Psi : A \wedge B \neq \mathbf{false}$

(ii) $\forall i \in \Sigma : \quad (\exists A \in \Phi : A \Rightarrow J_{i,}) \wedge (\exists B \in \Psi : B \Rightarrow J_{,i})$

(iii) $\forall i \in \Sigma : \quad (\forall A \in \Phi : S_{i+}.A \in \Phi) \wedge (\forall B \in \Psi : S_{i-}.B \in \Psi)$

Indeed, we can then prove by induction

$$\forall n \geqslant 1 : \forall \sigma, \tau \in \Sigma^n : \quad (\exists A \in \Phi : A \Rightarrow J_{\sigma,}) \wedge (\exists B \in \Psi : B \Rightarrow J_{,\tau})$$

The base case is given in (ii). Assume now the property holds for n, and let us prove it for $n+1$:

$$
\begin{aligned}
 & J_{\sigma i,} \\
 & \{\text{ defns (19) and (18) for } J_{\sigma i,} \text{ and } S_{\sigma i+}\} \\
= {} & S_{i+}.J_{\sigma,} \\
 & \{\text{ induction hypothesis, and monotonicity (4) of } S_{i+}\} \\
\Leftarrow {} & S_{i+}.A \\
 & \{\text{ condition (iii)}\} \\
\in {} & \Phi
\end{aligned}
$$

Similarly for $J_{,j\tau} \in \Psi$. From the induction thesis and (i), we conclude

$$\forall n \geqslant 1 : \forall \sigma, \tau \in \Sigma^n \quad : J_{\sigma,} \wedge J_{,\tau} \neq \mathbf{f}$$
$$\text{viz.} \quad \forall \sigma, \tau \in \Sigma^\infty \qquad : J_{\sigma,\tau} \neq \mathbf{f}$$

QED

4   Contraction

By definition (10), the iterates $J^{(n)}$ yielding the invariant J form a decreasing chain since $S_{+,-}$ is monotonous : $S_{+,-}.J^{(n)}$ is either equal to or strictly contained in $J^{(n)}$. Strict contraction arises in various ways; for example :

(i) Each transition S_i of S defines a contracting function; then S_+ contracts, $S_{+,-}$ too, and $J_-^{(n)}$ shrinks with increasing n since $J_-^{(n+1)} = S_+.J_-^{(n)}$.

(ii) Each transition S_i defines an expanding function; then S_- contracts, and $S_{+,-}$ also.

(iii) S_+ contracts along direction x; S_- contracts along direction y; S_+ and S_- neither contract nor expand along direction z; then $S_{+,-}$ contracts along x and y, but not along z.

These three cases respectively correspond to a sink, a source, and a saddle; the use of the post-pre-former $S_{+,-}$ abstracts from these variations.

4.1   Atomicity of invariants

Up to now, not much has been said about the size of a set $J_{\sigma,\tau}$: the latter may contain many states, a few states, one state, or no state at all. The liveness of the dynamics depends on the fineness of each limit component $J_{\sigma,\tau}$ $(\sigma, \tau \in \Sigma^\infty)$ excepting emptiness of course. The coarsest case is where each $J_{\sigma,\tau}$ is identical to J : the dynamics is then boring, as with

$$S = [0 \leqslant x \leqslant 1 \rightarrow x := x[]0 \leqslant x \leqslant 1 \rightarrow x := 1 - x] \text{ where } x \in \textit{Real}$$
$$J = 0 \leqslant x \leqslant 1$$

As a consequence, we focus on the case of maximal fineness. An invariant is **atomic** (viz. pulverized or atomized) iff each of its components is a singleton or is empty :

$$\forall \sigma, \tau \in \Sigma^{\infty} \quad : \quad card(J_{\sigma,\tau}) \leqslant 1 \tag{30}$$

Consider now a *full and atomic* invariant J. Each limit component $J_{\sigma,\tau}$ $(\sigma, \tau \in \Sigma^{\infty})$ is a singleton : it may not be empty (25) , and contains at most one element (30). The iterates $J_{\sigma,\tau}$ $(\sigma, \tau \in \Sigma^{*})$ form monotonous decreasing chains converging towards these singletons. Thus, the longer the finite trace (σ, τ) is, the closer $J_{\sigma,\tau}$ is to a singleton, viz. the smaller it is. This entails **sensitive dependence of initial conditions** : there exist states, in any small $J_{\sigma,\tau}$, which are transformed by a finite number of transitions into states distributed over all of J; see (29). Conversely, there are sets of states distributed over all of J which are transformed into any $J_{\sigma,\tau}$, however small; this entails sensitive dependence on **final** conditions.

We distinguish fullness from atomicity because there are cases where fullness is already revealing and easy to verify, whereas atomicity may be false or harder to prove. Fullness amounts to the invariance of non-emptiness, and atomicity in addition implies contraction towards singletons.

4.2 Sufficient conditions for atomicity

To prove the invariant J of a program S is atomic, it suffices to find two sets Φ and Ψ of predicates, a totally ordered set M with minimal element 0, and a function

$$\mu : \{A \wedge B | A \in \Phi, B \in \Psi\} \rightarrow M$$

such that

(i) $\forall A \in \Phi, B \in \Psi : \quad \mu(A \wedge B) = 0$ iff $card$ $(A \wedge B) \leqslant 1$

(ii) $\forall i \in \Sigma : \quad (\exists A \in \Phi : J_{i,} \Rightarrow A) \wedge (\exists B \in \Psi : J_{,i} \Rightarrow B)$

(iii) $\forall i \in \Sigma : \quad (\forall A \in \Phi : S_{i+}.A \in \Phi) \wedge (\forall B \in \Psi : S_{i-}.B \in \Psi)$

(iv) $\forall \sigma, \tau \in \Sigma^{\infty} : \forall A \in \Phi, B \in \Psi : \quad \mu(S_{\sigma+}.A \wedge S_{\tau-}.B) = 0$

Indeed, conditions (ii) and (iii) here are similar to (ii) and (iii) in Section 3.7 for fullness, and thus entail, by a similar proof,

$$\forall \sigma, \tau \in \Sigma^{\infty} : \quad (\exists A \in \Phi : J_{\sigma,} \Rightarrow A) \wedge (\exists B \in \Psi : J_{,\tau} \Rightarrow B)$$

Let us then prove $\forall \sigma, \tau \in \Sigma^{\infty} : card(J_{\sigma,\tau}) \leqslant 1$ using (i) and (iv). For any $\sigma, \tau \in \Sigma^{\infty}$, there are $i, j \in \Sigma$ and $\sigma_1, \tau_1 \in \Sigma^{\infty}$ such that $(\sigma, \tau) = (i\sigma_1, \tau_1 j)$; hence, there exist $A, A' \in \Phi$ and $B, B' \in \Psi$ such that

$$
\begin{aligned}
J_{\sigma,\tau} &= J_{i\sigma_1,\tau_1 j} \\
&= S_{\sigma_1+}.J_{i,} \wedge S_{\tau_1-}.J_{,j} \quad \{\ (19)\ \text{and}\ (18)\ \} \\
&\Rightarrow S_{\sigma_1+}.A \wedge S_{\tau_1-}.B \quad \{\ (ii)\ \text{and repeated}\ (4)\ \} \\
&= A' \wedge B' \quad\quad\quad\quad \{\ \text{repeated}\ (iii)\ \}
\end{aligned}
$$

By (iv), $\mu(A' \wedge B') = \mu(S_{\sigma_1+}.A, S_{\tau_1-}.B) = 0$.
Hence,

$$
\begin{aligned}
card(J_{\sigma,\tau}) & \\
\leqslant\ & card(A' \wedge B') \quad \{\ card\ \text{is monotone}\ \} \\
\leqslant\ & 1 \quad\quad\quad\quad\quad \{\ (i)\ \text{for}\ A', B'\ \}
\end{aligned}
$$

QED

There are two useful ways to ensure condition (iv), which respectively correspond to Floyd's termination functions [Fld] and to Liapunov's stability functions [Dvn, Wgg] :

(iv') Let M be the set of naturals; $\forall i, j \in \Sigma : \forall A \in \Phi, B \in \Psi$:
$$\mu(S_{i+}.A \wedge S_{j-}.B) = 0 \vee \mu(S_{i+}.A \wedge S_{j-}.B) < \mu(A \wedge B)$$

(iv") Let M be the set of non-negative reals, and let $0 < k < 1$;
$$\forall i, j \in \Sigma : \forall A \in \Phi, B \in \Psi : \quad \mu(S_{i+}.A \wedge S_{j-}.B) \leqslant k \times \mu(A \wedge B)$$

Measures [ArA], which are additive set-functions, could be used as functions μ. However, the latter ones are not required to be additive.

The conditions for fullness and atomicity, in Section 3.7 and in the present one, are akin to the Alekseev-Conley-Moser conditions [Wgg] but are defined in terms of approximating predicates; it is not claimed they are necessarily more effective.

The inverse of some functional transition S_i may well consists of two functional parts (or more); then, the pre-image $S_{i-}.P$ of a predicate P generally is the union of two disjoint predicates. In this case, it is useful to replace S_i by two transitions with functional inverses : the pre-images of P by the two new transitions generally are smaller predicates than $S_{i-}.P$, and atomicity is thus easier to prove.

5 Exercises

A few simple examples, based on classical ones [Dvn, Wgg], are presented. The main qualitative results of the analyses are summarized and discussed. Often, detailed formal developments are just hinted at, although such developments served as a useful source of intuitions for the results above.

In order to help understanding, transition-system programs are written with symmetric guards :

$$S = [\,\big[\,\big]\, i \in \Sigma : b_i.x \rightarrow x := e_i.x \rightarrow c_i.x\,]$$

$$\text{where } c_i = S_{i+}.b_i = \exists u : b_i.u \wedge (x = e_i.u)$$

We say b_i is a **pre-guard** and c_i is a **post-guard**; one could prefer to say **vanguard** and **rearguard**, respectively. Clearly,

$$b_i = S_{i-}.t$$
$$c_i = S_{i+}.t$$

5.1 The baker map

In one dimension, it is the doubling map, which amounts to a Bernoulli scheme [ArA], and is expressed as

$$S = \quad [\, S_1 : 0 \leqslant x \leqslant 1/2 \quad \to x := 2x \qquad \to 0 \leqslant x \leqslant 1$$
$$\quad []\, S_2 : 1/2 \leqslant x \leqslant 1 \quad \to x := 2x - 1 \quad \to 0 \leqslant x \leqslant 1$$
$$\quad]\, \text{where } x \in Real.$$

The chosen pre-guards allow a little non-determinism.

The invariant :

Given (17) and Section 2.2, we have
$$J_{\pm}^{(0)} = \mathbf{t}$$

$$\begin{aligned}
J_{-}^{(1)} &= S_{+}.J_{-}^{(0)} &&= S_{1+}.t \vee S_{2+}.t \\
&= c_1 \vee c_2 &&= 0 \leqslant x \leqslant 1 \\
J_{-}^{(2)} &= S_{+}.J_{-}^{(1)} &&= c_1 \vee c_2 \\
&= 0 \leqslant x \leqslant 1 &&= J_{-}^{(1)} = J_{-}
\end{aligned}$$

$$\begin{aligned}
J_{+}^{(1)} &= S_{-}.J_{+}^{(0)} &&= S_{1-}.t \vee S_{2-}.t \\
&= b_1 \vee b_2 &&= 0 \leqslant x \leqslant 1 \\
J_{+}^{(2)} &= S_{-}.J_{+}^{(1)} &&= (0 \leqslant x \leqslant 1/2 \wedge 0 \leqslant 2x \leqslant 1) \\
&&& \vee (1/2 \leqslant x \leqslant 1 \wedge 0 \leqslant 2x - 1 \leqslant 1) \\
&= 0 \leqslant x \leqslant 1 &&= J_{+}^{(1)} = J_{+}
\end{aligned}$$

$$J \quad = J_{-} \wedge J_{+} \quad = 0 \leqslant x \leqslant 1$$

Thus, each point in [0,1] has an admissible infinite past and an admissible infinite future, when applying the baker map. But this does not say much about the dynamics.

Fullness of the invariant :

We use the sufficient conditions 3.7. After some simple experiments, the following choices appear natural:

Φ : the predicate $0 \leqslant x \leqslant 1$,
Ψ : the predicates $p \leqslant x \leqslant q$ where $0 \leqslant p \leqslant q \leqslant 1$.

Condition (i) holds since $p \leqslant q$. Condition (ii) is verified as follows :

$$\begin{aligned}
J_{1,} &= S_{1+}.t = & 0 \leqslant x \leqslant 1 & \quad \in \Phi \\
J_{2,} &= S_{2+}.t = & 0 \leqslant x \leqslant 1 & \quad \in \Phi \\
J_{,1} &= S_{1-}.t = & 0 \leqslant x \leqslant 1/2 & \quad \in \Psi \\
J_{,2} &= S_{2-}.t = & 1/2 \leqslant x \leqslant 1 & \quad \in \Psi
\end{aligned}$$

Condition (iii) w.r.t. Φ is also verified easily (see Section 2.2) :

$$S_{1+}.(0 \leqslant x \leqslant 1) \quad = \exists u : 0 \leqslant u \leqslant 1/2 \wedge (x = 2u) \wedge 0 \leqslant u \leqslant 1$$
$$= \exists u : 0 \leqslant 2u \leqslant 1 \wedge (x = 2u)$$
$$= 0 \leqslant x \leqslant 1$$
$$\in \Phi$$

$$S_{2+}.(0 \leqslant x \leqslant 1) \quad = \exists u : 1/2 \leqslant u \leqslant 1 \wedge (x = 2u - 1) \wedge 0 \leqslant u \leqslant 1$$
$$= \exists u : 0 \leqslant 2u - 1 \leqslant 1 \wedge (x = 2u - 1)$$
$$= 0 \leqslant x \leqslant 1$$
$$\in \Phi$$

The following verification of condition (iii) w.r.t. Ψ shows the recursive structure of the invariant :

$$S_{1-}.(p \leqslant x \leqslant q)$$
$$= 0 \leqslant x \leqslant 1/2 \wedge p \leqslant 2x \leqslant q \qquad \{\,\text{section 2.2}\,\}$$
$$= p/2 \leqslant x \leqslant q/2 \qquad\qquad \{\,0 \leqslant p/2 \leqslant q/2 \leqslant 1/2\,\}$$
$$= p_1 \leqslant x \leqslant q_1 \qquad\qquad \{\,p_1 = p/2 \text{ and } q_1 = q/2\,\}$$
$$\in \Psi \qquad\qquad\qquad \{\,0 \leqslant p_1 \leqslant q_1 \leqslant 1\,\}$$

$$S_{2-}.(p \leqslant x \leqslant q)$$
$$= 1/2 \leqslant x \leqslant 1 \wedge p \leqslant 2x - 1 \leqslant q \quad \{\,\text{section 2.2}\,\}$$
$$= p/2 + 1/2 \leqslant x \leqslant q/2 + 1/2 \qquad \{\,1/2 \leqslant p/2 + 1/2 \leqslant q/2 + 1/2 \leqslant 1\,\}$$
$$= p_2 \leqslant x \leqslant q_2 \qquad\qquad\quad \{\,p_2 = p/2 + 1/2 \text{ and } q_2 = q/2 + 1/2\,\}$$
$$\in \Psi \qquad\qquad\qquad\quad \{\,0 \leqslant p_2 \leqslant q_2 \leqslant 1\,\}$$

QED

Thus, in the invariant J, no component $J_{\sigma,\tau}$ $(\sigma, \tau \in \Sigma^\infty)$ is empty : all traces with infinite past and infinite future can be realized. But this does not yet say much about the intensity of the dynamics within J.

Atomicity of the invariant :

We apply the conditions 4.2, using

Φ : the predicate $0 \leqslant x \leqslant 1$,
Ψ : the predicates $p \leqslant x \leqslant q$ where $0 \leqslant p \leqslant q \leqslant 1$,
M : the non-negative real numbers,
$\mu.(p \leqslant x \leqslant q) = q - p$.

Condition (i) holds since the interval $[p, q]$ reduces to one point when $q - p = 0$. Condition (ii) and (iii) have been proven above. Condition (iv) is verified using (iv") with $k = 1/2$; indeed, for $A = 0 \leqslant x \leqslant 1$ and $B = p \leqslant x \leqslant q$,

$$\mu.(S_{1+}.A \wedge S_{1-}.B)$$
$$= \mu.(0 \leqslant x \leqslant 1 \wedge p/2 \leqslant x \leqslant q/2)$$
$$= (q - p)/2$$

Similarly, $\mu.(S_{2+}.A \wedge S_{1-}.B) = \mu.(S_{1+}.A \wedge S_{2-}.B) = \mu.(S_{2+}.A \wedge S_{2-}.B) = (q - p)/2$.

From the fullness and the atomicity of the invariant, we conclude the baker map has a dense multitude of traces and is sensitively dependent on initial or final conditions; see Sections 3 and 4. This is of course not surprising, but is obtained for a (slightly) non-deterministic version of the baker map. The deterministic case, e.g. with the pre-guard

$0 \leqslant x < 1/2$ in S_1, is analyzed in the same way. In this example, the issue of determinism vs. non-determinism is thus secondary.

The simplicity of the baker map allows to derive explicit expressions for the trace-based iterates : for each $\sigma, \tau \in \Sigma^n$, there is some $0 \leqslant m < 2^n$ such that

$$J_{\sigma,\tau} = \tfrac{m}{2^n} \leqslant x \leqslant \tfrac{m+1}{2^n}$$

In general, it is difficult to derive such exact formulae, also for J; this is why the sufficient conditions for fullness and atomicity use the sets Φ and Ψ of approximating predicates.

5.2 Variants of the baker map

The baker map can be transformed in various related forms, without influencing the fullness and the atomicity of the invariant.

5.2.1 The rekab map

We obtain a less deterministic program by inversing the baker map:

$$S = \begin{array}{llll} [\, S_1 : 0 \leqslant x \leqslant 1 & \rightarrow x := x/2 & \rightarrow 0 \leqslant x \leqslant 1/2 \\ [\!] S_2 : 0 \leqslant x \leqslant 1 & \rightarrow x := x/2 + 1/2 & \rightarrow 1/2 \leqslant x \leqslant 1 \\ ]\, \text{where } x \in \text{Real} \end{array}$$

The analysis of this inverse program is directly given by that in Section 5.1, simply exchanging the indices $-$ and $+$, viz. exchanging the past and the future. The fullness and the atomicity of the invariant $0 \leqslant x \leqslant 1$ of the rekab map are thus verified forthwith.

The direct baker-map can well be taken to be deterministic, whereas its inverse in any case must be non-deterministic. Yet, both have the same full and atomic invariant. Again, the issue is thus not determinism vs. non-determinism, but well contraction in the past-with-future vs. no contraction.

The main difference between the baker and rekab maps is that the former is repulsing and the latter is attracting.

We can also combine the baker map and its inverse without perturbing the fullness and atomicity of the invariant:

$$S = \begin{array}{llll} [\, S_1 : 0 \leqslant x \leqslant 1/2 & \rightarrow x := 2x & \rightarrow 0 \leqslant x \leqslant 1 \\ [\!] S_2 : 1/2 \leqslant x \leqslant 1 & \rightarrow x := 2x - 1 & \rightarrow 0 \leqslant x \leqslant 1 \\ [\!] S_3 : 0 \leqslant x \leqslant 1 & \rightarrow x := x/2 & \rightarrow 0 \leqslant x \leqslant 1/2 \\ [\!] S_4 : 0 \leqslant x \leqslant 1 & \rightarrow x := x/2 + 1/2 & \rightarrow 1/2 \leqslant x \leqslant 1 \\ ]\, \text{where } x \in \text{Real} \end{array}$$

5.2.2 Fat and thin baker-maps

The baker-map in section 5.1.1 is slightly non-deterministic : the state $x = 1/2$ is the only one belonging to both pre-guards. Let us replace this common point by an interval, say $[1/3, 2/3]$, so as to obtain a fat map :

$$S = \begin{array}{llll} [\, S_1 : 0 \leqslant x \leqslant 2/3 \rightarrow & x := 3x/2 & \rightarrow 0 \leqslant x \leqslant 1 \\ [\!] S_2 : 1/3 \leqslant x \leqslant 1 \rightarrow & x := 3x/2 - 1/2 & \rightarrow 0 \leqslant x \leqslant 1 \\ ]\, \text{where } x \in \text{Real} \end{array}$$

The invariant :

$$J_{\pm}^{(0)} = t$$

$$
\begin{aligned}
J_{-}^{(1)} &= S_{1+}.t \vee S_{2+}.t && = c_1 \vee c_2 \\
&= 0 \leqslant x \leqslant 1 \\
J_{-}^{(2)} &= S_{1+}.(\,0 \leqslant x \leqslant 1) \vee S_{2+}.(0 \leqslant x \leqslant 1) && = 0 \leqslant x \leqslant 1 \\
&= J_{-}^{(1)} && = J_{-}
\end{aligned}
$$

$$
\begin{aligned}
J_{+}^{(1)} &= S_{1-}.t \vee S_{2-}.t && = b_1 \vee b_2 \\
&= 0 \leqslant x \leqslant 1 \\
J_{+}^{(2)} &= S_{1-}.(0 \leqslant x \leqslant 1) \vee S_{2-}.(\,0 \leqslant x \leqslant 1) && = 0 \leqslant x \leqslant 1 \\
&= J_{+}^{(1)} && = J_{+}
\end{aligned}
$$

$$
\begin{aligned}
J &= J_{-} \wedge J_{+} && = 0 \leqslant x \leqslant 1
\end{aligned}
$$

Fullness and atomicity of the invariant :

We choose Φ, Ψ, and μ as for the baker map (Section 5.1), but replace $k = 1/2$ by $k = 2/3$. Again, the drastic increase of non-determinism w.r.t. the baker map does not modify the overall dynamics. Simply, the rate of contraction has been slowed down from $1/2$ to $2/3$.

The iterates $J_{\sigma,\tau}$ $(\sigma, \tau \in \Sigma^*)$ are not mutually exclusive : different transitions can be applied to the states in $[1/3, 2/3]$. Hence, many singletons $J_{\sigma,\tau}$ $(\sigma, \tau \in \Sigma^\infty)$ are identical.

Symmetrically, a thin version of the baker map is obtained when the pre-guards are disjoint and their union is strictly contained within $[0, 1]$; such a thin map is deterministic and may yield a full, atomic invariant which is a Cantor subset of $[0, 1]$.

5.2.3 The tent map

This is obtained from the baker map after replacing the monotone increasing transition S_2 by a monotone decreasing one :

$$
S = \begin{array}{l}
[\, S_1 : 0 \leqslant x \leqslant 1/2 \quad \rightarrow x := 2x \quad \rightarrow 0 \leqslant x \leqslant 1 \\
[\!]\, S_2 : 1/2 \leqslant x \leqslant 1 \quad \rightarrow x := 2 - 2x \quad \rightarrow 1 \geqslant x \geqslant 0 \\
\,]\ \text{where } x \in \mathit{Real}
\end{array}
$$

An analysis similar to that of the baker map proves the invariant is $0 \leqslant x \leqslant 1$, and is full and atomic; the rate k of contraction in (iv") can again be $1/2$.

We could as well study an upside-down tent-map, viz. a valley map. Not much new would appear. And we could combine all these baker-like maps and their inverses, without modifying the fullness and the atomicity of the invariant.

5.2.4 The logistic map

This example is included among the variants of the baker map because it can be transformed into the tent map, using a.o. a trigonometric function [Dvn].

$$S = \begin{cases} S_1 : 0 \leqslant x \leqslant 1/2 & \to x := 4x(1-x) & \to 0 \leqslant x \leqslant 1 \\ S_2 : 1/2 \leqslant x \leqslant 1 & \to x := 4x(1-x) & \to 1 \geqslant x \geqslant 0 \end{cases}$$

The logistic map is decomposed into two transitions which correspond to the monotonic parts of the map and which are invertible; see the end of Section 4.

The invariant :

$$
\begin{aligned}
J_{\pm}^{(0)} &= \mathbf{t} \\
J_{-}^{(1)} &= S_{1+}.\mathbf{t} \vee S_{2+}.\mathbf{t} && = 0 \leqslant x \leqslant 1 \\
&= J_{-}^{(1)} && = J_{-} \\
J_{+}^{(1)} &= S_{1-}.\mathbf{t} \vee S_{2-}.\mathbf{t} && = 0 \leqslant x \leqslant 1 \\
J_{+}^{(2)} &= S_{1-}.(0 \leqslant x \leqslant 1) \vee S_{2-}.(0 \leqslant x \leqslant 1) && = 0 \leqslant x \leqslant 1 \\
&= J_{+}^{(1)} && = J_{+} \\
\\
J &= J_{-} \wedge J_{+} && = 0 \leqslant x \leqslant 1
\end{aligned}
$$

Fullness of the invariant :

We use again

Φ : the predicate $0 \leqslant x \leqslant 1$,

Ψ : the predicates $p \leqslant x \leqslant q$ where $0 \leqslant p \leqslant q \leqslant 1$.

Condition(i) in Section 3.7 clearly holds since $p \leqslant q$. Condition (ii) and condition (iii) for Φ are easy to verify. Condition (iii) for Ψ is verified as follows :

$$
\begin{aligned}
& S_{1-}.(p \leqslant x \leqslant q) \\
& \{ \text{section 2.2} \} \\
=\ & 0 \leqslant x \leqslant 1/2 \wedge p \leqslant 4x - 4x^2 \leqslant q \\
& \{ \text{algebra} \} \\
=\ & 0 \leqslant x \leqslant 1/2 \wedge 4x^2 - 4x + p \leqslant 0 \wedge 4x^2 - 4x + q \geqslant 0 \\
& \{ \text{discussion of quadratic inequations} \} \\
=\ & \tfrac{1-\sqrt{1-p}}{2} \leqslant x \leqslant \tfrac{1-\sqrt{1-q}}{2} \\
& \{ 0 \leqslant \tfrac{1-\sqrt{1-p}}{2} \leqslant \tfrac{1-\sqrt{1-q}}{2} \leqslant 1 \text{ since } 0 \leqslant p \leqslant q \leqslant 1 \} \\
\in\ & \Psi
\end{aligned}
$$

By a similar reasoning,

$$
\begin{aligned}
& S_{2-}.(p \leqslant x \leqslant q) \\
=\ & \tfrac{1+\sqrt{1-q}}{2} \leqslant x \leqslant \tfrac{1+\sqrt{1-p}}{2} \\
\in\ & \Psi
\end{aligned}
$$

Any $J_{\sigma,\tau}(\sigma, \tau \in \Sigma^*)$ takes the form $p \leqslant x \leqslant q$ where $0 \leqslant p \leqslant q \leqslant 1$ and where p and q are generated by recursive compositions of the functions $x \to \frac{1 \pm \sqrt{1-x}}{2}$: each formula $J_{\sigma,\tau}$ ($\sigma, \tau \in \Sigma^{\infty}$) is infinitely recursive, viz. fractal.

Atomicity of the invariant :

Here, it is harder to define an adequate function μ : the contraction of the successive $J_{\sigma,\tau}$ ($\sigma, \tau \in \Sigma^*$) does slow down in the neighbourhood of $x = 1/2$. A solution is then to use the trigonometric transformation [Dvn] from the tent map to the logistic map in order to derive a function μ on the basis of the one used for the tent map. This is left as an exercise.

This example shows again that the qualitative dynamics of systems depends on the possible compositions of transitions and on the rate of contraction of components of invariants. The specific nature of the various transitions is less important.

5.2.5 N-dimensional baker-maps

We obtain various 2-dimensional baker-maps by using a baker map, or its inverse, along the axis x and the axis y. The composition of two direct baker-maps yields

$$
\begin{aligned}
S = \ [\, &S_1 : 0 \leqslant x \leqslant 1/2 \wedge 0 \leqslant y \leqslant 1/2 && \to (x,y) := (2x, 2y) \\
& && \to 0 \leqslant x \leqslant 1 \wedge 0 \leqslant y \leqslant 1 \\
[]\, &S_2 : 1/2 \leqslant x \leqslant 1 \wedge 0 \leqslant y \leqslant 1/2 && \to (x,y) := (2x-1, 2y) \\
& && \to 0 \leqslant x \leqslant 1 \wedge 0 \leqslant y \leqslant 1 \\
[]\, &S_3 : 0 \leqslant x \leqslant 1/2 \wedge 1/2 \leqslant y \leqslant 1 && \to (x,y) := (2x, 2y-1) \\
& && \to 0 \leqslant x \leqslant 1 \wedge 0 \leqslant y \leqslant 1 \\
[]\, &S_4 : 1/2 \leqslant x \leqslant 1 \wedge 1/2 \leqslant y \leqslant 1 && \to (x,y) := (2x-1, 2y-1) \\
& && \to 0 \leqslant x \leqslant 1 \wedge 0 \leqslant y \leqslant 1
\end{aligned}
$$

$]$ where $x, y \in Real$

For this 2-dimensional baker-map, the invariant is $0 \leqslant x \leqslant 1 \wedge 0 \leqslant y \leqslant 1$, and is full and atomic. The verification simply combines for x and for y the proofs given in Section 5.1; the function μ becomes a product of functions μ_x and μ_y :

$$
\begin{aligned}
\mu.(\, p \leqslant x \leqslant q \wedge r \leqslant y \leqslant s) \ &= \mu_x.(\, p \leqslant x \leqslant q) \times \mu_y.(\, r \leqslant y \leqslant s) \\
&= (q-p) \times (s-r)
\end{aligned}
$$

We can take the inverse of the above S, viz. inverse baker-maps along x and along y. We can also use two fat baker-maps (Section 5.2.2) : the invariant remains full and atomic; similarly with two thin maps. We can combine a direct baker-map along x and an inverse one along y; this yields a hyperbolic system [Wgg]. We can generalize such variants to more dimensions.

5.3 Interesting classes

The following exercises, based on those of the previous sections, illustrate other kinds of dynamical systems. They again show how the dynamics remains invariant when determinism is replaced by non-determinism after an inversion, when conservative hyperbolic systems become dissipative or accumulative, when continuous spaces are reduced to large discrete spaces, and when programs with similar dynamics are composed. The dynamics essentially depends on the fullness and the atomicity of the invariant, and these characteristics are stable under the considered changes.

5.3.1 Hyperbolic systems

As already suggested, a horseshoe-like map is obtained by composing the baker map along the axis x and the rekab map along y :

$$S = \quad [\,S_1 : 0 \leqslant x \leqslant 1/2 \wedge 0 \leqslant y \leqslant 1/2 \quad \rightarrow (x,y) := (2x, y/2)$$
$$\rightarrow 0 \leqslant x \leqslant 1 \wedge 0 \leqslant y \leqslant 1/4$$
$$[]\,S_2 : 0 \leqslant x \leqslant 1/2 \wedge 1/2 \leqslant y \leqslant 1 \quad \rightarrow (x,y) := (2x, y/2)$$
$$\rightarrow 0 \leqslant x \leqslant 1 \wedge 1/4 \leqslant y \leqslant 1/2$$
$$[]\,S_3 : 1/2 \leqslant x \leqslant 1 \wedge 0 \leqslant y \leqslant 1/2 \quad \rightarrow (x,y) := (2x - 1, y/2 + 1/2)$$
$$\rightarrow 0 \leqslant x \leqslant 1 \wedge 1/2 \leqslant y \leqslant 3/4$$
$$[]\,S_4 : 1/2 \leqslant x \leqslant 1 \wedge 1/2 \leqslant y \leqslant 1 \quad \rightarrow (x,y) := (2x - 1, y/2 + 1/2)$$
$$\rightarrow 0 \leqslant x \leqslant 1 \wedge 3/4 \leqslant y \leqslant 1$$
$$]\ \text{where } x, y \in Real$$

$$J = \quad 0 \leqslant x \leqslant 1 \wedge 0 \leqslant y \leqslant 1$$

The fullness and atomicity of J are proved by the sufficient conditions 3.7 and 4.2, using

Φ : the predicates $r \leqslant y \leqslant s$ where $0 \leqslant r \leqslant s \leqslant 1$,
Ψ : the predicates $p \leqslant x \leqslant q$ where $0 \leqslant p \leqslant q \leqslant 1$,
$\mu(A \wedge B) = \mu_x(A) \times \mu_y(B)$, $k = k_x \times k_y = 1/2 \times 1/2 = 1/4$.

The pre-guards determine four squares which are transformed by S_+ into four horizontal rectangles corresponding to the post-guards; indeed, S_+ is dilating along x and contracting along y; by S_-, the four squares are transformed into four vertical rectangles; by $S_{+,-}$, they are transformed into sixteen squares, and into 4^{n+1} ones by $S_{+,-}^{(n)}$.

The program analyzed here is conservative : four squares are mapped into four rectangles having the same total area as the four squares. If we use the fat or thin versions (Section 5.2.2) of the baker or rekab maps, we may obtain dissipative or accumulative programs : the sum of areas may decrease or increase, but the invariant remains full and atomic.

5.3.2 Non-determinism without atomicity

Sensitive dependence on initial or final conditions results from fullness **and** atomicity. Without the latter, the dynamics remains very simple, even in the presence of non-determinism. An illustration is the cross map, which amounts to a tent map (Section 5.3.2) without any contraction :

$$S \quad = \quad [\,S_1 : 0 \leqslant x \leqslant 1 \quad \rightarrow x := 1 - x \quad \rightarrow 1 \geqslant x \geqslant 0$$
$$[]\,S_2 : 0 \leqslant x \leqslant 1 \quad \rightarrow x := x \quad \rightarrow 0 \leqslant x \leqslant 1$$
$$]\ \text{where } x \in Real$$

$$J \quad = \quad 0 \leqslant x \leqslant 1$$
$$J_{\sigma,\tau} \quad = \quad 0 \leqslant x \leqslant 1 \qquad\qquad (\sigma, \tau \in \{1, 2\}^\infty)$$

The invariant is full but not at all atomic : neighbour points may remain neighbour forever, and to reach points distributed over all of J, one must begin with points already distributed over all of J. There is no sensitive dependence on initial conditions, although the cross map is non-deterministic.

5.3.3 Discrete state-spaces

As with the alternative determinism vs non-determinism, the choice between continuous spaces vs discrete ones is not essential w.r.t. sufficient fullness and atomicity.

For instance, a discrete version of the baker map can be the following; ev and od respectively characterize evenness and oddness of integers, and N is any positive integer :

$$
\begin{aligned}
S = \quad & [\, S_1 : 0 \leqslant x \leqslant N && \to x := 2x && \to 0 \leqslant x \leqslant 2N \wedge ev(x) \\
& [\!] S_2 : 0 \leqslant x \leqslant N-1 && \to x := 2x+1 && \to 0 \leqslant x \leqslant 2N \wedge od(x) \\
& [\!] S_3 : N \leqslant x \leqslant 2N && \to x := 2x-N && \to 0 \leqslant x \leqslant 2N \wedge ev(x) \\
& [\!] S_4 : 0 \leqslant x \leqslant 2N-1 && \to x := 2x-N+1 && \to 0 \leqslant x \leqslant 2N \wedge od(x) \\
&] \text{ where } x \in Nat
\end{aligned}
$$

$$
J = \quad 0 \leqslant x \leqslant 2N
$$

The additional transitions S_2 and S_4 yield odd integers, so as to ensure all integers in $[0, 2N]$ are reached by S; for this reason, the invariant J is sufficiently, but not strictly, full. It is atomic, since each $J_{\sigma,\tau}$ contains at most one integer for sufficiently long, yet finite, traces (σ, τ). The sensitive dependence on initial conditions increases with N.

An alternative example is a discrete version of the hereabove cross-map (Section 5.3.2) : for any positive integer N,

$$
\begin{aligned}
S \quad = \quad & [\, S_1 : 0 \leqslant x \leqslant N && \to x := N-x && \to N \geqslant x \geqslant 0 \\
& [\!] S_2 : 0 \leqslant x \leqslant N && \to x := x && \to 0 \leqslant x \leqslant N \\
&] \text{ where } x \in Nat
\end{aligned}
$$

$$
\begin{aligned}
J \quad &= \quad 0 \leqslant x \leqslant N \\
J_{\sigma,\tau} \quad &= \quad 0 \leqslant x \leqslant N \qquad (\sigma, \tau \in \{1,2\}^\infty)
\end{aligned}
$$

The system is still non-deterministic; its invariant remains full and coarse. The discretization of the state space does not change much in the dynamics.

6 Conclusions

For the dynamics of transition programs, the important issues are invariance and contraction, rather than questions such as determinism vs. non-determinism, or discretization vs continuity in state spaces. To determine fullness and atomicity, invariance and contraction must be considered in the past together with the future. Notwithstanding, attraction properties of invariants depend on contraction in the future only; this line has not been developed here.

Non-deterministic relations between states are tamed by deterministic functions between sets of states, viz. predicate-transformers. These benefit from simple duality rules obtained by reversing the relations programs define, viz. by exchanging the past and the future; this symmetry is especially useful in the structural analysis of invariants.

The sufficient conditions for proving fullness and atomicity of invariants, without deriving these, are based on the following techniques : manageable formulae serve as safe approximations of the exact predicates which describe components of invariants and which are often hard to deduce; contraction is detected using Liapunov-Floyd-like functions, viz. energy functions in the case of physical systems.

Thanks to the approach followed and the techniques used, the following results have have been obtained : non-deterministic systems are tackled without ado; symbolic dynamics is elaborated in general, not only for specific systems; more or less effective conditions help to prove the presence of dense multitudes of traces and of sensitive dependence on initial and final conditions; a continuum is established from discrete state-spaces to continuous ones.

Only elementary, classical examples have been re-constructed; the present work barely scratches the surface of relevant problems and only aims at a better understanding. The maximalist definitions of fullness and atomicity should be relaxed: Criteria of attraction should be defined. Composition laws for systems should be elaborated. Then, more substantial exercises could be carried out.

7 References

[ArA] Arnold, V. I., and A. Avez, *Ergodic Problems of Classical Mechanics*, Addison-Wesley, Redwood City CA., USA, 1989.

[Dij] Dijkstra, E.W., *A Discipline of Programming*, Prentice-Hall, Englewood Cliffs N.J., USA, 1976.

[Dvn] Devaney, R. L., *An Introduction to Chaotic Dynamical Systems*, 2nd ed., Addison-Wesley, Redwood City CA., USA, 1989.

[Fld] Floyd, R.W., Assigning meanings to programs, in: *Proc. Symp. in Appl. Maths.*, Vol.19, Amer. Math. Soc., Providence R.I., USA, 1967, pp. 19-32.

[Snt] Sintzoff, M., Ensuring correctness by arbitrary postfixed-points, in : *Proc. 7th Symp. Math. Found. Comput. Sci.*, LNCS 64, Springer-Verlag, Berlin, 1978, pp. 484-492.

[Trk] Tarski, A., A lattice theoretical fixpoint theorem and its applications, *Pacific J. Math.* 5(1955), pp. 285-310.

[vLS] van Lamsweerde, A., and M. Sintzoff, Formal derivation of strongly correct concurrent programs, *Acta Informatica* 12(1979), pp. 1-32.

[Wgg] Wiggins, S., *Introduction to Applied Nonlinear Dynamical Systems and Chaos*, Texts in Appl. Maths. 2, Springer-Verlag, Berlin, 1990.

CONSTRUCTING A PARALLEL SORT PROGRAM ON HYPERCUBE BY USING DISTRIBUTIVELY CALLABLE PROCEDURES

Daniel HERMAN* and Laurent TRILLING**

*IRISA/INSA Rennes and ** IMAG-LGI Grenoble, France

Abstract   The purpose of this paper is to describe an extension of the procedure concept through the design and implementation of a parallel sort. This extension, called a Distributively Callable Procedure (DCP), applies only to procedures having as many parameters as components in their result. Such procedures can be called by using a Distributed Procedure Call (DPC). A DPC is achieved by several partial calls issued from different processes, each of these partial calls having as result a component of the whole result. We show how a distributed and recursively expressed parallel sorting algorithm naturally can be designed by using DCPs. Futhermore, we derive a program from this algorithm to be loaded on each processor of a hypercube. In this case the DCPs serve to represent elementary communications among processors.

1. Notion of Distributively Callable Procedure

1.1 A first approach

We introduce this notion with an example. Consider the following procedure:

```
proc MinMax = (int a, int b) pair :
```

MinMax has 2 formal parameters a and b, both integers, and yields a result which is a pair of integers.
The result delivered by a procedure is the last value which is evaluated.

```
begin
  if a < b
      then (a, b)
      else (b, a)
  fi
end
```

In the language we use, a construct, called a **collateral** expression, can be used to express parallel executions. The notation:

```
( <p1> , <p2> )
```

means that the two calculations $<p1>$ and $<p2>$ are independant; and, as a consequence, they can be executed in parallel.

We consider that a procedure such as `MinMax`, which has exactly the same number of parameters and results, can be called in a distributed manner. In this case, each part of a collateral expression provides one of the actual parameters and receives the corresponding element of the result.

begin

    proc MinMax = ... ;

The following collateral has two parts p1 and p2

    (

p1 has its own context where two integers, i and j are declared. These two integers are not reachable by p2. The expression MinMax(i, -) is a partial call

      int i = 2;
      int j = MinMax(i, -)
      ... (1)

    ,

the context of p2 contains two integers a and b. The expression MinMax(-, a) is a second partial call.

      int a = 1;
      int b = MinMax(-, a)
      ... (2)
)

At (1) the value of j in p1 is 1 and, at (2), the value of b in p2 is 2

end

The corresponding execution can be pictured as follows:

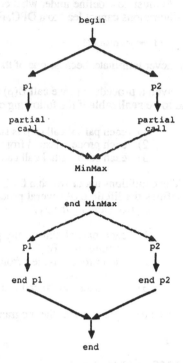

The group composed of the two partial calls which lead to the execution of MinMax is called a **Distributed Procedure Call** (DPC). A DPC can be considered as an extension of an ordinary procedure call. The latter is achieved by a single process whereas the former is achieved by several processes. Each process executes a **partial call** and provides one actual parameter. The result which is delivered by the called procedure is a tuple whose length **must** be equal to the number of parameters. The resulting tuple is dispatched among the calling processes so that each partial call delivers one element: the ith part of the result is given to the process which has provided the ith parameter.

A procedure which can be called by a DPC has the following general form:

    proc p = (**m1** x1, ..., **mk** xk) **k-tuple**: <body>

> *x1 ... xk are the formal parameters (of type m1 ... mk) and the result is a k-tuple (the type declaration of k-tuple must, of course, specify the types of all the results).*

We will call such procedures **Distributively Callable Procedures** (DCP). The syntax of a partial call providing the first actual parameter is p(a, -, ..., -), the second p(-, b, -, ..., -), and so on.

1.2. Realizable DPC

We must now define under what conditions a collection of partial calls can be a DPC. Some configurations cannot lead to a DPC. For instance, the collateral expression:

```
(i = MinMax(1, -), j = MinMax(2, -), k = MinMax(-, 3))
```

will never terminate, because one of the first partial calls will never find its partner.

Given a procedure p, we call $B(p)$ the block which defines the lifetime of p. A DPC of p is said to be **realizable** if the following conditions are satisfied:

1) each partial call of p is issued by a different process coming from $B(p)$;
2) each process issued from $B(p)$ does a partial call of p;
3) each such partial call can be incorporated in a unique DPC.

The conditions under which a DPC is realizable are easily extended to the case where a block B defines the lifetime of several procedures p_1, ..., p_n. Several DPCs of several procedures q_1, ..., q_m from among the p_1, ..., p_n are said to be realizable under the following conditions:

1) each partial call of any procedure q_1, ..., q_m is issued by a different process coming from B;
2) each process issued from B executes a partial call of one procedure from among q_1, ..., q_m;
3) each such partial call can be incorporated in a unique DPC.

As an example consider the program:

```
begin

    proc MinMax = … ;
    proc MaxMin = … ;

(1)     (MinMax(2,-), MinMax(-,1), MaxMin(1,-), MaxMin(-,2));
(2)     (MinMax(2,-), MinMax(-,1), MinMax(4,-), MinMax(-,3));

end
```

The collateral expression (1) is composed of two realizable DPCs and gives the result $(1, 2, 2, 1)$. Note that while the collateral expression (2) is also composed of two realizable DPCs, two different results $(1, 2, 3, 4)$ or $(2, 4, 1, 3)$ can be obtained, depending on the way in which DCPs are constructed.

2. A distributed expression for a sorting algorithm

In this section we will use DCPs to present and to program a parallel sort. In section 2.1, we apply the composition principle to present a parallel sort algorithm. This principle is applied here by using DCPs to construct a distributed algorithm in the same way as it is applied to construct a sequential algorithm by using ordinary procedures. In section 2.2, a precise formulation of this algoritm is given. In section 2.3, an example is applied to 4 elements and the associated sorting network is exhibited. In section 2.4, a unique program to be loaded on each processor of a hypercube is deduced by transformation .

2.1. Application of the composition principle to exhibit a parallel sort

Our aim is to construct procedures SE_0, SE_1, ..., SE_{2M-1} whose execution are independent as far as possible and such that (SE is for Sorted Element):

$$(SE_0(t_0), \; SE_1(t_1), \dots, SE_{2M-1}(t_{2M-1})) = (r_0, \; r_1, \dots, r_{2M-1})$$

where $(r_0, \; r_1, \dots, r_{2M-1})$ is the sorted array deduced from the original array $(t_0, t_1, \dots, t_{2M-1})$.

The first idea to apply aims to obtain the finest grain of parallelism. It is to single out the smallest decomposable entity and to assign it to a processor. In the case of a sort, the minimal entity is obviously a pair of elements of the array to be sorted since a pair can only be decomposable into two non-decomposable entities.

Then our parallel sorting problem is solved if we are able to construct procedures SP_0^M, SP_1^M, ..., SP_{M-1}^M (with $M = 2^P$) such that (SP is for Sorted Pair):

$$(SP_0^M(t_0, \; t_1), \quad SP_1^M(t_2, \; t_3), \dots, SP_{M-1}^M(t_{2M-2}, \; t_{2M-1})) =$$
$$((r_0, \; r_1), \; (r_2, \; r_3) \dots, \; (r_{2M-2}, \; r_{2M-1}))$$

That is because, utilizing DCPs, we obtain

$$(SP_0^M(t_0, \; -), SP_0^M(-, \; t_1), \dots, SP_{M-1}^M(t_{2M-2}, \; -), SP_{M-1}^M(-, \; t_{2M-1})) =$$
$$(r_0, \; r_1, \dots, \; r_{2M-1})$$

and then

$$SE_0(t_0) = SP_0^M(t_0, \; -), \quad SE_1(t_1) = SP_0^M(-, \; t_1), \dots,$$
$$SE_{2M-2}(t_{2M-2}) = SP_{M-1}^M(t_{2M-2}, \; -), \quad SE_{2M-1}(t_{2M-1}) = SP_{M-1}^M(-, \; t_{2M-1})$$

Next we apply the composition principle, which, in our case,

-firstly permits us to assume that

(i) we know $M/2$ procedures $SP_0^{M/2}$, $SP_2^{M/2}$, ... such that:

$$(SP_0^{M/2}(t_0, \; t_2), \; SP_2^{M/2}(t_4, \; t_6), \dots, \; SP_{M/2-2}^{M/2}(t_{2M-4}, \; t_{2M-2})) =$$
$$((t_0', \; t_2'), \; (t_4', \; t_6'), \dots, \; (t_{2M-4}', \; t_{2M-2}'))$$

where $(t_0', \; t_2', \dots, \; t_{2M-2}')$ is the sorted array deduced from the array $(t_0, t_2, \dots, t_{2M-2})$,

(ii) we know $M/2$ procedures $SP_1^{M/2}$, $SP_3^{M/2}$,... such that:

$$(SP_1^{M/2}(t_1, t_3), SP_3^{M/2}(t_5, t_7),...,SP_{M/2-1}^{M/2}(t_{2M-3}, t_{2M-1})) =$$
$$((t_1', t_3'), (t_5', t_7'),..., (t_{2M-3}', t_{2M-1}'))$$

where $(t_1', t_3', ..., t_{2M-1}')$ is the sorted array deduced from the array $(t_1, t_3, ..., t_{2M-1})$,

- secondly requires finding composition functions to apply to each pair (t_0', t_1'), ..., (t_{2M-2}', t_{2M-1}') in order to obtain (r_0, r_1), ..., (r_{2M-2}, r_{2M-1}).

For example, if $C_0^M(1, r)$ (resp. $C_1^M(1, r)$) is this composition function for the pair (t_0', t_1') (resp. (t_2', t_3')) then

$$SP_0^M(t_0, t_1) = C_0^M(t_0', t_1') = C_0^M(SP_0^{M/2}(t_0, -), SP_1^{M/2}(t_1, -))$$
$$= (r_0, r_1)$$

$$SP_0^M(t_2, t_3) = C_1^M(t_2', t_3') = C_1^M(SP_0^{M/2}(-, t_2), SP_1^{M/2}(-, t_3))$$
$$= (r_2, r_3)$$

Note that the first idea of composition functions that comes to mind does not work; namely, sort each pair (t_0', t_1'), ..., (t_{2M-2}', t_{2M-1}') and apply on each resulting pair the process which has been already applied to the original pair (that is, sort globally the first and second elements of pairs and then afterwards sort locally each pair).

Example:

$$(t_0,t_1,t_2,t_3,t_4,t_5,t_6,t_7) = (1,5,7,0,4,3,6,2)$$

$$(t_0',t_1',t_2',t_3',t_4',t_5',t_6',t_7') = (SP_0^{M/2}(1, -), SP_1^{M/2}(5, -),$$
$$SP_0^{M/2}(-, 7), SP_1^{M/2}(-, 0),$$
$$SP_2^{M/2}(4, -), SP_3^{M/2}(3, -),$$
$$SP_2^{M/2}(-, 6), SP_3^{M/2}(-, 2))$$

Since $SP_0^{M/2}, SP_1^{M/2}, SP_2^{M/2}, SP_3^{M/2}$ are such that:

$$(SP_0^{M/2}(1, 7), SP_2^{M/2}(4, 6)) = ((1,4), (6,7)) \quad \text{and}$$

$$(SP_1^{M/2}(5, 0), SP_3^{M/2}(3, 2)) = ((0,2), (3,5))$$

we have:

$$(t_0',t_1',t_2',t_3',t_4',t_5',t_6',t_7')= (1,0,4,2,6,3,7,5)$$

Local sorts on pairs give:

$$(0,1,2,4,3,6,5,7)$$

Then, sorting again first and second elements of pairs gives the same array which is clearly not sorted.

To obtain right composition functions, one can come back to the inital decomposition into independent entities and relax it by considering a less minimal one, namely quadruplets instead of pairs. Then a variant of the preceding idea can be used: that is, sort globally the outside and the middle two elements of quadruplets, then sort each quadruplet locally and proceed again on the resulting pairs in the same way (that is, sort globally the outside and the middle two elements of quadruplets and then afterwards sort each quadruplet).

Example: considering again

$(1,5,7,0,4,3,6,2)$

Sorting globally the outside and the middle elements of quadruplets gives:

$(0,3,5,1,2,6,7,4)$

Sorting quadruplets gives:

$(0,1,3,5,2,4,6,7)$

Sorting again globally the outside and the middle elements of quadruplets gives:

$(0,1,3,2,5,4,6,7)$

Sorting again quadruplets gives:

$(0,1,2,3,4,5,6,7)$

which is sorted.

However, a closer analysis [see Appendix 1] shows that, after a first phase giving as result the pairs (t_0', t_1'), ..., (t_{2M-2}', t_{2M-1}'), a second phase could make the decomposition which groups the outside elements of a quadruplet and the middle two elements of a quadruplet. More precisely, this second phase yields pairs (t_0'', t_1''), ..., (t_{2M-2}'', t_{2M-1}'') such that:

$$(SP_0^{M/2}(t_0', t_3'), \quad SP_2^{M/2}(t_4', t_7'), ..., SP_{M/2-2}^{M/2}(t_{2M-4}', t_{2M-1}'))$$
$$= ((t_0'', t_3''), (t_4'', t_7'')..., (t_{2M-4}'', t_{2M-1}''))$$

$$(SP_0^{M/2}(t_1', t_2'), \quad SP_2^{M/2}(t_5', t_6'), ..., SP_{M/2-2}^{M/2}(t_{2M-3}', t_{2M-2}'))$$
$$= ((t_1'', t_2''), (t_5'', t_6'')..., (t_{2M-3}'', t_{2M-2}''))$$

It remains then to apply a third phase which performs a local sorting on each pair; that is,

$$(MinMax(t_0'', t_1''), ..., MinMax(t_{2M-2}'', t_{2M-1}'')) =$$
$$((r_0, r_1), ..., (r_{2M-2}, r_{2M-1}))$$

Example: as it was given above, the first phase gives:

$(t_0', t_1', t_2', t_3', t_4', t_5', t_6', t_7') = (1,0,4,2,6,3,7,5)$

The second phase gives:

$(t_0'', t_1'', t_2'', t_3'', t_4'', t_5'', t_6'', t_7'') = (1,0,3,2,5,4,7,6)$

And the third phase gives:

$(r_0, r_1, r_2, r_3, r_4, r_5, r_6, r_7) = (0,1,2,3,4,5,6,7)$

Finally, a further improvement [see Appendix 1] can be made by simplifying the second phase: processes to be applied on pairs, instead to be composed of the three indicated phases, can be composed only of the second and the third phases.

2.2 Precise formulation of the parallel sorting algorithm

Finally, procedures $SP_i{}^m(l, r)$ must be defined according to the following pre and post conditions. For $k = M/m$,

-if (l, r) is the pair numbered i/k of an array t of m elements numbered from 0 to $m-1$ (pre-condition),

-then $SP_i{}^m(l, r)$ delivers the pair numbered i/k of the sorted array deduced from t (post-condition).

In the same way, procedures $MP_i{}^m(l, r)$ (MP is for Merging Pair) must be defined according to pre and post conditions:

-if (l, r) is the pair numbered i/k of an array $t = ((l_0, r_0),\ldots,(l_{m-1}, r_{m-1}))$ such that $l_j \le l_{j+1}$ and $r_j \le r_{j+1}$ for $0 \le j \le m-1$ (pre-condition),

-then $MP_i{}^m(l, r)$ gives the pair numbered i/k of the sorted array deduced from t (post-condition).

Recursive definitions of $SP_i{}^m(l, r)$ and $MP_i{}^m(l, r)$ follow:

$SP_i{}^1(l, r) = MP_i{}^1(l, r) = MinMax(l, r)$

if $m > 1$ then

- if i/k is even then

$$SP_i{}^m(l, r) = MinMax(MP_i{}^{m/2}(SP_i{}^{m/2}(l, -), -),$$
$$MP_{i+k}{}^{m/2}(SP_{i+k}{}^{m/2}(r, -), -))$$

$$MP_i{}^m(l, r) = MinMax(MP_i{}^{m/2}(l, -), MP_{i+k}{}^{m/2}(r, -))$$

- if i/k is odd then

$$SP_i{}^m(l, r) = MinMax(MP_i{}^{m/2}(-, SP_{i-k}{}^{m/2}(-, l)),$$
$$MP_{i-k}{}^{m/2}(-, SP_i{}^{m/2}(-, r)))$$

$$MP_i{}^m(l, r) = MinMax(MP_i{}^{m/2}(-, l), MP_{i-k}{}^{m/2}(-, r))$$

What remains is to construct the procedures $SP_i{}^m(l, r)$ and $MP_i{}^m(l, r)$ (with $m \le M$) such that

$$(SP_0{}^M(t_0, -), SP_0{}^M(-, t1),\ldots, SP_{M-1}{}^M(t_{N-2}, -), SP_{M-1}{}^M(-, t_{N-1}))$$

produces the sorted array deduced from t. The procedure NetSort (M) which delivers the array of pairs of procedures $((SP_0{}^M, MP_0{}^M),\ldots, (SP_{M-1}{}^M, MP_{M-1}{}^M))$ is easily derived from the preceding recursive definitions [see Appendix 2].

2.3. An example

To sort four elements t_0, t_1, t_2, t_3, the initial call should be:

$$(SP_0^2(t_0, -), SP_0^2(-, t_1), SP_1^2(t_2, -), SP_1^2(-, t_3))$$

where SP_0^2 and SP_1^2 should be:

proc SP_0^2 = (**int** l, r) **pair**:
 MinMax(MP$_0^1$(SP$_0^1$(l, -), -), MP$_1^1$(SP$_1^1$(r, -), -))

proc SP_1^2 = (**int** l, r) **pair**:
 MinMax(MP$_1^1$(-, SP$_0^1$(-, l)), MP$_0^1$(-, SP$_1^1$(-, r)))

with $SP_0^1 = SP_1^1 = MP_0^1 = MP_1^1 = MinMax$

The associated sorting network can be pictured as follows:

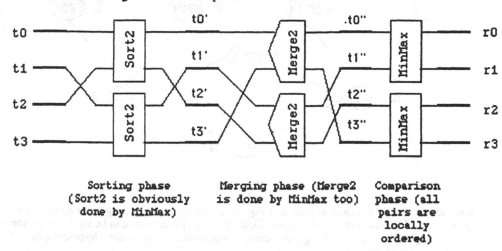

Sorting phase   Merging phase (Merge2   Comparison
(Sort2 is obviously   is done by MinMax too)   phase (all
done by MinMax)   pairs are
                                                           locally
                                                           ordered)

Figure 1. Sorting network for N=4.

N.B. This network is close to the odd-even network presented by BATCHER [BATCHER 68] for "odd-even" parallel sorting. It is a little more expensive but it has a more regular structure. Its execution time is asymptotically equivalent ($O(\log^2(N))$). What should be noted is that it is by using DPCs that our program takes into account both the independence of the comparisons and the absence of shared memory graphically expressed by this sorting network.

2.4. Implementation on a hypercube

That these recursive definitions lead naturally to regular structures of computation is worthy of note. For instance, an execution of NetSort(4) generates the following communication structure (so-called "butterfly") for the $SP_i{}^m$ procedures:

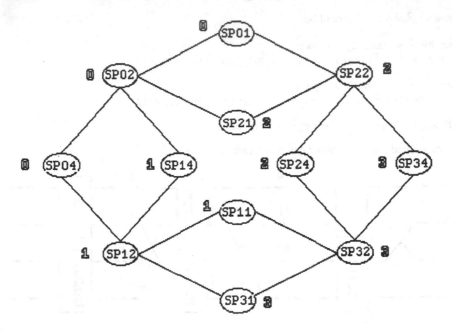

Figure 2

It is then easy to understand, as shown in Figure 2, that by implementing procedures $SP_i{}^m$ on the processor i (indicated by a **i** on figure 2), a square of processors can be used to execute a parallel sorting of 8 integers. In the general case, it will be necessary to use a hypercube of 2^{P-1} processors to sort 2^P integers.

To obtain an implementation in which the same code PSP_i (for Program for Sorted Pair on processor i) is loaded on each processor, we need to express elementary communication procedures between processors. This is easily done by implementing on each processor i an array Ex_i of distributively procedures such that:

$$Ex_i[s] = (\textbf{int } lp, rp) \textbf{ pair: } (rp,lp), \text{ for } s:1,\dots,P$$

with $Ex_i[s] = Ex_{i+K}[s]$, where $K = k$ if i/k is even and $-k$ if k is odd for $k = M/2^s$.

To derive $PSP_i(m, l, r)$ and analagously $PMP_i(m, l, r)$ from $SP_i{}^m(l, r)$ and $MP_i{}^m(l, r)$, one must first note that the execution of $SP_i{}^m(l, r)$ may be serialized so that:

$$PSP_i(1, l, r) = PMP_i(1, l, r) = MinMax(l, r)$$

and if $m > 1$ then

- if i/k is even then

$$PSP_i(m, 1, r) = MinMax((11, r1) = (SP_i^{m/2}(1,-), SP_{i+k}^{m/2}(r,-));$$
$$(MP_i^{m/2}(11,-), MP_{i+k}^{m/2}(r1,-)))$$

$$PMP_i(m, 1, r) = MinMax(MP_i^{m/2}(1,-), MP_{i+k}^{m/2}(r,-))$$

- if i/k is odd then

$$PSP_i(m, 1, r) = MinMax((11, r1) = (SP_{i-k}^{m/2}(-,1), SP_i^{m/2}(,r));$$
$$(MP_i^{m/2}(-,11), MP_{i-k}^{m/2}(-,r1)))$$

$$PMP_i(m, 1, r) = MinMax(MP_i^{m/2}(-, 1), MP_{i-k}^{m/2}(-, r))$$

Then, transformation rules forcing execution of procedures PSP_i and PMP_i on processor i have to be introduced. For example, if F stands for SP (or MP) then

$$(F_i^{m/2}(1,-), F_{i+K}^{m/2}(r,-))$$

may be replaced by

$$((L, R) = PF_i(m/2, 1, Ex_i[s](r, -));$$
$$(L, Ex_i[s](R, -)))$$

where $s = \log(m)$

Similar rules can be introduced for

$$(F_i^{m/2}(-,1), F_{i+K}^{m/2}(-,r)) \text{ and } (F_{i+K}^{m/2}(-,1), F_i^{m/2}(-,r)).$$

Finally, we obtain:

$$PSP_i(1, 1, r) = PMP_i(1, 1, r) = MinMax(1, r)$$

and if $m > 1$ then

- if i/k is even then

$$PSP_i(m, 1, r) = MinMax((L1,R1) = PSP_i(m/2,1,Ex_i[s](r,-));$$
$$(11, r1) = (L1, Ex_i[s](R1,-));$$
$$(L2, R2) = PMP_i(m/2,11,Ex_i[s](r1,-));$$
$$(L2, Ex_i[s](R2,-)))$$

$$PMP_i(m, 1, r) = MinMax((L, R) = PMP_i(m/2,1,Ex_i[s](r,-));$$
$$(L, Ex_i[s](R,-)))$$

- if i/k is odd then

$$PSP_i(m, 1, r) = MinMax((L1, R1) = PSP_i(m/2,Ex_i[s](-,1),r);$$
$$(11, r1) = (Ex_i[s](-,L1),R1);$$
$$(L2, R2) = PMP_i(m/2,Ex_i[s](-,r1),11);$$
$$(R2, Ex[s](-,L2)))$$

$$PMP_i(m, 1, r) = MinMax((L,R) = PMP_i(m/2,Ex_i[s](-,r), 1);$$
$$(R, Ex_i[s](-,L)))$$

3. Conclusion

Our purpose was to show that the concept of DPCs can be useful in designing and programming a parallel sort algorithm (SP_i^m). We transformed the resulting program into an additional program running on a hypercube (PSP_i).

First, the fact that the final program as well as initial specification is recursively expressed, is noteworthy. This appears to us to represent a higher level of expression than is normally the case for sequential programs and not normally the case when it comes to distributed programs.

This can simply be explained by the fact that if adequate tools to write recursive distributed programs are not provided, people are not tempted to imagine recursive distributed algorithms! BATCHER's sorting network is clearly recursively expressed. But they are drawings which need to be programmed. DPCs appear to be a good tool for that since they permit us to derive finally a recursive distributed algoritm on a hypercube. Procedures PSP_i have been quite rapidly implemented and tested on a hypercube FPS T40 [BARRAUD 91]: all that is necessary is just to write elementary communication procedures $Ex_i[s]$. Also derived by the usual means is an iterative version from PSP_i and it has been tested.

A second point, in the same line of reasoning, concerns the functional aspects of the program. These aspects appear clearly since the main problem is in designing the procedures SP_i^m and MP_i^m from elementary ones($MinMax$). From our viewpoint, the main benefit seems to be a better understanding. To see the value of this improvement, one can see how similar algorithms to the one given in section 2 are presented in [BATCHER 68, AKL 85, GIBBONS 88]. These presentations clearly illustrate the underlying ideas of these algorithms, but they cannot be exactly considered as programs giving the full possibilities of asynchronism.

DCPs may be seen as an intermediate concurrent control structure lying between a rather well-structured but too weak one(collateral expression) and more powerful but too primitive ones(like semaphores or monitors). To the authors' knowledge, there is little related work. If some authors, like[FRANCEZ 86], propose a general framework in which DPCs could be modelized, they do not focus on them. The original idea of this extension of procedure call is due to J.P.BANATRE[BANATRE 81]. He and his colleagues propose similar, nevertheless somewhat different, linguistic constructions [BANATRE 89] to be embedded into a concurrent object oriented language for system programming. Apart from their work, one can cite [QUINIOU 88] who describes embedding DCPs into PROLOG for OR-processes communication and applies the resulting facilities to program the heuristic search algorithm A^*.

Finally, as the success of a new programming construction depends mainly on its understandability, the issue could be: is DCP a simple enough notion to be of value? The notion of partial call itself seems easily understandable. The difficulty may come from the definition of the family of processes involved in a realizable DPC. Recall that this definition restricts this family to the descendants of a common ancestor. In the example developed in section 2, this difficulty does not appear since all procedures SP_i^m and MP_i^m are different. So, the processes to be assembled to compose a realizable DPC are easily identified. Nevertheless, two delicate points must be cleared. The first one concerns procedures SP_1^m and MP_1^m which must be different, despite the fact their associated fonction is the same(e.g. $MinMax$). The second one concerns the fact that all procedures SP_i^m and MP_i^m, as we have defined them, have the same lifetime. Consequently, a cautious implementation verifying at run-time the realizability of DPCs would impose too strong a synchronization. Because of the lack of space, we cannot enter into the details of the remedy. The basic idea is to prefix the definition of these procedures by a newly introduced operator **loc**. The expression **loc** p, where p is a procedure, delivers a procedure different from p, having the same function and whose execution block $E(p)$ is fixed to the current block. Also, since it becomes then possible for a programmer to fix the execution block of a procedure, a slight modification of a realizable DPCs definition by remplacing $B(p)$ by $E(p)$ must be carried out.

Hence, a more precise semantics of DPCs has to be given. Our idea is to introduce a dual expression of collateral expressions, namely **anticollateral expression**. Just as an ordinary call is defined as as a block, a DPC would be defined as such an expression.

References

[AKL 85] S.G. AKL, *Parallel Sorting Algorithms*, Academic Press (1985).

[BANATRE 81] J.P. BANATRE, *Contribution à l'étude d'outils de construction de programmes parallèles et fiables*, Thèse, Université de Rennes (1981).

[BANATRE 89] J.P. BANATRE, M. BENVENISTE, *Multiprocedures: generalized procedures for concurrent programming*, 3rd workshop on Large Grain Parallelism, Software Engineering Institut, CMU (1989).

[BARRAUD 91] S. BARRAUD, J. MARLIERE, *Transformation d'un algorithme de tri parallèle et mise en œuvre sur hypercube*, Projet Maîtrise MLA, Université Joseph Fourier (Grenoble)(1991).

[BATCHER 68] K. BATCHER, *Sorting Networks and their Applications*, AFIPS Spring Joint Computing Conference **32** 307-14 (1968).

[FRANCEZ 86] N. FRANCEZ, B. HALPERN, G. TAUBENFELD, *Script: A communication abstraction mechanism and its verification*, Science of Computer Programming, (6):35-88 (1986).

[[GIBBONS 88] A. GIBBONS, W. RYTTER, *Efficient Parallel Algorithms*, Cambridge University Press (1988).

[QUINIOU 89] R. QUINIOU, L. TRILLING, *Collective predicates for expressing control of OR-parallelism in PROLOG*, 3rd Conference on Artificial Intelligence: Methodology, Systems and aplication, Varna, T. O'SHEA, V. SGUREV(eds), 159-167 North-Holland (1988).

Appendix 1. Sketch of proof of $SP_i{}^M$.

The array t' verifies the following condition $PreMerge(t')$:

$$t' = (t_0', t_1' \ldots, t_{2k}', t_{2k+1}', \ldots, t_{2M}')$$
$$= (a_0, b_0, \ldots, a_s, b_s, \ldots, a_k, b_k, \ldots, a_{M-1}, b_{M-1})$$

where the array $(a_0, a_1, \ldots, a_{M-1})$ (resp. $(b_0, b_1, \ldots, b_{M-1})$) is ordered.

1. Firstly, we have to show that if $(a_0', b_1', a_2', b_3', \ldots)$ (resp. $(b_0', a_1', b_2', a_3', \ldots)$) is the ordered array deduced from $(a_0, b_1, a_2, b_3, \ldots)$ (resp. $(b_0, a_1, b_2, a_3, \ldots)$) then the resulting array r is such that:

$$r = (Min(a_0', b_0'), Max(a_0', b_0'), Min(a_1', b_1'), Max(a_1', b_1') \ldots)$$

It is true if in the array t'' such that

$$t'' = a_0', b_0', a_1', b_1', \ldots$$

each element is in its final pair; that is, if any element a_k (resp. b_k) of the array t' has a pair position f in the array t'' such that all elements in left pairs(whose pair position is smaller than f) are smaller than a_k and all elements in right pairs are greater than a_k. We consider the case where there exists a leftmost element b_s greater than a_k in t' (such that $b_s > a_k$ and $b_{s'} < a_k$ for $s' < s \leq k$); the other case is symmetrical. Then we must have $f = k - \lceil (k-s)/2 \rceil$. By definition of t'' the position f' of a_k in t'' is such that if $k-s$ is even then $f' = k - \lceil (k-s)/2 \rceil$ and such that if $k-s$ is odd then $f' = k - (\lceil (k-(s+1))/2 \rceil + 1) = f$.

2. Secondly, we have to show that $MP_i{}^m$ is deduced from $SP_i{}^m$ by avoiding the first phase. This is due to the fact that for each DPC of the form

$$(MP_0{}^m(t_0', -), MP_1{}^m(t_1', -), MP_0{}^m(-, t_2'), MP_1{}^m(t_3', -), \ldots)$$

the precondition $PreMerge(t')$ is verified. And this is easily deduced from the fact that if $PreMerge(t')$ is verified then $PreMerge((a_0, b_1, a_2, b_3, \ldots))$ (resp. $PreMerge((b_0, a_1, b_2, a_3, \ldots))$) is verified.

Appendix 2. Procedure NetSort (m) whose the call NetSort (M) gives as result:

$$((SP_0{}^M, MP_0{}^M), \ldots, (SP_{M-1}{}^M, MP_{M-1}{}^M))$$

```
type SPMPprocarray = [] ( procpp SP, MP),

type procpp = proc (int , int) pair,

proc NetSort = (int m) SPMPprocarray:
 if m=1 then (MinMax, MinMax)
 else
   (SPMPprocarray la, ra) = (NetSort(m/2), NetSort(m/2));
   constructarrayfor i from 0 to m-1
    do
     if even(i) then
     ((int l, r) pair: MinMax(MP of la[i/2](SP of la[i/2](l,-),-),
                       MP of ra[i/2](SP of ra[i/2](r,-),-)),
      (int l, r) pair: MinMax(MP of la[i/2](l,-),
                       MP of ra[i/2](r,-)))
      else
     ((int l, r) pair: MinMax(MP of ra[i/2](-,SP of la[i/2](-,l)),
                       MP of la[i/2](-,SP of la[i/2](-,r)),
      (int l, r) pair: MinMax(MP of ra[i/2](-,l),
                       MP of ra[i/2](-,r)))
     fi
    od
 fi
```

N.B. The loop **constructarrayfor** is such that

```
constructarrayfor i from a to b do f(i) od
= (f(a), f(a+1), ..., f(b))
```

Lecture Notes in Computer Science

For information about Vols. 1–481
please contact your bookseller or Springer-Verlag

Vol. 524: G. Rozenberg (Ed.), Advances in Petri Nets 1991. VIII, 572 pages. 1991.

Vol. 525: O. Günther, H.-J. Schek (Eds.), Advances in Spatial Databases. Proceedings, 1991. XI, 471 pages. 1991.

Vol. 526: T. Ito, A. R. Meyer (Eds.), Theoretical Aspects of Computer Software. Proceedings, 1991. X, 772 pages. 1991.

Vol. 527: J.C.M. Baeten, J. F. Groote (Eds.), CONCUR '91. Proceedings, 1991. VIII, 541 pages. 1991.

Vol. 528: J. Maluszynski, M. Wirsing (Eds.), Programming Language Implementation and Logic Programming. Proceedings, 1991. XI, 433 pages. 1991.

Vol. 529: L. Budach (Ed.), Fundamentals of Computation Theory. Proceedings, 1991. XII, 426 pages. 1991.

Vol. 530: D. H. Pitt, P.-L. Curien, S. Abramsky, A. M. Pitts, A. Poigné, D. E. Rydeheard (Eds.), Category Theory and Computer Science. Proceedings, 1991. VII, 301 pages. 1991.

Vol. 531: E. M. Clarke, R. P. Kurshan (Eds.), Computer-Aided Verification. Proceedings, 1990. XIII, 372 pages. 1991.

Vol. 532: H. Ehrig, H.-J. Kreowski, G. Rozenberg (Eds.), Graph Grammars and Their Application to Computer Science. Proceedings, 1990. X, 703 pages. 1991.

Vol. 533: E. Börger, H. Kleine Büning, M. M. Richter, W. Schönfeld (Eds.), Computer Science Logic. Proceedings, 1990. VIII, 399 pages. 1991.

Vol. 534: H. Ehrig, K. P. Jantke, F. Orejas, H. Reichel (Eds.), Recent Trends in Data Type Specification. Proceedings, 1990. VIII, 379 pages. 1991.

Vol. 535: P. Jorrand, J. Kelemen (Eds.), Fundamentals of Artificial Intelligence Research. Proceedings, 1991. VIII, 255 pages. 1991. (Subseries LNAI).

Vol. 536: J. E. Tomayko, Software Engineering Education. Proceedings, 1991. VIII, 296 pages. 1991.

Vol. 537: A. J. Menezes, S. A. Vanstone (Eds.), Advances in Cryptology – CRYPTO '90. Proceedings. XIII, 644 pages. 1991.

Vol. 538: M. Kojima, N. Megiddo, T. Noma, A. Yoshise, A Unified Approach to Interior Point Algorithms for Linear Complementarity Problems. VIII, 108 pages. 1991.

Vol. 539: H. F. Mattson, T. Mora, T. R. N. Rao (Eds.), Applied Algebra, Algebraic Algorithms and Error-Correcting Codes. Proceedings, 1991. XI, 489 pages. 1991.

Vol. 540: A. Prieto (Ed.), Artificial Neural Networks. Proceedings, 1991. XIII, 476 pages. 1991.

Vol. 541: P. Barahona, L. Moniz Pereira, A. Porto (Eds.), EPIA '91. Proceedings, 1991. VIII, 292 pages. 1991. (Subseries LNAI).

Vol. 543: J. Dix, K. P. Jantke, P. H. Schmitt (Eds.), Nonmonotonic and Inductive Logic. Proceedings, 1990. X, 243 pages. 1991. (Subseries LNAI).

Vol. 544: M. Broy, M. Wirsing (Eds.), Methods of Programming. XII, 268 pages. 1991.

Vol. 545: H. Alblas, B. Melichar (Eds.), Attribute Grammars, Applications and Systems. Proceedings, 1991. IX, 513 pages. 1991.

Vol. 547: D. W. Davies (Ed.), Advances in Cryptology – EUROCRYPT '91. Proceedings, 1991. XII, 556 pages. 1991.

Vol. 548: R. Kruse, P. Siegel (Eds.), Symbolic and Quantitative Approaches to Uncertainty. Proceedings, 1991. XI, 362 pages. 1991.

Vol. 550: A. van Lamsweerde, A. Fugetta (Eds.), ESEC '91. Proceedings, 1991. XII, 515 pages. 1991.

Vol. 551: S. Prehn, W. J. Toetenel (Eds.), VDM '91. Formal Software Development Methods. Volume 1. Proceedings, 1991. XIII, 699 pages. 1991.

Vol. 552: S. Prehn, W. J. Toetenel (Eds.), VDM '91. Formal Software Development Methods. Volume 2. Proceedings, 1991. XIV, 430 pages. 1991.

Vol. 553: H. Bieri, H. Noltemeier (Eds.), Computational Geometry - Methods, Algorithms and Applications '91. Proceedings, 1991. VIII, 320 pages. 1991.

Vol. 554: G. Grahne, The Problem of Incomplete Information in Relational Databases. VIII, 156 pages. 1991.

Vol. 555: H. Maurer (Ed.), New Results and New Trends in Computer Science. Proceedings, 1991. VIII, 403 pages. 1991.

Vol. 556: J.-M. Jacquet, Conclog: A Methodological Approach to Concurrent Logic Programming. XII, 781 pages. 1991.

Vol. 557: W. L. Hsu, R. C. T. Lee (Eds.), ISA '91 Algorithms. Proceedings, 1991. X, 396 pages. 1991.

Vol. 558: J. Hooman, Specification and Compositional Verification of Real-Time Systems. VIII, 235 pages. 1991.

Vol. 559: G. Butler, Fundamental Algorithms for Permutation Groups. XII, 238 pages. 1991.

Vol. 560: S. Biswas, K. V. Nori (Eds.), Foundations of Software Technology and Theoretical Computer Science. Proceedings, 1991. X, 420 pages. 1991.

Vol. 561: C. Ding, G. Xiao, W. Shan, The Stability Theory of Stream Ciphers. IX, 187 pages. 1991.

Vol. 562: R. Breu, Algebraic Specification Techniques in Object Oriented Programming Environments. XI, 228 pages. 1991.

Vol. 563: A. Karshmer, J. Nehmer (Eds.), Operating Systems of the 90s and Beyond. Proceedings, 1991. X, 285 pages. 1991.

Vol. 564: I. Herman, The Use of Projective Geometry in Computer Graphics. VIII, 146 pages. 1992.

Vol. 565: J. D. Becker, I. Eisele, F. W. Mündemann (Eds.), Parallelism, Learning, Evolution. Proceedings, 1989. VIII, 525 pages. 1991. (Subseries LNAI).

Vol. 566: C. Delobel, M. Kifer, Y. Masunaga (Eds.), Deductive and Object-Oriented Databases. Proceedings, 1991. XV, 581 pages. 1991.

Vol. 567: H. Boley, M. M. Richter (Eds.), Processing Declarative Kowledge. Proceedings, 1991. XII, 427 pages. 1991. (Subseries LNAI).

Vol. 568: H.-J. Bürckert, A Resolution Principle for a Logic with Restricted Quantifiers. X, 116 pages. 1991. (Subseries LNAI).

Vol. 569: A. Beaumont, G. Gupta (Eds.), Parallel Execution of Logic Programs. Proceedings, 1991. VII, 195 pages. 1991.

Vol. 570: R. Berghammer, G. Schmidt (Eds.), Graph-Theoretic Concepts in Computer Science. Proceedings, 1991. VIII, 253 pages. 1992.

Vol. 571: J. Vytopil (Ed.), Formal Techniques in Real-Time and Fault-Tolerant Systems. Proceedings, 1992. IX, 620 pages. 1991.

Vol. 572: K. U. Schulz (Ed.), Word Equations and Related Topics. Proceedings, 1990. VII, 256 pages. 1992.

Vol. 573: G. Cohen, S. N. Litsyn, A. Lobstein, G. Zémor (Eds.), Algebraic Coding. Proceedings, 1991. X, 158 pages. 1992.

Vol. 574: J. P. Banâtre, D. Le Métayer (Eds.), Research Directions in High-Level Parallel Programming Languages. Proceedings, 1991. VIII, 387 pages. 1992.